ENDORSEMENTS

Groen van Prinsterer's classic text, Unbelief and Revolution, is one of many attempts of nineteenth-century European intellectuals to come to terms with the French Revolution and its aftermath. Harry Van Dyke deftly situates the book in its political, religious, and historiographical contexts, thereby doing readers a great service. Puzzling allusions, ideas, and assumptions in Groen's narrative begin to make sense when read against their historical background. But Van Dyke not only takes his readers on a tour of nineteenth-century intellectual culture, he also invites them to take some Groenian wisdom with them back into the twenty-first century. Could it be, Van Dyke asks, that Groen's struggle with emerging forms of secularism is of utmost relevance in a world in which religion and secularism are still competing forces?

—**Herman Paul**, Professor of the History of the Humanities,
Leiden University

This present edition is also timely, due to the growing interest in Groen's disciple, Abraham Kuyper. Kuyper's famous identification of Calvinism as a *Weltanschauung* (as comprehensive as Modernism) inspired a generation of Christian intellectuals to go beyond their forebear's otherworldly spirituality in a search for a distinctly biblical perspective on contemporary social and political issues. As Van Dyke shows in *Challenging the Spirit of Modernity*, this movement is rooted in Groen's lectures on the "religion" of the French Revolution—a secular religion of unbelief, in competition with Christianity for the hearts and minds of Western culture. Van Dyke is not only a skillful translator of these lectures, but also a meticulous biographer, an adept intellectual historian of an important Dutch political theorist, and a literary critic engaged in exacting textual analysis. Even as he recounts the history of Groen's world, Van Dyke is in the position of a historiographer—critically evaluating Groen's own historical writing. The result for the reader is that Groen van Prinsterer comes to life—his education and political career, the reason for his focus on the French Revolution, and his conviction that Christianity is a guide to all of life.

—**David S. Caudill**, Professor and Goldberg Family Chair in Law, Villanova University Charles Widger School of Law

Groen van Prinsterer's classic text, Unbelief and Revolution, is one of many attempts of nineteenth-century European intellectuals to come to terms with the French Revolution and its aftermath. Harry Van Dyke deftly situates the book in its political, religious, and historiographical contexts, thereby doing readers a great service. Puzzling allusions, ideas, and assumptions in Groen's narrative begin to make sense when read against their historical background. But Van Dyke not only takes his readers on a tour of nineteenth-century intellectual culture, he also invites them to take some Groenian wisdom with them back into the twenty-first century. Could it be, Van Dyke asks, that Groen's struggle with emerging forms of secularism is of utmost relevance in a world in which religion and secularism are still competing forces?

—**Herman Paul**, Professor of the History of the Humanities, Leiden University

Van Dyke's analysis of, and commentary on, Groen van Prinsterer's lectures on Unbelief and Revolution were timely when they first appeared in 1989—during the Bicentennial of the French Revolution. This present edition is also timely, due to the growing interest in Groen's disciple, Abraham Kuyper. Kuyper's famous identification of Calvinism as a *Weltanschauung* (as comprehensive as Modernism) inspired a generation of Christian intellectuals to go beyond their forebear's otherworldly spirituality in a search for a distinctly biblical perspective on contemporary social and political issues. As Van Dyke shows in *Challenging the Spirit of Modernity*, this movement is rooted in Groen's lectures on the "religion" of the French Revolution—a secular religion of unbelief, in competition with Christianity for the hearts and minds of Western culture. Van Dyke is not only a skillful translator of these lectures, but also a meticulous biographer, an adept intellectual historian of an important Dutch political theorist, and a literary critic engaged in exacting textual analysis. Even as he recounts the history of Groen's world, Van Dyke is in the position of a historiographer—critically evaluating Groen's own historical writing. The result for the reader is that Groen van Prinsterer comes to life—his education and political career, the reason for his focus on the French Revolution, and his conviction that Christianity is a guide to all of life.

—**David S. Caudill**, Professor and Goldberg Family Chair in Law, Villanova University Charles Widger School of Law

Groen van Prinsterer's *Unbelief and Revolution* deserves to be better known in the English-speaking world. Harry van Dyke's fascinating introduction to this seminal work had been out of print for decades, but I am pleased to see it available once again for a new generation of readers. I pray that it will stimulate the needed communal reflection on the relationship between our faith commitments and the current condition of our civilization.

—**David T. Koyzis**, St. George's Centre for Biblical and Public Theology, Hamilton, ON

Challenging the Spirit of Modernity

A Study of Groen van Prinsterer's Unbelief and Revolution

STUDIES IN HISTORICAL & SYSTEMATIC THEOLOGY

H
S ✚ S
T

Challenging the Spirit of Modernity

A Study of Groen van Prinsterer's Unbelief *and* Revolution

HARRY VAN DYKE

LEXHAM PRESS

Challenging the Spirit of Modernity
Studies in Historical and Systematic Theology

Copyright 2019 Harry Van Dyke

Lexham Press, 1313 Commercial St., Bellingham, WA 98225
LexhamPress.com

This book is a revised edition of *Groen van Prinsterer's Lectures on Unbelief and Revolution* (Jordan Station, ON: Wedge Publishing Foundation, 1989).

Print ISBN 978-1-68-359320-1
Digital ISBN 978-1-68-359321-8

Lexham Editorial Team: Todd Hains, Eric Bosell, Danielle Thevenaz
Cover Design: Bryan Hintz
Typesetting: Kathy Curtis

To Nienke

We do not want a theocracy, but recognition of the connection between religion, authority, and freedom.

Contents

Contents

PREFACE TO THE NEW EDITION

Nearly three decades have passed since this book was first published. It appeared simultaneously in a trade edition as well as an academic edition in partial fulfillment of the requirements for the degree of D.Litt. at the Free University of Amsterdam. The second half of my book contained an English translation of Groen van Prinsterer's lectures on *Unbelief and Revolution*; the first half was a commentary on that classic text, describing its content and its context. The translation has been published separately as *Unbelief and Revolution* in Lexham Classics. The commentary is reprinted in the present work.

The dissertation was soon out of print, but demand for it never died out. Thus I welcomed the offer by Lexham Press to republish both the translation and the commentary. Below, I have used the occasion to correct a few stylistic details and to expand some footnotes with more recent information. Apart from that, the text remains unchanged.

Groen van Prinsterer (1801–1876) was a trailblazer in the struggle for the preservation of the Christian roots of Western culture against the encroachment of secularism since the eighteenth-century Enlightenment. His lectures traced the origin and nature of this intellectual and spiritual revolution and articulated the principles by which to respond to it. In his native country, the Netherlands, his book and his career inspired an "anti-revolutionary" movement that engaged society and politics from a distinctively "Christian-historical" orientation. This movement would eventually have a significant impact on Dutch society in the areas of education, industrial relations, social justice and democratic politics under the leadership of Groen's disciple Abraham Kuyper (1837–1920).

In light of the current revival of interest in the life and thought of Kuyper, Groen van Prinsterer's seminal work will no doubt find new readers. I hope that the following pages will be of help in understanding and appreciating Groen's work.

Harry Van Dyke
Summer 2018

INTRODUCTION

The book *Ongeloof en Revolutie* is the text of a series of historical lectures presented in 1845–46 and published in 1847. Its historical context is Holland during the Restoration and its author is Guillaume Groen van Prinsterer (1801–76). A Dutch classic, it has never had an unabridged translation into another language. The purpose of the present study is to make *Ongeloof en Revolutie* accessible to the modern English reader who may be interested in its origin and contents in light of its historical impact. My abridged translation of *Unbelief and Revolution* was published as a stand-alone volume in 2018.[1]

NATURE OF GROEN'S BOOK

Like a much smaller but rather more famous publication of the following year, the *Communist Manifesto*, Groen van Prinsterer's book defies all categories of conventional classification. *Unbelief and Revolution* might be called a political or philosophical work if it were not so obviously also a historical study. Conversely, many historians feel that the work contains too little description of empirical phenomena and too much analysis in terms of recurring phases and logical relationships to rank it among history proper. Again, although it is expressly Christian in its message, it is neither a theological treatise nor merely a 'tract for the times.'

Unbelief and Revolution is at once a protest against the increasingly secular spirit of the times, an attack on the prevailing liberalism in church and state, and a plea for reform in a historically sensitive direction guided by Christian principles. Like the works of Tocqueville that would come out a decade later, *Unbelief and Revolution* confidently weaves in and out of

---

1. Guillaume Groen van Prinsterer, *Unbelief and Revolution*, trans. Harry Van Dyke, Lexham Classics (Bellingham, WA: Lexham Press, 2018).

historical description and theoretical analysis, achieving a synthesis that gives its pages their unique and enduring significance. Reminiscent of Burckhardt's gloomy premonitions, *Unbelief and Revolution*'s ominous predictions about the inevitability of future tyranny if contemporary trends continued mark it as a prophetic work of an astute mid-nineteenth-century observer. Twentieth-century parallels of the book are Christopher Dawson's *Gods of Revolution* with its religious penetration and Eric Voegelin's *From Enlightenment to Revolution* with its original periodization of the history of Western Civilization. In its sustained explication of the Enlightenment as a new gospel Groen's book resembles Paul Hazard's twin works, *La Crise de la conscience européenne* and *La Pensée européenne au XVIIIe siècle*, Carl Becker's *The Heavenly City of the Eighteenth-Century Philosophers*, and Crane Brinton's *The Shaping of the Modern Mind*. A contemporary of Groen's book was *Sybil, or the Two Nations* (1845) by Benjamin Disraeli, which formulated a similar socio-political prescription for treating its country's malaise: neither liberalism nor socialism but "a free Monarchy and a privileged and prosperous People." A closer parallel in terms of an avowed Christian orientation is Gladstone's *The State in Its Relation to the Church* of 1837, albeit that Groen did not later have to make quite so drastic a turnabout on the issue of the church's "public rights" as Gladstone did.

Unbelief and Revolution, as I hope to show, is one of those seminal works which are written only once in a generation and which so capture the central issue emerging from the past that they help set the debate for future generations. In point of fact, *Unbelief and Revolution* is today a major source document for the history of the rise of the anti-revolutionary movement in the Netherlands. This movement, whose peculiar name betrays its Groenian origin, is essentially an early, Dutch Calvinist manifestation of that multi-faceted phenomenon of modern times variously known as Christian action, Christian social action, Christian politics, Christian democracy—the conscious, organized resistance of European Christians to modern secularism.

If the above comments serve to introduce the book's general thrust and historical significance, its spirit, tone and style can perhaps best be indicated through further comparisons with works more generally known, some of which constituted its sources. *Unbelief and Revolution*, then, resembles Burke's *Reflections on the Revolution in France* in historical approach, and Burke's *Letters on a Regicide Peace* in unflinching opposition to prevailing policy. In passionate eloquence it resembles Lamennais's *Essay on Religious Indifference*, and in monarchical sympathies it is a belated footnote to Haller's *Restoration of Political Science*. Antedating the following by at least half a decade, Groen's work is as sure-handed as Stahl's *What is the Revolution?* in pinpointing the nature of the spiritual crisis of European Civilization, and it is as firm-minded as Stahl's *Protestantism as a Political Principle* in advocating the introduction into modern politics of a party committed to a biblical confession and a biblical worldview for the purpose of competing with the traditional parties of left and right which have a non-biblical, humanistic orientation of one sort or another. As a spirited repudiation of secular humanism Groen's book of 1847 constitutes the polemical prelude to Abraham Kuyper's positive espousal of Calvinism as a political creed and program in his third Stone Lecture of 1898. Finally, in diction and style, tone and appeal, *Unbelief and Revolution* of 1847 falls somewhere between Coleridge's magnificent *On the constitution of the church and state* of 1830 and Newman's masterful *Apologia* of 1864.

CENTRAL THESIS OF *UNBELIEF AND REVOLUTION*

The very title of Groen's work has the ring of a manifesto and hints at a grand indictment of the age. Its theme is the secular roots of the age of revolution. Its central thesis is that the French Revolution of 1789 was the mature fruit of Europe's *intellectual* revolution which had subverted the *spiritual* foundation of society. The subjectivism and consequent skepticism as a result of which the Enlightenment had dismissed divine revelation and Christian traditions were followed—very logically, according to Groen—by a political philosophy which brooked no authority beyond man and his reason and which generated the novel creeds of religious atheism and political radicalism. The new "theory of liberty" was responsible for an insatiable desire to reconstruct everything—religion, morality, state, society—on a new foundation, in a crusade for the final emancipation and salvation of mankind. This intellectual-spiritual revolution is pictured by the author as surfacing in 1789 with all the enthusiasm, determination and rigor of a religious movement having its day. On this view, *"the Revolution"* was secularism's bid for control of European civilization.

In the lectures, Groen developed a unique and profound interpretation. The case he argued was that the root cause of the malaise of his age was *unbelief*—unbelief as it was first elaborated into a system and then applied in a wholesale social experiment. According to the author, a correct appraisal of the French Revolution—and, for that matter, of its entire aftermath—must lay bare its profoundly *religious* character. Groen's own analysis consistently identified religion—in the broad sense of man's ultimate concern and commitment—as the underlying, all-determining driving force behind the events that rocked the world in the generation immediately preceding his. But the uniqueness of this interpretation comes out especially in what follows. The heady days of 1789 were long gone, but, insisted Groen, since the secular ideology that shaped that dramatic history was not repudiated when the revolution was contained by the Reaction under Napoleon and subdued by the Restoration of 1815, therefore the same subversive ideas continued to erode the foundations of society and would eventually lead to fresh flare-ups of revolutionary violence. Like Tocqueville, a favorite author of his later years, Groen came to the disturbing conclusion that, humanly speaking, the revolution had become a permanent feature of European civilization. We are living in a condition of permanent revolution, is the conclusion of his book of 1847; revolutions are here to stay and will grow much worse in scope and intensity unless men can be persuaded to return to Christianity, to practice its precepts and to obey the gospel in its full implications for human life and civilized society. Barring such a revival, the future would belong to socialism and communism, which on this view were but the most consistent sects of the new secular religion. To Groen, therefore, the political spectrum that presented itself to his generation offered no meaningful choice. In terms of his analysis, the *radical left* was composed of fanatical believers in the godless ideology; the *liberal centre*, by comparison, was occupied by warm believers who warned against excesses and preached moderation; while the *conservative right* embraced all those who lacked either the insight, the prudence, or the will to break with the modern tenets yet who recoiled from the consequences whenever the ideology was practiced and implemented in any consistent way. None of the three "shades" or "nuances" of secular liberalism represented a valid option for Christian citizens. Groen ends his book with a compelling invitation—to resist "the revolution" *in whatever form it manifests itself* and to work for a radical alternative in politics, along anti-revolutionary, Christian-historical lines.

RECEPTION

Groen's book pointed a direction and promoted a realignment of forces. Its effect in the practical domain is hard to overestimate once we realize that its statement of the problem of modern secular culture became the basis of a wide politico-cultural movement in the Netherlands that is still in evidence today. By reformulating the basic issue of modern society it relocated the battlefront for the struggle to maintain some form of Christian civilization. As it did so it was instrumental in bringing about a renewed involvement in the life of the nation on the part of one of its most creative minorities, the orthodox Calvinists. Groen broke the stranglehold of conservatism on them without delivering them up to the social gospel. His spiritual sons were in the vanguard of those who in the 1870s laid the foundations of a Christian labor movement.[2] In the political realm Groen's life-work bore fruit before the century was out in the popular crusades and electoral victories led by the great emancipator Abraham Kuyper under the Anti-Revolutionary standard. A veritable groundswell of Neo-Calvinist thought and action saw the founding of the Free University in 1880 and the formation of a distinct school of Calvinist philosophy in the 1930s, to name but a few of its more outstanding landmarks.

If this is the record of *Unbelief and Revolution* as a historical catalyst, as a scholarly piece of work it has generally stood very low in the estimation of those who have bothered to examine it. Early reviews were on the whole negative. One conservative critic, while agreeing with parts of it, called it one-sided and immoderate, and unlikely to get a hearing in any case, overtaken as it had been by the very events it seemed to predict: namely, the new wave of revolutions of 1848.[3] Reviewers of liberal sympathies judged it "derivative, internally contradictory and apodictic"[4] or powerful indeed

---

2. Hagoort, *Gedenkboek Patrimonium*, pp. 104–80; idem, *De Christelijk-sociale beweging*, pp. 50–75; cf. Fogarty, *Christian Democracy in Western Europe*, chaps. xv–xviii. For full bibliographical data on publications mentioned in short form in the footnotes of the present work, see the Select Bibliography.

3. Bakker Korff (1848), pp. 401–04.

4. De Witte Van Citters (1848), pp. 109–11.

because "never wavering in the resolution of the most difficult questions" yet owing that power chiefly to its misleading historical evidence and its selective appeal to historical development.[5]

Since those early reviews, colored by the political debate of the day, the assessments by a number of professional historians have not improved the book's reputation. Fruin called the work vague and shallow, unscientific in its use of the Bible, unreliable in its depiction of the old regime, misguided in its deduction of the French Revolution from ideas, illiberal as regards the relation between church and state, and reactionary with respect to free enterprise—in short, a work representative of a party that should never be entrusted with political power.[6] The best Huizinga ever said about Groen's work was that as an interpretation of the French Revolution it introduced the concept "the revolution," an image which, "born of wrath and alarm, takes from the historical fact only the point of departure, in order to give a name to the romantic-apocalyptic conception that is the modern form of the Augustinian concept of the *civitas terrena*."[7] Geyl dismissed the work as "one grand mistake," a specimen of history-writing whose unhistorical method and religious bias doomed it to sterility and whose account of the revolution betrayed little "intimate knowledge or even notice of the events or the social relations" involved in it.[8]

Modern-day sympathizers with Groen have not been much kinder to his major work. Smitskamp conceded that it suffered from logicistic reasoning and that it was improvisational, uneven, and grandiosely one-sided.[9] A group of Christian scholars who "revisited" the book on the occasion of the hundredth anniversary of its publication was unanimous in its verdict that as a witness to the secular world the work has abiding significance, but that as a piece of historical scholarship it suffers from grave shortcomings. Consider: it misconstrues medieval political developments; it overestimates the historical significance of the Reformation; it explains events according to a "mechanical idealism" which totally ignores

5. De Bosch Kemper (1849), pp. 192–94, 200f.

6. Fruin (1853), *Verspreide Geschriften*, X, 76–167.

7. Huizinga (1914), *Verzamelde Werken*, VIII, 265.

8. Geyl (1952), *Reacties*, pp. 6–11.

9. Smitskamp, *Groen van Prinsterer als historicus*, p. 74; idem, "Het boek 'Ongeloof en Revolutie,'" p. 26.

the socio-economic factor and virtually eliminates the influence of persons on the course of history; it is hopelessly entangled in the unsuspected
implications of the historical relativism and sociological universalism of its
day; it fails to demonstrate the putative link between unbelief and revolution and short-circuits historical science and Christian faith.[10] Indeed, the
general impression one carries away from the commemorative volume is
that Groen van Prinsterer was more a seer than a historian: "Groen is the
prophet who saw the Great Truth in history but had difficulty finding the
right arguments" is a fair summary of the volume's general thrust.[11] The
modern detractors have not been left unanswered,[12] but the mainstream of
the historical profession has left the work in the category to which it has
long been assigned: a work fundamentally flawed. The conclusion seems
as inescapable as it is intriguing: a book of far-reaching impact and enduring relevance has exercised its enormous influence in spite of its intrinsic
validity, or rather invalidity.

THE PRESENT STUDY

One purpose of the present study is to determine to what extent the historians' verdict is correct or in need of revision. A related purpose is to make
the work accessible to a wider audience than it has hitherto had, in the
hope of realizing two further aims: to open the discussion of its historiographic merits to non-Dutch scholars; and to help put an end to its almost
total neglect (beyond its country of origin) in histories of the period and
of the movement to which the book belongs. To this end our study contex-
tualizes the book and analyzes its contents. An English translation of the
work was published by Lexham Press in 2018.

   To put the book in its context, then, we review some of the relevant
aspects of Restoration Holland and the period's religious awakening,
taking special note of themes and topics directly referred to in the book
(chapters 1 and 2). These historical sketches are followed by an overview

---

10. *Lustrumbundel* of the Society of Christian Historians (1949), pp. 71 (Dr. H. J. Smit), 81
(Professor A. A. van Schelven), 103, 108f (Dr. J. C. H. de Pater), 127 (Professor H. Dooyeweerd),
and 142f (Professor A. M. Donner).

11. Van Deursen, "De Vrije Universiteit en de geschiedwetenschappen," p. 388.

12. See Select Bibliography *sub nomine* Aalders, Algra, Bremmer, Kamphuis.

of the author's life, in which we concentrate on the period leading up to his decision to lecture on the topic of unbelief and revolution (chapter 3).

The remainder of our study is devoted to the book itself. First comes a discussion of the lectures as such: their purpose, prototypes, sources, audience and style (chapters 4-8). We continue with a discussion of the work as a published book: its structure and argument, editions and translations (chapters 9-12). We conclude by exploring the controversial issues raised in debates about the book (chapter 13).

1
—

RESTORATION HOLLAND

Books, no less than people and ideas, must be judged in the light of their times. The reader of *Unbelief and Revolution* will want to be familiar with the main features of the days in which Groen van Prinsterer lived, labored and lectured. Now the immediate historical context of the work was Restoration Holland. In the history of the Netherlands, it should be borne in mind, the Restoration period stretches from 1813 to 1848. Unlike France, the Netherlands did not in 1830 undergo a political metamorphosis marking the end of an era. Holland did see the break-up that year of the "misalliance" with Belgium, devised by the Powers at the end of the Napoleonic era to serve as a buffer on France's northern frontier. But its social and political structures continued well into the forties. Thus Restoration Holland did not make the transition to a more modern phase of national life until the revolution of 1848. *Unbelief and Revolution*, conceived during the Belgian Revolt and its aftermath, was born in the twilight years 1845–46, just before Holland saw the dawn of a new age.

Given this setting of the work, at least two trends are of paramount importance for understanding it. First, the 1840s mark the years when conservatism had spent itself and liberalism stood poised to assume leadership. Second, these were the years when the religious awakening of the earlier decades of the century came to maturity and entered a new phase of practical involvement in society. To acquire familiarity with the background against which the book must be read, therefore, it will be useful to outline the period's main features as follows, in order of increasing complexity: the economic circumstances, the social conditions, the political framework, the intellectual climate, and the religious movements. The first four features are dealt with below, while the last is described in the next chapter.

1

ECONOMIC CIRCUMSTANCES

Economically, the Restoration years were trying times for Holland. Although the 1820s and 1830s had seen some revival of commerce and trade to pre-revolutionary levels, thanks in no small measure to personal initiatives of the energetic "merchant-king" William I, new developments had come to frustrate this economic restoration.

In 1815 the old staple trade had lain in ruins, never again to recover. The competition of American shipping and the port facilities of London and Hamburg seemed impossible to match, as did the quality and price of British manufactured goods in world markets. Holland's only hope of counting again in the world economy was to recapture its transit trade at the gateway to the Continent.

Such recapture was no small challenge. Amsterdam, on the decline since 1780, had seen its commissions trade finally destroyed by Napoleon's Continental System. Moreover, the port of Antwerp, closed to navigation since 1585, had been reopened in 1815 and had proved a significant rival to Amsterdam. This competition only increased after the Belgian troubles resulted in 1830 in the revolt and eventual secession of the southern provinces from the Kingdom of the Netherlands.

Trade across the North Sea with England was only modestly restored to former levels after the Commercial Treaty of 1837 removed a number of mutual protectionist barriers.

Turning from the open sea to its hinterland, Holland saw its prospects of full restoration decreased there as well. A Rhine Navigation Treaty with Prussia had stabilized relations in 1834 but also confirmed the loss of Holland's economic grip on this strategic waterway into the interior. The German Customs Union of 1831 further diminished Dutch trading opportunities in its immediate hinterland. Any strength it had recovered in transshipment traffic on the Rhine was seriously challenged when the construction of a railway linking Cologne to Antwerp was completed in 1843. Thus with the advent of the middle 1840s, Holland's economic prospects seemed if anything to grow worse.[1] By the middle of the decade the international downturn began to show its effects as well.

---

1. Boogman, "The Dutch Crisis in the Eighteen-Forties," pp. 196–99.

Holland's fishing industry, meanwhile, showed a mixed picture. With the coming of international peace in 1815, the cod fishing off the coast of Iceland had been resumed but remained insignificant, while the once-thriving whaling industry around Spitsbergen never revived. The herring fisheries fared much better; remarkable increases in annual catches (and sales!) restored the industry to former levels.

In the countryside, Holland's longstanding lead in advanced agriculture was still in evidence, but the depression of the 40s would hit hard here too. Nor was the old regime entirely gone; here and there manorial dues were still in force, road duty and compulsory use of the lord's mill were not yet extinct, and a kind of poll tax still rested on the inhabitants of certain rural villages. It is unlikely, however, that these vestiges of an outmoded order of things were any longer real obstacles to commercial farming. More serious was the international economic slump.

As a result of the Settlement of 1815, Holland's colonies were only partially restored; England returned Surinam in the West and the Indonesian Archipelago in the East, but retained Ceylon and the Cape. For a long time the British continued to dominate trade in the Indies, thanks to their superior cottons and linens. It was to take several decades before the independent but inexperienced Dutch merchants could make inroads in an area monopolized till 1795 by the now defunct East India Company. To stimulate overseas trade, the king, in addition to setting up agencies in the newly opened Latin American countries, took the initiative in 1824 of founding the *Nederlandsche Handelmaatschappij*, a shareholding company designed to serve commercial companies with information and loans but also to develop its own trade with new areas. The semi-public trading house developed a modest trade in tea with Canton, but when the Company entered on the market of the Indies it soon discovered that here it faced the same problems as the private firms: tough foreign competition. This led the company to try to meet the British competition head-on by developing domestic calicot manufacture, first in Flanders and, after the separation, in Holland's cities. Small factories were set up in Haarlem, Leyden and other places, later also in the eastern region of Twente after the Company's director De Clercq, in a meeting with Thomas Ainsworth, had been convinced of the viability of basing textile manufacture on local cottage industry using the flying shuttle.[2] Also, once the Cultivation System was introduced in the Indies, ensuring annual quotas of specified products to be grown by the natives, the Company was given a major role in shipping these goods to Europe and selling them there for the benefit of the state treasury. Not until 1840 did Holland regain its place as the leading market in at least one tropical product, coffee, a position she would hold till the 1870s. The recovery of shipbuilding, another of the Company's goals, was even slower. The craft had all but died out and foreigners had to be brought in. Shipowners reappeared in modest numbers. The Company guaranteed shipment, and through careful management which included the keeping of waiting lists of ships to be chartered, it was instrumental in gaining for Holland's merchant navy fourth place by 1850, behind the British, American and French.[3]

Throughout this period, Holland was still in the stage of early capitalism. Although the king had helped found the *Nederlandsche Bank* in Amsterdam for the purpose of stimulating credit as well as providing domestic commerce with (paper) means of exchange, the first purpose remained largely dormant as business and industry preferred the traditional method of funding new ventures exclusively with private capital. The limited liability company was rarely used. A contemporary observer, Potgieter, complained that Holland's commercial class remained stuck in its eighteenth-century rut and was "suffocating and wasting away in its stuffy counting-houses."[4]

Potgieter implied that those with capital to risk for gain were without initiative or enterprise. That judgment may be too harsh, for they also had to do without any incentive. Low returns discouraged investment, for example, in industrial ventures. Dutch industry was simply unable to be very competitive in the face of relatively costly production factors. Coal, to name one such factor, had to be imported, and transportation costs were high. Thus not just lack of enterprising spirit or capital investment but also structural factors help account for the country's industrial retardation.[5]

---

2. That the meeting took place by chance, as tradition would have it, is called "legendary" by Verberne, *Geschiedenis van Nederland in de jaren 1813-1850*, I, 185, and a "romantic invention" by Brugmans, *Paardenkracht en mensenmacht*, p. 78.

3. Verberne, *Geschiedenis van Nederland in de jaren 1813-1850*, I, 161-69.

4. Quoted in Wieringa, *Economische heroriëntering in Nederland in de 19e eeuw*, p. 15.

5. Griffiths, "Ambacht en nijverheid in de Noordelijke Nederlanden, 1770-1844," pp. 248-52.

Holland's infrastructure, to look at another factor, was still very primitive by the 1840s. The major cities and towns were not connected by cobbled roads till about 1848, while railroads took even longer to develop into a network: Amsterdam was connected south-westward with Haarlem ('39), The Hague ('43) and Rotterdam ('47), and south-eastward with Utrecht ('43) and Arnhem ('45), the crucial link with the German Rhinelands having to wait till 1856.[6] Much of the country would have remained isolated were it not for the age-old line service by stagecoach and tow-barge. The latter still handled most of the traffic in freight; even at that, a Dutch journal for political economy declared as late as 1846 that economically the most important domestic communication link was the footpath.[7]

Canal construction was easier in boggy Holland. Here, too, the head of state took energetic initiatives, often investing large private fortunes. Canals that linked provincial towns to nearby rivers, and canals that bypassed unnavigable stretches in the interior and chronically shifting sandbanks in the coastal water of the delta area did much to open backward regions, and gave both Amsterdam and Rotterdam more reliable links to the sea.

A special problem, of course, was the eternal struggle against the water. There always seemed to be too much water in the sea, during winter storms; too much water in the great rivers from the south, during spring thaw; too much water in the many inland lakes, at any season. Disastrous floods covered large areas in 1820 and 1825. When the waters receded, dykes were repaired and raised, and ancient schemes were revived and new plans laid for ambitious reclamation and drainage projects. Before these works could be tackled, however, the strong powers of the centralist government in Restoration Holland had to be enlisted to coordinate—or override—the jealously guarded jurisdictions of local polder boards, waterships, dyke watch committees, and even city councils who defended their hoary fishing rights and water tolls dating from the Middle Ages.

For all these reasons, industrialization was very slow in coming to an undeveloped country like Holland, even though its king had observed early in his reign with prophetic foresight: "The time of merchant shipping as

---

6. Verberne, *Geschiedenis van Nederland in de jaren 1813-1850*, I, 171–74.

7. Brugmans, *Paardenkracht en mensenmacht*, pp. 102f.

the nation's chief occupation is over; our national prosperity can only be regained by systematic industrialization."[8] William did what he could. He prescribed made-in-Holland textiles for the armed forces, the court, state orphanages, etc. He established a fund for loans and subsidies to industry. He helped organize exhibitions. He sent an envoy to England to study the iron industry. He invested in ventures large and small, becoming one of the major shareholders of John Cockerill's empire.[9] Yet by the time the international exhibition was organized in the Crystal Palace in 1851, Holland's entry still made a very poor showing.[10] Less than a quarter of her labor force was at that time involved in industrial occupations (as compared to 50% in agriculture).[11]

For the longest time, industrial production continued to rest on cottage industry and small workshops. Large factories were still rare in the 1840s and seldom employed more than 100 hands; only a few of the largest plants ranged between 200 to 600 workers.[12] Prior to the fifties, steam engines were the exception; machines ran on power provided by women, children and horses.[13] The country's lack of coal mines of any size made the cost of other sources of energy prohibitive for many years to come.

SOCIAL CONDITIONS

The working classes of this society led a harsh, dreary and precarious existence. Eager to escape sinking away into the dismal ranks of the paupers, one was happy with a subsistence wage. Massive unemployment was chronic and the proportion of the population living off public relief rose from 13% in 1841 to 27% in 1850.[14] Indirect taxes on all necessaries did

---

8. Verberne, *Geschiedenis van Nederland in de jaren 1813-1850*, I, 182.

9. Verberne, *Geschiedenis van Nederland in de jaren 1813-1850*, I, 183.

10. Brugmans, *Paardenkracht en mensenmacht*, p. 86.

11. Zappey, in *De economische geschiedenis van Nederland*, p. 208.

12. Verberne, *Geschiedenis van Nederland in de jaren 1813-1850*, I, 188-90.

13. Brugmans, *De Arbeidende klasse in Nederland in de 19e eeuw*, p. 41-60; idem, *Paardenkracht en mensenmacht*, pp. 69-83.

14. Verberne, *Geschiedenis van Nederland in de jaren 1813-1850*, I, 194; only slightly less somber figures in Boogman, *Rondom 1848*, p. 46: from 10% in 1842 to 15% in 1847. Griffiths cautions that such figures must also be interpreted in light of the rapid population increase of these years, while De Meere judges that in fact the rise in population entirely accounts for the rise in numbers of people on public relief; cf. *Algemene Geschiedenis der Nederlanden*, vol. 10 (1981), pp. 246f, 415.

little to help the plight of the thousands upon thousands who lived on the fringe of society.

Public relief was tied to residence requirements. If one failed to meet them, he could turn to the church, but deacons were often parsimonious and their inquisitorial methods humiliating.[15] Then there was organized charity and philanthrophy, the pride of the self-satisfied bourgeoisie and the condescending aristocracy, but the shame of the workingman who had lost his job. Failing all that, he and his dependants could join the throng of beggars and occasionally participate in looting during hunger riots, or else they could slink away into their humble home and slowly starve. The situation reached its lowest point during the notorious potato famine in the mid-forties.

To help remedy the hopeless situation, the enlightened physiocrat Johannes van den Bosch founded labor colonies in the eastern provinces, where urban paupers and their families were resettled to work the land, dig peat, and prepare the heaths and moors for cultivation. After a decade and a half of barely breaking even, the venture faced bankruptcy. The introduction to the area of textile manufacturing provided some relief, but by the time Van den Bosch died, in 1844, the future of his experiments was still problematic.

Not only the economic livelihood but also the physical health of the working classes left much to be desired. Their diet became increasingly one-sided. Except for pork, meat was rarely on the table.[16] As elsewhere, the potato was increasingly replacing wheat bread until it became the main— and sometimes only—course at all meals, washed down with weak tea or surrogate coffee. Serious malnutrition, going back a number of generations and aggravated by child labor, began in these decades to exact its toll. The home of the average workingman was less likely to be a clean-scrubbed city house or green-bordered country cottage than an ill-lit and ill-ventilated one-room tenement dwelling; and his place of work was more likely to be low-ceilinged and damp than bright and airy. His general health hardly improved when the more expensive beer and ale were gradually displaced

---

15. Cf. Van Loo, "De armenzorg in de Noordelijke Nederlanden, 1770-1854," pp. 426f.

16. De Meere, "Sociale ... structuren in de Noordelijke Nederlanden, 1814-1844," pp. 399-406.

as the popular drink by unwholesome gin distilled from potatoes. Finally, cholera epidemics, first in 1832 and then again in 1833 (from 1848 on returning almost annually) counted hundreds upon hundreds of victims among the most vulnerable of all classes.[17]

Conditions such as these have long been cited to explain the general "physical and mental apathy of the working masses," which in turn is held to be a major reason for Holland's economic backwardness before 1850.[18] The extent of this backwardness is still under investigation. New research methods have unearthed new facts. From 1830 on, both agriculture and shipping enjoyed a modest but steady rate of growth.[19] Industrial expansion, on the other hand, though significant enough to have contributed to some growth in per capita income, probably did so only very modestly,[20] while growth in income from all sources combined did not primarily benefit the upper classes.[21] Thus the picture must be nuanced.

Without any further nuance, however, the opening paragraphs of *Unbelief and Revolution* aver that a general decline in material prosperity was unmistakable. Was Groen van Prinsterer perhaps blind to the signs of economic growth around him, or were the rising trends invisible to him?[22] In any event, according to the testimony of not a few of his generation, who must have been tempted to look back with nostalgia to the

---

17. Verberne, *Geschiedenis van Nederland in de jaren 1813-1850*, I, 205-8; Brugmans, *De arbeidende klasse in Nederland in de 19e eeuw*, pp. 154-56; idem, *Stapvoets voorwaarts*, pp. 30-45.

18. Brugmans, in *Algemene Geschiedenis der Nederlanden*, vol. X (1955), pp. 264f.

19. Cf. Griffiths, *Achterlijk, achter of anders?*, pp. 16-28.

20. Cf. Griffiths, *Industrial Retardation in The Netherlands, 1830-1850*, chaps. 4-7.

21. Cf. De Meere, "Sociale ... structuren in de Noordelijke Nederlanden, 1814-1844," pp. 389-91.

22. We do not know how his personal investment portfolio fared during these years, but it is unlikely to have colored his assessment overly much. De Bosch Kemper, in his review of *Unbelief and Revolution*, would cite the 1848 Statistical Tables (published by the Ministry of Finance) as proof that Groen's picture was far too gloomy; cf. *Nederlandsche Jaarboeken voor Regtsgeleerdheid en Wetgeving* XI (1849): 199. Kemper's own picture, however, was sometimes too rosy: in his study of poverty, *Geschiedkundig onderzoek naar de armoede in ons vaderland* (1851), p. 18, he claimed that deaths from starvation did not occur in the Netherlands, thus ignoring the potato famine of the mid-forties; cf. Brugmans, in *Algemene Geschiedenis der Nederlanden*, vol. X (1955), p. 264.

Golden Age of the 17th and 18th centuries,[23] the economic picture of their own day looked bleak.[24]

POLITICAL FRAMEWORK

Between 1814 and 1848, the political arrangement of Restoration Holland remained essentially the same. When in November 1813 the Dutch, "stealing a march" on the approaching Prussian and Cossack liberators, had liberated themselves from the French occupying forces, they did not restore the former Republic but proclaimed William of Orange "sovereign prince." The constitution of 1814 provided for a strong monarch, assisted by ministers who were individually responsible to him. Retained of the Napoleonic regime were not only the uniformity in justice, taxation, finance and coinage, but also a strong central government. Provincial governors and local subprefects, appointed by the Crown, further strengthened centralist control. Parliamentary participation in government was kept at a minimum.

This arrangement remained basically intact with the constitution of 1815 for the newly created Kingdom of the Netherlands comprising Holland and Belgium. It provided for a bicameral legislature; an upper house or First Chamber, to be composed of notables two or three score in number

---

23. Cf. e.g. Huizinga's classic *Dutch Civilisation in the 17th Century* (1941; Eng. trans. 1968), Van Deursen's sobering *Plain Lives in a Golden Age* (1991), and Schama's lavish *Embarrassment of Riches* (1987).

24. Recent economic historians, making skillful and patient use of (naturally "anachronistic") tools of analysis, enable us today to see and understand—better, it is hoped, than contemporaries were able to—what was actually going on at the time. Their statistical analyses reveal new facts like the one noted above: modest but steady growth in both agriculture and shipping for the years 1830–50; cf. Griffiths, *loc. cit.* (n. 19). Contemporary jeremiads about decline, therefore, ignored longer-term "trends" and cannot be taken at face-value, certainly not when they were aired during the recession of the mid-forties. Nor should one commit a doubly unwarranted generalization—as much historiography about the period seems to have done till recently—by extrapolating backward, as it were, from data known about Holland's late industrial take-off (c. 1895) to infer that its economy *as a whole* was stagnant *throughout* the nineteenth century. On the contrary, current research points to a "lagging" but by no means "backward" economy; cf. Griffiths, *ibid.*, p. 10. In fairness to Groen and other observers before 1850, however, it should be noted here that Griffith's graphs show at the same time that no sector of the Dutch economy (with the possible exception of agriculture) saw any kind of *accelerated growth* or *dramatic upswing* until the third or even the last quarter of the century. Nor is the revisionist account as yet part of the general consensus. In a recent collection of essays on Dutch society since 1815, De Hen gives the updated, rosier picture while Daalder still presents the traditional, gloomier version of pre-1850 economic conditions; cf. F. L. van Holthoon, ed., *De Nederlandse samenleving sinds 1815; wording en samenhang* (Assen: Van Gorcum, 1985), reviewed by H. v. Dijk in *Tijdschrift voor Geschiedenis* 100 (1987): 628f.

and appointed by the king, could review, debate, and vote on bills; the right to initiate bills and interpellate ministers of the Crown *was* reserved for the Second Chamber or lower house, consisting of slightly over 100 members and chosen by the provincial estates. Its sessions were to be public and it was given the right to approve budgets—but in the case of "ordinary expenditures" only, and for ten years at a time. The administration of the colonies was placed directly under the Crown. Education was declared to be an "abiding concern" of the government. Limited freedom of the press would be enjoyed, and religious denominations were given equal protection.

The rule of King William I has been called an enlightened despotism. Both liberals and Catholics in the Belgian provinces grew to hate it with a passion. William's language policy and his meddling with the seminaries reminded them of the days (still within living memory) when Emperor Joseph II ruled the southern Netherlands. The Belgian Revolt and the formation of an independent Kingdom of Belgium in the end forced the king— after a decade of stubborn resistance—to restrict his paternalistic rule to Holland. This unpleasant fact, however, did not induce him or his advisers to alter the nature of that rule. Thus his benign administration from the top down, designed to foster not only economic prosperity but also unity, concord and public tranquility through religious uniformity,[25] led to the persecution of religious dissenters such as the Seceders of 1834.

Once William accepted the separation of Belgium, in 1839, his government initiated the process of adjusting the constitution to fit the kingdom which was now reduced to the northern half. The proceedings of 1840 soon revealed, however, that parliament would use the opportunity to press for more extensive revisions. In response, the government proposed a dozen or so changes, which both chambers approved, and which were ratified later that year by the constitutionally prescribed "chamber double in number." The month-long Double Chamber was a forum for airing views and developing principles that would linger long after. Among the more outstanding participants in the debates were Thorbecke and Groen van Prinsterer, each of whom seemed to represent a distinct school of thought proceeding from more or less articulate premises. This marked the beginning of a revival of political discussion which would engage many minds

---

25. A. de Groot, "Het vroegnegentiende-eeuwse Nederland," p. 29.

throughout the forties and which came to a provisional conclusion in the dramatic revision of 1848.[26]

The constitutional changes of 1840 were not insignificant. Parliament made some gains in strengthening its control over public finance, over colonial administration, over the king's ministers (they were henceforth responsible "before the law" and were to co-sign all laws and edicts pertaining to their department), and over the franchise (it was transferred from local jurisdiction to the national level). Tired and disappointed, the king decided his time was up and abdicated in favor of his son.

King William II was not the man to continue some form of autocratic rule, now tempered by the new restrictions. Even if he had wanted to do so, the hero of Waterloo lacked his father's political sense, financial insight, dedication to administrative detail, and above all, firmness of character.[27] Royal edicts early in the reign of William II gave some relief from the caesaropapism of his predecessor by meeting conscientious objectors halfway in both church and education.[28] In general, the policy of William II was characterized by conciliation and compromise. It was executed by conservatives drawn mainly from the upper classes. His most prominent minister was Floris van Hall, a skillfull debater and shrewd politician whose drastic financial reforms of 1844 probably saved the country from serious trouble bordering on bankruptcy. This clean-up, long overdue,[29] also had the effect that the reform-minded opposition would no longer be sidetracked by the battle for balanced budgets and tighter financial control but could now concentrate on the broader issue of the kingdom's political structure as such. Replies to speeches from the throne urged a revision of the constitution—meekly in 1843, more pointedly in 1844. The government of the day ignored it, or protested that the time was not ripe. In December 1844, nine members of the Second Chamber, led by Thorbecke, used their right of

---

26. Boogman, *Rondom 1848*, pp. 23–49.

27. Cf. Boogman, "The Dutch Crisis in the Eighteen-Forties," p. 196.

28. Groen's friend Elout van Soeterwoude remembered in his old age that as secretary to the Crown Prince in the thirties he had spoken in favor of freedom of religion and Christian schools, "not without harming my ... career yet neither without effect on the later acts of William II." *Briefwisseling*, IV, 483.

29. Zappey estimates that between 1830–39 the average cost to the state of the unresolved Belgian question had amounted to over 40% of its entire annual budget; cf. *De economische geschiedenis van Nederland*, p. 213.

initiative to table a full-fledged proposal for revision, including ministerial responsibility, annual budgets, the right of amendment, and direct elections. The proposal was voted down, but the public debate continued—as is reflected, for example, in Lectures I and XV (12f, 414-21)[30] of *Unbelief and Revolution*. New life was stirring, the middle class was awakening, a long-felt general discontent was being aired, and long-range visions, argued on the basis of a variety of political outlooks, began to compete for the public's attention and favor. Were Thorbecke and associates, were the leading dailies of Amsterdam, Rotterdam and Arnhem right in arguing that the long-awaited natural complement of constitutional monarchy was undisputed rule by parliament, to be wielded by enlightened and well-to-do burghers, preferably of liberal persuasion? Were the numerous minor papers and pamphlets correct in prophesying that universal suffrage and democratic participation in government was the wave of the future and that Holland should prepare itself to fall in line lest it fall behind? The constitutional impasse, accompanied in other areas by uncertainty, half-heartedness, irresolution and even defeatism, continued to mark the decade as a period of crisis with little prospect of resolution.[31] This too was part of the context, this too determined the climate in which *Unbelief and Revolution* was born.

INTELLECTUAL CLIMATE

The intellectual and spiritual temper of Restoration Holland was tame and dull. In many accounts of the period, the years 1815-1848 are depicted as a time of smugness and sluggishness, of phlegmatic complacency and lethargic stagnation. The euphoria of the liberation of 1813 proved short-lived when the challenges of economic reconstruction made it apparent very quickly that a speedy and easy restoration of former prosperity was out of the question. A general inertia was witnessed throughout society. Universities at this time, for example, saw few exciting developments; though holding their own in medicine and the study of the classics they proved quite unreceptive to any of the new ideas in philosophy and little more than imitative with regard to the new discoveries in natural science

---

30. A roman numeral followed by an arabic numeral refers to lecture and page in the first edition of 1847. Page numbers marked by a superscript "2" refer to pages in the second edition of 1868.

31. Boogman, "The Dutch Crisis in the Eighteen-Forties," passim.

that were attracting attention in neighboring countries. Brief spurts of nationalism alone seemed able to ripple the quiet waters of mental life. When Dutch forces under the Crown Prince distinguished themselves in the June days of 1815 at Quatre Bras and Waterloo, the martial feats were celebrated in prayer services, pageants and bombastic poetry. The Ten-Day Campaign of 1831 into the rebelling southern provinces, though hardly victorious when it was concluded by a full-scale withdrawal of troops the moment the Great Powers allowed a French force to invade northward in aid of the rebels, nevertheless provided a powerful injection to boost the flagging national spirit. The author of *Unbelief and Revolution* complains, in both the opening and concluding lectures, of a spirit of listlessness that hung over the nation. Unimaginative complacency and lack of energy and initiative set the tone. A much-cited couplet of the time, from a poem by a Barend Klyn entitled "To Our Country's Young Men," betrays the mood of the period:

> If calm in spirit you remain
> at home in palace or in hut,
> you may regard yourself as blessed,
> for peace is bliss and bliss is peace.[32]

In his Preface (xii), Groen talks of this general frame of mind as one "for which it is difficult to find an appropriate name." It took the poet-novelist Potgieter to symbolize the era in a name which has stuck: in an "allegorical sketch" of the Dutch people, composed in 1842, he introduced the character of Jan Salie, a cross between a self-satisfied milksop and a hidebound stick-in-the-mud whose favorite drink was neither Schiedam nor Schnapps but wholesome "saliemelk" (sage-milk) and for whom the present was the best of all possible worlds and any yearning for "progress" a sure sign of ingratitude. The mood of the time is also captured in the gently satirical *Camera Obscura* of Hildebrand (pseudonym of Nicolaas Beets), with its

---

32. "Gij in paleis of stulp gezeten / Gij kunt door 't kalm gemoed u zelven zalig heeten / Want rust is zaligheid en zaligheid is rust." Quoted in M. Elisabeth Kluit, *Het Protestantse Réveil in Nederland en daarbuiten, 1815-1865* (Amsterdam: H. J. Paris, 1970).

entertaining sketches of the stuffy Stastok clan and the self-satisfied airs of the parvenu family Kegge.[33]

On the whole, the literature of the time was stamped by sentimentalism rather than Romanticism. The poets of "hearth and home" were more popular than the writers of epics and lyrics. Both subject-matter and its treatment often bordered on the banal. Other arts suffered from the same anemia. It was indeed the Biedermeier period in which architecture, for example, was in the grip of a pseudo-monumental neo-classicism and music was appreciated for its ability to offer gentle amusement rather than sublime art.[34]

Raised in the polite society of The Hague, Groen van Prinsterer had first-hand knowledge of the socially acceptable opinions of his day: one was expected to be moderately modernist in religious beliefs and moderately liberal in political views. A general tolerance prevailed: one was willing to respect, if not embrace, most any creed—except those held with fervor: these were spurned as symptomatic of uncultured "enthusiasm."

The practical rationalism of the eighteenth century lived on in mitigated form among the staid burgher class, whose personal creed was often limited to the Kantian triad of "God, virtue, and immortality." Academic philosophy was for decades dominated by Philip Willem van Heusde, whose lectures in Utrecht between 1804-39 emphasized beauty and simplicity, common sense and respect for received religious opinion.[35] Van Heusde's eclectic philosophy aimed at a synthesis of Christianity and Platonism. A gifted teacher who employed a gentle version of the Socratic method, he believed that a revival of Greek letters would help young people develop their full potentials ("germs") of "common sense." In combination with a "purified Christianity" such a *paideia* would enable individuals to approximate "conformity to the Deity" and progressively transform the human race into a true humanity. Mankind's greatest teacher was Christ, who showed by his example how man may employ his potential for self-mastery and self-improvement to attain to moral perfection: Christ's supernatural pedagogy of mankind was the consummation of the preparatory work

---

33. Cf. Meijer, *Literature of the Low Countries*, pp. 209-15.

34. The more positive sides to this period in the literary arts are persuasively presented by Buitendijk in "De jonge Da Costa, romanticus in de biedermeiertijd," pp. 53-62.

35. Sassen, *Geschiedenis van de wijsbegeerte in Nederland*, pp. 298-303.

performed by all natural theology in its best exponents, notably Plato. In his educational philosophy, Van Heusde taught that the phase of childhood was best suited for nurturing religious sentiments, free of doctrines and focused on the noble life of Christ. Thus the elementary school, since it serves childhood, should stress faith as a childlike trust in God and avoid doctrinal niceties and other theoretical exercises, which are better suited for young men who pursue higher education, the intermediate school being reserved for boyhood training in practical subjects such as the commercial and medical arts.[36]

Such was the only home-grown philosophy of the period. Van Heusde's pupils greedily imbibed his cocktail of Plato, Lessing, Hemsterhuis and Herder, which they spiked with an ingredient lately introduced by Schleiermacher: *feeling*.[37] The best of them soon filled university chairs, notably in Groningen, where they developed a distinctive academic theology that came to be known as the Groningen School. This school claimed to be the legitimate heir of "indigenous Dutch evangelicalism" dating back to the pre-Reformation movement of the Brethren of the Common Life. The Groningen divines regretted that the supposedly native Netherlandic strain of tolerant and mild Christianity, as exemplified in Wessel Gansfort and Erasmus, had later been overrun by aggressive creeds imported from alien soil, such as Lutheranism and especially Calvinism.[38] In 1837 they started a quarterly, *Waarheid in Liefde* (Truth in Love), subtitled "A theological journal for cultured Christians." Their chief maxims amounted to "no creed but Christ" and "not doctrine but life," and their main tenets were that revelation aimed at the education of mankind to become children of God and that Christ was the perfect Educator: He had not died to satisfy divine justice but to exemplify divine love. Although they rejected the higher criticism of a David Friedrich Strauss, maintaining, for example, the historicity of Christ's bodily resurrection, at the same time they allowed that Scripture was not necessarily infallible and insisted that man was not totally depraved. In line with their teacher, Van Heusde, they appealed to

36. Lakke, *Philip Willem van Heusde*, pp. 52–69, 190–225, 283–90.

37. From Benjamin Constant they first learned to view religion as a *"sentiment intérieur"*; from Schleiermacher they learned to give a systematic elaboration of religion as having its seat in the human breast; cf. Vree, *De Groninger godgeleerden*, pp. 30f, 153–60, 338.

38. Vree, *De Groninger godgeleerden*, pp. 244, 280–82, 285–89, 328f, 341.

the "germ of the holy" with which every man is endowed, rendering him susceptible to higher revelation.[39] A humanistic strain colored their entire theology. In the spiritual climate of the day, their emphasis on the human potential would soon eclipse divine revelation, as human goals would come to replace supernatural ends. Already the empiricism of Utrecht and the modernism of Leyden were taking shape in the younger minds of future leaders like Opzoomer, Kuenen and Scholten.[40]

Irenic in spirit and broadly tolerant in confessional definition, the adherents of the Groningen School were influential for several decades, filling many pulpits and university chairs and often dominating the Reformed synod by sheer numbers. They were active in home and foreign missions and in the dissemination of Bibles. In particular, they devoted their energies to the establishment and inspection of government schools, the common schools for primary education.[41] The influence of the Groningen divines is reflected in a number of polemical comments in *Unbelief and Revolution*, notably in Lecture VII (155).

In these years of steering a safe middle course between extremes of any kind, the *juste milieu* or golden mean was also recommended for religion. Van Heusde, while he rejected the "atheistic neologism" born in the age of reason, equally abhorred the "mystical fanaticism" so prevalent among orthodox Dutch Calvinists. Many of these people had for generations attended obscure conventicles in addition to public worship services, and since 1834 were even heard to be seceding from the Reformed Church altogether. Van Heusde approved heartily of the measures taken by the government to quell this religious rebellion and he openly attacked Groen van Prinsterer's critique of these measures.[42] The Groningen men, too, disapproved strongly of Secession, in which they recognized not only a revival of sixteenth- and seventeenth-century Calvinism but also the influence of the contemporary awakening known by its French name *Réveil* and imported, once again, from Geneva. In fact, in polemical opposition to the

39. Vree, *De Groninger godgeleerden*, passim, but esp. pp. 82–89, 153, 173, 178–80, 196–99, 201, 206f, 227, 254, 260–64, 325.

40. Cf. Bavinck, "Recent Dogmatic Thought in the Netherlands," pp. 212–18; Rasker, *De Nederlandse Hervormde Kerk vanaf 1795*, pp. 45–54.

41. Vree, *De Groninger godgeleerden*, pp. 208–21, 269–75.

42. Lakke, *Philip Willem van Heusde*, p. 44.

influence of that "Christian Réveil" with its reactionary theology espoused by mere "dilettantes,"[43] they referred to their own school as the mother of the "Evangelical Revival" whose historic mission it was to counter the reigning cold and arid rationalism with religious warmth and feeling, even with mystery and mysticism, provided it steered clear of the bigoted beliefs of a former, narrow-minded age which were wrong-headedly being revived by the Réveil.[44]

Having sketched the economic, social, political, and intellectual context of Groen's lecture series, we shall devote the next chapter to outlining the all-important religious backdrop.

---

43. Cf. Vree, *De Groninger godgeleerden*, pp. 205n, 305, 321.

44. Lakke, *Philip Willem van Heusde*, pp. 40, 325; Vree, *De Groninger godgeleerden*, pp. 17–23, 37–40, 162f, 330–42.

2
—
RELIGIOUS AWAKENING

While the Groningen divines worked arduously for an indigenous Evangelical Revival that had learned to relativize the restrictions placed on religion by reason, the religious movement that was to nurture Groen van Prinsterer was of a more radical type.

ROOTS OF THE DUTCH RÉVEIL

The Christian Réveil in Holland of 1820–50 was a blend of native Calvinism and the Methodist-inspired revival that appeared in various centers throughout Western Europe in the first quarter of the nineteenth century. Wherever the latter movement spread it questioned mere outward observance of religion and insisted on personal experience and inner conviction of the new life in Christ. The movement was further characterized by a rediscovery of the Bible as the guide for all of life, to be appropriated through personal study and communal sharing. Concentrating on the core of the gospel, on the fundamentals of biblical religion, the Réveil preached the gospel of free grace through Christ's atoning sacrifice. It warned against the tacit assumption underlying much contemporary Christianity that the merits of a virtuous life and good works ensured the Christian a place in heaven. Under the influence of Romanticism, participants in the Réveil were for a time heavily preoccupied with apocalyptic speculations about the end time; after 1830 this interest gradually receded before a growing concern with social evils and an urgent call to engage in practical philanthropy.

Although much research still needs to be done to clarify the question of the origins of the Dutch revival,[1] a number of strands can be identified that went into the weaving of this tapestry. As elsewhere, so in Holland

---

1. Cf. Schram, "Réveil-onderzoek," p. 9.

around 1800 efforts for revival were able to link up with existing "unofficial" religion as expressed in thriving conventicles and "exercises" (home gatherings for worship, often led by unordained men). Private meetings of the saints had been encouraged for more than a century by pietist movements of various stripes, in protest against the official churches—Reformed, but also Lutheran and Mennonite—which were reproached for giving stones for bread: that is, for providing sermons breathing cold and dry orthodoxy or (increasingly after 1750) optimistic and superficial rationalism. Earlier in the eighteenth century, small groups of Moravian Brethren had settled in various localities in Holland; their contacts with the Reformed Church influenced its spiritual life, particularly by encouraging the faithful to look beyond denominational walls for the sake of practicing communion of the saints. When John Wesley visited Holland in 1783, and again in 1786, he was well received, particularly in the homes of the well-to-do, who normally did not look kindly on "Arminian tendencies." In the same decade a number of local chapters were begun of the *Christentumsgesellschaft* of Basel, for the mutual edification of "lovers of Christian truth and godliness." Activities of this kind led in Amsterdam to a small split-off from the Lutheran church.[2] In 1797, the first Dutch missionary society was founded, in emulation of Christians in London.[3] Not long after Wilberforce had published his *Real Christianity* a Dutch translation was on the market.[4]

New indigenous developments could only foster these efforts at revival. When the Calvinist identity of the Reformed Church further eroded during the French period (1795-1813), a dramatic growth in the popularity of exercises and conventicles testified to the continued resistance to the spirit of the age. One instance of this was to prove of special significance later: starting in 1801, a textile manufacturer in Leyden by the name of Lefébure led a weekly Bible study and prayer group in his home which was attended by some thirty to eighty people from various walks of life, including university students.[5]

---

2. P. N. Holtrop, *Tussen Piëtisme en Réveil* (Amsterdam, 1975).
3. A. D. Martin, *Doctor Vanderkemp* (Westminster, n. d.), pp. 53–60.
4. Kluit, *Het Protestantse Réveil in Nederland en daarbuiten*, pp. 42–46, 82.
5. Kluit, *Het Protestantse Réveil in Nederland en daarbuiten*, pp. 58, 66.

A book which receives favorable mention in Groen van Prinsterer's Lecture II (30) also dates from this time: the warm and devout *Preach the Gospel to Every Creature* by Hieronymus van Alphen.[6] Many years of correspondence with the Swiss pastor Johann Kaspar Lavater of Zurich had confirmed Van Alphen in the gospel of grace, and he spent the last decade of his life writing tracts and broadsheets critical of the thinking of his day. Though Van Alphen owed his reputation to a charming collection of verses for children—moralistic poems admonishing Dutch boys and girls to be industrious, studious, grateful, kind and good—his political and philosophical writings attacked autonomous morality, agnostic freethought and optimistic egalitarianism. Operating from an eclectic and pious version of common-sense philosophy infused with a Calvinist theology, he evolved from a defender of the Enlightenment "properly understood" to a courageous spokesman of the Counter-Enlightenment. By the time Van Alphen was editing his *Christelijke Spectator* in 1799, his stance also implied a critique of the revolution in his country. In his book of 1801 he condemned the revolution explicitly because of its connection with the "false philosophy" of the age.[7] Curiously, as early as 1768 one of the theses appended to his doctoral dissertation ran: "We defend, against Rousseau, *Du Contrat Social*, IV, viii, that a republic of Christians who are truly such can be stable."[8] Groen's friend Koenen devoted a full-length monograph to him in 1844, which Groen read with "uncommon interest."[9]

Personal contacts and both learned and popular publications from another Swiss city added to the Dutch awakening. Geneva, the city of Calvin (and Rousseau) saw a remarkable revival of evangelical faith in the early years of the Restoration. A visit by the mystic Madame de Krüdener helped ignite the smouldering flames in 1813.[10] A few years later a small circle of students and young pastors began to meet regularly for Bible study; it included Jean-Henri Merle d'Aubigné, Frédéric Monod, and César

---

6. H. van Alphen, *Predikt het Euangelium allen Creaturen! Eene staatsmaxime in het Rijk van Waarheid en Deugd* (The Hague: Thierry en Mensing, 1801).

7. *Predikt het Euangelium*, pp. 162f, 353; quoted in Smitskamp, *Groen van Prinsterer als historicus*, p. 53n.

8. P. J. Buijnsters, *Hieronymus van Alphen (1746-1803)* (Assen: Van Gorcum, 1973), pp. 44, 99-113, 259-64, 312-30.

9. *Briefwisseling*, II, 585.

10. Gäbler, "De weg naar het Réveil in Genève," p. 40.

Malan. It was to this circle that the Scottish baron Robert Haldane, an itinerant lay preacher of Calvinist Baptist tenets, lectured on the Epistle to the Romans in the winter season of 1817.[11] When the official church clamped down on these and similar activities, Merle went to Berlin where he studied briefly under Neander and Schleiermacher; in 1819 he became pastor of the Walloon church in Hamburg, and in 1828 he moved to Brussels to become court preacher, where he was instrumental in the spiritual awakening of Groen van Prinsterer.[12] Merle attained an international reputation through his *History of the Reformation*. César Malan, who seceded from the state church, wrote many tracts and hymns and made Geneva his home base for missionary journeys through France. Visiting Holland in 1842, Malan preached in the Walloon Church of The Hague (much to the delight of the Groens, who invited him to dinner) and in the English Episcopal Church in Amsterdam. Malan repeated his visit in the following year and was again warmly received in every Réveil circle, whose members felt blessed and strengthened by his ministry; among them was the founder of a Christian elementary school in Nymegen, J. J. L. van der Brugghen.[13]

LEADING PERSONALITIES

All these foreign injections stimulated and encouraged a growing number of Dutch Christians who held fast to the faith of the fathers. Yet leadership, let alone organization and communal action, was slow in developing. One of the more prominent and eloquent spokesmen of Dutch Calvinism since the turn of the century had been the poet-scholar Willem Bilderdijk (1756–1831), who as non-juring barrister had lived in exile between 1795–1806. Excluded from every university chair or public post in the Restoration years, he had made his home in Leyden where he lectured privately to a small circle of students. The thrust of his lectures was at once an impassioned pro-Orange, pro-Calvinist reading of Dutch history and a scathing impeachment of the liberalism current in church, state and academy. For a time the young student Guillaume Groen van Prinsterer was among his audience, critically assessing the refreshingly and sometimes outrageously

---

11. Alexander Haldane, *The Lives of Robert Haldane of Airthrey, and of His Brother James Alexander Haldane* (London, 1853), chap. xviii.

12. *Briefwisseling*, II, 182.

13. Kluit, *Het Protestantse Réveil in Nederland en daarbuiten*, pp. 94, 431f, 489.

new views and opinions.[14] Bilderdijk's small but devoted following carried his ideas into the citadels of official learning. Looking back many years later, Groen would credit Bilderdijk for having "dissipated the prestige of infallibility in which the dominant opinion had found its safeguard" and for making even the opposing camp conscious of the "necessity to re-examine questions presumed settled"; thus his significance for historical studies, even if largely negative, was nevertheless immense: "We may deplore the acrimony which, on both sides, often turned the discussions into disputes, but at least, and that was an immense gain, science, long stationary because men thought they had attained the limits of truth, resumed its march by the impulse of doubt."[15] Besides his poetry, Bilderdijk wrote many tracts contending for the Reformation faith and fulminating against its modern detractors. One of the last projects he completed was an annotated translation of Thomas Chalmers's *Evidence and Authority of the Christian Revelation*.

The lasting reputation of the "school of Bilderdijk" was in no small measure due to another of his pupils, Isaac da Costa (1798–1860), who came to rival the master in Calvinist convictions, romantic poetry, patriotic fervor, and iconoclastic *Zeitkritik*. When Da Costa published his *Grievances Against the Spirit of the Age*[16] it struck like a bombshell. Often called the "birth-cry" of the Dutch Réveil proper, the tract inveighed against the easy optimism of the time and derided the comforting beliefs in social progress and human perfectibility. Its pages bristled with strident denunciations of the period's arrogant self-delusion and moral laxity, but also with fervent exhortations to acknowledge man's utter depravity and his desperate need of true enlightenment by the eternal Word and Spirit.

Isaac da Costa, and his friend, the young medical doctor Abraham Capadose (1795–1874), had together attended Bilderdijk's lectures in Leyden, and after starting their respective careers in their home town Amsterdam, had publicly embraced Christianity through baptism. Both men came from the Sephardic Jewish community of Amsterdam, where their conversion caused quite a stir. Much greater, however, was the stir aroused throughout the land by Da Costa's *Grievances* which had become an overnight bestseller.

---

14. Tazelaar, *De Jeugd van Groen*, pp. 74–86; Van Essen, "Bilderdijk en Groen van Prinsterer," passim.

15. Groen van Prinsterer, *Archives*, I (2nd ed., 1840), 26.

16. *Bezwaren tegen de Geest der Eeuw* (Leyden: Herdingh en Zoon, 1823).

A spate of articles and reviews, pamphlets, even sermons, lampooned the author as the "conceited monkey of the old baboon" Bilderdijk, and both master and pupil were declared to be obscurantists, enemies of enlightenment, extinguishers of light and lovers of the dark night of ignorance and bigotry. His reputation ruined, the young lawyer Da Costa had to look for a different source of income. He became a private lecturer, regaling small groups of friends with series of lectures on language, church and national history, the book of Acts, and so on. Friends helped out discreetly, in return for his frequent meditations at religious soirées. Indeed, the regular "Sunday evenings" held at Da Costa's home from 1826 on may be regarded as the real beginning of the Amsterdam Réveil. Da Costa had come to the idea of hosting such gatherings after a visit that year by the Swiss pastor Chavannes, who told him of similar evenings in the canton of Vaud which were organized even at the risk of prosecution by the authorities. Da Costa's Sunday evenings continued for decades. They were spent in prayer, much singing, and Bible study led by the host, and were frequented by individuals even from outside Amsterdam.[17]

If the revival in the nation's capital emphasized personal salvation, the revival in Holland's administrative center, The Hague, was from the beginning colored by an interest in ecclesiastical and political affairs. One of its central figures was Cornelis baron van Zuylen van Nijevelt (1777-1833), who published a tract in 1828 entitled *Het Liberalismus*, which contained sentences like: "Liberalism presses people and nations together, incites them against one another, and after causing the foundations of all religion and social life to totter, ends by bringing about that general apostasy and disorder which has long been clearly foretold ..."[18] In the unpublished, expanded manuscript we read: "The Dutch church is perishing from delicacy."[19]

Two preachers of The Hague who exerted an influence on Groen's life and thought were Jean Charles Isaac Secrétan and Dirk Molenaar. Molenaar was the Reformed minister who in 1827 published (anonymously) an *Address to All My Reformed Fellow-Believers*, in which he castigated the

---

17. Kluit, *Het Protestantse Réveil in Nederland en daarbuiten*, p. 167; Evenhuis, *Ook dat was Amsterdam*, V, 116–18.

18. *Het Liberalismus* (Amsterdam: J. H. den Ouden, 1828), p. 37.

19. Orig.: "... gaat ten onder aan kiesheid"; quoted in Kluit, *Het Protestantse Réveil in Nederland en daarbuiten*, p. 191.

church's latitudinarianism, a policy which went so far as to tolerate even the denial of the divinity of Christ. Molenaar publicly raised the question, Is it honest to continue to call oneself Reformed while believing the Synod of Dort to have erred? adding almost defiantly: Why not convene a general assembly and calmly propose to all members to change the church's teachings and then, in light of those who would not choose for this, simply and calmly divide the church's property and in that way promote peace and love? The authorities were not amused and had the police track down the identity of the author. A chastened Molenaar explained in a conciliatory letter to the king that he had not intended to cause a schism. Before the year's end the "libellous" tract went through seven printings.[20]

Isaac Secrétan (1798-1875) was pastor of the Walloon Church, a congregation of the francophone branch of the Dutch Reformed Church. He had accepted a call to The Hague in 1828. A man of milder views, especially on worldly amusements, he did succeed after a while in convincing the circle around Molenaar that he too was a son of the awakening. For years he conducted Bible studies on Friday evenings for some forty participants. Here Groen and his wife first met De Clercq and Van der Kemp.

Willem de Clercq (1795-1844) was originally a Mennonite from Amsterdam who had befriended Da Costa for literary reasons, but had undergone his spiritual influence as well, to the point of accepting infant baptism. After an early and successful start as a grain merchant in the family firm, De Clercq was appointed acting director of the crown corporation of the *Nederlandsche Handelmaatschappij*, that personal creation of the king intended to boost trade with the colonies. This appointment had brought De Clercq and his family to The Hague, where they resided till 1831 and participated in the life of the awakening there.[21]

Carel Maria van der Kemp (1799-1862) had been a student in Leyden contemporary with Groen. His law practice in The Hague allowed him to indulge in the study of history, which seems to have been sparked by a publication attacking Da Costa's interpretation of Prince Maurice's role in the Arminian controversy of 1618-19. When the standard work on Dutch church

---

20. Kluit, *Het Protestantse Réveil in Nederland en daarbuiten*, pp. 211-13.

21. Kluit, *Het Protestantse Réveil in Nederland en daarbuiten*, pp. 133f, 193.

history by Ypey and Dermout came out, Van der Kemp was so incensed that he wrote a three-volume work refuting "Arminian misrepresentations."[22]

PRACTICAL ACTION

The author on the Dutch Réveil from whom we have derived many details above, Elisabeth Kluit, has concluded that it was the awakening in The Hague, particularly in the person of Groen van Prinsterer after his publication of *Nederlandsche Gedachten* (about which more later), that first broadened the Réveil's concerns from personal piety to social and political issues; a mainly negative attitude with respect to "the world" and "the times" gradually made way for positive involvement in public affairs.[23] If The Hague was first, however, other centers followed suit. In 1834 the Amsterdam revivalists had launched their periodical *Nederlandsche Stemmen*, which from the start devoted a disproportionately high number of articles to political questions.[24]

To the credit of the Amsterdam circle it must also be recorded that they soon enlarged their outreach for souls to embrace the organizing of sewing classes for young girls, Christian nursery schools, and tuition-free dayschools for children of the lower classes—all of which included in their curriculum a heavy dose of Bible stories and Christian doctrines at the appropriate—and sometimes not so appropriate—level.[25] In The Hague, the wives of Groen and De Clercq had taken it upon themselves, as early as 1832, to start a nursery school for pre-schoolers and a seamstress academy for older girls. Groen himself, and his friend Elout, in the late thirties, began to make personal visits to the homes of the poor, especially in long, cold winters which often left such people without means to keep their families warm and fed. The two benefactors would inquire into the circumstances of families that had come to their attention, give money where it seemed responsible, dispense practical advice, and … speak to them of

---

22. Kluit, *Het Protestantse Réveil in Nederland en daarbuiten*, pp. 200–02; cf. C. M. van der Kemp, *De Eere der Nederlandsche Hervormde Kerk gehandhaafd tegen Ypey en Dermout* (3 vols.; 1830–1833).

23. Kluit, *Het Protestantse Réveil in Nederland en daarbuiten*, p. 205.

24. De Gaay Fortman, *Figuren uit het Réveil*, p. 322; the journal's full name reads in translation: Netherlandic Voices on Religion, Politics, History and Literature.

25. Kluit, *Het Protestantse Réveil in Nederland en daarbuiten*, p. 416; for the many-sided activities of the Amsterdam circle after 1845, see Evenhuis, *Ook dat was Amsterdam*, V, 244–51, 264–71.

Jesus.[26] Activities like these caused the name of the Groen van Prinsterers to be uttered with affectionate respect in the poorer wards of the city, and reportedly may have saved them, when a riot threatened, from having the windows of their stately mansion smashed.[27]

Contacts with the lower classes only strengthened the friends' resolve to work for improving not just the church but also the schools, for to orthodox Christians the "mixed" or common schools of The Hague were fast becoming as unsatisfactory as Holland's public schools in general. Conceived in 1806 in an atmosphere of enlightened, non-sectarian Christianity, the public school's instruction in the "basic principles of religion and morality" had over the years evolved into the same namby-pamby Protestantism that they found so objectionable in the church. But to their dismay they came to the discovery that their application to the local authorities for permission to erect a separate private Christian school—a legal step required by the constitution—repeatedly met with refusal. Behind this refusal lay fear of sectarian divisiveness in the nation.

In 1840, with the formal separation of Belgium a fact, Holland's constitution had to be revised. Groen used the occasion to argue for a clause providing full freedom of education: if parents feel in conscience bound to seek more positive Christian instruction for their offspring they should not be hindered; children are not the property of the state, as the revolution holds.[28] Later that year Groen was appointed to a royal commission to draw up recommendations for introducing desired changes in the education system of the land. Within days he was swamped with advice, both solicited and unsolicited, from diverse correspondents.[29] Personally, he was at a loss; he hesitated to recommend a religiously pluralist school system, preferring instead a local option for a specific form of religious instruction during school hours. In a letter to his friend Da Costa he raised the possibility of recommending yet another "middle" course: namely, that government schools be required to give instruction "in those principal truths

---

26. An early instance of "patronage," which became a more common method of practicing charity after 1840; cf. Van Loo, "De armenzorg in de Noordelijke Nederlanden, 1770-1854," pp. 424, 432.

27. Mulder, *Groen van Prinsterer, staatsman en profeet*, p. 131.

28. *Adviezen 1840*, p. 57.

29. *Briefwisseling*, II, 336-61.

on which Lutherans, Calvinists and also Catholics like St. Augustine, St. Bernard, Bossuet and Fénelon agree."[30] In the end, the commission made no concrete proposals for change, although it did achieve, as we shall see, by royal decree of January 1842, the possibility of appeal to the provincial authorities in case local governments refused permission for whatever reason. Even then, the laborious process did not always yield the desired result, since the same prejudices and arbitrariness reigned at the provincial level.

In these years Groen made or renewed the acquaintance of brothers who would attend his lecture series midway through the decade: Pieter Jacob Elout van Soeterwoude, appointed attorney at the Provincial Court; Aeneas baron Mackay, who also served as chamberlain to Crown Prince (after 1840 King) Willem and his wife; Johan Anne Singendonck, clerk with the Council of State; and Lord Bylandt, a medical doctor of German extraction who set up residence in The Hague. Groen's old friend Van der Kemp, meanwhile, had become a deputy district judge. A spatially more distant yet no less intimate relationship developed between Groen and the Amsterdam merchant and city councillor Hendrik Jacob Koenen (1809–74). The two had met for the first time in the summer of 1829, when Koenen was still studying law at Leyden. It appeared that they shared a common interest not only in the Réveil but also in scholarly studies. Koenen reintroduced himself to Groen by letter in early 1830, expressing the hope that they could come to a periodic exchange of ideas. He explained that his studies, too, were in the areas of both literature and law. In philosophical jurisprudence especially he was reading a wide range of authors, both recommended and scorned, and he had come to the tentative conclusion that in every age jurisprudence seemed to stay in step with developments in theology. Koenen confided to the older man that he leaned toward the Historical School after saying farewell to Wolffianism because it put natural theology on a par with revealed religion. Groen answered encouragingly.[31] Over the years the Groen-Koenen correspondence increased in frequency as both men saw their involvement in public responsibilities increase.

---

30. *Brieven van Da Costa*, I, 68.
31. *Briefwisseling*, I, 262f, 267.

In the spring of 1840, new areas of Christian work had been brought to the attention of the friends when leading men of the British and Foreign Anti-Slavery Society visited their country. On this occasion George Alexander expressed the hope that Mr. Groen might be for Holland what Mr. Wilberforce had been for England: the pivot of a national protest against slavery. Then, in April, Elizabeth Fry visited Holland. Crusading on behalf of prison reform and abolitionism, she met Groen and others in The Hague, and Da Costa and De Clercq in Amsterdam. They remembered that two years earlier their friend Gefken had written in *Nederlandsche Stemmen* that slavery caused the loss of nothing less than "man's personality, which according to Christianity has its ground and origin in the image of God in which man is created." A visit by John Scoble in 1841 again laid the deplorable condition of African slaves upon their conscience. The friends consulted and came to the unanimous conclusion that abolition for the slaves of Surinam was desirable since their present status impeded efforts to evangelize them. An Abolition Society was founded and a request for a charter sent to the king, for the time being without result.[32]

THE BATTLE FOR CHURCH REFORM

In 1842, Groen and six of his friends in The Hague sent an overture to Synod requesting maintenance of the church's doctrinal standards, particularly against tenets of the Groningen School. Would the friends in Amsterdam follow suit and file a notification of concurrence or else a similar petition? Da Costa demurred. No healing can be expected, he wrote Groen, by restoring a former situation; confessions are no safeguards against rationalism, only the living Christ is. Moreover, their role is played out; the new age is bound to see a wholesale revamping of theology. Besides, has history not shown that dead orthodoxy invariably ensues once believers' living confessions are enshrined into official creeds?[33]

---

32. Reinsma, *Een merkwaardige episode uit de geschiedenis van de slavenemancipatie*, pp. 7–14, 28–40; *Briefwisseling*, II, 419, 944–46; V, 115–18, 793–95. The Society would be revived in 1853 under the chairmanship of Groen; when emancipation finally came to Surinam in 1863, it was Gefken who, as attorney general in Paramaribo, was given an *aubade* by the grateful ex-slaves. Cf. De Gaay Fortman, *Figuren uit het Réveil*, p. 215.

33. Kluit, *Het Protestantse Réveil in Nederland en daarbuiten*, pp. 436–38; *Brieven van Da Costa*, I, 105, 176–84.

Da Costa would not fight on the basis of creedal formulations. That this refusal did not stem from theological indifference on his part, however, he proved a few years later when he published a short treatise attacking the *Handbook for Christian Apologetics and Dogmatics*, written in Latin by Hofstede De Groot and Pareau, professors of theology in Groningen. Da Costa accused the Groningen divines of teaching a false Christology, a one-sided doctrine of the Trinity, a Pelagian anthropology, and a subversive doctrine of Scripture. "What will become of Christianity," he asked, "if its objective foundations are thus undermined and a reconstruction of Christianity is attempted on the basis of a mystical subjectivism?" Before long, the leading men of the Réveil (most of whom, as we have seen, were not professional theologians) began to hold the Groningen "reconstruction of Christianity" directly responsible for the far worse forms of negation represented by an increasing number of vocal Dutch disciples of Strauss and Bauer. The Groningen men retorted with bitter irony that in that case one would have to hold the orthodox at least equally responsible, since their confessional rigidity had kept them from joining forces in the pressing cause of theological renewal, driving many well-intentioned contemporaries straight into the arms of modernism.[34]

A man like Groen could only deplore the lack of a united front in the battle for the restoration of the church. But perhaps other activities could unite the friends? Thus he welcomed the initiative taken by a relative newcomer to the campaign for Christian action. Otto Gerhard Heldring (1804–76) had begun to correspond with several Réveil members. He was serving a large rural parish in Gelderland, where he had become intimately acquainted with the plight of lowly peasants and day-laborers sunk in poverty, illiteracy and superstition. A man of practical bent, Heldring looked for effective remedies and soon became involved in running evening classes, setting up homes for orphans and neglected children, breaking the soil of the Veluwe moors, digging village wells, and so on. In May 1845 came his circular letter begging the friends of revival for united support for these

---

34. Cf. J. van den Berg, "P. Hofstede de Groot en het Réveil," pp. 16, 30f. See also Johan Huizinga, *Verzamelde Werken*, VIII, 139–63.

works of Christian mercy and social amelioration. What must we do? the circular asked; continue our separate ways, or is united action possible?[35]

The result of this rallying cry was a meeting in the nation's capital on 26 August 1845. Interdenominational in make-up, it was chaired by Groen. It adopted the name "Christian Friends" and started a tradition of meeting twice a year to consult on social projects, to set up small institutions, and to collect monies for the same. Groen was pleased that already at the second meeting, in January 1846, the whole question of education was thoroughly discussed and a few practical steps were taken to promote private Christian schools and train Christian teachers. Nevertheless, he was disappointed that the church issue was studiously avoided as too controversial.[36] Few Reformed laymen and even fewer Reformed pastors favored the "juridical-confessional" strategy Groen wanted to follow: namely, to protest to the church boards that modernists had unlawfully gained access to the pulpits of the denomination and ought by right to be subjected to church discipline. A sizable group advocated instead a more spiritual and irenic approach: work from within by proclaiming the full gospel and letting it bear fruit over time. Da Costa called this the "medical" way: more effective than fighting legal battles was to let truth and error grapple in a fair exchange, and God would bless such testimony in His own good time. Groen was inclined to call this approach deplorable passivity and dereliction of duty. The issue remained a bone of contention among the Christian Friends and was to lead to a parting of the ways before a decade was past. In the meantime, their meetings were devoted to discussing such topics as: Should we form temperance unions or are prohibition societies the need of our time? How can lotteries be combated, Sunday observance be promoted? And, in the meeting of April 1850, the interesting question: What are we to think, relative to the Netherlands, of the opinion of Professor Stahl of Berlin that Christians should form a political party?[37] The early fifties saw the establishment of Christian electoral associations in a number of urban districts; a nation-wide federation of such associations did not become a fact until 1879, when the Anti-Revolutionary Party became the

35. *Briefwisseling*, V, 141–44.

36. *Brieven van Da Costa*, I, 238.

37. Kluit, *Het Protestantse Réveil in Nederland en daarbuiten*, p. 482.

first organized political party of the Netherlands. The peculiar name of this party is a direct fruit of Groen van Prinsterer's lifework.

Groen van Prinsterer was a lifelong member of the Dutch Reformed Church, the post-revolutionary continuation of the denomination which during the Republic (1576–1795) had been, though not officially established, both favored and monitored by the civil authorities.

The Reformed Church, put on a par with the Lutheran, Mennonite, Remonstrant Arminian and Roman Catholic communions as a result of the revolution of 1795, was given a new administrative organization by royal decree of 1816. Its presbyterian polity was replaced by an annual synod supervised by the government's Ministry of Public Worship; the president of the synod as well as the members of a permanent synodical committee were appointed by the Crown. Under this administrative apparatus the Reformed Church entered a historical phase that would be marked by an ever-widening gap between the official church organs and the spiritual life of the local congregations.[38]

The subscription formula for prospective pastors was revised in 1816 to bring it up to date. In effect it now freely admitted candidates for the ministry who preferred enlightened supernaturalism to Calvinist orthodoxy by asking them to declare their agreement with "the doctrine which in conformity with God's holy word is contained in the received forms of unity of the Dutch Reformed Church." This new wording gave rise to the well-known *quia-quatenus* debate, for it clearly allowed the dual interpretation of agreeing with the confessional standards of the church either *inasmuch as* or only *insofar as* these standards conformed to God's Word. The ambiguity thus introduced and legitimized a degree of doctrinal freedom in pulpit and seminary that was increasingly more at odds with historic Christianity, while those who began to lodge official protests discovered that the church courts tended to side with latitudinarians of various stripes.

The wording was advisedly and necessarily ambiguous, one of the framers of the Form of Subscription "confessed" twenty years later, when increasing unrest and contention had repeatedly centered on the charge that the Form was equivocal—a charge to which former members of the Synod of 1816 had so far haughtily replied that they would never have

---

38. Cf. Vree, "De Nederlandse Hervormde Kerk in de jaren voor de Afscheiding," pp. 34–47.

stooped to such "tricks of Jesuitry." In 1835, however, one of their number, the Reverend H. H. Donker Curtius, felt it was time to lay this charge to rest by openly setting forth that, if not equivocation, at least ambiguity had been the very thing needed back in 1816. Referring to the actual state of the Reformed Church in 1816, Donker Curtius explained that pastors and professors at the time *de facto* enjoyed a good measure of doctrinal freedom, which was the irreversible outcome of two centuries of theological development. Few office-bearers still followed the sixteenth-century confessions, for example, in an Athanasian formula of the Trinity and an Anselmian doctrine of satisfaction. It was therefore more ethical in 1816, argued Donker Curtius, to formulate a pledge that was in line with the state of theological science and in harmony with widely held interpretations of Reformed doctrine. What strict confessionalists wanted was to reassert and restore an old pledge which in practice had not been adhered to in any case. By not requiring, through formal subscription, what had long been left free in practice, Synod wisely adjusted law to fact. Faced with a delicate task, however, Synod could not very well dispel all ambiguity and expose its liberal spirit by expressly inserting in the subscription form a qualifier like "insofar as." "One word too little or too much could easily have spoiled much good and ignited discord throughout the church." With commendable caution Synod had "contented itself with a *sapienti sat* while avoiding what some people's ears could not endure."[39]

Not surprisingly, this explanation did little to achieve the goals of peace and concord. The orthodox were scandalized. Synod published a report later that year to reassure the faithful that the intended "ambiguity" was not meant, then or now, to condone "duplicity." This pacifier seemed only to add fuel to the flames of indignation.[40] The champions of confessional purity became more vociferous than ever. Publicly censured as unloving disturbers of the peace, they were privately derided as intolerant obscurantists, out of step with the times. Open letters, such as the one of 1842 signed by Groen and six of his friends in The Hague, petitioned Synod to keep "neology" out of the church, but to no avail.

---

39. H. H. Donker Curtius, "Geschied- en oordeelkundige aanmerkingen betreffende het Formulier van verbindtenis, vastgesteld door de Algemeene Synode van de Nederlands Hervormde Kerk in 1816," *Godgeleerde Bijdragen* 9 (1835): 1–50, esp. 3–5, 25f, 36–41.

40. Cf. *Briefwisseling*, II, 144.

It also deserves mention that a good number of pastorates, especially in the outlying provinces, were still subject to patronage; vacancies were filled at the discretion of a local lord, and orthodox congregations for years might be saddled with a modernist preacher.

SECESSION AND RÉVEIL

Meanwhile, in 1834, things had come to a head. Disciplinary measures against recalcitrant preachers resulted in the Secession of a significant number of Reformed people—in places whole congregations—from the main church of the land. For a while, the churches of the Secession (*Afscheiding*) were not recognized: the authorities had their meetings dispersed, their leaders fined and imprisoned, and troops billeted in members' homes. As we shall see, Groen publicly protested against these measures, allegedly taken in the interest of religious unity and ecclesiastical tranquility, but Thorbecke, the leader of the progressive liberals, wrote in the French daily of The Hague in defense of the government's policy. We owe a particularly passionate outburst in Lecture XV (419) to this affair.

By 1840, under the new king, persecution of the Seceders ceased, but separate worship was permitted only on condition that the Seceders renounce all claims to being the true and lawful continuation of the Reformed Church of old. Failure to register with the authorities as a separate denomination remained a punishable offence. When midway through the decade, economic depression and potato blight added to their woes, large groups of *Afgescheidenen* decided with pain in their hearts to quit their beloved country long known for its religious liberty, and, after ascertaining that re-settlement under the beloved and revered House of Orange, on Java, would still not guarantee them the right to establish separate day-schools for their children, they emigrated to the New World across the Atlantic, to settle under a foreign flag, in Michigan and Iowa.[41]

---

41. Cf. Smits, "Secession, Quarrels, Emigration and Personalities," pp. 100–107. On the eve of his departure for America in 1846, Secession leader the Rev. A. C. van Raalte informed Groen that the needs of the emigrating brothers constrained him, the hope of finding relief for many "cheers my path," and the provision of my family, "especially the need of school instruction ... supplies a sharp spur." He added with an unusual show of emotion: "Amid my sorrows you, brother, comforted my soul ... you were not ashamed of us, and although differing in standpoint I found in you, amid libel and abuse, a fraternal love which gave off warmth." *Briefwisseling*, II, 745.

There were now three movements for religious renewal in the Netherlands: the theological one centerd in Groningen, the revivalist, and the reformist. The latter two movements converged in the colorful figure of Hendrik Peter Scholte (1805-68).[42] Scholte had been a theological student in Amsterdam who frequented the Sunday evenings at the Da Costas. A fellow student who joined him was Anthonie Brummelkamp. Going up to Leyden to complete their theological training, the two had become regular visitors to Leféburé's exercises. When like-minded students joined their company, the "Club of Scholte" was born. It included men like Simon van Velzen and Albertus van Raalte, also future pastors who, together with Scholte and Brummelkamp, became leaders of the Secession movement.[43]

The traumatic process of Secession was first set in motion when Hendrik de Cock, the Reformed pastor of Ulrum, a small village in the northern province of Groningen, wrote an ill-tempered pamphlet against two colleagues ("wolves in sheep's clothing") who denied total depravity and condemned attendance at conventicles. Much like Abraham Kuyper later in the century, Rev. de Cock, though trained in a liberalizing theology, had come to a Calvinist position under the influence of his parishioners, whose old-style religion had induced him to make a study of the Canons of Dort and Calvin's *Institutes*. His subsequent activities led to his arraignment before the provincial church board. He was suspended without salary, and when he would not desist from publishing divisive pamphlets he was defrocked. Thereupon, his congregation took a drastic step: in October of 1834 they seceded from the "Church of 1816" to return to the "teaching, discipline and worship of the Reformed fathers." Within weeks, Scholte and his congregation in the south followed suit.

Interestingly enough, the Réveil friends called the step premature and unwarranted. Earlier in the year, the friends had come out with the first issue of a learned periodical called *Nederlandsche Stemmen*. Its editors were Da Costa, Koenen, De Clercq, and young Maurits van Hall. As soon as news of the events in Ulrum reached the western seaboard, Groen wrote to Koenen urging him to write in the *Stemmen* against this "ill-advised step":

---

42. Cf. Smits, *De Afscheiding van 1834*, VI, 14-21.

43. Cf. Rullmann, *De Afscheiding*, pp. 33-7; Oostendorp, *H. P. Scholte: Leader of the Secession of 1834 and Founder of Pella*, pp. 37-43; TenZythoff, *Sources of Secession*, pp. 129-35.

the periodical should openly disapprove of this separatism, this "excommunication of the church." Koenen replied that it was editorial policy to wait with comment on any news item until it was made public; meanwhile, he added, you must have heard of the "liberal" measures taken by the government: several hundred soldiers have been billeted in the homes of De Cock's followers; the remedy surely is worse than the evil![44] This early exchange between Koenen and Groen prefigured the pattern of the Réveil's reaction to the Secession: disapproval both of the separation and of the persecution.[45]

One man whose personal life was profoundly affected by the events was Anne Maurits Cornelis van Hall (1808–38). Many contemporaries agreed that this gifted lawyer was seriously jeopardizing his promising career by appearing repeatedly as counsel for the defense in court cases involving Seceders. But Van Hall's conscience was struck; as a member of the establishment, he felt implicated in the persecution measures, and so before a year was out, he left the Reformed Church and joined the Secession. When his brother Floris terminated their partnership in the law firm with the promise of helping him set up a practice elsewhere, Maurits moved to The Hague to start on his own. At the same time he also resigned as co-editor of the *Stemmen*.[46]

Another counsel for the defense in a number of these cases was Jan Willem Gefken (1807–87). Both Gefken and Van Hall published the full text of some of their defense pleas delivered in court.[47]

Groen's sense of justice was outraged by the persecution. But he was the king's "privy counsellor extraordinary" and so did not feel free to go public with his feelings. Instead, he submitted a private memorandum to His Majesty in which he protested against the government measures. When he got no reaction, he hesitated no longer and published his *The Measures Against the Seceders Tested Against Constitutional Law*.[48] It was a masterpiece of logical argument, discussing a number of key articles

---

44. *Briefwisseling*, II, 90f.

45. Cf. Knetsch, "Het Réveil en de Afscheiding," pp. 80–83.

46. *Briefwisseling*, II, 172, 174.

47. Kluit, *Het Protestantse Réveil in Nederland en daarbuiten*, pp. 397, 408.

48. *De Maatregelen tegen de Afgescheidenen aan het Staatsregt getoetst* (Leyden, 1837). Favorably reviewed by Heinrich Leo in the *Berliner Politisches Wochenblatt*, 3 Feb. 1838.

from the constitution often cited in defense of the government and showing how inapplicable they were to the case at hand. As mentioned earlier,
Thorbecke countered in the *Journal de la Haye*, defending the official position. Groen replied with two articles in the same journal.[49] A functionary
at the Ministry of Justice (A. W. van Appeltere) wrote a defense in the form
of a lengthy brochure.[50]

Was it any wonder, meanwhile, that some of the godfearing Secession
leaders began to have their doubts about the "powers ordained of God"?
When they began publishing *De Reformatie*, its pages included not only
Scripture studies and news of prosecutions but also philosophico-
theological discussions of the state and civil authority. Scholte, before his
emigration, was an active contributor, and one of his diatribes against civil
authority provoked Groen's comment in Lecture III (59).[51]

Toward the end of 1842, Groen had taken up contact with a "man of the
people," Johan Adam Wormser (1807-62). This was a rather unusual step
for a man of Groen's social position since Wormser was but a "common"
bailiff with the Amsterdam court. But Groen greatly admired Wormser's
recent articles on education in *De Reformatie* and eagerly sought to make
his personal acquaintance. The initial contact would grow into a cordial
friendship and close collaboration. Wormser had been an elder and catechism teacher in the local Secession church but had left it when dissension
within the denomination had broken out. He was a lifelong proponent
of associations of believers based on the Reformed confessions—first in
the church, but also in other areas of life. It was at Groen's urging that
Wormser, a mere administrative official, was invited to the meetings of
the Christian Friends in 1845.

---

49. See the issues of 23 Sept. and 7 Oct. 1837; reprinted in *Verspreide Geschriften*, II, 49-69.

50. Countered by A. M. C. van Hall in *De Reformatie* II (1837): 283-317, and by C. M. van
der Kemp in a two-part *Beoordeling van het geschil over de maatregelen tegen de Afgescheidenen*
(Rotterdam, 1837, 1838).

51. Years later, in spite (or because?) of his tenure as a Justice of the Peace in Iowa and his
active campaigning for the Democratic Party in Michigan (see Oostendorp, pp. 183f), Scholte
reiterated his opinion that the "governments of this world are under the influence of the
Prince of this world"; cf. H. P. Scholte to J. J. L. van der Brugghen, 22 Oct. 1857, published in
Nieuw Nederland, 5 Dec. 1947, pp. 1f.

THE SCHOOLS ISSUE

In the 1840s, the struggle for Christian elementary education, too, began increasingly to demand the attention of friends of the Réveil.

The deprotestantization of the mixed state school was visibly accelerating. Not only was the catechism banned and all doctrinal instruction, however occasional and fragmentary, frowned upon, but in one locality after another, Bible reading was prohibited, often at the request of the Catholic clergy who were offended by nothing so much as the teacher's "Protestant" commentary which often accompanied such readings. Lack of trust marked relations between many Catholic parents and non-Catholic teachers, especially in the preponderantly Catholic provinces of the south. North of the rivers, liberal Protestant parents persuaded school superintendents and school boards more and more to muzzle any "religious fanatics" among the teachers; orthodox parents, on the other hand, not blessed with the support of the reigning elite, chafed under the growing emphasis in the schools on maintaining "unbiblical" neutrality toward religion and on giving "unprotestant" treatment of the glorious history of the nation. The royal decree of 2 January 1842 provided for one hour of doctrinal instruction a week, to be given by a local clergyman acceptable to the majority; it further allowed the religious color of state schools to reflect local conditions by providing for greater religious pluriformity in the composition of school boards and in the appointment of teachers. In practice, however, one dissenting voice was enough to remove anything "offensive" from curriculum and classroom. Of their own accord, or else on strict orders, teachers avoided "controversial" points and retreated to the safety of a bland neutrality. Private schools began to appear in some localities, but in others the authorities refused to license such initiatives on the grounds that the mixed school was "sufficiently Christian" to render a private Christian school quite superfluous. This arbitrary treatment occurred also in The Hague, when Groen and a number of associates wished to start a private school. They dug in their heels and renewed their requests and appeals for six long years.

Roman Catholics at this time were still subject to political disabilities. In the civil service they were highly underrepresented. As under the Republic, they lived the life of a minority north of the Rhine and Meuse rivers, where they clung together to preserve their identity. By the 1840s, however, increasing self-confidence was also unmistakable, aided by the rise of self-assertive ultramontanism. New monasteries were founded, new churches built; a Catholic periodical, in 1846 even a Catholic daily, was available to a group that amounted at this time to nearly two-fifths of the population.[52] In Lecture XV (406), Groen would single them out as a possible future threat to the evangelical hope of recapturing the lost patrimony of a Protestant Holland.

FOREIGN CONTACTS

Dutch revivalists were also very conscious of their co-religionists in other countries. Koenen for a while served as Dutch correspondent to the *Evangelische Kirchenzeitung* of Berlin.[53] The Prussian *Kreuzzeitung* likewise was followed with lively interest and approval. More puzzling to them were the views and behavior of the Crown Prince who ascended the throne in 1840. That Frederick William IV was a declared enemy of liberal theology and liberal constitutions they could only applaud, but that he restored the medieval Order of the Swan and dreamed of enlarging the Union Church of 1830 into a supra-confessional Church of Practical Christianity embracing not only Lutherans and Calvinists but also all Catholics seemed less orthodox. On the other hand, his cooperation with the British government in establishing a "Bishop of the Church of St. James at Jerusalem" was clearly an important venture for promoting Christianity among the Jews. Important also were the publications, beginning in 1840, by a Friedrich Julius Stahl, who carried on a high-level debate about the demands of a Christian state as opposed to a liberal secular state.[54] Although Groen was only dimly aware of Stahl and his views when he gave his lectures on *Unbelief and Revolution*, his discovery of the German shortly thereafter immediately made him recognize Stahl as a kindred spirit from whom, moreover, he could learn much, especially in coming to a proper assessment of the validity of the anti-revolutionary theories of Von Haller.[55]

---

52. Boogman, *Rondom 1848*, p. 35.

53. Cf. *Briefwisseling*, II, 134, 174.

54. Kluit, *Het Protestantse Réveil in Nederland en daarbuiten*, pp. 358–65, 397.

55. Fafié, *Friedrich Julius Stahl*, pp. 127, 135.

Groen made the personal acquaintance of Hengstenberg, editor of the *Evangelische Kirchenzeitung*, in the summer of 1834, when the latter was "taking the baths" at the seacoast near The Hague.[56]

Another foreigner who wielded a large influence among Dutch revivalists was Alexandre Rodolphe Vinet (1797-1847). For many years a teacher of French in the Gymnasium of Basel, Vinet had established his reputation as a writer on religious liberty in the Paris revival journal *Le Semeur*, which circulated wherever French was read. In 1837, Vinet was appointed professor of practical theology in the University of Lausanne, in the canton of Vaud whose Grand Council had just abolished the Helvetic Confession as doctrinal standard of the church. With many others, Vinet believed the time was ripe for severing all state ties and establishing a Free Swiss Reformed Church.[57] His treatise of 1839, published a few years later under the title *Essai sur la manifestation des convictions religieuses et sur la séparation de l'Eglise et de l'Etat*, was an eloquent plea for a strict separation between church and state. In light of Vinet's status among evangelicals (Groen himself included),[58] Groen felt it incumbent upon himself to devote a special discussion to this treatise in Lecture III (59-65).

The weal and woe of the Swiss brothers continued to rank high in the interest of their Dutch beneficiaries. Thus, when in 1832 Merle and Gaussen sought to safeguard orthodoxy in seminary training by founding the School of Theology in Geneva, their Dutch contact De Clercq helped to raise funds for this project in Holland by writing pamphlets explaining the venture of the brothers in Geneva.[59] The Walloon pastor, L. G. James of Breda, a convert under Haldane when a student in Geneva,[60] did the same. In the course of time, a number of Dutch students went to receive their training in Geneva.[61] "Small history" has a way of repeating itself: this educational hegira was a resurrection, on a smaller scale, of an identical movement

---

56. *Briefwisseling*, II, 85.

57. Kluit, *Het Protestantse Réveil in Nederland en daarbuiten*, pp. 103-5, 310-14.

58. Cf. Keijzer, *Vinet en Hollande*, passim; idem, *Alexandre Rodolphe Vinet, 1797-1847*, pp. 204-53, esp. 215, 225f, 233-39.

59. Kluit, *Het Protestantse Réveil en Nederland in daarbuiten*, p. 286.

60. Cf. Knetsch, "Louis Gabriel James (1795-1867)," p. 128.

61. Cf. Schram, "Réveil-relaties met Genève en Neuchâtel," pp. 34, 37.

almost three centuries earlier, when students from the Low Countries attended Calvin's Academy.

3
—

GROEN VAN PRINSTERER

Guillaume Groen van Prinsterer was born in Voorburg, a village near
The Hague, on 21 August 1801, the eldest child (and only son) of a medical
doctor and a wealthy heiress of a Rotterdam banking family. Father Groen,
who descended from a long line of preachers, was a man of progressive
views; as court physician, and later as an inspector of public health and a
member of both the city council and the provincial government, he successfully propagated such new practices as sea-bathing and the use of burial
plots outside of sanctuaries.[1] A member of the Reformed Church, he shared
the moderately rationalist approach to religion of many of his generation.

FORMATIVE YEARS

It became apparent at a very early age that the young Willem—his French
name, given at baptism, was never used except for official purposes—was
a gifted child. He received the education that went with his class; attending
school four evenings a week once he had turned eight, the child was chiefly
taught at home: geography and Dutch by his papa, and French, English and
German by his governess, while his mama conversed and corresponded
with him in French.[2] Between the ages of 12 and 16, Willem attended a Latin
school, first in The Hague and then in Utrecht, where he mastered Greek
and Latin and was introduced to history and natural science. His papa spe-
cially arranged catechism instruction by the court preacher, which resulted

---

1. Mulder, *Groen van Prinsterer, staatsman en profeet*, p. 15.

2. Mulder, *Groen van Prinsterer, staatsman en profeet*, p. 17. Thus French was almost his
"mother tongue." German came less easy to him; cf. Lohman, "Groen's reis naar Parijs en
Besançon in 1836... ," p. 84. Inability to converse in English once kept him from holidaying
in Britain. When he finally did go, in August 1855, he reported to a friend that London was
"frightfully busy," that public works throughout England were "astonishing," and that the
location of Edinburgh, with its panoramas overlooking land and sea, was simply "ravishing,
einzig"; *Briefwisseling*, II, 790; III, 201; V, 307.

in Willem Groen's public profession of faith at the age of 17—a faith which, on his own testimony many years later, was sincere but conventional and therefore shallowly optimistic and moralistic.

In the fall of 1817, Willem Groen went up to Leyden to study law and letters. Soon favored by professors and students alike, he enjoyed his university days to the full, participating in several debating societies, the usual parties, and sports (horseback riding, swimming, golf, fives). He studied hard and after six years submitted two separate doctoral dissertations which he defended on one and the same day, earning his Dr.Jur. with a study of *The Excellence of the Justinian Code as Manifest from Its Principles* and his D.Litt. with a study of *Proper Names in Plato, or an Exposition of the Assessment of Persons either Introduced as Speakers or Mentioned for Whatever Reason in the Writings of Plato*; both studies were written in impeccable Latin and both subjects were treated with a decided historical slant.

Three lasting influences from his years at the academy must be noted. First, there was his induction into the thinking of the rising Historical Law School, to which he seemed to have been particularly congenial. His reading of Savigny and other members of the school inoculated him against the constructionistic rationalism that had grown out of the Enlightenment and that had been put into practice in the French Revolution. His mentor, Professor Van Assen, taught him to be critical of (premature) codification of law and skeptical about written constitutions that were the work of committees and assemblies.[3] This last point may not have required much power of persuasion, for the fatherland had survived no less than six constitutions since the Revolution of 1795,[4] a record in political experimentation which drew several scathing comments from Groen in the opening remarks of Lecture I (4) and which did not predispose him to join in with the clamor for revision in the 1840s, as his sarcastic comments show in Lecture XV (416-21).

---

3. Brants, *Groen's geestelijke groei*, pp. 27, 31, 35-37; Zwaan, *Groen van Prinsterer en de klassieke Oudheid*, pp. 255-61, 379n184.

4. The fundamental laws of 1798, 1799, 1801, 1805, 1806 and 1810—not counting the constitution of 1814 to serve the new kingdom, overhauled again in 1815 to accommodate the incorporation of Belgium; the revision of 1840, after the formal recognition of Belgian independence, was constitution number nine.

Secondly, there had been his exposure to and in some sense his participation in the ongoing revival in the learned world of the study of Plato,
a revival which, though centered in Utrecht, did not bypass Leyden. The
renewed interest in the Platonic dialogues left a permanent mark on the
young man Groen. Although it did not shape his worldview to the extent
of turning him into a philosophical realist, it did reinforce his natural predisposition to have no dealings with any form of "Sophism" — a dangerous
doctrine that despises objective norms, a subversive skepticism that "ren-
ders the whole range of human knowledge unstable and subjective," as he
would put it halfway through Lecture II (27). At the same time his love of
Plato's writings, while enriching his appreciation of style, especially helped
sharpen his critical faculties and put him on guard for the rest of his life
against the "sophistry" of brilliant genius.[5]

This last point tempered the third influence he underwent at Leyden.
Curiosity drove him to find out for himself what was being taught at
the notorious private seminar of the eccentric Bilderdijk. This fervent
Calvinist, loyal Orangist and reactionary monarchist attracted students of
some of the better families and (as one critic put it) was "corrupting the
best of our youth" by his bitter invectives against the spirit of the age and
every possible "received opinion" in history and philosophy, law and politics. His high-flying harangues were delivered harum-scarum in a dazzling
display of astonishing erudition. Young Willem Groen attended Bilderdijk's
lectures for more than a year and although he kept his reserve in the face of
so much hypercritical revisionism, yet almost in spite of himself he found
that the old man's vehement attacks, as he would acknowledge years later
(toward the close of Lecture II, p. 40), "first made me doubt the things I
had hitherto accepted without questioning."[6]

After graduating from Leyden, Groen spent the next four years on a
variety of activities. He joined a respected law office in The Hague and
pleaded as counsel for the defense in a number of cases[7]; he wrote a few

---

5. Gerretson, "Groens aanleg," pp. 22f; Tazelaar, *De Jeugd van Groen*, pp. 103, 132–39; Zwaan,
Groen van Prinsterer en de klassieke Oudheid, pp. 132–61.

6. Tazelaar, *De Jeugd van Groen*, pp. 74–86; Brants, *Groen's geestelijke groei*, pp. 19–50;
Van Essen, "Bilderdijk en Groen van Prinsterer," passim.

7. Groen was sworn in on 22 Dec. 1823. His short career as barrister, in both civil and
criminal cases, 1824–25, is briefly documented by Gerretson, *Briefwisseling*, I, 40n3. Details
will have to wait till the Archief-Van der Hoop (Rijksarchief, Groningen) is opened.

articles on civil law for a law journal; he was almost appointed professor of law in Leyden, but one of the king's most influential ministers advised against it (either because of suspected Bilderdijkian sympathies or simply because of youth and inexperience); he gave two or three lectures to fashionable culture societies. On a pleasure trip to Paris he made the acquaintance of a number of prominent people (Victor Cousin, who admired his dissertation on Plato; Guizot, then professor of history in the Sorbonne; and others) and thoroughly enjoyed the theater and the opera. Back in The Hague he circulated in high society and attended balls and parties.[8]

Secretly Groen hoped for a career related to historical studies. When the government in 1826 opened a competition for the best scheme for compiling a well-documented and patriotic Dutch history, he eagerly set to work, for the prize-winning essayist was to be appointed official national historian.[9] The announcement that he was one of the top five would not come till four years later.

Meanwhile, other matters occupied his attention. He had made the acquaintance of Elisabeth van der Hoop, a well-educated, clear-headed and very pious young woman, to whom he became engaged in the summer of 1827. The marriage took place the following spring. "Betsy" was to be his right hand throughout his life: she helped look after the estate consisting of land, houses and bonds; she kept records and ran the household; she nursed him through many a sickness; she was his copyist and secretary when his writing hand was incapacitated.[10] Above all, Betsy was instrumental in Willem's gradual growth from "laodiceanism" to a whole-hearted surrender to Christ. The couple would have no children.

Between the engagement and wedding had come the appointment to the Royal Cabinet. This was a kind of clearinghouse for all state papers

---

8. Mulder, *Groen van Prinsterer, staatsman en profeet*, pp. 32f.

9. Cf. Blaas, in *Britain and the Netherlands*, VIII, 134f. By fostering a sense of a shared past reaching back to the Middle Ages the government hoped to compensate for the lack of a heritage common to the north and the south in that most artificial creation of 1815, the United Kingdom of the Low Countries; but of the forty entries received, Groen's alone "betrays some sign of romantic influence" with its plea for evoking the past for moral and political purposes.

10. Groen seems to have enjoyed anything but robust health. According to the published correspondence (cf. e.g. *Briefwisseling*, I, 578, 648–50; II, 648f, 655; III, 673, 895; V, 541, 585), many a raw winter saw him confined indoors, racked by coughing spells. He was also small in stature, measuring only "1 el 5 palm 7 duim," i.e. 1 meter 57, or 5 feet 2 inches; cf. Schutte, *Mr. G. Groen van Prinsterer*, opposite p. 35.

passing between the monarch and the various departments, offices and civil services. Not keen on what looked like a strenuous and slavish clerical position, Groen accepted with reluctance—"almost in spite of myself," he wrote in his autobiographical notes at the end of his life, adding that by this providential route he would be shaped for the career of his real choice as it would give him access to the treasures of the family archives of the House of Orange and put him in touch with the historical record of the religious faith that had given birth to and provided the backbone for the Dutch nation.[11] On 1 November 1827 Groen was appointed referendary or reporting clerk of the Royal Cabinet and a year and a half later its secretary or director. The work entailed sorting documents and correspondence, analyzing reports and making extracts of memoranda, and on occasion composing texts of royal replies, advice, decrees. The position required its holder to follow the court and thus to reside alternately in Brussels and The Hague for a year at a time.[12]

These were the years of the preparation and outbreak of the Belgian Revolt. In his position, which brought him into daily contact with the king, Groen was privy to many deliberations in the highest government circles. His duties also took him to the public gallery of parliament, where he witnessed the rising tide of discontent and defiance among representatives from the southern half of the kingdom. During lulls in the debates, he would read the works of Edmund Burke, probably recommended to him by the court chaplain Merle d'Aubigné. The young couple were very much edified by the latter's preaching, and closer personal contact with the Merles developed into a friendship for life.

Residing in the center of the accelerating vortex, Groen craved firm guidance, both for mind and heart. He devoured Burke's *Reflections*, also Pascal's *Pensées*, and a recent work by Lamennais, *Des Progrès de la révolution et de la guerre contre l'église*. He began more and more to disagree with the opportunistic shilly-shallying of the government and he communicated this to his royal taskmaster. In the fall of 1829, back in The Hague, Groen decided to begin editing a new small journal for political comment, *Nederlandsche Gedachten* ("Netherlandic Thoughts" or "Dutch Reflections").

---

11. *Nederlandsche Gedachten*, 1873/74, V, 161–67, 249, 313.
12. *Briefwisseling*, I, 151, 166.

In the first year of its existence, the paper urged the government to persevere in its language and educational policies repressive of French and Catholic subjects in the south, and not to give in to the cry for parliamentary sovereignty which was but another name for popular sovereignty and which conflicted not only with the constitution but also with history and the national character. At the same time, the paper openly criticized the government for not *consulting* parliament seriously and regularly, in fact, for wielding an excessively centralized and autocratic regime. Gradually, in part under the mounting influence of a redirection in his personal outlook which we shall examine in a moment, Groen's journal grew more critical of the ideological assumptions common to both sides of the dispute. King William's state centralism had liberal roots no less than did the views and program of the rebels in Brussels; meanwhile it had deprived him of the support of his loyal Flemish subjects whose justified grievances as Catholics had driven them into the arms of the liberal opposition.[13] Not many months after the secession of the Belgians was a fact, *Nederlandsche Gedachten* recommended making a clean break by cutting all ties with Belgium and recognizing its independence before the revolution would spread northward.[14]

The revolutionary flare-ups of 1830, only fifteen years after Waterloo, were a brutal reminder to many politically sensitive Christians that all was not well with European civilization. The German Catholic, Joseph Maria von Radowitz, recorded in his private memoirs that it was the revolution of 1830, and particularly the shock of witnessing the revolt in Brussels while traveling through in those very August days, that ultimately led him to help establish the *Berliner Politisches Wochenblatt*.[15] For Groen van Prinsterer, the Belgian Revolt with its aftermath was a crucial event in his formative years; like 1914 to the Edwardians, 1830 was to him a point of no return. It drew the scales from his eyes and set his feet on a path that

---

13. Cf. Gerretson, *Verzamelde Werken*, II, 33–35.

14. In our own time, the historian Pieter Geyl saw much sense in Groen's reasoning at this point, even though he deplored the fact that the cause of liberalism could triumph in the Belgian Revolt only at the expense of Dutch nationalism; cf. Geyl, *Kernproblemen van onze geschiedenis*, pp. 245–65. Geyl was a "Great Netherlander" who championed the concept of a Netherlandic nationality embracing all Dutch-speaking peoples; cf. Von der Dunk, in *Britain and the Netherlands*, VIII, 191–201.

15. Scheel, *Das Berliner Politische Wochenblatt*, p. 18.

he would travel the rest of his days. Apart from the shake-up it gave to his worldview, it also sharpened his insight into the realities of the new age Europe had entered upon. For a Dutchman, moreover, the traumatic experience was both instructive and difficult to lay to rest. Not only the military intervention by the French and the diplomatic intervention by the British, but especially the opportunistic dealings of the Powers following the armistice which saw the callous sacrifice of Dutch interests and the cynical violation of the principle of legitimacy and of former treaties, would rankle long in the minds of Groen's generation; no doubt the whole painful episode accounts for the acrid tone of certain passages in Lectures XIV and XV (387ff, 410f).

His friend and former mentor Van Assen, meanwhile, attributed the "calamities that afflict Europe" to the "immoderate desire for liberty" and chose this theme as the subject for an academic oration at Leyden. In a confidential memorandum to the king the conservative law professor ascribed the Belgian Revolt to the sinister collusion of two different emancipation movements, the one political and the other religious; this collusion was evident in the monstrous alliance in the south: "the bizarre union between two principles which are eternally at war with one another, Jacobinism and Catholicism." And in case the king had missed it he added, with a hint of a teacher's pride in the growing accomplishments of one of his students: "All this is capably set forth in such excellent journals as *Nederlandsche Gedachten.*"

Confident in the pleasing assurance that the best minds were seeing things right, Professor Van Assen would yet be in for a surprise. His former student was in the process of making the discovery of his life and was soon analyzing the crisis of the age in terms of a much profounder cause. Exactly a year after his note to the king, as the pages of *Nederlandsche Gedachten* began to lay out the editor's fundamental insight, Van Assen confided to Groen: "I wish I could challenge more than I am able your [thesis about] *unbelief* as the characteristic feature of the last fifty years."[16] It is a measure of Groen's greatness, and the index of his historic significance, that while his whole milieu was pulling him in the direction of a conservative reaction he persisted in his ponderings until he had gained a firm hold of the

---

16. Cf. *Briefwisseling,* I, 462, 484f, 786 (emphasis added).

key insight that would unlock the secret of his revolutionary times. This insight once gained, he never looked back.

For indeed, the turbulent events that he was now witnessing at such close range drove an independent, searching mind like Groen's to inquire more deeply into the inner coherence and ultimate cause of the chronic disruptions of his age. His search was at once intellectual and existential and ended in nurturing a spiritual turnabout in his life under the influence of two potent injections. The first of these was a re-reading of modern history through the eyes of writers against the great French Revolution of 1789. The second was a new reading of the Scriptures under the fresh impression of weekly sermons by revival preachers like Molenaar, Merle d'Aubigné and Secrétan. This twofold injection had the effect that with ever increasing clarity and conviction Groen learned two things: first, to see a link between the day-to-day occurrences and the underlying ideology of liberalism with its roots in the revolutionary philosophy of the Enlightenment; but, secondly, to lay another crucial link as well, viz. between that revolution and unbelief. He learned to see that the intellectual revolution of the eighteenth century was directly related to the decline of Christianity after its short-lived revival in the sixteenth century, that in fact it represented its wholesale substitute aiming at founding a new society, one without God.

Groen and his wife had "joined" the Réveil, almost without realizing it. But while Betsy's faith flourished, her husband's followed only from a distance. The same critical independence of mind which as a student had kept him from embracing the extreme views of a Bilderdijk or, for that matter, from yielding to the vogue of Romanticism, now kept him from surrendering without reserve to the uninhibited piety and single-minded devotion of his wife and friends. Coming out of an atmosphere of much lukewarm Christianity, Groen sensed he did not have what they had—a personal relationship with Christ—and so he could not measure up to what seemed to be the criteria of a true Christian as defined by the revivalists: total commitment, inner joy and peace, a readiness at all times to testify of the hope within one and to renounce the world of refined culture and pleasure. The Groens did adopt an ascetic lifestyle at this time: they went to as few parties and dinners as possible; those court functions which they could not avoid they found empty and "meaningless in the light of eternity." The two lived soberly and shared of their riches with the poor, so that over the years, as we have noted, their name came to be held in honor even among the most radical elements in the working-class quarters of The Hague. Of course, they were people of independent means, and from 1835 on they would occupy the stately mansion along the Korte Vijverberg where Betsy would have the help of several maids, a cook, a cook's help and a chambermaid; in addition, they purchased a country home maintained by two gardeners and a livery man.[17]

We are fortunate to have an important document from these transition years. In September 1831, the young editor of *Nederlandsche Gedachten* decided to explain to his (dwindling) readership what "system" the journal was basing itself on. Some outside prodding lay behind this decision. Koenen had remarked to De Clercq, in a letter of 15 May 1831, that *Nederlandsche Gedachten* lacked a systematic expression of its working principles. Some issues were drawing the public's attention, he observed in Amsterdam, while others evoked but little interest. He believed he could explain this fickleness. The editor of *Nederlandsche Gedachten* claims repeatedly that his judgments of the facts are based on firm principles, yet he does not show this link concretely. By contrast, Koenen pointed out, "the writers of the *Evangelische Kirchenzeitung* have set us an example in a detailed piece entitled "Vom göttlichen Rechte der Obrigkeit nach protestantischen Grundsätzen." ... Something of this kind, affirmed and proved by the testimony of wise men and believers of all ages ... can be very fruitful, though it should go beyond a mere theological treatment: what we need is a historical, juridical and practical exposition, otherwise those principles will only get through to a few of the initiate ...[18] If they were truly developed with firm consistency, maintained with dignity, and accepted everywhere, then I should say Our Fatherland can remain free."[19]

Quite possibly, this suggestion was passed on by De Clercq to the editor of *Nederlandsche Gedachten*. By August, Koenen felt confident enough to

---

17. Upon Groen's death in 1876, succession duties had to be paid over an estate estimated in a probate inventory at a little under two million guilders; cf. Steur, "De geldelijke nalatenschap van Groen van Prinsterer," *Tot Vrijheid Geroepen* 22 (1976): 78–87, esp. 83.

18. This perceptive comment echoed a sentiment of Emil Ludwig von Gerlach, one of the editors of the *Kirchenzeitung* who was engaged at this very time in preparations for an explicitly political weekly which would come out that fall; cf. Scheel, *Das Berliner Politische Wochenblatt*, p. 42.

19. Rullmann, "De politieke leiding onzer christelijke periodieken in de 19e eeuw," p. 539.

convey this opinion to the editor personally. Readers respect your religious views, he wrote Groen, and they also affirm your practical commentary on political affairs, but they do not see the connection. They are unacquainted with your entire way of thinking, or with the how of applying the lofty principles of religion to the questions of order and law, so they regard as separate the very thing you wish to unite.[20]

The implied challenge stung Groen into action. He would explain his "entire way of thinking." The explanation turned into a series of seven articles, under the collective title *Overzigt* (Overview), to which we shall return in chapter 5 below. The periodical ran for another fifteen issues, then ceased publication for lack of interest.

GROEN'S AWAKENING

The completion of the *Overzigt* of 1831 marked an important stage in Groen's pilgrimage. He had resolutely passed a fork in the road but wondered whether he would prove fit for the journey that lay ahead. Groen had found the key to a Christian worldview as applied to the crisis of his time: *unbelief the deepest cause, the gospel the only answer*. Yet he felt keenly that Christianity had to be more than an intellectual truth, a correct worldview. It had not sufficiently touched his heart and become his life-principle, he confessed to friends, quasi-objectively yet plaintively.

What probably stood in the way was the realization that to embrace a childlike faith entailed some kind of sacrifice of the intellect. But what kind? This problem could easily have turned into an insuperable stone of offence for one whose life thus far had displayed such an unusual degree of intellectual independence.[21] It is fascinating to follow the ebb and flow of this crisis in Groen's life as reflected in the published correspondence. The way it was handled and resolved guaranteed that the spiritual reorientation he was undergoing never seriously jeopardized what would be his life's calling—his natural and wholehearted involvement in historical learning and public issues. Yet it was not without a pointed challenge to bring that part of his life, too, under the discipline of a Christian pedagogy. Fortunately, his Mennonite-Réveil friend was there to keep him on the straight course

---

20. *Briefwisseling*, I, 463; see also 443, 467, 510, 543.
21. Cf. Schaeffer, "Groens zelfportret," p. 227.

between a dualistic pietism that leads to anti-intellectualism and cultural withdrawal and a pietistic dualism that separates the "Christian life" from one's unavoidable "life in the world."

It was De Clercq who wrote Groen in those years of introspective self-examination and spiritual self-reproach that one must be prepared to discard everything in order to know Christ. "Must it all be discarded?" Groen asked by return mail; "can it not rather be quite properly united with the truth of the gospel?" To which De Clercq replied with disarming candor:

> Understand me well, I do not wish that you become *stupid*, but that all your *gifts* may become sanctified. ... If we have learned and studied history apart from Christ, we must now learn to see that Christ is the center of history ... if we have studied philosophy and come to admire it, we must now learn that ... this same philosophy can teach us the vanity of all human knowledge and the insufficiency of its power to re-create man. ... What was truth outside of us must become truth inside us. What was a vision of the mind must become a feeling that fills our hearts.[22]

This message did not fall on deaf ears; Groen's life would become one long struggle to put on the mind of Christ and to lead every thought captive to the obedience of Christ. But what about that *feeling that fills the heart*?

In the very days that he was composing his *Overzigt* Groen communicated to his friend and co-editor, a nominal Christian as he himself had been, that although he had come to realize religion was a "life-principle that ought to be united and interwoven with our entire existence," he himself did not possess the faith "by which a person becomes a new creation, has one's own will and passion replaced by a desire to serve God and is made to feel wholly content, peaceful and happy ..." However, he added that he was daily making greater use of the means of attaining such faith, namely prayer and Bible reading, and was beginning to have more trust "in the help of Him who will finish His good work in me."[23]

Conversions have a way of following the pattern expected of them by the already converted. In January 1832, Groen wrote to De Clercq that in comparison with his friend's conviction his own faith was weak. I can see

---

22. *Briefwisseling*, I, 284.
23. *Briefwisseling*, I, 503.

clearly, he wrote, that most of the time at least "I have little more than a historical faith, a general and vague assent of the mind, a faith which cannot exert the kind of influence on our heart and walk that we all do need. I hope and pray that by God's grace that purely intellectual conviction may soon be personally applied to myself and genuinely appropriated."[24]

Scarcely two weeks later he wrote the following lines in a cordial, almost fatherly letter to a younger brother-in-law who was going through miserable times serving with the militia in the field:

> ... a joy that the world knows not of yet cannot take away, that joy is given by faith in Christ, through which we are saved from an otherwise inescapable and eternal perdition; and that faith is promised to everyone who is sensible of being a sinner and totally depraved, who prays for redemption, and who joins to that sincere and humble prayer constant and attentive Bible reading. The superficial Christianity, dear David, that has become common also in our country is meaningless, in fact is even dangerous in that it often deludes one into thinking that one already has what one still lacks. ... You wonder perhaps about the tone of this letter but I assure you that ever since I by God's grace have received the beginnings of that faith I blame myself and am ashamed that I so seldom and so weakly speak and write about that which alone is really important for someone who is mortal and immortal and who without Christ is irreparably lost.[25]

Some months later, De Clercq's happiness was almost made full by a note from his dear friend Willem which said: "I am experiencing that for several months now I no longer regard Christianity as something completely external to me."[26]

In January 1833, during a severe illness, Willem consoled his anxious Betsy: "Do not be anxious. I believe in Christ, without much influence in my life, it is true, but still, in recent weeks, with greater influence upon my heart, so that there is also no reason in that respect why I should be shut out; the statements of the Bible are sure."[27] After his illness he confided to De Clercq that "my faith is not lively enough. But I am persuaded, just as

---

24. *Briefwisseling*, I, 529.
25. *Briefwisseling*, V, 20f.
26. *Briefwisseling*, I, 569.
27. *Briefwisseling*, I, 648; Betsy reporting to De Clercq.

much [now] as on my sickbed, that apart from Christ all is vanity."[28] To Koenen, who was coming over for a visit during these months, he wrote in advance not yet to expect to see him leading the family devotions; "I lack the confidence," he confided, and explained that in these matters he deferred to his wife.[29]

His recovery took many months and was concluded by a trip to Switzerland. Having renewed his acquaintance with Merle in Geneva, he traveled to Basel to visit Vinet and on the way chanced to meet Blumhardt Sr. in Lausanne.[30] Conversations with these men punctuated the beginning of a wholly new direction in his life.

Groen's conversion—if that is the word—was slow and gradual, and cannot be pinned down to one day; it was an awakening that stretched from 1827 to 1833. As Groen appropriated the faith, he slowly shed some of his natural reserve, to become a vocal witness of the hope that was in him.[31] To a Christian who he knew was less advanced than he was, his beloved Professor Van Assen, Groen wrote gently but firmly: "Faith in Christ is absolutely essential; there is but one name given by which man can be saved, as the apostle says. Don't look for truth everywhere; in that flitting about one so easily overlooks it; seek it first and in earnest where so many are convinced it is found ..."[32] To a former friend of university days, P. J. J. Mounier, Walloon preacher in Amsterdam, he felt constrained that winter to write a letter about one of his sermons he happened to have heard. Mounier had preached on the necessity and utility of prayer without once pointing to Christ as the One who has restored access to God's throne and in Whom alone the promises of God are yea and amen. To proclaim the fatherhood of God apart from atonement in Christ, admonished Groen, is to proclaim a deceptive generalization. Your sermon distressed me, wrote Groen sadly, because it preached a religion built on imagination and feeling, not Christ.[33]

---

28. *Briefwisseling*, I, 661.

29. *Briefwisseling*, I, 666.

30. Mulder, *Groen van Prinsterer, staatsman en profeet*, p. 54.

31. In a letter to a friend he quoted a maxim of Hannah More in her book *Practical Piety*: "Restrain your outward profession till you have formed *habits* of piety." *Briefwisseling*, I, 598.

32. *Briefwisseling*, I, 700.

33. *Briefwisseling*, II, 24f.

During his convalescence Groen made use of his prerogative to enter the family archives of the House of Orange. There he spent many quiet hours perusing letters from the sixteenth century. They confirmed and consoled him, for many of them spoke of a faith that held fast amid trial, danger, fire and sword. What is more, they put him in touch with a glorious tradition that he could now claim as his own. Reflecting on these years in old age, Groen recorded that it was then he learned to understand the secrets of the faith of the Reformation and its martyrs and was induced to join the "Christian-historical *party* which rests on the Anchor of the soul and endures the ages." It was all, he had learned to see, a providential preparation for the next phase of his life in which he would discover his life-calling.[34]

By 1834, then, Groen's conversion to the truth of the gospel was in principle complete: his intellectual conviction had deepened into a conviction of the heart. Up to this time, Groen's active mind had absorbed many of the intellectual currents of his day and had brought them to some workable synthesis—the best of everything, of nothing too much. He now struggled with the question of the implications of the Christian faith for his mental equipment, his scholarly learning, and his worldview. And so he came to compose his *Essay on the Means by Which Truth Is Known and Confirmed*.[35] It would remain the only theoretical treatise he ever published. Eclectic in nature, the *Essay on Truth* can hardly be said to give a consistent "theory" or well-rounded "system." Yet it does give a reliable picture of where the young convert chose to take his "Archimedean point" in the welter of conflicting intellectual currents of his time.[36]

The *Essay on Truth* addresses the question how man may arrive at sure knowledge. Man, according to Groen, has four distinct yet interrelated tests of truth at his disposal: *philosophy*, or what can be demonstrated, not by autonomous reason or metaphysics, but by believing philosophy that operates within the bounds of religion; *history*, or what has stood the test of time and is confirmed by the experience of mankind both in the absence and in the presence of (faith in) the gospel; *consensus omnium*, or what has

---

34. *Nederlandsche Gedachten*, 1873/74, V, 313, 357.

35. *Proeve over de middelen waardoor de waarheid wordt gekend en gestaafd* (Leyden, 1834). Hereafter cited in the notes as *Proeve* (1834).

36. Cf. Zwaan, *Groen van Prinsterer en de klassieke Oudheid*, pp. 574f.

been accepted by all men always and everywhere; and *revelation*, or what God has vouchsafed to disclose to man from the beginning of time and now is inscripturated in the Bible. The greatest of these, the final and definitive standard which guides and corrects all the rest, is revelation (147–50, 188).[37]

Ultimately, maintains Groen, all truth is Christianity's truth. On this basis, one can be "an eclectic thinker in a good sense" (36). Although he rejects the notion of a natural theology, Groen does believe that philosophy outside the pale of Christian revelation has historically given voice to truthful insights. He accounts for this by saying that all philosophies are derivations of religion and that all religions are derivations of the one true religion given to man—borrowings from the original, primordial revelation given in Paradise (34–37, 76, 97).

Notions and formulations like the latter would seem to place Groen in the camp of Christian romantic historicism, were it not for his Calvinian awareness of the radical corruption of sin.[38] Fallen man's natural religion is enmity against God; he has darkened primordial revelation, holds the truth in unrighteousness, and corrupts his good insights through the direction followed by his thought as a whole (36, 39–42).[39]

If the *Essay*'s philosophical system seems rudimentary and sketchy, its articulation of a Christian view of history is consistent, comprehensive, and very traditional. In these pages Groen shows himself in decided opposition to secularized historical science. He deals with the question in two parts: (1) "history without Christ"; (2) "history in the light of the gospel."

(1) The negation of Christianity in the last century, he expounds, brought such a diversity of views that an arbitrary theory was adopted to regain a sense of meaning in history: God's providential plan was replaced by the doctrine of perfectibility (99–107). But this belief in progress could not be maintained for long, and the undeceived have since opted

---

37. Cf. Zwaan, "Groen van Prinsterer over de wijsbegeerte," pp. 33f; idem, *Groen van Prinsterer en de klassieke Oudheid*, p. 231. Numbers in parentheses in the main text refer to pages in the work under discussion.

38. Cf. J. Klapwijk, "Calvin and Neo-Calvinism on Non-Christian Philosophy," pp. 49–51; Zwaan, *Groen van Prinsterer en de klassieke Oudheid*, pp. 27, 43f, 108–10, 112f.

39. This important restriction in Groen's defense of a healthy eclecticism weakens the charge leveled by Dengerink, *De sociologische ontwikkeling van het beginsel der S.i.e.k.*, p. 72, that the *Essay on Truth* betrays "lack of insight into the truth that neither history nor science nor the universal consensus develop independently of people's fundamental religious motivation."

for fatalism or indifferentism. The fatalist school reduces men to mere tools, and virtue and vice to the necessary resultants of relations and circumstances (108–26). The school of indifferentism obliviates the distinction between good and evil, mingles truth and falsehood, highlights only what has vitality, greatness, power and success, and confines itself to pure description, banning all feeling or judgments: accustomed to false commentary, these historians have become averse to all commentary (127–30).

(2) History properly viewed, Groen continues, has Christianity at its very center. Christ is its beginning and end, and God's redemptive plan is its main issue, to which human designs and efforts are subordinated (131). The sum of history is the triumph of Christ over Satan, and therefore its core is the history of the church, that is, the continuous formation and preservation of the body of Christ through the operation of the gospel. The unity of history is visible already in the promise in Paradise: the final outcome is the defeat of evil, the condition of victory is enmity and war, while the seed of the woman points to the victorious Redeemer. To the practicing Christian historian, therefore, the gospel is history's unifying principle. It is the ray of light which sometimes illumines the whole field of history, at other times gleams as through a haze (132–36).

From this vantage point, says Groen, history reveals a ceaseless struggle of truth against unbelief and superstition. Before Christ, God entrusted his oracles to Israel and suffered the nations to walk in their own ways. After Christ, the heathen world sank deeper into barbarism or else kept its forms but lost its inner vitality, whereas Christianity conquered Europe, stemmed anarchy, tamed savageness, and restored law, order and morality, a rejuvenation that was nothing short of a miracle. But corruption set in with the papal hierarchy, the veneration of saints and the abuse of indulgences; the truth was darkened and its witnesses were burned at the stake. Once the Protestant Reformation restored the Bible to its rightful place, however, there followed an era which testifies to the beneficent influence of the gospel. Yet even before the wars of religion had ended, the corruption resumed in the form of Catholic superstition and Protestant orthodoxism. Soon apostasy reared its head, giving rise to atheism and the present-day materialism (137–41).

Nevertheless—such is the hopeful note on which this historical vision ends—a new triumph of Christianity is in the making. Unbelief dominates but cannot finally conquer. In revivals everywhere, the fundamental truths of Scripture are being reaffirmed. Israel still stands, as a confirmation of what it denies; Islam lies prostrate, its existence artificially prolonged. The Bible is traveling to the ends of the earth and the good news is reaching the remotest peoples. The last great battle may be closer, Christ's second coming nearer, than many think. If the times are uncertain, the outcome is not: every event must serve the coming victory. World history is but the receptacle for the unfolding gospel, like the blade of corn or the butterfly's cocoon (141–44). Certainly this was a vision of history that could inspire its author, if he so chose, to practice history with unity of outlook and catholicity of scope as well as Protestant convictions and evangelical fervor.

The *Essay on Truth* in some sense marked the close of Groen's formative years. His formal education behind him, he had served a short season as a practicing lawyer and a longer period as a senior civil servant, neither of which had satisfied him. He had tried his hand at editing a journal, and it had become a journal largely of dissent. He had embraced the faith of the fathers and had testified privately and publicly to the fixed point of his new life. What would the future hold?

HISTORIAN AND PUBLICIST

In December 1833, Groen had resigned from the Royal Cabinet. In addition to being appointed "privy councillor extraordinary" he retained an earlier appointment as curator of the Archives of the House of Orange, a position to which he now turned with all his energies. King William gave permission to publish from the rich holdings in the family archives, and in 1835, the first volume appeared of a series entitled *Archives ou Correspondance inédite de la Maison d'Orange-Nassau*, a publication which immediately established Groen's international reputation as a historian. The series would run till 1839 and consist of seven volumes, followed after a long interval by Volume VIII as well as a Supplement in 1847. A second series would be published by Groen between 1857–61 in five volumes. Together these volumes published correspondence by members of the House of Orange between 1566 to 1688, from William the Silent, Prince of Orange, and his brothers of Nassau, to William III, Dutch stadtholder and king of England.

These primary sources enabled the practitioners of the new scientific history for the first time to clear up many obscurities about the Dutch Revolt and, in particular, to topple several legends surrounding William the Silent. When William H. Prescott dealt with the Dutch Revolt in his *History of the Reign of Philip the Second* (1855), he had this to say about the *Archives*: "The editor is at no pains to conceal his own opinions; and we have no difficulty in determining the religious sect to which he belongs. But it is not the less true that he is ready to render justice to the opinions of others, and that he is entitled to the praise of having executed his task with impartiality."[40] Another historian of international reputation, Guizot, said of the editor's extended introductions to each of the volumes—the "Prolégomènes"—that they were marked by a strict as well as generous impartiality, a scrupulous and unswerving fairness—all the more meritorious "from a Dutchman and a zealous Protestant, busied in the records of the sufferings and the heroic struggles of his forefathers."[41]

In its country of publication, meanwhile, the appearance of the *Archives* occasioned an open collision between the old and the new conception of the historical profession. In a published polemic with a gentleman of the old school, the aged patrician Maurits Cornelis van Hall (1768-1858), Groen had to come to the defense of the rights and duties of an editor-publisher of primary sources.[42] Van Hall upbraided the editor of the *Archives* for extenuating Spanish atrocities during the Dutch Revolt and particularly for excusing the crimes of that Machiavellian monster Philip II. Groen countered that one must judge historical actors in the light of their time

---

40. Kirk ed.; London, 1894, p. 377. To Groen personally Prescott wrote: "The work indeed under your hands is possessed of a much higher value than what is derived from the mere reproduction of the text; although we can not praise too highly the apparently faithful and accurate manner in which this has been accomplished. But your own notes and preliminary dissertations furnish stores of information to the historian and to the student of history for which he might look in vain elsewhere: and although in some points there are some of your readers who may come to a different conclusion from yourself, there is no one who will refuse to you the credit of having conducted your investigations with thoroughness, candor and conscientious love of truth." Quoted by Groen in his *Maurice et Barnevelt*, p. clxxxi; the original in Algemeen Rijksarchief, The Hague, Archief Groen van Prinsterer, Prescott to Groen, 2 July 1857.

41. *Edinburgh Review*, 1847; as quoted by Groen in his *Maurice et Barnevelt*, p. clxxx.

42. Cf. *Hendrick, Graaf van Brederode, medegrondlegger der Nederlandsche vrijheid, verdedigd door Mr. M. C. van Hall* (Amsterdam, 1844); G. Groen van Prinsterer, *Antwoord aan Mr. M. C. van Hall* (Leyden, 1844).

and its prevailing ideas and, consequently, that Philip should be seen as a ruler who sincerely believed it his duty to persecute heretics and to uphold his authority in a sprawling empire preyed upon from many sides. By the same canon, Groen pointed out, he had refused to conceal things that he had discovered were censurable in the conduct of William the Silent and contemporary Protestant leaders.

More serious, while more fundamental, was Van Hall's censure of the editor's "impropriety" in making private correspondence public. Van Hall appeared piqued by Groen's debunking of one of the traditional heroes of the Dutch Revolt, the Count of Brederode, who emerged from the published correspondence in the *Archives* as a man of mediocre talents, loose morals and questionable character. According to Van Hall, delicacy dictated that an editor suppress certain domestic details appearing in personal letters and content himself in given cases with providing only extracts and abstracts. Groen's rejoinder was a firm repudiation of this once fashionable standpoint. Historical scholarship, he replied, was served only by the original text and the whole truth, complete and authentic, unvarnished by the subjective opinions of the editor; with this policy alone could one hope to correct long-standing misconceptions and so advance historical knowledge.[43] In general, Groen supported the new scientific history and welcomed its search for truthful accuracy. In Lecture VII (161) he would hail the publication of new source materials and scholarly monographs regarding the history of the Reformation and the Reformers, in the confident expectation that continued research would only enhance the reputation of Protestantism's beginnings.

Younger colleagues in the historical profession sided with Groen against Van Hall. Reinier Cornelis Bakhuizen van den Brink (1810-65) judged the publication of the *Archives* "invaluable" and its mode of editing "in many respects not to be improved upon." Robert Jacobus Fruin (1823-99) would speak, years later, of Groen's "undying merit" as the "pioneer of our present-day historiography." And Coenraad Busken Huet (1826-86) named Groen the "father of modern Dutch historical research."[44] Groen

---

43. Cf. Smitskamp, *Groen van Prinsterer als historicus*, pp. 115f, 126f, 141; Schutte, *Mr. G. Groen van Prinsterer*, pp. 38-40; Van Essen, "Guillaume Groen van Prinsterer and His Conception of History," pp. 243f.

44. Quoted in Smitskamp, *Groen van Prinsterer als historicus*, pp. 130, 143.

in turn praised the works of the rising generation of Dutch critical historians and encouraged their scholarly endeavors, unreservedly giving his
recommendation for Bakhuizen's appointment to the national archives
and Fruin's to the history chair at Leyden.[45] In addition, thanks to his social
position and wide contacts he was able to help open doors to a number of
Europe's archives and gladly offered his mediation to any serious scholar
who contacted him for this purpose.[46]

Understandably, Groen was a lifelong admirer of the man whom some
regard as the greatest historian of his age, Leopold von Ranke (1795-1886).
Although in later years Groen thought he could detect in the German grand-
master of modern critical history too much influence of "the atmosphere of
the court of Berlin,"[47] Groen always had immense respect for Ranke, whom
he considered a model above all of objectivity in the sense of impartiality
and whose guarded language and coolly formulated judgments he greatly
admired.[48] The respect was mutual.[49]

RESEARCH JOURNEY

In 1836, the king authorized Groen to visit a number of archives in France
and Germany to hunt down historical documents related to the royal house
and Dutch history. Accompanied by his wife (and her chambermaid), he
departed early April, to return toward the middle of October. Let us take
a moment to follow him on this tour, to get an indication of the kind of
society he moved in and the kind of people he wished to associate with.[50]

---

45. In the case of Bakhuizen, cf. *Briefwisseling*, II, 851; III, 71, 132, 867; V, 270; in the case of
Fruin, cf. *Briefwisseling*, III, 330, 334, 343, 384, 390, 395, 550, 586; IV, 757, 762f, 894; V, 392. See
also Smitskamp, *Groen van Prinsterer als historicus*, pp. 167f.

46. His first contact with Dr. Abraham Kuyper stemmed from his role in this capacity;
cf. *Briefwisseling*, V, 607. For his occasional assistance to Ranke in gaining access to archival
collections in The Hague, cf. *Briefwisseling*, II, 403; IV, 353; see also "Vier Briefe Leopold von
Rankes an Willem Groen van Prinsterer," *Historische Zeitschrift* 150 (1934): 559-63.

47. *Briefwisseling*, IV, 628, 630, 755, 765.

48. Cf. *Briefwisseling*, II, 275, 404, 588; IV, 488; *Nederlandsche Gedachten*, 1873/74, V, 145f;
Maurice et Barnevelt, p. 149.

49. Cf. *Briefwisseling*, II, 550; III, 438; IV, 924.

50. In the following paragraphs, numbers in parentheses refer to pages in W. H. de
Savornin Lohman, "Groen's reis naar Parijs en Besançon in 1836 ten behoeve der 'Archives,'"
which is the edited text of Groen's own journal of the trip.

The Groens arrived in Paris on 21 April 1836, after several stopovers, notably in Cologne where Groen paid a visit to August von Schlegel. In Paris they visited the graves of Racine and Pascal and by only minutes missed being witnesses to an attempt on Louis Philippe's life (26, 58). Many days were spent in sparsely lit rooms copying rare documents, occasionally assisted by one or two hired copyists. (The same activity was repeated at Baden, Stuttgart, and especially Besançon, where a two-week visit was rewarded with many copies of letters by Cardinal Granvelle, advisor to Philip II and opponent of William the Silent.) In Paris, the Groens attended worship services conducted by Réveil preachers like Malan and the brothers Monod. Here, too, Groen called on Guizot, who talked excitedly about continuing his *History of England*, and Victor Cousin, who shared his thoughts on education and reminisced about his visits to the Low Countries. Michelet came to pay his respects to Groen in his hotel suite and the evening passed quickly as the men talked shop. Groen obtained a pass to the Chamber of Peers to hear Thiers speak. He attended the trial sessions of would-be regicide Alibaud whom they had seen taken away in handcuffs moments after the attempted assassination on June 25. Groen recorded in his journal that evening that the accused's final speech had been so moving that he could not remember exactly all he said (63; cf. Lecture XIV, p. 390).

On Corpus Christi Day, the Groens witnessed, with mixed feelings, the procession at the Notre Dame. At a dinner in Fleury, as the guest of Marquis de Pastoret, Groen met Berryer (mentioned in Lecture XIV, p. 390) and a Madame Monbreton, who shared anecdotes about Napoleon and about the pecuniary circumstances that induced Chateaubriand to write his *Génie du christianisme*. They visited the school started five years before by the Evangelical Society; in his journal Groen made a point of noting its enrolment statistics and operating costs. They visited the zoo, the Invalides, and Versailles (which impressed the Dutch visitors with its gigantic proportions but less so with its ostentatious artificiality) (48, 55, 57).

A side trip to Switzerland allowed the Groens to look up their friends Merle d'Aubigné and his wife and to be present at the baptism of their infant son, named Willem in honor of Groen (75). They met other revival leaders such as Gautiers, Trochin, and Gaussen. Crossing Lake Geneva by steam ferry, they traveled to Lausanne and from there to Freiburg, Zurich,

Baden, Schaffhausen, and Tübingen, where Groen paid a visit to Professor K. F. Haug.

Next came Stuttgart in Württemberg, where he met the famous classicist Professor Creuzer, had an audience with the king, and spent several evenings with Pfarrer Knapp, but where searches in the local libraries for useful manuscripts yielded only a few. After a week in Stuttgart, they traveled to Karlsruhe and then to Heidelberg, where he paid a courtesy call on old Professor Thibaut, the opponent of Savigny. Over Darmstadt, they arrived in Frankfort; here he had a long conversation with the pious J. H. von Meyer, from whose lips Groen recorded the earnest words, later echoed in *Unbelief and Revolution*: "There will be no peace for princes and peoples so long as the gospel is not the foundation of politics"; and: "We are heading for hard times; unbelief has spread much farther than before the first French Revolution" (96).

In Frankfort, Groen made a point of calling on Professor Ranke of Berlin, in town for archival research, but he did not find him in. Traveling next to Cassel, on September 19, they were visited there on the 28th by Ranke, a "small, lively, generous, garrulous" man, who during a trip to a local ruin that afternoon "much to my regret, said some very unfavorable things about the *Berliner Politisches Wochenblatt* and accused it especially of wanting to build on a historical foundation without knowing any history" (101–02).

In Cassel, Groen spent many long mornings copying useful documents in the government archives and went on long walks in the afternoon with his wife. Twice they dined in the palace of the Elector. October 6 took them to Elberfeld, where they heard sermons by Kohlbrugge and Krummacher. When Krummacher looked them up later in the week, one point of conversation was the sensational impact of Strauss's *Leben Jesu*: "It speaks for thousands who had not dared to be open about it or who had not made an orderly system of it but who now no longer acknowledge the Bible to be the Word of God" (105). On the 11th of October, the Groens took the steamer at Düsseldorf, to arrive in Rotterdam one day later; after three more hours they were in The Hague—home at last.[51]

---

51. See also Groen's paper, "Reis in Frankrijk en Duitschland, voor het Huis-Archief des Konings," in which he reports enthusiastically on his discoveries in the various archives he visited; *Verspreide Geschriften*, II, 263–80.

CHALLENGING THE ESTABLISHMENT

Refreshed and encouraged by brothers in the faith and stimulated by
fellow historians, Groen published his third volume of the *Archives* and
set to work on the fourth. The following year, however, a work of a different genre flowed from his pen. He felt constrained to record his protest against the religious persecution of Seceders by offering the public a
tract about *The Measures Against the Seceders Tested Against Constitutional
Law*. The author carefully examined the grounds which were commonly
adduced in government circles and by public prosecutors during court
proceedings in defense of the repressive measures taken against the dissenters, and demonstrated point by point that the measures were ineffectual, illegal, unconstitutional, un-Dutch and unchristian (41-45, 47-58).
He demolished the appeal that had been made to certain articles in the
penal code and in the constitution of 1815: they neither now, nor ever have,
sanctioned interference with the exercise of religious worship, and for
that reason alone the king will surely live up to his oath to uphold the
constitution and stop the tyrannical measures (52f). But, more importantly, the Seceders may not be denied the right to serve God according to their conscience; there must be justice for all (2). Holland, Groen
wrote, has always been a free country (4), especially in religious affairs:
during the Republic the church enjoyed the protection of the House of
Orange against interference by ambitious magistrates (14); the Seceders
are protesting against an unpresbyterian polity which, shortly after the
national liberation of 1813, when its introduction was first suggested, had
been (rightly) condemned by the Council of State as in conflict with the
history, experience, and spirit of the National Church (17f). Groen saved
his climax for the end. What have I to do, he exclaimed with abandon—
what have I to do with ponderous arguments, with the subtle distinctions
of jurisprudence and the painstaking interpretation of statutes! These
measures are out of place in Holland, under Orange. They fly in the face
of the *intention and spirit* of the constitution of 1815 (59). The case of the
Seceders, he concluded, touches upon the most cherished and sacred
of our constitutional safeguards and, what is more, is symptomatic of
the condition of church and state: after an age of predominant unbelief a return to the simple gospel is everywhere visible and at work; the

question is: which will have to yield? Will our institutions gradually be altered in accordance with the gospel, or will the gospel be cast out? (66).

Since he was addressing a question of church and state, Groen felt justified in raising another issue as well, one which would constitute a major concern for the rest of his days, *public education*, or: what is to be the nature of the instruction provided by the state for a Christian nation? To sketch the situation, his short treatise opened with a characterization of the Dutch state since 1795, the year that the old Republic of the Seven United Netherlands had succumbed to the revolution. The equality of all religions then introduced had meant that the Reformed Church was separated from both state and school. The major part of the first half of the tract is devoted to the demonstration that the church, though nominally separated from the state, had in fact become "part of the state machine," with the result that the Seceders were persecuted not so much for being dissenting church members as for being rebellious subjects (15). This argument was preceded by a short description of an analogous situation in education. It is an exceptionally courageous section in the tract and deserves special notice.

The schools of the land, separated from the church, had become parts of the state machine as well. The School Act of 1806 had instituted the common, public, non-sectarian school. Non-sectarian had meant neutral with respect to the doctrines of the various denominations: the school had to be acceptable to Catholics as well as Protestants, and even Jewish children (and parents) were not to be offended in their religious sentiments. Thus gradually all doctrine had been banned, though "Bible History" remained on the curriculum—which could not be real history, said Groen, if deprived of the teachings which illumine and explain it. Similarly, Groen went on, moral instruction that was not rooted in Christian doctrine could not teach true morality, and to illustrate how widely accepted this notion was abroad he quoted, among others, Robert Peel, who had said in a speech about the inhabitants of Scotland: "My earnest prayer has been that to his children and his children's children might be long preserved that system of education, which taught the first lesson of infancy in the book of life and founded moral obligations on the revealed will of God" (12n). Exactly contrary to the intention of the legislator, Groen continued, the system of 1806 did not respect but rather affronted the religious sensibilities of earnest Protestants and Catholics. The common school had degenerated into a place of instruction that was based not on commonly held Christian beliefs but on common unbelief and indifference. Nor would the addition of an extra hour of religious instruction by a clergyman remedy the situation, for religious teaching was the basis and soul of nurture, not an isolated part of instruction. Therefore, Groen concluded, there was an unbreakable connection between freedom of conscience, freedom of worship, and freedom of education (13). Thus far the *Measures*.

The standpoint here taken with respect to education was not new in those days, but it had seldom been argued so cogently and forcefully. Groen returned to the subject in 1840, when he temporarily exchanged his concentrated work on the *Archives* (by then seven volumes in number) for a seat in the Double Chamber of that year, which was mandated to prepare a revision of the constitution necessitated by the secession of Belgium.

In advance of the coming session, to influence opinion, Groen published his *Contribution Toward a Constitutional Revision in Line with the Dutch Spirit.*[52] In this 120-page work he argued that what the country needed first of all was not a revised constitution but a different spirit among its responsible statesmen. The constitution of 1815, for all its merits, had never been fully and fairly implemented. And why not? Because "a general and harmful principle has been more powerful than the nature of institutions and the intentions of people" (42). Yet many were blind to this underlying factor and blamed calamitous circumstances for the neglect of the constitution. By contrast, Groen contended that "the many political disasters that have afflicted our country," while they could be traced to secondary causes such as foreign intervention, overbearing government, or public apathy, had a "main cause" as well: all that calamity had been the "necessary result of the ideas by which men, amid general applause, allowed themselves to be guided" (61f). These ideas were unhistorical, revolutionary. Hence, what Holland needed was an anti-revolutionary attitude with regard to political institutions and arrangements. Groen argued for principles that had proved their worth in the past and were in tune with the character of the Dutch people and their history. For that reason he proposed, among other things, that the composition of the upper house be changed to make it

---

52. *Bijdrage tot herziening der Grondwet in Nederlandschen zin* (Leyden, 1840).

truly representative of the various sectors of society and that the manner of electing the lower house be changed to link it more closely and directly to the people (103–05). He also emphasized that the Netherlands was a tempered monarchy, which meant kingly rule tempered by the demands of justice and equity, restricted by acquired rights, and regulated by a constitution; such rule required government by a responsible and homogeneous ministry. He further argued for genuine autonomy for the several provinces and municipalities, in order to honor their distinctive character and counteract bureaucratic centralism (77–83).

In his *Contribution* Groen particularly defended freedom of conscience. This freedom was eminently Dutch and entailed nothing short of full freedom of the press, of worship, of church organization, and of education. The latter he defined simply as "freedom of religion with respect to one's children." According to Groen, the common school of 1806 had had its day. It had been the product of the religious indifference of the time. Since then, the consciences had been aroused from their slumber; more and more people were averse to a type of education that lacked the highest truth. Therefore separate schools for positive Christian education should be allowed rather than prohibited by local authorities who high-handedly deemed the present school "Christian enough." The whole idea of wanting to control the moral and religious education of the nation "is but another one of those ideas that derive from the system of the Revolution." Instead, what the state ought to recognize was the "natural competence" or right of parents to educate their children, "an obligation placed upon them by God himself" (89–95). Returning to the subject in his concluding chapter, Groen stated his ideal solution: "The separation of schools, sooner or later, has become imperative" (125). A plural system of state schools which respected the religious diversity of the nation, rather than a monopoly for the common school which satisfied but few, was the solution for the future, according to Groen in 1840.

In a passage reminiscent of the last quarter of Lecture XV, Groen sketched the political spectrum as he saw it. Since the liberal theory prevails among us, he said, people belong to one of two schools: either they are "conservative," though not in the sense of the gospel ("Prove all things; conserve that which is good"), for they wish to preserve *whatever is*, good and bad, without distinction; or they pride themselves on being "liberal," a label which Groen did not want to refuse or begrudge them, except that he wished they had given more evidence of their love of liberty in resisting existing injustices (120–22).

One further striking passage in the *Contribution* of 1840 deserves to be noted here. At the beginning of chapter III, entitled "Indispensability of True Principles," Groen wrote that any revision would be a futile exercise "so long as the ideas are followed that have guided the government and the nation thus far." He continued: "When the Revolution principles, which *invert* the essence and natural relation of things, are applied, a revolutionary state is the result, that is to say, a state in which, despite all safeguards and forms, arbitrary power defends itself by physical means, first, against everything which in the nature of things and in the history of the nation possesses lawful existence; second, against the further development of the very theories that have produced it. An adequate indication of those principles in their nature, application, and pernicious character with respect to religion, learning, society, and state would require a volume." And then follow some six pages (44–50) which essentially give a summary of the main theme of *Unbelief and Revolution*.

The close of this work of 1840 is also noteworthy. As his final conclusion the author wished to state the following:

> To accept or reject the gospel is to reject or retain the liberal misconceptions. To accept the latter is to be plunged into the vortex of misery in which Europe has been dragged around since they became general. … The history of the last half century, also in our country, can be summarized in two words: a struggle against the consequences of the principles we have approved of. What the Netherlands has become, in consequence, can be seen all around us. What she will become if she continues on this course can be foreseen without unusual perspicacity: perhaps, if her people remain indifferent, she will flourish through commerce and industry; certainly, if her people become agitated, she will suffer discord—until one of the neighbouring states, *or a confederation of the Powers,* covets the prosperity of the powerless, or takes pity on the senseless quarrelers. What the Netherlands might become, if her people show Christian spirit, may be calculated by him who thinks it is

possible to calculate the vastness of God's promises to nations that serve Him (150f).

With this high-sounding note Groen ended his advance contribution to the upcoming constitutional debate.

That summer Groen was appointed by the States of Holland to the Double Chamber. In August, the special sessions began; a month later a number of relatively minor constitutional revisions were passed and the chamber was discharged. Seven weeks later Groen published his edited and annotated speeches or *Adviezen*.[53] This volume revealed that many of the things set forth in his earlier *Contribution* had been reiterated on the floor of the house. Unavailing liberalism, was his constant theme, must be repudiated if a constitutional revision is to be at all useful (45–51). Nor was conservative reaction the answer. "We do not want to restore rightly abolished abuses or destroy the good that has been brought about in revolutionary times," explained the novice parliamentarian who impressed everyone by the maturity of his contributions to the debate; "we do not want a theocracy ... but recognition of the connection between religion, authority, and freedom, and God's supreme authority made the foundation of government and legislation" (45f). At the same time he pleaded for the emancipation of the Reformed Church from state tutelage (63–5), which had in practice led to the coercion of conscience (142–45). The Seceders, in Groen's firm opinion, were entitled to a parliamentary inquiry, as their petition requested (28–35). On other questions as well Groen was forthright in stating his views. He argued and voted in favor of a more responsive ministry which would unite on a common policy and announce its program in advance (75, 114–16, 151). He contrasted his ideal of "tempered monarchy" with the reality of "revolutionary autocracy" which had been the practice for the last quarter century (11, 43, 117).

Several speakers distanced themselves in the strongest terms from Groen and his ideas. Apart from their complaint that his speeches were difficult to grasp or that he wrongly kept dragging religious issues and theological differences into the parliamentary debates, they accused Groen of

---

53. *Adviezen in de Tweede Kamer der Staten-Generaal in dubbelen getale* (Leyden, 1840).

disparaging the Christian elements of the existing constitution (the oath, the spirit of toleration evident in the equality of religions, the provisions for education and pauperism), of defending principles in the abstract, of ignoring the pressing circumstances of the day which urged a speedy revision, of appealing to "Netherlandic principles" without specifying what they were, of invoking "Christian principles" that remained vague and indistinct, of being a representative of the "revolutionary Historical School" (sic), of really aiming at overturning the constitution, of secretly aspiring to introduce a dominant church and compulsion of conscience. Extracts of these attacks on his views and person were faithfully reproduced in Groen's edition of his speeches (94, 98, 108f, 117f, 132). Groen replied to them as well as he was able, but each of these indictments would be given extensive rebuttal in *Unbelief and Revolution* five years later.

Again we see how the central themes of *Unbelief and Revolution* were beginning to be formulated by Groen at this time. The Dutch state had been subjected for half a century to revolutionary experiments. Unbelief had been applied to politics: men had set aside the gospel, accepted the liberal theories, rejected historic principles. Struggling against nature and law, they had fallen into a maelstrom of revolutions, were at last suffering from a condition of exhaustion and despair, and since 1830 had entered a phase of suspicion, reluctance, and despondency. For these disillusioning results, however, they had blamed impersonal circumstances or human exaggeration. The revolutionary state of today, in the name of "public safety" or the "common good," wielded an unlimited authority, evident in a choking centralism and a meddling interference with everything (39f, 50, 69, 98f, 108, 119).

Finally, the house debates provoked Groen to be very clear about his objections to the common school system. He explained that its enforced union of all religious persuasions was harmful; "it replaces what each persuasion regards as the salt of education with a flat surrogate." The common school had perforce to ban the doctrines peculiar to each persuasion. If the local priest insisted, even the Bible was banned. Without doctrine, God becomes a Supreme Being and is invoked as Father without a Mediator. Without doctrine, all moral instruction becomes indoctrination in autonomous morality, whereby children are taught to observe ethical rules without knowing their ground, their purpose, or the power by which one may live up to them (57, 80–82). Compulsion in education had been a major cause of discontent leading to the Belgian Revolt, Groen reminded his fellow parliamentarians, and yet the policy was continued in Holland (60). Whether one thought the reasons given were valid or not, dissatisfaction with the existing school system was a fact.[54] In one way or another, this grievance must be redressed. Forcefully he drove the point home:

> Parents who, with or without adequate grounds, are honestly convinced that the character of the instruction in the existing schools is non-Christian, must not be prevented, directly or indirectly, from providing their children with the kind of education they believe they can justify before God. That coercion, to put it bluntly, is intolerable and must stop. It is a presumption springing from the Revolution doctrine which, disregarding the rights of parents, considers children the property of the state (57).

With scornful indignation Groen dismissed the observation made by a fellow member that surely home instruction was free for anyone who chose not to make use of the public instruction provided in state schools. A useless suggestion for nine-tenth of the nation, retorted Groen, for how is this freedom to be enjoyed by the peasant or the artisan who can scarcely make a sober living by toiling from dawn to dusk by the sweat of his brow? With ironic wit he added: "I am very much in favor of the distinction between classes, but with respect to freedom of conscience I wish all classes to be equal" (78).

Thus spoke Groen in the session of 31 August 1840. That fall he was given the opportunity to follow up his parliamentary counsels. The king had abdicated and, it will be remembered, under the new king Groen was appointed to a royal commission to study existing grievances concerning elementary education and to make recommendations for redressing them. Groen found the task difficult. He had not come to a firm position on the whole question. Numerous letters, solicited and unsolicited, were sent to him containing information, opinion and advice from sympathizers and

---

54. One group, the non-conformists of the Secession, after 1835 increasingly boycotted the public school; cf. Van Gelderen, "Scheuring en Vereniging, 1837–1869," pp. 118–23.

non-sympathizers, teachers and ministers, lawyers and scholars.[55] Many avowed attachment to the common school yet favored granting the right to establish privately funded schools. The more he thought about it, the more Groen began to hesitate about his own, more radical, proposal: splitting the public school into three "denominational" (Catholic, Protestant, Jewish) branches, as a local option. "The Roman Catholics will press for it," he wrote his friend De Clercq, "but what about us? Can there be Christian education without that separation?" But then again, how risky! The Reformed Church is weak and divided, Catholicism is united and strong.

> Pray for me that I may acquire wisdom, caution; let me know your
> ideas, send me any materials you deem useful to read, inform me of
> the opinion of others whom you deem creditable. What is at stake
> here, I may not hide it from myself, is in a certain sense the future
> of the nation.[56]

To his friend Da Costa, too, he communicated his growing misgivings about separate school systems for the major religions, each supervised by its respective clergy. "What benefit would we derive from seeing the Protestant, or if you will Reformed, schools brought under the influence of the church, of the Clergy?" It might make people more watchful of the confessional orthodoxy of Reformed pastors, that was true; yet would it not be hazardous, to say the least, to strengthen the influence of that profession, such as it was?[57]

Ever forthright, friend Koenen gave as his opinion that a restoration of a parochial school system as before 1795 would be "counter-revolutionary." Nor was it, he agreed, advisable, seeing the "run-down condition of the church and the inactivity of her pastors, especially in the large towns." The operation of truly Protestant schools would have to involve a considerable number of elders. He advised Groen to await local initiatives and developments rather than try to reform the national system at one stroke from The Hague.[58]

In the end, Groen added his signature to the commission's report—which merely enumerated the variety of complaints and recommended

---

55. *Briefwisseling*, II, 336–61.
56. *Briefwisseling*, II, 363.
57. *Brieven van Da Costa*, I, 68.
58. *Briefwisseling*, II, 342.

continuance of the common, non-denominational government school, with extra assurances that instruction be non-offensive to any creed—but, like the two Catholic members, he also submitted a supplementary memorandum of his own. In this "minority report" he made two additional recommendations: work toward splitting the public school according to religious persuasion wherever such was feasible and local residents requested it; prepare to end the government's monopoly in education by granting, without delay or restrictions, as a demand and a right of conscience, full freedom to establish and operate private schools. It is the Christian revival of our time, Groen explained to the king, that makes the common school of 1806 no longer satisfactory. Many Christians, be they Roman Catholic or Protestant, have become conscious of religion as a rule for conduct and life and are deeply concerned that in the public school Christian truth is being ignored if not violated. Since the days of the revolution the state has taken charge of education and more and more confined religious instruction to the narrow limits put on it by liberalism. Therefore let those of us laymen who take our religion seriously be granted the freedom to erect schools for instruction that is in keeping with the confession of our several church denominations. It is the least that the state can do. "Allow us to do at our own expense what our opponent does with Government subsidies for which our contribution, too, is demanded."[59]

The only visible effect of the work of the commission was a royal decree, promulgated on 2 January 1842, thus a full year later, facilitating the establishment of private Christian schools by providing for appeal to provincial authorities whenever local authorities refused authorization for unsatisfactory reasons (or for no reason at all). At the same time, the decree expressly prohibited the teaching in the common public school of anything that might be found offensive by any religious persuasion and

---

59. Groen's memorandum is dated 24 Dec. 1840 and was published by him in 1860, when private Christian schools seemed more than ever, given the Elementary School Act of 1857, to be the only alternative to an unsatisfactory public school system; *Verspreide Geschriften*, II, 157–80, esp. 163, 166, 178. See also A. A. de Bruin, *Het Ontstaan van de schoolstrijd* (Amsterdam: Ton Bolland, 1985), pp. 155, 242–44; this study emphasizes that the early schools' struggle was not so much a conflict between historic Christianity and Enlightenment humanism as an internal controversy among Christians: orthodox vs. modernizing theologians, anti-papists vs. ultramontanists, liberal vs. theocratic Protestants; but see the ensuing debate in *Tijdschrift voor Geschiedenis* 99 (1986): 205–13; 100 (1987): 580–88.

consequently it provided for the deletion—and, if agreement could be reached, for the substitution—of any passages in textbooks deemed offensive by any member of local school committees, the entire procedure to be supervised by a provincial committee and to be communicated *verbatim* to the teacher concerned. When the text of the decree was published in the *Staatscourant*, the friends of Christian education wondered what to make of it. Groen judged that on the score of Christian content the curriculum of the common school would in many localities "grow worse"; Bodel Nijenhuis, his publisher, referring to the deletion option, sneered that it would require a lot of work with scissors and paste.[60]

Groen's worst fears would soon be realized. Readers were expurgated and history lessons neutralized. The singing of psalms and hymns in school hours became the subject of bitter altercations and in more and more localities even Bible reading was banned from the classroom if the Catholic priest objected to it. Two years later, in the province of Groen's residence, South Holland, the Governor put an end to all wrangling by circulating an instruction forbidding the use of the Bible in all schools throughout the province, even in those attended only by children of Protestants.[61] Some hailed this drastic step as a permanent check on "meddlesome clerics" but in Lecture XV (419) Groen indicates that he considered this too high a price to pay for peace and justice on the educational front.

WRITING FOR SCHOOL AND CHURCH

Meanwhile, the year 1841 was a busy one for Groen. He worked on Volume VIII of the *Archives* and simultaneously on a revision of Volume I, in which he incorporated changes and additions that were the fruit of his trip through France and Germany five years earlier and for which he now wrote new, lengthy "Prolegomena."[62] Alongside these scholarly publications, his

---

60. *Briefwisseling*, II, 431f.

61. Cf. *Briefwisseling*, II, 635, 642; De Bruin, *Het Ontstaan van de schoolstrijd*, p. 244.

62. See the foreword to *Archives*, vol. VIII, v–vi. When Volume VIII finally came out in 1847 the librarian of the British Museum, Henry Ellis, himself a historian, wrote the editor of the *Archives*: "Your work does credit to your taste and labour, and will carry down to posterity the best materials for the history of your country during the period to which it relates." Ellis had himself, since 1824, edited a dozen volumes of similar royal letters, a publication which in some respects had served as a model for Groen. In October 1847, Ellis invited Groen to be a nominee for Honorary Membership of the Society of Antiquaries of London. I do not know whether Groen allowed his name to stand. *Briefwisseling*, II, 35, 831, 834.

practical involvement in the educational scene now induced him to try his hand at other works. Concerned about the religious content of public instruction both in Bible and in history, which in many localities, he had just learned, was far weaker than he had feared, he began to think of ways to serve the country's elementary schools and its Christian teachers.[63] The latter group especially he hoped to serve by composing a manual for Dutch history under the title "Handbook of the History of the Fatherland," to be written and published in installments. Halfway the appearance of the *Archives* volumes, Merle d'Aubigné had written him, "Won't you crown your labor with a book on the founding of the United Provinces? ... You owe it to the general public."[64] The first installment of Groen's *Handboek der Geschiedenis van het Vaderland*, covering the history of the Low Countries from earliest times to the Dutch Revolt, was published in July 1841, at the author's expense in order to ensure a low price and wide distribution. His friends were pleasantly surprised and praised the work for its concise detail, readable style, and Christian perspective (though one correspondent regretted the lack of proper documentation).[65] Openly Calvinistic in its periodization of Dutch history, in its estimate of the Protestant Reformation and the revolt against Spain, and in its unabashed quoting of Scripture passages to illumine the significance of events and periods, the work was bound to elicit critical comment. One Amsterdam periodical censured the "vain presumption" of the author in pointing to God's hand in history and the "dangerous tendency" to depict the rise of the Dutch Republic as originating in the "Reformation and the Christian principle."[66] It was on this occasion also that Groen and Koenen exchanged lengthy letters about the origin of feudalism and the Frankish monarchy as depicted in the *Handbook* and the revised volume of the *Archives*; Groen admitted

---

63. *Briefwisseling*, II, 390.

64. *Briefwisseling*, II, 165.

65. A favorable comparison was made, *qua* form, to Heeren's *Handbuch der Geschichte des Europäischen Staatensystems* (Göttingen, 1809), which it does indeed resemble. Later, Koenen drew the author's attention to a good review in the *Göttingische gelehrte Anzeigen*, 1844, II, 902–10. Wormser arranged for a popular edition, sold by subscription at a greatly reduced price, as the first volume in a publishing program to provide for a "home library for [everyone of] our people"; cf. *Nederlandsche Gedachten*, 1873/74, V, 386–92. In the late fifties, Koenen began to stimulate interest for a translation into French or German, but nothing came of it; cf. *Briefwisseling*, II, 600; III, 915; V, 388.

66. *Briefwisseling*, II, 407n2.

that he had made "no special or thorough" study of the Middle Ages but relied on A. Kluit, J. N. Moreau and F. Guizot, to which Koenen responded that in general Groen was "too monarchical" in his description of medieval kingship and that he ought to consult German scholars like K. F. Eichhorn, H. Leo and others.[67]

The *Handbook* would take till 1846 to complete. Realizing this schedule, Groen decided to try his hand first at lighter fare: a short but complete overview, for young readers. That fall he published a *Kort Overzigt* or "brief survey" of Dutch history ending with 1840. He had been shocked, he wrote his friend De Clercq, "by the way in which God's Word in our history is gradually being banned from our public schools. For the *mixed* school my *Overzigt* is certainly not suitable, but may it be serviceable for other schools and home instruction!" To another friend he wrote that his recent "examination of schoolbooks of Dutch history, I am compelled to say, filled me with indignation." As to level, the author intended it to be read by 10- to 12-year-olds. Both Professor Van Assen and Koenen reported to the generous donor of complimentary copies that their children were busy reading it,[68] while Da Costa wrote that he had begun using it "with great pleasure" in his daily private tutorial class.[69]

A sequel on world history, *Kort Overzigt der Algemeene Geschiedenis*, was written shortly thereafter, but was never published.[70] Another sequel which did see publication was a song book to accompany the Dutch history book (possibly in imitation of Zahn's Bible story book, mentioned below). The song book seems to have been compiled in a period of six weeks or less and was published in early 1842 under the title *Vaderlandsche Zangen*. These 138 patriotic songs, poems, occasional verse, sonnets, lyrics, psalms and hymns were slightly edited and annotated by Groen and supplied in the margin with the number of the section in the *Kort Overzigt* to which they were the companion pieces or commentaries.

---

67. *Briefwisseling*, II, 410–17.
68. *Briefwisseling*, II, 421f.
69. *Brieven van Da Costa*, I, 99.
70. It was published in 1990 in *Bescheiden*, ed. Zwaan, no. 57.

All these publications of 1841-42 reveal Groen as a Calvinist historian who was capable both of producing readable and reliable[71] syntheses and of structuring and casting them in accordance with his personal religious and political preconceptions. When the *Handbook* was complete, a history of Holland had been laid out in three parts: I. Before the Republic; II. The Republic; and III. The Revolution. The period of the Dutch Republic was divided into the following phases:

1. Suffering for the faith (1517-1568);
2. Contending for the faith (1568-1648);
3. Standing by the faith (1648-1713); and
4. Departing from the faith (1713-1795)

—a periodization which has been characterized as "in more than one respect typical" of Groen, whose "conception as a whole about the desired relation of church and state and the place of Catholics in our country, as well as his whole campaign within the Church, was decisively influenced by this historical interpretation."[72]

Groen was never to depart from his fervent belief that the Netherlands had its own providential mission to fulfill in world history.[73] His country was like a second Israel, albeit "not by identification but by comparison," he wrote in § 105 of the *Handbook*. And what, then, was Holland's peculiar mission? We read of it, among other places, in Lecture VII (175) of *Unbelief and Revolution*: "The Netherlands, more than any other country, was chosen and set apart by the mercies of God to be a seat of Protestantism."

As a further aid to Christian education, Groen looked for a useful school-book of Bible stories. He found it in the popular work by F. L. Zahn mentioned above: *Biblische Historien nach dem Kirchenjahre geordnet, mit Lehren und Liederversen versehen.*[74] With the assistance of the Nymegen lawyer and school commissioner J. J. L. van der Brugghen, he had it translated into

---

71. In the 1860s the *Handbook* would be prescribed reading for history students at Leyden; cf. *Briefwisseling*, III, 915.

72. Smitskamp, *Groen van Prinsterer als historicus*, pp. 144, 147n.

73. This is the theme that attracted the late Queen Wilhelmina (1880-1963) to Groen's *Handboek*; cf. Th. Booy, *Het is stil op het Loo … Overpeinzingen in memoriam koningin Wilhelmina* (Amsterdam: Ten Have, 1963), p. 153; idem, "Koningin Wilhelmina en de gereformeerden," *VU-Magazine* 1 (Nov 1972): 39-42.

74. Meurs, 1832; 2nd ed., 1840.

Dutch. Groen heavily subsidized its publication and wrote a foreword in which he recommended the work to all God-fearing parents and educators.

In these years, the fight against doctrinal laxness in the church also demanded his attention. The early part of 1842 produced the "Petition of Seven Gentlemen from The Hague" addressed to the Synod of the Reformed Church. The redaction of the text had been entrusted to Groen van Prinsterer. Its immediate occasion was the answer given by Synod the year before to a petition signed by more than 8,000 church members.[75] Synod's answer at that time had been curt: most of the petitioners, to judge from their signatures, are uneducated if not illiterate and therefore unqualified to judge of ecclesiastical matters; moreover, to ask for disciplinary measures against certain ministers is unfounded since all have pledged, at their ordination, to uphold the church's doctrine "only as it constitutes the essence and substance of the Confession of the Reformed Church."[76] The latter formulation ("essence and substance") gave Groen and his friends an opportunity to request Synod to do at least the minimum. Their petition protested calmly and eloquently against the inroads being made into the church by the Groningen school of theology and requested Synod to maintain both the cardinal truths of the gospel and, as a means to that end, the doctrinal standards of the denomination "in substance and essence." If Synod claimed that the latter was already being done, the petition went on, why was it that teachers in pulpit and seminary openly denied the authority of Scripture, the deity of the Savior, the forgiveness of sins through the blood of the cross? Did such fundamental doctrines fall *outside* the "substance and essence" of the Confession? If not, how were they to be upheld? Surely the answer was not difficult. The petition asked Synod to condemn all *contrary* teaching (in which connection it singled out the "doctrine presented by three professors" in the theological journal of the Groningen School) and to make a beginning with a revision of the church's governance.[77] The new teachings simply cannot hold a legitimate place in the church, it insisted, for they surreptitiously[78] substitute for

---

75. Rullmann, *De Strijd voor kerkherstel*, pp. 7–12.

76. Rullmann, *De Strijd voor kerkherstel*, p. 9.

77. Kluit, *Het Protestantse Réveil in Nederland en daarbuiten*, p. 436.

78. In private correspondence Groen accused the Groningen divines of "camouflaging" real differences by retaining many "evangelical locutions," thus "setting the minds of many

biblical truths "a sense and meaning opposite to those accepted by every Christian church" and, having eliminated the basis for union with God, speak only of His love and are silent about His righteous judgment.[79]

The petition of the seven was printed and sold to the public shortly after it had been duly deposited. By the time Synod dealt with the petition, it had to deal with many other supporting petitions as well as counter-petitions, signed by a total of 137 ministers and several thousands of members. Synod's response to all of them was the single decision which was no decision, to wit: "Whatever the respective value or want of value of the petitions may be, to let the matter rest without taking any further notice of the same."[80]

This supercilious answer prompted Groen and his six friends to turn directly to the church's membership throughout the land. Early in 1843 appeared the manifesto *To the Reformed Church*, written by Groen, with the imprimatur of the friends, as a "kind of sequel" to their petition.[81] This tract of 164 pages further explained the motives behind the petition and the several points at issue. Its tone was dignified yet forthright. Towards the close of the tract we read what one of the editors of the correspondence[82] has called one of the most moving sentences ever to flow from Groen's pen: "This battle for truth is at the same time a battle of love, because it is being waged for the salvation of souls, and a battle for peace, because it is being fought for the peace of God which passeth all understanding."[83]

Meanwhile, the second installment of the *Handbook* had come off the press. It had required much more work than the author had initially counted on. As usual, he sent complimentary copies far and wide, to sympathizers and opponents, to admirers, patrons and colleagues, to close and distant acquaintances. The Reverend Dr. W. Steven, former minister of the Scottish Church in Rotterdam and soon to be appointed chaplain to Trinity College, replied from Edinburgh in a thank-you note containing the following polite assessment: "It is pleasing to think that the rising

---

an unsuspecting reader at ease." *Briefwisseling*, II, 106, 207.

79. Quoted in Vree, *De Groninger godgeleerden*, p. 303.

80. Rullmann, *De Strijd voor kerkherstel*, p. 19.

81. *Aan de Hervormde Gemeente in Nederland* (Leyden, 1843); cf. *Briefwisseling*, II, 488.

82. C. Gerretson, to judge from the wording of the annotation.

83. Cf. *Briefwisseling*, II, 499n4, citing *Aan de Hervormde Gemeente in Nederland*, p. 138.

generation in Holland have as a schoolbook an elegant yet condensed view of the various fortunes of the Netherlands, with a vein of enlightened piety running through the whole work."[84]

It was a good thing that Groen and his friends were lawyers by training, for throughout these years they were in touch with the authorities, local and provincial, to obtain a permit for starting a Christian school in The Hague. The prescribed procedure did not forestall a great measure of arbitrariness in interpreting the law and the royal decree pertaining to such authorization. Friends in Nymegen, Nijkerk, Amsterdam and Bois-le-Duc were ultimately successful in their requests or appeals, but not the brothers in The Hague. They were informed that for a private Christian school to be authorized it was necessary that its religious character be as broad as the common public school—the very thing they wished to correct. The road of appeal and, finally, petition, was long and frustrating and in the end proved fruitless, at least for 1844-45. In 1844, Groen published the *Documents Relative to the Refusal of a Privately Endowed School in The Hague.*[85] Correspondence with influential men like De Bosch Kemper, solicitor-general in the district of Amsterdam, made Groen realize that even among self-styled liberals there was little sympathy for his efforts to realize freedom of education.[86] This episode in his life accounted for another passionate outburst toward the close of Lecture XV (420).

Yet another distinct disappointment of the last year or so for Groen had been the lack of coordinated activity by friends of the Réveil. While the petition to Synod had been pending, his gentlemen friends in Amsterdam, Da Costa, Koenen and De Clercq, had not, as he had hoped, sent in letters of support; instead, each had submitted a petition of his own, which, though not necessarily weakening the impact of that of the seven gentlemen from The Hague, had not helped very much in strengthening it either. Groen's hopes for a united front in the battle for church reform were dashed the year following publication of the tract *To the Reformed Church*, when Da Costa openly "broke ranks"[87] with his public apologia, in

---

84. *Briefwisseling*, II, 465, 467.

85. *Stukken beireffende de afwijzing eener bijzondere school der eerste klasse te 's Gravenhage* (The Hague, 1844).

86. *Briefwisseling*, II, 664, 678.

87. Thus Groen's associate, the Rev. Mr. G. Barger; cf. *Brieven van Da Costa*, III, 179.

which he rendered an "account of his sentiments" for not joining the gentlemen from The Hague.[88] As we have had occasion to note above, Da Costa
firmly believed that although the doctrinal standards were good in their
time, they should not be used in the present time as an instrument of
discipline in the church; rather, the "disease" in the church should be
allowed to take its course and not be opposed except by its only "medicine,"
preaching the Word. As he explained to Groen in private correspondence,
Da Costa felt very strongly that it was wrong to press for adherence to
human creeds "apart from the Divine Word from which they derive their
validity." Moreover, the appeal to historic confessions created the impression of not admitting progress and tended to remain formal anyway; it
would be better to defend *specific* teachings of Scripture, and much better
still to use *new* formulations in doing so. To insist on full and unqualified
subscription would not restore the purity of preaching. We must, argued
Da Costa, demand fidelity to the distinctive *truths* of the gospel, not to
tradition. Personally he was convinced that a "wholesale transformation
in the field of theology is imminent, which will bring to light, perhaps
more splendidly than ever before, the truth as it is in the Word, as it is in
Christ." Vibrant life, not frozen formularies, were the means to restoration.
Therefore he just could not agree with the principle of the seven's petition
to Synod. "Neology is not conquered by paleology."[89]

    This open division among the Réveil brethren was clearly a tactical
weakness in their struggle to reform the church from within. Groen enter-
tained the hope that communal consultation on a regular basis would result
in fuller agreement and then in collective action. At the same time, he went
on record as deeming it premature and forced to found an Evangelical
Society analogous to the one in France, adding that he expected the gospel
to bear fruit sooner or later in some association or other of that kind. To
help prepare for such fruit-bearing, however, Groen began in his correspondence of the summer of 1842 to raise the possibility of organizing a
"meeting" (he used the English word). Secession leaders such as H. P. Scholte
wrote him in reply that the existing ecclesiastical division would make

---

88. I. da Costa, *Rekenschap van gevoelens bij gelegenheid van den strijd over het adres aan de
Hervormde Gemeente in Nederland* (Amsterdam, 1843).

89. *Brieven van Da Costa*, I, 12, 73, 78–85, 105–8; see also 274–85.

his participation in any such association very difficult; other correspondents gave mixed reactions to his cautious overtures for a meeting.[90] Not so Heldring, his friend the country pastor.

As early as 31 May 1842, when the petition had just appeared in print, Heldring had written Groen of the desirability of "setting a date for a meeting of all those who sympathize with the cause for the purpose of discussing many issues."[91] The moment passed, but the idea seems to have lingered. It was at this time, too, that a correspondence began to develop on a more or less regular basis between Groen and the Amsterdam bailiff Wormser. A former elder in the local church of the Secession and for a while the leader of an independent group until he returned to the Reformed fold, Wormser was an astute and largely self-taught man who took a great interest in the church question and in the struggle for Christian education.[92] Between 1842–45, in the dozen or so letters exchanged between them, Wormser encouraged Groen to call a meeting for all Christians in the land, irrespective of denomination, to discuss mutual concerns, especially in education. Groen replied that there seemed to be too little enthusiasm for the idea among his contacts to warrant the undertaking.[93] The time did not seem ripe for Heldring's idea of calling a "meeting." When would it be?

THE YEAR 1845

Meanwhile, Groen filled his days with historical studies. Installment three of the *Handbook* had appeared in October 1843, and installment four, for which he had to do pioneering work on the eighteenth century, came out in May 1845.[94] In that month Groen received a visit of Heldring which would at last launch an effort at coordinated activity in the practical domain. In

---

90. *Briefwisseling*, II, 461, 464f, 470, 474.

91. *Briefwisseling*, II, 449.

92. Over the years, a large measure of confidentiality, based on comradeship and cooperative ventures, would develop between this "man of the people" and the learned gentleman from The Hague; only half in jest Groen once referred to Wormser as "my privy councillor." His significance is well sketched in Evenhuis, *Ook dat was Amsterdam*, V, 152–67; his ecclesiastical pilgrimage is analyzed in Te Velde, "J. A. Wormser en zijn Vrije Gemeente in Amsterdam (1840–1851)," passim.

93. *Brieven van Wormser*, II, 4, 19, 21.

94. Installments 1–4 were reviewed in the *Allgemeine Zeitschrift für Geschichte* (Berlin) VII (1847): 53–79, 97–148, by E. M. Arndt, whose sympathies for the orthodoxy of Dort and for the social contract were opposite to Groen's; cf. *Briefwisseling*, II, 802.

Groen's study on the Korte Vijverberg, and perhaps also at the dinner table of his host, Pastor Heldring unburdened himself of a long-felt inner conflict: should he continue to be involved in the existing societies for philanthropy, education, abolition, missions and Bible distribution, societies which were half-Christian, half-humanistic; or should he work toward separate agencies for these causes on an uncompromisingly biblical basis? In the former his contributions were appreciated if he played down his orthodoxy; the latter would require concerted action and interdenominational goodwill.[95] Heldring admitted that his conscience leaned toward the solution of separate action and that he longed to have its feasibility investigated. Groen responded by saying that he had long felt the same and he invited Heldring to draw up a circular letter to test the waters. The letter was soon circulated by Groen among his many Réveil and Secession contacts, and this time the probings were encouraging.[96] In August 1845, the first meeting was held in Amsterdam, followed by a second already in January 1846.

Chairman at the meetings of the Christian Friends was Groen van Prinsterer. Cautious as ever, he was mildly optimistic. He noticed anxiously that discussion avoided the thorny ecclesiastical question, but at least a start had been made to complement individual with joint deliberation and action. Groen took hope for the future. Reflecting on what had now commenced, he began to feel that perhaps the Calvinistic character of the nation, the Calvinistic presence in public life and in the public institutions, would not have to be given up entirely, at least not without a fight. To what extent further "disestablishment" of Calvinism in the Netherlands would have to be accepted he could not foresee. The clear-headed Wormser wrote him in those very days:

> I am by no means insensitive to what is called the national church and our national schools, institutions and character. The memory of what God in his grace has done in our land, and of the public institutions which arose as a result of that, always has much that is precious and appealing to me.

But the problem, Wormser continued (and Groen could only have agreed), was that amid much spiritual awakening and revival of *persons,*

---

95. Rullmann, *De Strijd voor kerkherstel,* p. 45.
96. *Briefwisseling,* II, 680, 687–89; V, 141–44.

the reformation and revival of time-honored *institutions* was proving much more difficult. We need to practice communion of the saints, Wormser urged, and avoid pouring new wine into old bottles. In the growing confrontation about the spiritual direction of Dutch society and culture, the nominal Christian character of many institutions may be removed by the Lord Himself, and through the crisis the members of His Body will grow to greater solidity and independence. For this reason Wormser expected a great deal from the ongoing struggle for complete freedom of religion and education. If we meet with much opposition in society in setting up Christian schools, for example, it may be that the Lord wants to break and remove that opposition utterly. "What benefit would there be, if our institutions were freely admitted, only to remain under the supervision of unbelievers? We would risk falling asleep again, as our fathers did."[97]

And so we see Groen, in 1845, at the center of a possible regrouping of forces in the country, of a consorting together of fellow believers for the purpose of making a cultural-institutional impact on the nation. In part, their endeavors aimed to restore what was lost; in part, their minds were turning to new ways and means of countering what was a new development in the world, a revolution in Christendom. Since Holyoake in England first coined the term in 1851, we have been accustomed to calling the new development "secularism." Groen at this time revived the rhetoric of his *Overzigt* of 1831 and talked of *unbelief, revolt against God, the Revolution.* Years of thought, study and debate seemed to come to fruition. Let us now turn to the antecedents immediately prior to his decision to lecture on unbelief and revolution.

In the summer of 1845, Groen began to work on the fifth and final installment of his *Handbook*. It was to cover events from the coming of the revolution to Holland in 1795 to the liberation from French occupation in 1813, and "possibly beyond that year, if only in summary account."

Although he kept being urged from various quarters to resume publication of the *Archives* (the last volume of which had appeared back in 1839), Groen decided that the *Archives* must wait till the *Handbook* was complete.[98] As he studied the period, however, he felt the need to delve more deeply into

---

97. *Brieven van Wormser,* I, 17f.
98. *Brieven van Wormser,* I, 56f.

the French Revolution which had impinged so strongly on Dutch history as to result, finally, in the absorption of Holland into the Empire of Napoleon (1810–13). Already during the final stages of writing the fourth installment he had written his publisher: "I do realize that I must take care not to delve too deeply into the French Revolution; however, I feel that especially from 1787 on, our history, and in particular the history of the fall of the Republic, cannot be properly understood without looking continually at events in France."[99] Now, as he set himself to continue the story for installment five, the events in France began to absorb him completely. He reread the *History* by Thiers; he began to read the *History* by Alison. Professor Van Assen drew his attention to the *History* by Wachsmuth. The various studies in manuscripts of the age of revolution in which he had engaged off and on since 1835 were brought out again. Throughout the summer and well into October he worked feverishly in his country-house Oud-Wassenaar (a recent purchase, an hour's drive from The Hague). The grand conception was there: the age of revolution, with all its ups and downs, right up to the present, was the direct product of the revolutionary ideas of the Enlightenment which had been able to supplant the age-old principles of European Christendom owing to the spread of unbelief. Basically, it was still the conception of the *Nederlandsche Gedachten* as outlined in the *Overzigt* of 1831 and confirmed in Groen's mind ever since. It had clearly outgrown the scope of the *Handbook* and begged separate treatment. Very well, if Da Costa and others lectured on literary and biblical topics, perhaps here was a topic *he* could lecture on. He quietly told his friend Elout that he was planning a lecture series to set forth his basic views and that it would be all right to let the other friends know.

But how to organize the material and present the evidence as convincingly as possible? Groen adopted a form of discourse that came natural to him. It would be the same one as had crystallized into the manuscript studies composed since 1835. He would argue his case both logically and

---

99. *Briefwisseling*, II, 660. It should be remembered that throughout the revolutionary era, the history of the Netherlands closely followed that of France. In fact, some years before 1789, Holland had its own (abortive) democratic revolution. In 1795, the Great Revolution came to Holland as French armies, aided by Dutch revolutionary "patriots," overran the country and helped set up the Batavian Republic. In 1806, Napoleon created the Kingdom of Holland, placing his brother Louis on the throne, and in 1810 he simply incorporated the Netherlands into the French Empire.

historically, in the form of a "natural history" followed by a "biography" of the spiritual revolution he wished to expose. Thus he would show, first, how the fruits can be known beforehand by examining the tree on which they grow, and then, how the peculiar tree is known by looking at its fruits as they ripen and mature one by one. But, of course, the argument as a whole would only gain in cogency if he could manage first to demolish the contrary case: namely, that the revolution arose in reaction to the divine-right monarchy and oppressive absolutism of the *ancien régime*. Consequently, Groen resumed his study of the pre-revolutionary forms of government and their purported shortcomings and abuses. He asked an acquaintance (De Bosch Kemper) to return the copy he had lent him of the anonymous work on the constitutional place and function of the estates in the German lands, *Die ständische Verfassung und die deutsche Constitutionen*,[100] because, he explained, "I use it quite often and need it right now." On September 1, he was ploughing his way through the proceedings of the National Assembly of Revolutionary Holland. This detour toward completing the *Handbook* seemed more and more mandatory. The more he read about the period starting with 1795, he wrote to Da Costa on 12 October 1845, the more he was afraid as yet to pick up the thread of his Dutch history—"less so on account of the events to be related than in regard to the principles to be outlined: the latter is a precarious business and I will have to be especially mindful to 'make haste slowly.' "[101]

This is approximately how one can reconstruct the gestation of *Unbelief and Revolution* in the summer and fall of 1845 from bits and pieces of information scattered through Groen's correspondence of this time.[102]

By November, Groen was back in The Hague. Much was still uncertain, many details still needed sifting to allow the larger picture to emerge, but armed with folios of notes, extracts and trial runs, he made the plunge and quietly informed his friends that he was going ahead with his plan to host a series of lectures and that the first meeting would be at his winter home on Saturday the 8th.

---

100. Offprint from the *Berliner Politisches Wochenblatt*, 1833.
101. *Brieven van Da Costa*, I, 239f; III, 267.
102. Cf. *Briefwisseling*, II, 682, 698, 702, 703, 704.

Late that fall, while the series was in progress, his publisher friend, J. T. Bodel Nijenhuis of the firm S. en J. Luchtmans of Leyden, grew worried. When would the concluding installment of the *Handbook* get done? On November 25, Groen wrote Bodel that he was "extremely busy" with lectures for his friends on Saturday evenings, and on December 4 he admitted that he had had to put aside all other activities "for the time being." On December 9, Groen wrote:

> I understand your difficulty about my lectures very well. I felt the need, and perhaps also the duty, for once to communicate *viva voce* the ensemble of my convictions about constitutional law and history—at least to make the attempt. I own it is now demanding all my energies. But this spring, the Lord willing, I earnestly hope to resume work on one of the installments. However, is that the right word? Could I not consider my *Handbook* complete as it is, under the title *Handbook of the History of the United Netherlands*, even though I would then not be permitted to finish the whole as *planned*?[103]

THE YEARS AFTER 1845

Apparently, this last idea found little favor with either author or publisher. Yet, as it turned out, Groen would not return to his book on Dutch history until the late spring of 1846, when he had recuperated somewhat from the strain of the lecture series. "I have been completely engrossed this winter," he wrote to Merle d'Aubigné on 22 March 1846, "by a series of lectures in which I attempt to prove that the history of the last half century has been but the development of the revolutionary principles which have their root in unbelief and which cannot be effectively combatted except by a return to the truth of the gospel."[104] That spring of 1846, back at Oud-Wassenaar, he filed away his lecture manuscripts and resumed work on the *Handbook*. By June, enough of it was written to warrant starting to print, and the first sheets rolled off the presses.[105] The pace was slow, owing to a tremor in his right hand, but by the middle of November the end was in sight and Groen communicated to Bodel: "The more I have had to work on the *Handbook*, the more I have had to nurse my hand. ... I may come to Leyden one of these

---

103. *Briefwisseling*, II, 714f.
104. *Briefwisseling*, II, 735.
105. *Brieven van Da Costa*, I, 252.

days, or else after completing the *Handbook*. P.S. What font do you advise for the Preface?"[106]

The picture is now clear. To be able to write the concluding part of the *Handbook* about the age of revolution in Holland, Groen allowed himself— or saw himself compelled—to deal first with the age of revolution in its wider, European scope. In one sense, therefore, *Unbelief and Revolution* is a companion piece and backdrop for the last part of the *Handbook*, which probably benefited from critical reactions received as he gave the lectures.

What else happened between the filing away of his lecture manuscripts in the spring of 1846 and the publication of the book *Ongeloof en Revolutie* in the summer of 1847? To encourage his Amsterdam friends in their recent venture of launching the periodical *De Vereeniging: Christelijke Stemmen* (for which they had tried in vain to get his participation on the editorial board), he submitted the text of Lecture II; the article, bearing the title "The Abiding Protest of Knowledge and Science against the Revolution," opened the very first issue of the *Stemmen*, was continued in the second, and concluded in the third.[107] Later that year, the *Stemmen* printed part three of Lecture III: "On the Divine Right of Government."[108] For the time being, the manuscript of the remaining lectures gathered dust in the drawer. Would it remain there for nine years, or possibly for ever?

It is difficult to determine exactly what finally induced Groen to go public with his lectures. As he apologetically explained in the Preface, he realized he was rushing into print but it was time he put his weapons to use; he then mentioned certain events in Switzerland and Prussia and the appearance of certain books in Berlin and Paris that had borne out the correctness of his basic position. Looking at these clues, we note that at most two of the items mentioned could possibly antedate his decision to actually publish the lectures. First, early in March he had become acquainted with Radowitz's *Gespräche aus der Gegenwart über Staat und Kirche*, whereas the first mention of his decision to publish his lectures occurs in a letter to Bodel dated 16 March.[109] Also, the first volume of Louis Blanc's

---

106. *Briefwisseling*, II, 731, 744, 751.
107. *De Vereeniging: Christelijke Stemmen*, Volume I, 1847, 1–9, 65–71, 129–34.
108. *De Vereeniging: Christelijke Stemmen*, Volume I, 1847, 747–55.
109. *Briefwisseling*, II, 784f; see also 781, letter 1082.

Histoire de la Révolution française was released on 6 February 1847,[110] hence may have been known to Groen prior to his decision to publish. As for the remaining items referred to in the Preface: the address to the United Diet by Frederick William IV dates from April 11, while the earliest that Groen could have heard of the confrontation by the Swiss confederacy of the Catholic *Sonderbund* would have been after July 20; finally, it is not until July that the correspondence makes mention of his reading of Lamartine's *Histoire des Girondins*.[111] Thus only the appearance of the books by Radowitz and Blanc may have influenced the initial decision. Perhaps he felt his own work was as good if not better.

Be that as it may, it was midway through March, as noted above, that Groen informed Bodel of his desire to publish, at his own expense, the text of the lectures of the previous winter. Apparently Bodel was able to offer a satisfactory contract, for on April 19 we find Groen eagerly awaiting galley proofs and on May 25 further explaining to his publisher, "I am giving the lectures without recasting them, just as they are: that is why I retain those expressions which do not regard the public but which exempt me from additions, etc."[112]

Why the rush all of a sudden? one cannot help but wonder. Perhaps the meetings of the Christian Friends, the sixth of which had been held 14–15 April 1847, were giving Groen increasing hope of united action in church, state and society. It would therefore be all the more important to ensure unity of outlook among the friends, to dispel illusions about an easy victory for their Christian principles, to plumb the real depth and grasp the true nature of the crisis afflicting their country.

A spiritual diagnosis of the contemporary scene could certainly prove useful. The year before, large groups of Seceders had emigrated to the United States and their leaders had explained their motives and said goodbye to Groen.[113] Although he disapproved of their departure, he was

---

110. Leo A. Loubère, *Louis Blanc* (Northwestern University Press, 1961), p. 63.

111. *Briefwisseling*, II, 802. Lamartine's first two volumes appeared *post* March 18; cf. William Fortescue, *Alphonse de Lamartine: A Political Biography* (New York: St. Martin's, 1983), p. 128.

112. *Briefwisseling*, II, 783, 788, 790.

113. *Briefwisseling*, II, 744–50, 766.

willing to agree with their somber estimate of the country's condition.[114] Meanwhile, the liberal theologian, Scholten, had been inaugurated in Leyden, and Opzoomer's star was rising in Utrecht. Synod persisted in its latitudinarianism and the Groningen School was gaining in prominence. Was modernism the irrepressible wave of the future? Politically, restoration conservatism was in its death-throes and the king's autocratic rule was rapidly losing favor and prestige. Would Holland gravitate to liberalism, in the wake of France, where strident liberals were staging defiant demonstrations against the July Monarchy at election meetings and (when these were prohibited) political banquets, and where new books by Lamartine and Louis Blanc were coming out in praise of the first French Revolution— the Reign of Terror not excepted. At home, Thorbecke's voice, in publications and occasional speeches, grew more insistent and self-confident.[115] Bread riots in Friesland and Groningen resulted in casualties, both in lives and property; the specter of creeping communism haunted the minds.[116] What would Groen van Prinsterer do in times like these?

The scholar in history and constitutional law made his contribution by publishing his "system" for all his countrymen to read. He had to swallow his pride of workmanship as he felt the lectures really needed further study and polishing, but he put these "selfish scruples" aside. As soon as the book was out, he sent no less than eighty-seven complimentary copies to men of influence in church, state and academy—friends and colleagues, sympathizers and critics, potential allies and adversaries alike.

That same summer of 1847 saw the completion of the first series of the *Archives*. It symbolized more than the end of a scholarly project. Looking back we can say that by 1847 the groundwork had been laid for a new phase in Groen's life. Moving from his study to the floor of parliament, the author of *Unbelief and Revolution* was to become a participant in the public debate about the laws that would govern the Dutch state and society in the second half of the nineteenth century and beyond. For our purposes,

---

114. *Briefwisseling*, II, 752.
115. Cf. Boogman, *Rondom 1848*, pp. 44–49.
116. Cf. *Briefwisseling*, II, 449f.

the remainder of our author's career beyond the year 1847 need only be sketched in broad outline, highlighting the more salient features.[117]

In the revolution, 1848, Groen openly stated that the peaceful *coup d'état* of King William II and the Dutch liberals was an overreaction to events in the capitals of Europe and to mock demonstrations in the streets of The Hague. Once the new constitution became a fact, he loyally resolved to abide by it but continued to repudiate the spirit in which it had been conceived. He declared himself opposed to its tacit endorsement of popular sovereignty and the majoritarian principle in its provisions for direct elections, even though he himself had earlier been an advocate of both ministerial responsibility and greater popular influence on government. To explain his position he wrote a series of nine tracts, *Constitutional Revision and National Concord* (1849). Its more than 500 pages formulated few alternative policies and measures, but argued first of all for a reversal of mentality, an acknowledgment of royal sovereignty, and a respect for the "ancient liberties" and "true needs" of the people.

Except for brief intervals, Groen van Prinsterer served as a member of the Second Chamber between the years 1849-57 and 1862-65. (The years 1857-61 were mainly spent on a second series of *Archives*, in five volumes.) A loyal adherent of constitutional monarchy and a declared enemy of parliamentary sovereignty, he nevertheless became a champion of parliament in its fight for the right to criticize every action of government without restriction, including royal appointments,[118] and for the right to vote down a budget, if need be for purely political reasons as a last resort. Novel for their time, election "promises" were defended by Groen, who insisted that the electorate had the right to inquire of candidates what political platform they would pledge to uphold.[119] Between 1850-55, as editor-in-chief of a

---

117. See also Schutte, *Mr. G. Groen van Prinsterer*, chapters IV-VII; the bibliographical essay on pp. 156-63 of this book is a useful guide for further reading.

118. During the parliamentary crisis of 1866-67, occasioned by the celebrated "motie-Keuchenius," Groen threw his weight behind the anti-conservative campaign which permanently prevented the Netherlands from following the example of Prussia, where Bismarck was continually defying parliamentary majorities; cf. S. van der Wal, *De motie-Keuchenius; een koloniaal-historische studie over de jaren 1854-1866* (diss. Utrecht; Groningen and Batavia: Wolters, 1934), passim.

119. Fruin attacked this encouragement of "political immorality" and pointed to the constitutional stipulation that members of parliament should sit "without instruction or consultation."

daily, *De Nederlander*, Groen established himself as a feared, admired and hated political journalist. Groen believed in "ideological polarization" for the sake of political clarity. While such political "isolation" allowed him to enter into short-term pragmatic alliances with "adversaries" for promoting specific solutions, it enabled him above all to lay a durable foundation for growing cooperation and united action on the part of Christians otherwise separated by traditional divisions and denominational loyalties. Thanks to Groen, the term "revolution" came to be applied in the Netherlands to the whole of the secular spectrum of politics, not just to its radical wing.

Groen's years in parliament were intensely frustrating. Thorbecke's first ministry (1849-53) proposed a new Poor Law, which Groen opposed because it reinforced state powers and encroached on the rights of the church and its diaconate. During the debates Groen went out on a limb when he defended as an inalienable right of conscience the declared intention of a Secession church that under no circumstances would it obey the bill before parliament if it were to become law.

Groen's position was marked by ambivalence both before and during the no-popery movement of April 1853 that followed the papal announcement about restoring the episcopal hierarchy in the Netherlands after three centuries of desolation "inflicted by the Calvinian heresy." Although he considered the measure ill-advised and certainly ill-timed, he defended the church's constitutional right to enact it. But he also noted in his paper that Roman Catholicism, particularly in its temporal aspirations which it had never renounced, needed to be combated by every spiritual means available. At the same time, the evident vitality in the land of Protestant sentiments, so rudely awakened, gave him hope that forces could be mobilized to work in the *state* for the preservation of the Protestant character of the *nation* by not only permitting religious equality now, but also by safeguarding religious equality in the future against possible "popish aggression."[120]

The public agitation of 1853 resulted in a new government which, after acquiescing in the restoration of bishoprics, in its turn came to an untimely end when it introduced an education bill that did little to redress grievances about the religious character of the public school. It rained petitions. In the course of this session Groen failed to win a majority for his

---

120. Bruins Slot, *Groen van Prinsterer bij het herstel der hierarchie*, pp. 69–71, 86–92, 95–101.

private member's bill that would have allowed appeals against refusals by local or provincial authorities to permit the erection of private Christian schools.[121] After the elections of 1856, a new government was headed by Van der Brugghen, who was widely regarded as an anti-revolutionary but who personally located himself in the ethical-irenical wing of the school. Groen had suffered defeat at the polls but regained a seat in a by-election later that year for the express purpose of helping a satisfactory education bill through the chamber and the committees. The Van der Brugghen Ministry, regarding its task to be conciliatory, submitted a compromise bill, allowed a number of amendments that weakened it further, and in the end sponsored a Primary Education Act which for all practical purposes did not differ from the bill to whose impopularity it owed its existence.[122] Appealing to the "actuality" of the situation—the conditions and circumstances to be taken into account by the legislator—Van der Brugghen argued that the times did not permit a better law. In a larger sense, his conflict with Groen reflected his profound disagreement with the notion of a "Christian state"; not unfairly, he compared himself to Bunsen and Groen to Stahl.[123] Grievously disappointed and mortally offended, Groen resigned his seat on the day it passed the chamber—as a protest against what he termed political improbity and parliamentary impotence in responding to popular petitions. The tactical merit of his unusual step is debated to this day.[124] He himself explained to his constituents that the final vote marked the end of his mandate and called for a deed "the meaning of which would not be unclear"; what he now needed was "peace, or at least a change of arena."[125]

This painful experience, and similar if less dramatic episodes in the following decade, gradually persuaded Groen, almost in spite of himself, that his co-religionists who were of the so-called ethical-irenical party

---

121. P. J. Oud, *Honderd jaren; een eeuw van staatkundige vormgeving in Nederland, 1840–1940*, 5th impr. (Assen: Van Gorcum, 1971), pp. 51f.

122. Diepenhorst, *Onze strijd in de Staten-Generaal*, I, 247–49.

123. Cf. J. J. R. Schmal, *Tweeërlei staatsbeschouwing in het Réveil* (2nd ed.; The Hague: Blommendaal, 1946), p. 93. The intermittant debate about the conflict has not been conducted without rancor. New perspectives have been opened by L. Kalsbeek, *Theologisch-wijsgerige achtergronden van de verhouding van Kerk, Staat en School in Nederland* (Kampen: Kok, n.d. [1976]), pp. 201–18.

124. Cf. W. F. de Gaay Fortman, "Groen van Prinsterer als staatsman," in *Een staatsman ter navolging*, p. 54.

125. Open *Brief aan de Kiezersvereeniging: Nederland en Oranje te Leiden*, p. 7.

were unreliable allies in the battle against the "permanent revolution." From 1860 on, he campaigned openly for strict religious neutrality in the public schools, now that a nominal Christianity, inoffensive to people of any creed as well as to those of no creed, was by law prescribed. According to his new orientation, alongside the public school the state should provide equal support for a parallel system of distinctly Christian schools erected through private initiative, according to the maxim: "Separate schools the rule, state schools a supplement." To that end he began to agitate for a partial revision of the constitution.[126] His untiring agitation in behalf of this cause was especially intended to provide relief for all those parents who preferred Christian schooling for their children yet could not afford it. Groen decried the inequity of the public school's monopoly on state financing, which made Christian day-school education not a real freedom but a privilege of the well-to-do (or a charity for those supported by the well-to-do). In time, Groen's restless agitation bore fruit in the Anti-School Law League of 1872, which developed into a nation-wide organization of local action committees, the grass-roots basis for the rise of the Anti-Revolutionary Party in 1879. His lingering influence is also evident in the great People's Petition of 1878, and still later in the equalization legislation of 1889, 1905 and 1920. In his own lifetime Groen continued his struggle for anti-revolutionary causes, though without notable success.

By 1868 Groen, though he continued his lifelong habit of commenting publicly on affairs of the day, considered himself retired from active life. In an important sense he had not been sucessful in any of his causes. He had been disappointed in politicians who were anti-revolutionary in sympathies and reputation yet who in his eyes conducted themselves like compliant conservatives or crypto-liberals in practice. He had been thwarted in his all-out attempt to bolster the Christian character of the state school, which was now rapidly becoming a breeding ground for the religion of secular humanism. Although the state had released its hold over the church, a bureaucratic Synod continued to shield unorthodox pastors—now no longer merely members of the Groningen School but increasingly also adherents of blatant modernism. In 1865, Groen gave his failing powers to

---

126. Cf. Van Essen, "Groens gedragslijn in zijn strijd voor de vrijheid van onderwijs," *Uitleg*, 19 May 1976, p. 18.

a Confessional Association that defended, among other things, the right of
Reformed consistories to refuse admittance to modernist ministers, if need
be in defiance of the higher church boards. In spite of a series of setbacks
in several fields, Groen was not beaten. His words and actions in the twilight years of his life are marked, not by bitter disillusionment or a spirit
of defeatism, but by grave earnestness coupled with belligerent defiance.
The occasional polemical pamphlet spoke of unabated mental and spiritual energy. To Groen's mind, the effects of unbelief and revolution in
society were becoming more evident every day—in his own country and
beyond. In addition, the growing strength of ultramontanism filled him
with alarm, and the violations of international law during the unification
processes of Italy and Germany made him fear the worst for the future of
European society. Against this background he produced his second edition
of *Unbelief and Revolution*.

One of his friends, Professor Gratama of the law faculty of Groningen,
was delighted by the tenor and scope of the additional material in the new
edition. He had found it most useful just the other night, he wrote Groen
from his northern domicile on 8 January 1869, for he had had a visit of Dr.
Beets. Nicolaas Beets, in town for a lecture, had complained (in the privacy of Gratama's drawing room) that too many orthodox leaders sided
with conservatism and aristocracy. His host had disputed this in general,
and particularly in the case of Groen van Prinsterer. To prove his point,
he had his guest read some of the new material in the 2nd edition. "Beets
appeared surprised and amazed by those statements of yours."[127]

Eventually, however, Groen's uncompromising stand led to a definitive
break with Christian conservatives, notably over the schools issue. Groen
remained to the end a tireless defender of a pluralist educational system in
which distinctly Christian schools would be able to compete on fair terms
with nominally Christian or neutral schools. He was one of the founding fathers and the first president of a national Association for Christian
Primary Education. Biographers point to a growing radicalism in the aging
Groen; in his last years he was in sympathy with only a handful of younger
leaders of middle-class background who championed his own "lost" causes
with fresh vigor and without compromise and to whom he gladly passed

---

127. *Briefwisseling*, IV, 303f. The new material is discussed in chap. 11 below.

the torch.[128] When Abraham Kuyper made his appearance on the national stage, Groen was happy to retire permanently from the public eye.

He continued to publish to the very last: shorter historical works; occasional pieces for national commemorations; a second edition of *Unbelief and Revolution*; a thorough revision of the *Handbook* (completed in 1873); annotated editions of a lifetime of correspondence with Da Costa, Wormser, and Thorbecke; finally his devastating historical critique of Motley's *Life and Death of John of Barneveld*, in the form of the profuse monograph *Maurice et Barnevelt* (1876). Groen van Prinsterer entered his rest on 19 May 1876.

---

128. For his surprise move in the closing weeks of the election campaign of 1871, when he disowned all anti-revolutionary candidates except three, see Den Hartogh, *Groen van Prinsterer en de verkiezingen van 1871*.

4

PURPOSE OF THE LECTURES

Although the story thus far has given us some indications of the motivation behind the composition and publication of *Unbelief and Revolution* midway through Groen's career, nevertheless it is worthwhile to consider this subject by itself for a moment. It is not really difficult to infer from statements in the book itself, as well as from comments in other writings and in his personal correspondence, what motivated Groen to elaborate the "ensemble of [his] convictions" at this time. His lectures aim to be at least three things: a confession of political principles; a witness to the saving power of the gospel; and an exercise in Christian apologetics.

A CONFESSION OF PRINCIPLES

As in 1830, so in 1845 Groen felt he had something to contribute to the ongoing debate about long-range decisions to be made. He wished to give guidance and leadership to kindred spirits in responsible positions, so that he and they could influence the direction the country would take. Far more than in 1830 he felt equipped after long years of study and reflection to diagnose the real ailment of the body politic and the public mind and to recommend what he saw as the only real remedy. Groen wanted to demonstrate that only by returning to "Christian-historical principles" could society avoid the dilemma of anarchy and despotism, could leaders chart a third way in public affairs, a way that would be marked off from the sluggish conservatism of the *status quo* with its perpetuation of serious injustices, especially in church and education, and a way that would be no less distinct from the progressive liberalism of Thorbecke and associates, which might promise improvement in the short term but would prove disastrous in the long run since it represented only a more conscious and wholehearted endorsement of the same underlying philosophy. Constitutional revision and parliamentary reform were welcome to Groen, but only within the larger framework of principled opposition to the dominant ideology. The centralist, bureaucratic, revolutionary state had to be attacked in its roots, not just in its symptoms. If Christians defaulted now and denied themselves their legitimate influence by holding back their political witness, matters would only grow worse as the helm of state would pass to progressive liberalism, which would prove to be but a halfway station to radicalism. The stakes were much higher, announced Groen in Lecture I (12), than the acquisition of certain constitutional safeguards, of "invaluable supports of political liberty": at bottom the Christian foundations of society were at issue, and with that the very future of Christian civilization, the eternal destiny of souls, and the honor of God.

The seemingly inevitable shift in power to progressivist forces, Groen was convinced, would only abandon the country outright to a permanently revolutionary situation. By exposing the root error of his contemporaries Groen hoped to pave the way for a radical alternative to the existing political spectrum and to mobilize all men of Christian allegiance to get the country moving again on a Christian-historical path of reform and renewal.

A WITNESS TO THE GOSPEL

Groen wanted to serve his Lord, and through that his country. In the concluding pages of both Lecture I and Lecture XV he gave voice to the same aspiration to serve his country in a Christian sense as he had so eloquently expressed already in 1831 in the concluding paragraph of the *Overzigt*:

> Let us close with one wish. The Netherlands was formed and reformed by Christianity. When she deviated and departed [from the faith] and was dragged into the abyss, she was rescued by God's mighty arm when He had broken the violence of the despot; and since the days that the storm of revolution has once again risen over the world she has been spared, shielded, guided in a remarkable way, as though she were being prepared and nurtured, both by evil and the mitigation of evil, for an important future. Where principles are at issue, how much has a single person, leaning on God, not been able to accomplish! How much might a single nation, however small, not be able to achieve if in defence of justice and interest she were also to raise the banner of Christianity before

the eyes of the nations of the world! May that destiny be reserved for the Netherlands; may she in God's hand be serviceable to that Christian regeneration which mankind needs in order to triumph over unbelief and destruction.[1]

As *Unbelief and Revolution* went to press, Groen wrote his publisher, "I am happy that you also approve of the Preface. May this work be blessed and may our country be heading for a better future by turning back to Him who alone spares and exalts the nations! To offer even the least contribution to that end is a duty; and it is a privilege to be permitted to confess Him in whom alone is all our hope."[2]

That last sentence points to the very personal motivation that impelled Groen. He felt called upon to be a witness of the gospel, to give a testimony to the truth of Scripture in its implications for individuals and nations—for the conversion of men's hearts and, consequently, for the healing of society. Was he permitted, he asked his audience, to remain silent when divine grace had drawn him from darkness into marvelous light, had transferred him from a conventional, rationalistic Christianity to a vital Christian *faith* that urged him on to be *working by love*? In his opening lecture (9) he assured his friends, "There is but one thing needful for us all: it is not as statesmen or as scholars but as sinners that we seek to be saved." He added that, for his part, he found rest and peace for his soul in the good news of free grace. "I say this at the very outset because in no way would I want to escape the shame of this confession." "Our standpoint," he said at the beginning of Lecture XI for the benefit of newcomers to the series, "is that of the Christian who desires to glory in nothing but Christ and him crucified"; but this confession implies for the Christian that he "acknowledges no wisdom or truth in religion, morality and justice, in home or state, unless it begins by submitting heart and mind to Revelation." Quoting 1 Peter 4:10, he went on to state, "After all the labour I have spent on historical studies I consider it my calling to witness on this terrain to the truth that is in Christ." And how, then, did he propose to witness to this truth on the terrain of historical studies?

---

1. *Nederlandsche Gedachten*, 1831, III, 108.
2. *Briefwisseling*, II, 802.

By offering a demonstration, from the march of ideas and the course of events, "that the history of the past sixty years, with its outpourings of wickedness, is the peculiar unfolding of ideas, ideas which in turn are the peculiar fruit of the rejection of Christian truth, a fruit and manifestation of systematic unbelief."

AN EXERCISE IN APOLOGETICS

That very history of the past sixty years, finally, was what motivated Groen to give his testimony at this time. The time was most propitious, he believed, for Christian apologetics. "Would it not prepare the philosopher of our time," Groen asked, "to bow his proud head before the beneficent gospel, if the darkness of his enlightenment and the foolishness of his wisdom were to be exhibited in the narrative sequence of indisputable facts?" In the same passage in Lecture I (11) the audience is reminded that if the heavens declare the glory of God, so does history. To Groen's mind, God's glory is declared by showing from the history of the revolution era "that to forsake the Word of God is enough to plunge apostate man, who lacks neither intellect and ingenuity nor favorable circumstances, into an abyss of misery." There we have the grand and unmistakable lesson to be drawn from the experience of the age of revolution: apart from God man can only work his own destruction. The entire revolution stems from unbelief; therefore, Groen reasoned in Lecture XI (271), the only foolproof remedy lies in belief: "Man must break out of the vicious revolutionary circle; he must turn to God ..."

And here we see his threefold motive—to be an apologist of Christianity, a witness to the gospel, and an advocate of Christian-historical principles—blend into the single purpose of the entire work. The "historical lectures" carry an eminently practical message. As Groen says on one of the closing pages: "If it has been my wish to guide you by the light of the gospel along the path of history through the various phases of revolutionary predominance, I was less interested in the journey itself than in its destination" (413).

In other words, the historical survey has been in vain unless the listeners draw the lesson of their time. That lesson is spelled out succinctly in the appraisal of the age of reason and revolution in Lecture VIII (190): Resist beginnings! Unbelief gave power to the *philosophes*. Philosophical teachings led to 1789. And 1789 produced 1793. Such is Groen's burden. Let us never forget, he urges his audience, that our Christian heritage, even our civil rights, are not safe in the revolutionary state. The various revolutions are facts that cannot be undone without sinning against the law of history. But the revolution must be resisted. In this battle of the spirits it is our duty today to contend for the highest Truth and seek to save the future by pointing to the "sole road which leads to the happiness of nations" (191).

5

—

PROTOTYPES AND PARAPHRASES

Because *Unbelief and Revolution* represents a key work in Groen's oeuvre, it is possible to go to other works written during his long and productive career to find different versions—prototypes and ectypes, preliminary drafts and paraphrases—of his main work. He himself mentioned in the Preface that he had recorded his Christian-historical viewpoint "briefly" in *Nederlandsche Gedachten*, volume III, numbers 21-27. In the 2nd edition he dropped a footnote informing the reader that a "synopsis of the present work" had since appeared on pages 33-41 of *Le Parti anti-révolutionnaire* (1860) and on pages 27 and following of *Ter Nagedachtenis van Stahl* (1862). With some justification he might have added that a popularization of the work had been attempted in his five-part tract of 1848 entitled *Vrijheid, Gelijkheid, Broederschap; toelichting van de spreuk der Revolutie*. And, to be complete, Groen also summarized the book's main thesis in his *Grondwetherziening en eensgezindheid* of 1849.

Before examining these shortened versions, we will go back to Groen's formative years to trace some of the intellectual ingredients that went into the making of the mind that composed *Unbelief and Revolution*.

When we reviewed Groen's life and career we had occasion to enumerate the influential currents he was exposed to in his university days: largely negative were the rejection by Platonism of modern forms of sophism, and the repudiation by Bilderdijkianism of received views of Dutch history, particularly as regards its republican traditions and the role of the Reformed Church; more positively, the reading of Savigny had turned Groen into a sympathizer with the Historical Law School. Each of these three ingredients helped shape and strengthen Groen's critical and historical bent of mind; but none induced the young man to elaborate a system for himself or even to formulate any firm views or interpretations.

GROEN'S EARLIEST WRITINGS

To gain some idea of Groen's intellectual maturation between his university days and the composition of the *Overview* (i.e. between 1822 and 1831), we shall take a closer look at his earliest writings.[1]

In the year 1822, the Greeks revolted against the Turks. As elsewhere, so in the Netherlands, the forces of philhellenism and "Christian civilization" established a national committee of support. Groen wrote a pamphlet in 1825 which he entitled *Objections to an Appeal to Support the Greeks*[2] and in which he raised some critical questions: Are the Greek rebels indeed Christians? Is Islam then not a force for civilization? Is it in keeping with the gospel to launch a crusade? And, of critical importance before all else: Have the implications for international law been taken into account?— Such a skeptical reaction to the popular appeal for helping the Greeks would not have been very well received in Dutch society of the time. On the advice of a friend, who felt it might jeopardize his career prospects (Bilderdijk had publicly defended a similar position), Groen decided not to publish his pamphlet.[3]

A short treatise of the following year was devoted to the question of codification: *Thoughts on the Difficulty and Importance of Compiling a Criminal Code.*[4] Here Groen urged patience and caution, for such a code, on which work had recently begun in Holland, must serve the nation on sensitive questions of justice for many years to come, and it would be imprudent to repeat the mistakes made in France and Germany, where a number of such codes had in recent times been adopted only to be discarded again.— This treatise, too, which may have been intended for a law journal, was never published.

---

1. We omit from consideration the theses or debating resolutions he defended in official seminars or in student clubs during his years at Leyden; cf. Tazelaar, *De Jeugd van Groen*, pp. 101–22; *Bescheiden*, ed. Gerretson, pp. 3–14, esp. theses 48, 61, 70, 73, 87 and 88.

2. *Bedenkingen tegen een oproeping tot ondersteuning der Grieken*; in *Bescheiden*, ed. Gerretson, pp. 32–79.

3. Cf. Zwaan, "Groen van Prinsterer over Grieken en Turken," p. 23. Zwaan notes a "questionable legitimism" throughout the entire essay, which moreover "teems with contradictions"; *Groen van Prinsterer en de klassieke Oudheid*, p. 90n211; for Groen's qualified endorsement of legitimism, cf. *ibid.*, pp. 245–47.

4. *Gedachten over de moeyelijkheid en belangrijkheid van het ontwerpen der Wetboeken van Strafregt en van Lijfstraffelijke Regtspleging*; in *Bescheiden*, ed. Gerretson, pp. 81–87.

Another short article of 1826 did make its way into the pages of a journal.[5] It argued that in any sale of real estate the vendor's privilege took priority over earlier mortgages, provided it was duly transferred before closing the transaction. The brief was a careful but firm defense of a not unimportant detail of existing property rights.

Again in 1826, Groen contributed several articles to a local daily, which published them. Two are devoted to the Greek revolt and present the gist of the unpublished essay. Half a dozen others comment on French affairs and criticize the reign of Charles X from a liberalist perspective: Groen argues, for example, that the ultra-royalists are dangerous, for by reintroducing primogeniture "they seek to go back to the Middle Ages" and suppress the aristocracy of ability and merit in favor of the aristocracy of wealth and heredity, thereby both subverting the charter and ignoring the "voice and law of nature"; hence the Chamber of Peers is to be commended for voting it down. Some other opinions defended in the articles are: the rising influence of the Jesuits is deplorable; freedom of the press should be safeguarded, certainly against charges of calumny with respect to people already dead; the intrinsic value of a parliamentary vote lies in the grounds adduced, not in the tally of votes it receives; and so on.—Groen would include these articles in his *Selected Writings* of 1859 as specimens of "my first contribution to the periodical press."[6]

Still another unpublished manuscript consists of *Notes* taken on a journey to Van den Bosch's labor colonies.[7] Here Groen challenged the right of the state to press vagrants into forced labor: if they want to live on charity, who can forbid them? The beggar too has rights, which may not be arbitrarily removed by a simple police order. According to the young author-observer, neither the interest of the state nor the general utility or common good can excuse the curtailment of "private rights." And then followed a sentence which expressed a thought that would form one of the cornerstones of *Unbelief and Revolution*:

---

5. "Het Privilege des verkoopers heeft den voorrang ook voor de vroeger ingeschrevene Hypotheken, mits hetzelve vóór het sluiten van de order worde overgeschreven," *Bijdragen tot Regtsgeleerdheid en Wetgeving* 1 (1826): 229-37.

6. Groen van Prinsterer, *Verspreide Geschriften*, I, v, 1-26.

7. *Aanteekeningen op een reisje naar de Coloniën der Maatschappij van Weldadigheid in 1826*; in *Bescheiden*, ed. Gerretson, pp. 87-92.

If along with the philosophers of the previous century one assumes a social contract, whereby everyone has alienated his private rights for the benefit of society and thus has, as it were, subjected himself unconditionally to the government of that society, then such propositions can be granted; but for that very same reason it is equally true that that philosophy, which would commend itself as the champion of liberty, from the nature of the case gives occasion to the most terrible despotism. (88f)

A longer treatise, which also went unpublished, was called an *Essay on the History and Consequences of the Growing Unity of Civilized Nations*.[8] It sketched the formation of a unified European civilization, from the barbarian invasions, through the coming of Christianity and feudalism, Renaissance, the invention of printing, and the Reformation, to modern times. This broad perspective was then said to be a wholesome reminder of the unity of world history. In general, the essay was a nuanced statement of the idea of progress. Western culture was a "holy fire" that had spread its civilizing impact into more and more departments of human society and to more and more places on the globe (107), though Groen ended by saying that it remained an open question whether it had promoted "true enlightenment, genuine virtue, and real happiness," adding the consoling sentiment of the pious suprarationalism of his milieu that, fortunately, our peaceful assurance of the perfectibility of our race does not depend on the march of history but rests on the sure ground that "for every man the link between this and a future life of bliss can be made by one's own personal perfectibility" (153). These considerations aside, the historian can note that as the nations drew closer together, the effect has been most beneficial for learning and the arts, and particularly for the exact sciences. For languages and literature, however, it has tended also to be harmful: corruption of the native tongue is a high price to pay for the enjoyment of foreign drama and poetry and for the purification of grammar resulting from comparative linguistics. In general, Groen concluded in the spirit of Romanticism, slavish imitation of foreign models has suppressed the full development of each individual

---

8. *Historische proeve over de geschiedenis en gevolgen der steeds naauwer gewordene vereeniging van de beschaafde Volken*; in *Bescheiden*, ed. Gerretson, pp. 92–153.

nation's brilliance and genius (136–52). The essay in passing censured religious persecution, church establishment, slavery and the slave trade as "contrary to reason" (116, 138). More significantly, though still quite typical for a Restoration author, the future lecturer on unbelief and revolution decried the recent infatuation with "deceptive reasonings and chimerical projects [which had] called into question every principle of religion as well as of constitutional law—first in England, afterward in France, then in Germany, finally everywhere," and which had caused revolutions and the violent overthrow of legitimate governments throughout the civilized world. With what appears like objective detachment the young essayist noted matter-of-factly:

> In a certain sense the revolution has not yet ended. Men disagree whether to conserve the old or adopt the new or follow a middle course. That disagreement, the germ of subsequent revolutions, persists: it is becoming more widespread in proportion as civilization embraces more countries. (106)

Finally, Groen deplored the tendency of the mid-1820s to thwart the activity of the European Congresses with what he considered a misapplication of the principle of non-intervention (116–18).

Still dating from 1826 is a forty-page pamphlet entitled *On the Present War in Portugal*.[9] Written in the same month (December) as Canning's threat to intervene on behalf of Portugal, which had been attacked by Spain, the tract was a plea for moderation. France was aroused and might aid Spain; would this crisis escalate into a general European war? (30). Groen expressed the hope that reason, not passion, would prevail, but he was anything but sure. In the threatening crisis, brought on by what he chose to depict chiefly as an immanent *clash of principles*—a clash between constitutionalism and anti-constitutionalism—he called upon his fellow countrymen to rally around the constitutional throne of Holland (41). The exhortation of the 25-year-old freelance journalist was published the same week, on the advice of his friend and with permission of his father—albeit

---

9. *Iets over den tegenwoordigen oorlog in Portugal* (The Hague, 1826); reprinted in *Verspreide Geschriften*, I, 27–41.

anonymously.[10] Complimentary copies were sent to a circle of friends and acquaintances, but Groen left it to the discretion of Professor Van Assen in Leyden whether to pass a copy on to the aged Bilderdijk, for, "who would not be afraid of a Genius who could, if he so pleased, demolish it?"[11]

Next, in early 1827 there appeared the text of a lecture held in Voorburg about *Constantine Huygens, Principally as the Occupant of [the country-house] Hofwyck*.[12] In it, the local people were exhorted to treasure the "homes and graves in our midst of our most glorious forebears." In words reminiscent of Burke (with whose writings he was not yet acquainted), the youthful speaker closed with the assurance that once we recognize their greatness, "a lasting memorial will have been erected in our grateful hearts, and we shall all cherish the plots of which our patriotic sentiments testify, 'holy is this ground.'"

A special case among Groen's earliest productions is the *Oration on the Reasons for Making Known the Nation's History*,[13] a paper which he had given in Brussels and now submitted to the king on hearing of the royal decree that announced a contest for the appointment of a 'historian of the realm.' The oration discusses four reasons for making known the history of Holland: its excellent content, expecially in terms of its inspiring examples of men and women; the present ignorance of it, aggravated by the growing gap between scholars and the general public; the fact that since 1795 the Netherlands has entered a new phase which leaves the story of the Republic a finished whole; and the possibility it would afford to identify, safeguard, and develop the historical roots of the present constitution, which has not been the product of a "constitution factory" but indeed gives expression in many respects to "what existed before" (255). Taken together, these reasons add up to a single moral-pedagogical purpose: make known the country's history to make better citizens. Indeed, a "utilitarian" motive is revealed in every line of the oration.[14] Our interest in this essay is further

10. Tazelaar, *De Jeugd van Groen*, pp. 230–32.

11. *Briefwisseling*, I, 68.

12. *Constantijn Huijgens, voornamelijk als bewoner van Hofwijck* (The Hague, 1827); reprinted in *Verspreide Geschriften*, II, 225–41.

13. *Redevoering over de redenen om de Geschiedenis der Natie bekend te maken* (Brussels, 1829); here quoted as reprinted in *Verspreide Geschriften*, II, 242–56.

14. Smitskamp, *Groen van Prinsterer als historicus*, p. 18.

aroused when we see Groen mention in passing that a previous generation, "under the illusion of its higher enlightenment, believed it was called upon to overturn everything which former wisdom and experience had gradually given shape," when it should have realized that "gradual improvement" rather than "sudden change" ensure durable reform (253). Again, it is with heightened interest that we read his opinion that "the present is but the continuation and development of the past; it unites ancestors and progeny" (251). When Groen included this piece in his *Selected Writings* in 1859, he noted that one important reason to which he now admitted he had paid too little attention was the "instructive character of Dutch history as evidence of the blessing that rested on the confession of the pure gospel."[15]

Groen's official entry in the contest for the appointment as "historian of the realm" was three times as long as the oration. Entitled *Essay on the Compilation of a History of the Netherlands,*[16] it was printed at the state's expense three years later, along with volumes containing the essays of four other finalists. As with the oration, of which it is an expanded version, a partial excuse for the essay's self-congratulatory patriotism is the fact that the royal decree had expressly called for a scheme that would "cultivate love of the fatherland, promote civic virtue, and uphold the national interest." Again, Groen censured the previous generation for having preferred sudden change to slow improvement (139). The same criterion of historical continuity is used by the author to justify the Dutch Revolt against Spain, since it proceeded from the principle that resistance had to be offered to such "novelties" as inquisition, constraint of conscience, and destruction of local rights (87).

What do all these products of the 1820s show us? They show that Groen employed key concepts of the Historical School to the extent that it had emphasized the organic nature of history and law, and that he voiced ideas borrowed from German idealism to the extent that it had drawn attention to the uniqueness of individual nations. Groen's study of transitional figures between Enlightenment and Romanticism such as Rousseau and

---

15. *Verspreide Geschriften,* II, vi.

16. *Proeve over de zamenstelling eener Algemeene Nederlandsche Geschiedenis* (The Hague, 1830); selected portions reprinted in *Bescheiden,* ed. Gerretson, pp. 240–84.

Madame de Staël was reflected, on the one hand, in his appreciation of the progress of reason in the development of civilization and, on the other hand, in his adoption of at least three anti-Enlightenment corrections: to recognize recurring periods of decay and corruption, to be milder than usual in assessing the Middle Ages, and in general to judge the past in the light of its time. Over the years a tendency is noticeable toward greater appreciation for the process of history as such and for the need to enter into it "with sympathetic understanding."[17]

But also in a more formal sense these early writings tell us a great deal about their author. They demonstrate in many ways that the child is father of the man—that the bent of mind of the mature man of the 1840s is everywhere in evidence in the young man of the 1820s. There is, first of all, the broad sweep of his historical outlook, guided everywhere by the unquestioned assumption that *religion*, particularly the Christian religion, rather than being a private creed of personal significance only, has to be counted among the most formative influences in the rise of nations and the development of society—that its public presence can only be denied at the peril of violating reality and that its decline inevitably spells the decline of the culture it suffuses. Secondly, there is the unmistakable trait of exercising *critical judgment* and avoiding speculative dogmatism; the young Groen constantly weighs the pros and cons of issues, tries to be objective in his sympathies, carefully examines popular opinions, and displays little fear— at most modesty—in submitting contrary ideas not currently in favor with informed public opinion. Like the mature man, the young Groen has a lively *interest in current European events*, is eager to reflect and comment on them in documented studies, and seems very keen on asserting his personal freedom and independence of mind. In the third place, there is the assessment of his own day and age as a period fraught with deep-seated tensions caused by his generation's historic mission to find the proper response to the democratic revolution: should that response take the form of negative *reaction*, positive *progress*, or a cautious *juste milieu*? Groen appears to lean toward the middle-of-the-road solution, but for any future revolutions he is especially concerned that *respect for law* be observed, in constitutional as well as international law. Above all, fourthly, his early writings already

---

17. Smitskamp, *Groen van Prinsterer als historicus*, pp. 28–30.

show his overriding concern for a cause that he would champion the rest of his life: *freedom of conscience*; this concern is evident from his consistent condemnation of moral compulsion and religious persecution, royal tyranny and popular pressure, intolerance of dissenters, and oppression of slaves abroad and paupers at home. In sum, the early writings give us a picture of the "complete personality in its formative stage."[18]

However, the spiritual center, the animating and regulating dynamo of this personality was still to undergo a radical transformation. Groen's self-assessment of his youth, written in old age, is insightful:

> Until 1828 I was more or less like Guizot before the lightning bolt of 1848 taught him to see the satanic nature of the Revolution; like the Protestant majority I was *liberal and Christian*, under the motto, *medio tutissimus ibis* [you will go most safely in the middle]; like almost everyone in the Reformed Church, I belonged to the *Great Protestant* party; depending on the thermometer, I was a *conservative* liberal or a *liberal* conservative.[19]

"Until 1828." That was the year that first brought Groen to Brussels, where the Royal Cabinet's referendary and his young bride, attending the court chapel services, were exposed to the preaching of Merle d'Aubigné which watered the seed sown in the Réveil circle of The Hague. And, of equal importance, it was the year that brought Groen to the brink of the volcano about to erupt in the Belgian Revolt.

THE *OVERVIEW* OF 1831

The revolt of the Southern Netherlands, as we have seen, occasioned Groen's *Nederlandsche Gedachten*, whose underlying principles he tried to sketch in a seven-part *Overview* during the fall of 1831. As the first clear prototype of *Unbelief and Revolution*, this *Overview* deserves a closer look. In old age Groen himself called *Unbelief and Revolution* "the amplified Sketch of 1831."[20]

---

18. Tazelaar, *De Jeugd van Groen*, p. 258; see also Gerretson, "Groen's aanleg," *Verzamelde Werken*, II, 38–41.

19. *Nederlandsche Gedachten*, 1873/74, V, 255.

20. *Nederlandsche Gedachten* (second series), 1873/74, V, 25, 158, 348, 351.

Like many a writer and public figure of strong convictions if not dogmatic systems, Groen prided himself on always having been the same (since
1828). His first series of *Nederlandsche Gedachten*, written between the ages
of 28 and 30, are his earliest sustained endeavor to influence the opinion
of his contemporaries, and they do indeed show remarkable consistency
with his later work *Unbelief and Revolution*, composed when he was 44 (or,
for that matter, as we shall see below, with the French synopsis written
when he was 58).

The date of the Sketch or Overview is astonishing. After all, in 1831
Groen, on his own testimony, was not yet a committed Christian. He was
a *convinced* Christian, one who gave his intellectual assent to the gospel;
as he had confided to a friend in a letter of 1829: "I adhere with heart and
soul to the Christian religion as to our only comfort in life and death, and
in particular sincerely profess the Reformed doctrine as contained in the
Confessions of our church."[21] But he had not yet become a Christian in possession of the kind of faith "by which a person becomes a new creation,"
someone for whom religion has become a "life principle" which is "united
and interwoven with [one's] entire existence."[22] Could such a man be in
possession of a genuine Christian-historical worldview—a worldview that
required seven installments in a journal to be adequately summarized; and
that was worth reviving, expanding and publicizing more than a decade
after his real conversion; and still later was worth broadcasting to the
world in an international language? This circumstance sheds a curious
light on Groen's worldview and, for that matter, on his conversion. For if a
certain worldview can be embraced and warmly propagated as eminently
Christian while at the same time the propagator on his own admission has
but a growing "persuasion of the mind" that the whole of history is "a continuous confirmation of the truths which Scripture reveals,"[23] then does
that not imply that the worldview in question is susceptible of demonstration to anyone, regardless of belief—that a convincing case can be made for
it irrespective of the faith of the hearer? The question will be raised later
by certain critics of *Unbelief and Revolution*, who would disqualify the work

---

21. *Briefwisseling*, I, 528.
22. *Briefwisseling*, I, 503.
23. *Briefwisseling*, I, 503.

for that reason alone. Curiously, the question seems not to have occurred to Groen. In any event it did not deter him from lecturing in 1845 with all the more conviction on what he had "seen" as early as 1831, just as he would state in 1868, in the Preface to the second edition of the 1845 lectures, that his "Christian-historical worldview has not merely remained the same but has actually been reinforced" by events of the intervening years. Groen never doubted that his viewpoint could be demonstrated irrefutably from the facts of history and that his position, based on history in combination with Scripture, was invincible.

As mentioned earlier, the *Overview* of 1831 appeared in seven install-ments toward the end of the third and virtually last volume of *Nederlandsche Gedachten*.

Already in the late winter of 1831 Groen's *Nederlandsche Gedachten* pos-ited that the modern age was characterized by a ceaseless struggle between factions of liberalism (II, 160). Beginning with the March issues of that year, objections to liberalism appear on its pages in formulations that are strongly reminiscent of *Unbelief and Revolution*: liberalism promises lib-erty but brings slavery; it reduces the variety of social institutions to an undefined mass; it is a false doctrine that throws society into disarray and aspires not to a new form of government but to a total reorganization of society; it gives rise to a state that is an artificial mechanism rather than an organic whole, thus stifling all interest and involvement on the part of the citizen (III, 12, 26, 48, 59).

The issues that appeared between 27 September–19 November 1831 car-ried the "*Overzigt*," which was announced as an overview of the "overall system" of the paper (III, 79). The *Overview* concentrates on the heart of the matter. At once the reader is told that the main feature of the last half century is *unbelief*. While many blame the period's calamities on the per-nicious belief in popular sovereignty, "one ought to go one step further and acknowledge that this false idea is but the result of unbelief, is one of the forms in which unbelief manifests itself." In European Christendom of old, the gospel had been considered the foundation of states and the law-code of nations: governments, even deficient governments, were honored as ministers of God. Then came modern philosophy. It made the human intellect the criterion of truth and justice and thus gave rise to a parallel development in religion and politics: neology, deism, atheism in the one,

Jacobinism and liberalism in the other. The detestable philosophy was systematically developed in France and disseminated throughout Europe, a not surprising spread since in most countries Christian faith had seriously declined. This overturning of men's minds was bound to result in the overturning of society's institutions. The resulting revolutions are repeated failures, yet are constantly renewed (III, 79f). Why have men not learned the unmistakable lesson of history? Because they have never taken issue with the basic principle of this harmful doctrine but only with the *degree*, *manner* and *timing* of its application. Thus the revolutionary principle has survived to this day.

The first French Revolution, the *Overview* continues, had long been in the making through the general sympathy with revolutionary premises. The court and all three orders contributed to a movement for reform based on the notion of a social contract, with its requirements of absolute freedom and equality. Once the revolution broke out and got underway, anarchy developed, followed by reaction which ended in Napoleon. In the meantime the rest of Europe allied to oppose it, but only out of self-defense, not out of opposition to the revolutionary theory.

The so-called *restoration* did not break with it either, asserts the *Overview* of 1831. It retained the revolutionary state machine and grafted legitimate dynasties onto the revolutionary trunk. The Powers carried on the arbitrary diplomacy of liberalism and promoted liberalism's gradual triumph in a number of countries (III, 83f). Particularly in France the revolution festered on, until it succeeded the year before in toppling the Bourbons. Steering a middle course between extremes, the July Monarchy to date has had to resort to despotic measures to preserve itself. By recognizing Louis Philippe, the European Powers have actually *intervened in favor of the revolution* (III, 88f).

How to call a halt to the destructive theory? *The liberal theory cannot be successfully combatted except by means of Christianity*. It alone can preserve Christendom, its order and its respect for law. At bottom we face a *war of religion*, this time between belief and unbelief. If the revolution is to be vanquished Christian faith must revive, the gospel must triumph. And it may well triumph, for its necessity is again felt everywhere, and its essence is eminently *historical* and will therefore prove to be *practical* and realistic (III, 93f).

Thus far the first four installments of the *Overview*. It is indeed as though we are reading a summary of *Unbelief and Revolution*, notably the second half, Lectures VIII–XIV. In the three remaining installments of the *Overview* Groen develops more positive arguments for the Christian position.

The cultural impact of a return to Christianity, the *Overview* continues, is not limited to the indirect influence of personal piety but will show up in a redirection of public affairs and social relations and will illumine every branch of learning and practice. Christianity destroys the liberal theory by providing a basis for authority, freedom, national solidarity and true enlightenment. It does not resist nature and time but rather allows them to do their beneficial work. Instead of fighting the laws established by God, it rests on firm *historical* ground and returns from a purely ideal to the real, *positive* (by no means just *material*) world (III, 97f). The present world crisis cannot be ended by restoring material prosperity or former boundaries, nor by pacifying the rivalry between nationalities or between monarchical and republican forms of government, nor yet by mediating between Protestantism and Catholicism or between conservatism and radicalism. The cardinal question is: to be revolutionary or anti-revolutionary, that is to say, to accept or reject genuine authority, to acknowledge or deny the supremacy of self-sufficient reason, to submit to a Higher Being or to accept only laws of one's own making. "When men seek to accommodate the one with the other, they have already decided against God, who will not suffer any other gods beside Him" (III, 101–4).

In conclusion, Groen writes that his paper stands for immutable *principles* as against human *opinion*. It opposes the revolution theory, the doctrine of unbelief, with belief, taken "in the broadest and philosophical sense of the word," with truths whose certainty is not so much demonstrated as intuited (*gevoeld*) and on which all human knowledge must build. The presumptuous philosophy of unbelief *inverts* the natural order: here the deified individual determines what is truth, guided solely by his fallible and finite understanding. We, by contrast, do not rely on our own insight. We have Holy Scripture. We know that every deed which combats Scripture's commandments is a crime, every opinion which contradicts its teaching a delusion. Whereas modern philosophy acknowledges no *objective* truth or revelation, the Christian needs no further proof. But our battle can even be carried onto the terrain of unbelief and before the vaunted tribunal of public opinion. In opposition to the spirit of the present age we invoke the spirit of the ages. With the exception of the Greek sophists, the philosophy of the eighteenth century is a novelty in world history. Liberalism is a doctrine that exalts itself against eternal principles and universal consensus; it flies in the face of the whole of history and human experience and when practiced brings only dissolution in its wake. For all that, the fact remains that it is dominant at the present time. On its continuation or destruction hinges the future of the world. Either truth is restored and liberalism collapses; or liberalism will extend its conquests and usher in a period of anarchy, compulsion, or apathy; or else the struggle between true principles and false theories will lead to exhaustion, and the repression of the Concert of Europe will evolve into a benign despotism as the nations sink away again into the kind of listless indifference and narcotic peace that we have witnessed since 1815 (III, 105ff).

All these statements in the last half of the *Overzigt* (the whole is summarized once more in two large columns in the periodical's Index to Vol. III[24]) return in elaborated form in *Unbelief and Revolution*, particularly in Lectures I–III, just as Lectures VIII–XIV, we concluded above, appear in skeletal form in the first half of the *Overzigt*. Thus we can conclude that the only portions of *Unbelief and Revolution* that do not have their prototype in the *Overzigt* are Lectures IV–VII, that is to say, the lectures which discuss the political arrangements and abuses under the *ancien régime*, the perversion of constitutional law in modern times, and the historical significance of the Protestant Reformation. Indeed, Groen did not say too much when he stated in 1847 that he had outlined his position already in 1831 in the pages of *Nederlandsche Gedachten*. The gaps just noted were filled in the intervening years.

Nederlandsche Gedachten meanwhile had become at once too potent and less than relevant for its contemporaries. Since by 1831 the separation of Belgium seemed an accomplished fact, the paper was no longer being written at the cutting-edge of history. Its increasingly unconventional views caused interest to drop even more rapidly. Its readership, which had never amounted to more than three hundred odd subscriptions, now fell to levels where publication seemed hardly warranted. Groen gave up and ceased

---

24. The Index entry was reproduced in full in *Nederlandsche Gedachten*, 1873/74, V, 346–48.

its publication. Reminiscing many years later about this early journalistic venture, Groen recalled that the "asphyxiating atmosphere of a returning laodiceanism" had silenced him.[25] I discontinued *Nederlandsche Gedachten*, Groen wrote to Koenen more than a year afterward, "much less because of financial considerations than because of the conviction that in the long run I would not be able to find much agreement with my ideas about the events of the day until I had provided a more extensive and scholarly exposition of my principles."[26] He appears to have prepared for just such a more scholarly presentation, first, by launching his *Essay on Truth* (1834), and, secondly, by working steadily, from 1835 on, alongside his labors for the *Archives*, on an extended treatment of the whole phenomenon of the modern revolution. Both of these "prototypes" are examined immediately below.

How pleased Groen must have been, after putting a definitive end to his *Nederlandsche Gedachten* in the spring of 1832, to make the acquaintance shortly thereafter of a new German weekly which bore the motto, "Not the counter-revolution but that which runs counter to the revolution," and which offered much fare that met with his warm approval: the *Berliner Politisches Wochenblatt*. He read the copy that arrived weekly at the Royal Cabinet. Later he acquired the bound volumes, and many tiny pencil marks in the margin testify to Groen's ample use of it. In *Unbelief and Revolution* he would quote with approval its praise of Haller, its defense of right over history, its opposition to the absolute state born of the French Revolution and maintained in the Restoration, its characterization of Robespierre as a believer more consistent than the rest, and finally its apocalyptic warning against future developments in comparison with which the French Revolution would appear "a pleasant idyll."[27]

---

25. *Nederlandsche Gedachten*, 1873/74, V, 350.

26. *Briefwisseling*, II, 78.

27. Cf. footnotes, 1st ed., pp. 37, 46, 255, 268, 341, 342, 393, 405—respectively in Lectures II, III, X, XI, XIII, XIV, and XV.

THE *ESSAY ON TRUTH* OF 1834

This treatise sets forth Groen's prolegomena to public law. The title page advertises it as the first volume of a larger work under the collective title *Considerations on Constitutional and International Law*,[28] and the Preface identifies the work as an "introduction to future considerations" and the "continuation in altered form" of the *Nederlandsche Gedachten*, written for the same object and resting on the same foundations (pp. vi, x). The first chapter, entitled "Principles," covers the same ground as the *Overview* of 1831. Straightway Groen shows his hand. It was rationalism that corrupted all learning and, "since theory is never without influence on action," ensured the fall of states. Received truth was replaced by a dizzying succession of a thousand systems, inspiring at last a general despair of all truth. The repeated attempts to erect the new state in conformity with the theory all ended in despotism; liberty proved an idle dream and was abandoned for material pursuits (7–9). Anticipating his later work, Groen notes that it would be very important to show in greater detail how that same atheistic philosophy lies at the *origin* of "all the revolutions that have succeeded one another in France and whose *cause* is still looked for in the *occasions*" (10n). Later sections are given over to a defense of Protestantism and its world-historical role (43–68, 136–42). In extended footnotes in chapter IV, part II, Groen formulates some of the basic weaknesses he has come to see in the political theory of liberal writers (144–71). Of the many other passages reminiscent of *Unbelief and Revolution* we mention only the scorn for the "anglo-revolutionary" parliamentarianism of the Restoration (198–201) and the fulminations against liberalism's contract theory as well as its arbitrary diplomacy since 1830 (209–12). It was clear to the reader that these *Considerations* of 1834 held a promise of further studies.

---

28. *Beschouwingen over Staats- en Volkerenregt* (Leyden, 1834). For works that may be regarded as other volumes under the same general title, see Zwaan, *Groen van Prinsterer en de klassieke Oudheid*, p. 470.

THE MANUSCRIPT "STUDIES
ON THE REVOLUTION"

Groen's literary remains include a bulky folder containing hundreds of sheets of notes, extracts and draft essays in manuscript form. Portions of this material, reworked and expanded, at times condensed, are incorporated in *Unbelief and Revolution*, mostly in a reworded version but on occasion also nearly verbatim. The folder's cover bears the author's handwritten label: "Studies on the revolution—unfit for publication."[29] These studies give evidence of the fact that at least some of the lectures as they were finally given had been preceded[30] by a number of "trial runs"; in the case of some of the other manuscripts, their fragmentary and repetitive nature warrants viewing them as "false starts," thus demonstrating how Groen wrestled with his material in order to achieve a well-rounded and satisfying conception of "the Revolution."[31] They are all the more interesting as no manuscript is extant of *Unbelief and Revolution* itself. A short discussion of the seven studies follows here, in order of their increasing degree of completeness.[32]

Study VI. (French text.) This manuscript reads like a long telegram. At the head Groen writes: "Institutions. Preparatory work. To clear path. Purely historical. Noting the facts. But results to be related to general purpose." Then follow many sheets of notes (often mere catchwords and phrases) grouped in a more or less orderly sequence of paragraphs. Under *I. Institutions* Groen lists points to cover in connection with Great Britain, the Netherlands, the United States and France; hints of these points are scattered throughout Lectures III–V. Under *II. Ideas* he itemizes points to discuss in connection with the Protestant Reformation and the development of modern political theory; here, hints of what would turn up in

---

29. *Studiën over de Revolutie, niet voor uitgave geschikt.* Algemeen Rijksarchief, The Hague, Archief Groen van Prinsterer, no. 29. The mss. have been separated into Studies I to VII and prepared by J. Zwaan for integral publication, with a critical apparatus, as nos. 39-45 in a volume of G. Groen van Prinsterer, *Bescheiden*, in the series *Rijks Geschiedkundige Publicatiën*, no. 209, pp. 388-595. I thank Dr. Zwaan for allowing me to consult his manuscript prior to its publication in 1990.

30. Though none of the mss. bears a date, internal evidence places one in 1839, another *post* 1835, another *ante* 1841, and so on; cf. *Bescheiden*, ed. Zwaan, p. 388n1.

31. Cf. Smitskamp, "Het boek 'Ongeloof en Revolutie,'" p. 17.

32. The unsatisfactory numbering I, II, III, etc. ultimately goes back to De Vries, *Mr. G. Groen van Prinsterer; een bibliografie* (Utrecht: Wentzel, 1908), sub no. 36.

Lectures VI–VII begin to appear. Coming to *"systematic unbelief,"* he jots down its downward steps toward atheism and social upheaval (cf. Lectures VIII and IX), followed by the characterization of the ensuing history as an oscillation between movement and resistance (cf. Lecture X). Next, the "irresistible development" of stages or phases is outlined: demolition (till 1789), diversity of opinions (1789–95), submission (1795–1813), despair (1814–30), and indifference (since 1830). Already the framework of Lectures XI–XIV is taking shape. What follows resembles a labyrinth of topics to be treated in detail: copious notes on the fortunes of the French monarchy, the rise of the English Parliament, the constitution of the Dutch Republic, the growth of medieval society, the historical context of the Reformation—all foreshadowing very dimly what would ultimately be set forth in Lectures III–VII.

Study VII. (French text.) This study is of a mixed nature. Halfway its cluttered sheets there is a noticeable shift in focus. The opening paragraph identifies the envisioned essay as an examination of the charge that the revolution was caused by the very nature, or else the abuses, of the institutions of modern Europe. After a page or so of general observations, the "purpose of the work" is formulated: namely, to show that the root cause of the present age of revolution is the "abandonment of the Christian principle" and the "unfolding of practical atheism." The remaining first half of this draft essay then proceeds to deal with a number of fundamental topics treated in full in chapters 2–5 of the *Essay on Truth* of 1834 and here presented as the starting principles and point of view adopted by the author.[33] The second half offers a series of short sketches outlining basic concepts of constitutional law identical to those covered in Lectures III and IV: divine right, the nature and origin of government and sovereignty, the classification of states, the object of civil government, the relation between church and state, and historic forms of government such as patriarchal rule, Asiatic monarchies, theocracies (with ancient Israel as a special case), and the republics of antiquity. The manuscript breaks off just after introducing the federative type of government and before advancing—as we may surmise from the parallel passages in *Unbelief and Revolution*—to the Germanic-Christian monarchy of Europe.

---

33. Cf. *Bescheiden*, ed. Zwaan, pp. 573-86.

Study V. (French text.) This compact sketch is a more streamlined combination of *VI* and *VII* (second half), composed for the most part this time in complete sentences. It has three distinct parts: the history of institutions, the march of ideas, and the revolutionary principle in action. Its opening sentence, "For fifty years the civilized world has been in permanent revolution," is followed by a thesis statement: "that the principle, the efficient cause of the turmoil that agitates us, is found in the natural unfolding of false doctrines," which doctrines are declared to be the "necessary consequence of abandoning divine truth, of unbelief ..." Next, the symbol of the tree and its fruit, so well known to readers of *Unbelief and Revolution*, makes its appearance: from a description of the tree, so we read, one can first get some idea of what is likely to be its fruit; this will enable one afterward, when investigating the fruit, to recognize with what tree it belongs. After these preliminaries, the *history of institutions* begins by describing some general principles on which pre-revolutionary political constitutions rested and then sketches their common elements: king, clergy, nobility, third estate; the historic rise of many political features peculiar to Germany, England, the Low Countries and France are outlined, issuing in the conclusion that will reappear on the closing pages of Lectures IV and V (90, 118): many abuses but possibility of reform; no need of a systematic revolution destructive of all social bonds. Next, the *march of ideas* is traced from the coming of Christianity, through the late medieval decadence, the Reformation, and the decline of faith, to the rise of unbelief and the acceptance of social contract thinking. Finally, a section on *the revolutionary principle in action* is divided into five phases: preparation (1750-89), movement (1789-95), resistance (1795-1813), continued revolution (1814-30), and reaction, indifference and materialism (since 1830). In short, in this manuscript the gist of *Unbelief and Revolution* is present. Only a separate treatment of the "perversion of constitutional law" (as in Lecture VI) is still missing.

Study III. (Dutch text.) This draft brings us even closer to the text of *Unbelief and Revolution*. Its prose is sedate, lacking all rhetorical agitation. The general framework is now formulated thus: "Long before 1789 the revolution had become inevitable. Men claim it was the wrong application of an excellent theory. We maintain: it was the correct application of a pernicious doctrine. Our proofs are the *nature* of this theory; the *nullity of the arguments* in which this claim is clothed; finally, the course of history, which is the steady *development* of the revolutionary germ." The image of tree and fruit is again applied: the present essay will deal with the tree from which a certain type of fruit may be expected. The text covers roughly the same ground as Lectures IV–IX—in cursory form, to be sure, but often with the same sequence of arguments, examples and refutations. The account of the Reformation, however, is limited here to a short passage about its impact on France, while there is even less about the (perverted) development of modern constitutional law. On the other hand, the essay does have a brief overview, not found in the lectures, of the growth of genuine monarchy in France from the early Franks to Louis XIV. As well, in trying to account for the spread of unbelief in eighteenth-century France the essay advances two reasons which were later suppressed in the lectures: the frivolous character of the French people and the immorality of the French court. Marginal notes reveal Groen's heavy dependence on the anonymous work *Geschichte der Staatsveränderung.*—*Study III* has a separate cover bearing an important note in Groen's hand: "The key to the French Revolution lies in the words of Rousseau, quoted in Kluit, IV, 15." Groen will quote Rousseau's words (using Lamennais, not Kluit[34]) in Lecture X (237): "This is the great problem to be solved in politics: to find a form of government that places the law above man. If that form cannot be found ... we must pass to the other extreme. ... In a word, I see no middle ground between the most austere democracy and the most complete Hobbism."

Study IV. (Dutch text.) This is the companion piece to *III* and is of the same quality. Sober in tone, it shows similar progress in research, thought and composition. It attempts to describe the "fruit by which the tree can be identified," hence offers a historical survey of the revolution. This it does in great detail, in jottings in point form, studded with references to volume and page in Thiers's *Histoire de la Révolution française* and the *Geschichte der Staatsveränderung*. A few references to Wachsmuth's *Geschichte Frankreichs im Revolutionszeitalter*, a work with which Groen was not familiar until September 1845, helps date the manuscript to a time period very close to the lectures.[35] In comparison with the parallel Lectures XI–XIV, there are many more details here about the progress of the debates and party struggles

---

34. A. Kluit, *Historie der Hollandsche Staatsregering*, IV (Amsterdam, 1804), p. 15.
35. Cf. *Bescheiden*, ed. Zwaan, p. 522n1; *Briefwisseling*, II, 702f.

as they developed from the opening phase of the revolution through the Terror to the end of the Directory. It must have been the very thoroughness of his preparatory studies that enabled Groen to compress his amassed material on the French Revolution into a few evenings' lectures.

Study I. (Dutch text.) This study marks a more definitive stage in Groen's studies but rounds off only one area of his researches. It looks like an amplification of *VII* (second half), holding forth as it does at considerable length and depth on such topics as the nature of authority and sovereignty, the origin and goal of states, the various forms of government, and the character of tempered monarchy as this arose in Europe. In its details and illustrations the essay goes far beyond what is to appear later in Lectures III and IV. Especially in the discussion of the separation of powers, of the mixed constitution, and of the requirements for viable constitutions in modern times, we encounter here the well-considered views of a seasoned student of political theory and constitutional history. The draft stage is still in evidence: some sections are spun-out and repetitious, the whole is uneven and disjointed. The rambling speculations at the opening about the *family* as the primordial species of the genus *state* can hardly have been satisfactory to the author himself. In any event, the audience at the future lectures would be spared this tedium: the allotted evening hours obliged Groen to concentrate on essentials and give his major conclusions only; whatever their intrinsic value, they faithfully reflect how far he had come in his reading and reflection.

Study II. (French text.) This is the maturest of them all. It is again written in French and is almost equal in length to the other six combined. It expands *III* and the bulk of *V.* Its topics are the same as those of Lectures III–IX but almost everywhere are treated at greater length, thus bringing out, more than the lectures will do, the gradual progress over time of the revolution under investigation.

The manuscript opens abruptly with a discussion of divine right and other principles underlying the pre-revolutionary states. In the course of this discussion, the abuses of those times are given ample attention, but the continual efforts at reforming them are contrasted with the method of revolution; this is done in a rhetorical flourish that is rare in the manuscripts: "They did not, in order to prune the tree, begin by cutting its roots. They did not, in order to improve the edifice, begin by overthrowing it.

They did not kill the patient in order to cure him." There follows[36] more than a score of sheets on the evolution of the French monarchy (summarized in less than a page in *Unbelief and Revolution*: Lecture IV, 81f) and almost half that many again on the constitutional history of England and the United Provinces. This first part ends with a short section on (again) alleged abuses under the old regimes; here, many a paragraph is identical in structure to its Dutch parallel in Lecture V.

The next part of this manuscript introduces something new. For the first time we meet with a distinct prototype of Lecture VI: a more or less self-contained sketch of the rise of the revolutionary theory in terms of the perversion of constitutional law whose fundamental error it was to "assimilate the modern states to the republics of Antiquity." Groen concludes the sketch with the cautionary observation that the new political theories (as well as the sensationalist branch of modern rationalist philosophy represented by Locke, Helvetius and Condillac—a point not made in Lecture VI) were at most "second causes" of the impending social revolution—contributing factors, swept up into the "efficient cause." That "major" or "superior" cause is then identified as the "abandonment of Christianity and its consequence, the reign of unbelief."

At this juncture Groen turns to a discussion of the question, What then is Christianity, and what had been its historic role up until that time in the shaping of European society? This leads Groen, naturally enough, to address the question, What then was the significance of the rejuvenation of Christianity in the Protestant Reformation?[37] His line of response is that the Reformation "momentarily suspended that pagan intellectual development which had invaded the higher classes who had seized control of art, science and culture." But Protestantism allowed its wholesome influence to flag and so left the field to unbelief. This whole section prefigures Lecture VII but in places is much more elaborate, with many more illustrations.

Next comes a *da capo* of the constitutional history of France. This time we are led straight into the intricacies of the debate between the autocratic-absolutist and the democratic-representative interpreters of early Frankish

---

36. According to the order in which this manuscript was first found and has now been published.

37. This sequence of topics discredits Smitskamp's conjecture that Lecture VII was a last-minute insertion; cf. "Het boek 'Ongeloof en Revolutie,' " p. 14.

monarchy. Groen sides with Moreau against Thierry and others. He contends, for instance, that royal power goes back to the earliest times following the collapse of the Roman Empire (it was not imposed by conquering Franks on freedom-loving Gauls); that the aristocrats did not share legislative power (the magnates of feudalism usurped it); that the early medieval assemblies were military reviews rather than forerunners of Estates General (the latter date from the fourteenth century and were convoked for the sole purpose of subventing in royal expenditures).

Inserted in the manuscript at this point are reams of critical notes on constitutional histories which Groen has consulted and plans to refute. He notes that while indeed his own dissenting opinion from so many current authorities obligates him to answer them, the task is made easier by the fact that they contradict each other. The notes afford a glance in Groen's scribbler, so to speak. Each time citing volume and page, he records, for example, where Kluit and Heeren praise Moreau but also where Savigny issues a caution; he lists six places where the *Vindiciae contra tyrannos* commits serious errors and eight opinions of historians on the untrustworthiness of Montesquieu; and so on. In general, Groen faults his "adversaries" for reading the present into the past and for offering a "republican" misreading of evidence that clearly documents the private-legal nature of medieval kingship. Thierry is praised for unmasking the "philosophical" historians, but his own racist theory and political bias is likewise documented. Specific places in Chateaubriand are listed as improving on Thierry, but Chateaubriand in turn is criticized for making bold assertions based on too little knowledge (eight instances are recorded). The list goes on.

On the remaining sheets it is relatively smooth sailing again for the reader of this manuscript. First, the examination of the impact of ideas is resumed. Then the subject-matter of the future Lecture VII is again gone over, as is that of Lecture VI immediately after, only to make way for yet another sketch of the role of Christianity and the Reformation: when Protestantism lost its vigor, unbelief spread quickly and "was soon to be systematic." For the first time in any of the manuscripts the outlines of Lectures VIII and IX now make their appearance (though not yet with any direct references to Lamennais and Rousseau, as in the lectures). This section ends with the bittersweet complaint that unbelief triumphed over a "phantom" of Christianity, "with weapons largely borrowed from her."

Groen notes: "There never was a battle between principles, but between a principle and dead institutions. The outcome was not doubtful." The manuscript then proceeds by introducing the next topic: the consequent development of "practical atheism" as this can be traced in the facts, that is to say, in the "history of the revolution," which is said to divide into a phase of liberty and a phase of order. Then *Study II* stops.

To sum up, the "Studies on the revolution" in manuscript form contain prototypes of many of the lectures. They reveal that Groen's preparatory labors involved many more authors, amassed far more historical detail, and elaborated much more of a thetic constitutional theory than were to appear in the pages of *Unbelief and Revolution*. The later lecture series, it will become apparent, is a condensed and polemical summation, in which the bookish scholar becomes the counsel for the prosecution who delivers his brief in as powerful and persuasive a manner as he can.

THE *PROLEGOMENA* OF 1841

Before turning to the paraphrases we should make mention of the "prototypical" passages in the *Archives*. By the time Groen reissues Volume I of this work, in 1841, he feels confident enough to preface his documents with helpful essays on aspects of the historical context. Two of the essays concern us here: one on the character of medieval monarchy as it entered the modern age, and another on the nature of the Protestant Reformation as it made its impact on that age. The essays are found on pages 76–118 of the Prolégomènes; the first includes as well a short passage, supported by a quotation from Haller, that sketches the "deterioration" of both constitutional practice and constitutional theory since the revival of Roman law (89–92). Thus these pages prefigure Lectures IV and VII and to a lesser degree Lecture VI.

The purpose of these editorial introductions is to fill in the background of the correspondence to follow: letters illustrative of the issues in the Dutch Revolt against Spain. At the same time the editor has his eye very much on the contemporary debate flowing out of the French Revolution. For the version of history that is being popularized by liberal writers impedes a proper understanding of the position not only of a Louis XIV but, by the same token, of a Philip II; the liberal view of old-regime monarchies as originally representative forms of government usurped by modern kings falsifies history. That is Groen's belief and so it is incumbent upon him as editor to demolish this myth of ancient "royal democracies." In the same vein, the misrepresentation by liberals of the Reformation as the forerunner of the revolution has to be set straight lest the reader misinterpret the correspondence now offered to the public.

The chief authorities invoked by Groen in these short treatises are Moreau and Guizot, and the targets of his polemic are Montesquieu and Mably, Madame de Staël and Chateaubriand. So pleased does Groen seem to have been with these pieces that the discussion of the same issues in *Unbelief and Revolution* is in places kept brief and the reader is referred seven times to this volume of the *Archives*.

For the sake of completeness we conclude this section by drawing attention to two prototypical *passages* in the *Handbook*, installment four, which was published just a few months before the lectures began. In § 599 Groen briefly develops the thought that when the people of the eighteenth century abandoned God, He left them to their own devices, to exhibit His glory even in the vanity of their plans and the disastrous outcome of all their deliberations. In § 822 he remarks that a rebellious people that runs after idols will be given up to the fruit of their own thoughts. These themes will be discussed in our concluding chapter.

POST-1847 PARAPHRASES

A few words, finally, about the author's own paraphrases of *Unbelief and Revolution* after the work was published. The five-part tract of 1848, *Liberty, Equality, Fraternity: Explanation of the Motto of the Revolution*,[38] was a popularization of Groen's "system" or "worldview." Written in the months when the storm of revolution swept across Europe,[39] it warned the common man that the revolutionary program of "Liberty, Equality, Fraternity" had so far brought nothing but enslavement and death, and that in "our more enlightened age" it was bringing widespread unemployment, pauperism and class antagonism as a direct result of unrestricted competition, the sway of the

---

38. *Vrijheid, Gelijkheid, Broederschap; toelichting op de spreuk der Revolutie* (The Hague, 1848).
39. During April and May 1848; cf. *Briefwisseling*, II, 879, 887.

rich, and the dominance of the banking houses. The five pamphlets were completed by June of that year and soon appeared also as a single volume of more than 120 pages. "People seem to be reading them diligently," wrote Professor Van Assen from Leyden,[40] from which we may conclude that perhaps not just the common man was taking note of their contents.[41]

The next recognizable paraphrase of key themes from *Unbelief and Revolution* occurs in a dozen pages of a work of 1849. In his dissenting *Constitutional Revision and National Concord*[42] Groen gave a summary of the revolution doctrine and its contemporary confessors on pages 68–79. Against the claim that there are three schools or parties in the country— conservatives, moderate liberals, and liberals in a hurry—Groen posits that there is a fourth one, the *anti-revolutionary* party, which stands opposed to all three. The latter rejects what the three *revolutionary* parties have in common, namely their assent to the theories of social contract, popular sovereignty, etc., which I, says Groen, regard as false and in conflict with history and revelation. He then proceeds to sketch the "genealogy of ideas"; the family relationship of liberalism and socialism; the necessity of development once the doctrine is accepted; and the inevitability of the final product as seen in the despotism of the revolutionary state. Much of this polemic dates from January 1849 and is a commentary from the sidelines on debates in parliament, of which Groen would soon be a member. In retrospect Groen said of the whole work that it "constitutes a single unity with *Unbelief and Revolution* or at least is closely tied to it."[43]

The French synopsis of *Unbelief and Revolution*, identified as such by the author himself, is found in the second chapter of the book *Le Parti anti-révolutionnaire et confessionnel dans l'Eglise Réformée des Pays-Bas* of 1860. This work was an apologia in response to an article on "the religious situation in Holland," published in a Lausanne daily and written by a pasteur Trottet who reported to his compatriots back home after serving for a year as pastor of the Walloon Church of The Hague. Trottet had characterized

---

40. *Briefwisseling*, II, 887.

41. The popular work was reprinted twice during Groen's lifetime (in 1859 and 1871) and four times since then (in 1903, 1931, 1939, and 1972); cf. the edition prepared by G. J. Schutte (Groningen: De Vuurbaak, n.d. [1972]), p. 123.

42. *Grondwetherziening en eensgezindheid* (Amsterdam, 1849).

43. Groen to J. A. Wormser, Jr., 5 July 1875; in *Briefwisseling*, VI.

the party of Mr. Groen as ultra-orthodox and Mr. Groen himself as an opiniated defender of an outdated system that obstructed true progress.

Groen answered in a six-chapter essay, three of which were published as a brochure of 107 pages, under the title mentioned above.[44] Chapter 2 basically sets forth his system. Section II of this chapter opens with the statement, "In 1831 my convictions regarding the particular character of our time were settled. I then tried to summarize them in an overview [aperçu] of the history since 1789, which I presented as the practical unfolding of the unbelieving philosophy, as the revolutionary theory in action." Section III begins: "In 1847 I dealt with the same subject more fully in a work whose title summed up my viewpoint: *Unbelief and Révolution* [*Incrédulité et Révolution*]. Unbelief the germ, revolution the fruit."

The last paraphrase dates from 1862. In his *In Memoriam* devoted to Friedrich Julius Stahl (1802-61),[45] Groen credits the German scholar and statesman for having articulated clearly and uncompromisingly the real nature of the revolution of modern times. Groen gives his own short characterization of the revolution on pages 27-31, which he concludes with two statements by Stahl: "Either the popular will is the highest law in the moral world, or there is a higher moral authority over man. ... However strange it may sound, there are but two political parties in Germany today: Christians and non-Christians." Related topics discussed in *Unbelief and Revolution* which here receive further elucidation are: the intimate connection between religion and politics (37-42), the fatal weakness of a Christian individualism (43-55), the relation of anti-revolutionaries to Rome (58-61), and the continuing subversion of historic Christianity by rationalism (100-11). The commemorative volume is everywhere illustrated with key quotations from Stahl. These reappear six years later in notes in the 2nd edition of *Unbelief and Revolution*.

---

44. Of the three remaining chapters, one was never finished, while the other two were not published till the present century, as appendixes in A. J. Dam's translation into Dutch of the French brochure of 1860: *De Anti-Revolutionnaire en Confessionele Partij in de Nederlands Hervormde Kerk* (Goes: Oosterbaan & Le Cointre, 1954), pp. 192-224. An English translation of the work was prepared by Colin Wright, *Christian Political Action in an Age of Revolution* (Aalten, Neth.: Woodbridge, 2015).

45. *Ter nagedachtenis van Stahl* (Amsterdam: Höveker, 1862); earlier version in *Nieuwe Bijdragen voor Regtsgeleerdheid en Wetgeving* XII (1862): 161-212.

6

SOURCES

What studies did Groen rely on when he came to compose his lectures? Two sets can be conveniently distinguished: sources on pre-revolutionary state and society—the Old Order; and sources on the new theory and practice of politics—the revolution. Our interest in this chapter focuses on *Unbelief and Revolution* as a piece of historical writing, and so we shall look closely at the sources Groen uses as well as the manner in which he uses them. But before we do so there is a more general question that needs to be addressed: Who or what inspired Groen to build the entire story around ideas? Whence his guiding vision?

THE GUIDING VISION

Groen's source for one of the fundamental assumptions on which he based his lectures cannot be traced with any precision—and understandably so. The notion of relating the French Revolution directly to the *ideas of the Enlightenment* was hardly original with Groen; it is as old as the revolution itself. We need think only of Burke.[1] And Louis XVI himself, having done his share in launching the revolution, lived long enough to make the same connection: in the memorandum he left behind when fleeing the country, June 1791, he complained that intricate institutions of long standing were being destroyed in the name of metaphysics and philosophical ideas; and the failure of his flight he came to look upon as a punishment from God "for having preferred insolent philosophy."[2] "What has led to the revolution," wrote another contemporary observer of royal blood, "is modern philosophy. This is what brought about the monstrous teachings which men dare

---

1. Cf. Alfred Cobban, *The Debate on the French Revolution: 1789-1800* (London, 1950), pp. 4-10; Hedva Ben-Israel, *English Historians on the French Revolution* (Cambridge, 1968), pp. 10-16; J. M. Roberts, *The French Revolution* (Oxford, 1978), pp. 138-40.
2. Quoted in Beik, *The French Revolution Seen from the Right*, p. 337.

to proclaim out loud in our days [and which] have had the most frightening
consequences and have led to appalling chaos and horrid crimes."[3] And the
spouse of the observer just quoted, Prince William V, is said to have warned
repeatedly against the endeavor of the democratic revolution of his time
"not only to invert the present form of government but even to undermine
and overthrow every foundation of government."[4] We shall return to this
whole matter in our concluding chapter; here we need only record that
Groen's "sources" for this "idealist" interpretation are countless.

The *religious deepening* of this common enough interpretation is no
easier to trace to any sources. It is equally unoriginal with Groen, though
no one before him gave such a consistent and sustained elaboration of it.
The notion of identifying religious apostasy as the driving force behind
the Enlightenment program is as old as the Counter-Enlightenment.
Groen himself honored the memory of Lavater, Klopstock and Stilling in
Lecture I (12), of Matthias Claudius and Albrecht von Haller in Lecture VIII
(186n, 199), and of his countrymen Van Alphen and Bilderdijk in Lecture II
(30, 38ff). In a sense, through his sustained scholarly analysis Groen formed
a bridge between these early Christian protestors against the securaliza-
tion of politics and the Dutch theorists of anti-revolutionary politics that
would come after him.

Again, the religious interpretation of the revolution is common enough
among early Dutch Réveil leaders. One student of Bilderdijk comments
that a few lines of the didactic poem *On Matrimony*[5]—"without the Christ
there is but spite, remorse and grief, no wisdom"—express what would be
the main theme of Groen van Prinsterer's *Unbelief and Revolution*.[6] Groen
certainly loved the poetry of the old bard; witness the many selections

---

3. Princess Wilhelmina of Prussia (wife of William V of Orange) to Princess Louise (her
daughter), from The Hague, some time in 1793; quoted by Fred Lammers in *Trouw*, 31 Dec. 1976
(article, based on archival research in The Hague and abroad; location of letter not specified).

4. Quoted in Groen van Prinsterer, *Handboek*, § 716.

5. *De Echt*; in Bilderdijk, *Dichtwerken*, V, 5.

6. J. Bosch, "Willem Bilderdijk als wijsgerig historievormer," p. 234; cf. also
A. Brummelkamp, "Bilderdijk beschouwd als profeet," pp. 195-208; both studies appeared
in *Mr. Willem Bilderdijk* (Pretoria, Amsterdam, Potchefstroom: Boekhandel v/h Höveker
& Wormser, 1906). See also *Grondwetherziening en eensgezindheid*, pp. 87-91, where Groen
quotes many lines by Bilderdijk (from the volumes *Navonkeling, Nalezingen, Krekelzangen* and
Rotsgalmen) in which the aging poet declaims against the new-fangled liberty.

from him in his *Vaderlandsche Zangen* of 1842.[7] Yet he felt constrained, in
Lecture II (39ff), to take distance from the counter-revolutionary stance
of Bilderdijk and his school.

At first blush, the following title would seem to be a very direct source for
the basic theme of Groen's work: *Le despotisme considéré comme le développe-
ment naturel du système liberal et comme le complément de la révolte de l'homme
contre Dieu.*[8] Our suspicion increases when we discover that this tract was
written by Abraham Capadose. Its contents, however, bespeak, if not a
different theme, at least a different spirit: it is the counter-revolutionary
philippic of Bilderdijk that is heard here, a largely negativist *exposé* of religious apostasy and new-fangled constitutionalism. The tract comes down
squarely on the side of absolute monarchy, of old-fashioned obedience
and authority, of the former ranks and orders in society (8-58). Thus if
anything it ranks alongside Da Costa's *Grievances* of 1823. It is also strongly
anti-papist. Certainly there is very little historical analysis here of the
development of political philosophy, of the Enlightenment, or of the French
Revolution, though in his chosen field of focus Capadose discerns the outlines of three distinguishable periods: (a) seduction, (b) separation from
God, and (c) enslavement to the power of Satan (72). Capadose's tract is
dogmatic, apodictic, and even apocalyptic in tone. By comparison, *Unbelief
and Revolution* is sober, scholarly, thorough, analytical. Nevertheless there
is an important basic theme that the two publications have in common: *the
natural development of liberalism leads to despotism and is an ever clearer manifestation of irreligion.* This common feature merited a reference when Groen
was giving his lectures on unbelief and revolution, yet Capadose's tract
is mentioned nowhere in the printed version of the lectures. We do not

---

7. Of the 160 selections (divided over 138 numbers), Bilderdijk's share is 26 (compare:
Valerius 3, Vondel 34, G. Brandt 8, Cats 6, Huygens 3, Van Alphen 10, Vollenhove 8, Onno Zwier
van Haren 8, Willem Zwier van Haren 7, Da Costa 14, versified psalms 5, other 28). Beets is
still conspicuous by his absence; but Groen did come to appreciate his poetry too, e.g. his
versification (in 1847) of Isaiah 45: "we have no hymn more beautiful" (*Brieven van Da Costa*, I,
267; see also III, 118n). Groen's correspondence with Da Costa contains frequent praise for the
poetry of Bilderdijk (cf. esp. I, 205f, 213, 247; III, 70, 136, 143; but see also III, 2-6, 27: regrettable
erotics) and for the poetry of Da Costa himself (cf. esp. I, 232n, 293, 300f, 356f; II, 110; III, 183,
195f, 236, 240f, 250-53). Groen was stirred by Da Costa's occasional poetry and would quote
from these "political poems" in the 2nd ed. of *Unbelief and Revolution*, pp. xvi, 310, 358, 420.
One has the impression that, generally speaking, Groen's tastes in poetry were determined
by the message more than by the medium.

8. Amsterdam: J. H. den Ouden, 1830.

know whether Capadose pointed out the affinity between the two works to Groen, but shortly after Groen had completed his lecture series Capadose published a Dutch translation of his own earlier work.[9]

Naturally, the 1828 brochure briefly mentioned in chapter 2 above, by Cornelis van Zuylen van Nyevelt, the nestor of the Réveil in The Hague, must have been known to Groen. Yet it, too, is nowhere cited by him. Because he did not agree with it? Or because it contained no "quotable quotes"? *Het Liberalismus* certainly touched on similar themes, for example that the revolution was rooted in autonomous reason and came with irresistible force:

> Human reason, puffed up, served as a vehicle for all the secret preparations made for that great eruption ... which took place in full force in the French Revolution, when all the delusions of philosophical understanding were turned into a dissolution of the whole social order and of every religious principle [and] reason was venerated as the goddess of the age, yea a very Temple was erected for her worship. ... The power of the evil which men had commenced was so great that they became entangled against their will in all the frightful consequences of this ruinous principle and were swept along in the great current. ... [O]ne should not ascribe the actual outcome of the turbulences of liberalism to a few mad hot-heads only, and so overlook the true goal that liberalism has set itself: to effect a *general* falling away, one into which all those too must be plunged who do not resist with all their might the influence of the spirit of the age which has been shaped by liberalism. (15f)

In general, of course, the very idea of linking historical cataclysms very concretely to *religious backsliding* was part of the Christian heritage also in the Netherlands. Calvinist preachers and teachers had done so throughout the two centuries of the Dutch Republic.[10] Groen's *Handbook* stands in that tradition—though purifying it of elements that modern research into the sources had since proved untenable.[11] The loss of Belgium in 1830 again

---

9. *Het Despotismus zich uit het liberalismus ontwikkelend* (The Hague, 1846).

10. J. C. Breen, "Gereformeerde populaire historiographie in de 17e en 18e eeuw," in *Christendom en Historie* (Amsterdam, 1925), pp. 213–42.

11. Smitskamp, *Groen van Prinsterer als historicus*, pp. 146, 167.

occasioned many a sermon and pamphlet that linked the event to national apostasy.[12] Thus Groen's comprehensive vision connecting revolution to unbelief fell into a familiar pattern of interpretation.

What was different about this interpretation, however, was that it concentrated on the actual historical links between unbelief and revolution, viz. secular political ideas. It described and analyzed these links in tracing the natural development of the new, "unbelieving" philosophy through its successive stages, from its birth in rationalism all the way to its practical implementation in the great experiment of 1789. These stages, finally, Groen believed could be empirically documented and verified. He would show that unbelief was the efficient cause—how it worked historically— though not the final cause, the divine purpose it was meant to serve.

SOURCES ON THE OLD ORDER

With a clear vision guiding his searches Groen spent many years studying the age of revolution he lived in. The first question to be addressed, obviously, was: What had brought it about? To answer this question required a thorough investigation into the evolution and condition of the old regimes in the various countries of Europe, notably in France. What helped was the fact that already at university Groen had read Ancillon, Bossuet, Chateaubriand, Heeren, Madame de Staël, Montesquieu and Rousseau.[13] The ever-widening range and scope of his reading up to the time of the lectures is evident from the early publications. For example, in the *Overview* of 1831 the authors quoted are Ancillon, Lamennais, Madame de Staël, and above all Pascal; but, in addition, Groen refers several times to two anonymous works, which he praises but also criticizes: *De nos réformes* (1829)[14] and *Appel à la France contre la division des opinions*, a reprint from the *Gazette de France* of 1831.[15] In the *Essay on Truth* of 1834, the authors most frequently

12. TenZythoff, *Sources of Secession*, pp. 114–20.

13. Tazelaar, *De Jeugd van Groen*, pp. 126–30.

14. By Jean Pierre Frédéric Ancillon (1767–1837), a conservative historian, publicist and man of affairs, now chiefly remembered for his *Tableau des révolutions* (4 vols.; 1803–05). The full title of his anonymous work is *De nos réformes des causes qui s'opposent à notre liberté politique, et des moyens qui nous restent pour acquérir une liberté raisonnable* (Leipzig: Brockhaus; Paris: Schabert et Heideloff, 1829). For his authorship I rely on Gerretson, in *Bescheiden*, I, 194n.

15. By Jacques Honoré Lelarge de Lourdoueix, a moderate liberal of independent mind who in the course of his career wrote against legitimists, Orleanists and utopian socialists.

cited, in addition to Ancillon, Lamennais and Madame de Staël, are Schlegel, Haller, Heeren, and the *Introduction générale à l'histoire du droit* (1829) by Jean Louis Eugène Lerminier (1803–57).

This list grows enormously after 1834 as the "Studies on the revolution" are being committed to paper.[16] These manuscripts reveal, first of all, that as his principal source for the old regime in France Groen has canvassed the twenty-one volumes of the *Discours sur l'histoire de France* (1777–89) by the official historiographer under Louis XVI, that "faithful servant of absolutism" Jacob Nicolas Moreau (1717–1803).[17] In part as foils to Moreau, Groen makes ample use both of the *Lettres sur l'histoire de France* (1827) and of the collection *Dix ans d'études historiques* (1834) by the romantic historian of liberal bourgeois sympathies, Augustin Thierry (1795–1856). The *Etudes historiques* (1831) by the romantic-turned-conservative François Réné de Chateaubriand (1768–1848) are his chief source for the views of a host of sixteenth- and seventeenth-century publicists (like Bignon, Brunet, Daniel, Domat, Fauchet, Loyseau, du Tillet, Valesius). For the British scene Groen's sources are George Buchanan's *Rerum scoticarum historia* (1571), William Blackstone's *Commentaries on the Laws of England* (1765–69), and David Hume's *History of England* (6 vols.; 1750–62); to his older contemporary Henry Hallam (1777–1859) Groen is indebted on account of his *View of the State of Europe During the Middle Ages* (1818) and his *Constitutional History of England* (1827). All in all, this enumeration tends to confirm the suspicions of a later critic of *Unbelief and Revolution* that Groen's knowledge of the Middle Ages is "second-hand"—though the same critic is clearly mistaken when he presumes that Groen "never made much study of the subject."[18] As is to be expected, for political theory Groen draws on the great classics in the field with the ease of long-standing familiarity: Plato and Aristotle, Cicero, Machiavelli, Bodin, the *Vindiciae contra tyrannos*, Grotius, Bossuet, Montesquieu and Rousseau. For the history of the Reformation one of his authorities is Jean Baptiste Honoré Raymond Capefigue (1802–72), whose *Histoire de la Réforme* (8 vols.; 1834–35) he admittedly appreciates less

His authorship of the *Appel* is identified in A. Barbier, *Dictionnaire des Ouvrages anonymes*, I, 258. About Lamennais and Madame de Staël more later.

16. Cf. esp. the annotation, *Bescheiden*, ed. Zwaan, pp. 388–595.

17. Cf. Beik, *The French Revolution Seen from the Right*, pp. 7–11.

18. Fruin, *Verspreide Geschriften*, X, 138f.

for its interpretation than for the many historical documents it reproduces.[19] For the history of modern philosophy in general and of the Enlightenment in particular he relies heavily on the works of a moderate disciple of Hegel, Victor Cousin (1792–1867).[20]

Turning now to *Unbelief and Revolution*, we note that in its pages many of these authors are scarcely mentioned, if at all. Yet the lectures show unmistakably, both in its pointed summaries of constitutional thought and in its sure-handed sketches of episodes in constitutional history, that the lecturer has steeped himself in the literature on the subject and draws heavily on it. The classics, of course, he has at his fingertips. Involving Aristotle in the debate, referring to Plato, quoting Tacitus and Cicero (a favorite in many of his writings!), and weaving in a verse from Horace here and an image from Virgil there—it is all second nature to Groen,[21] a nature which he tries to restrain to some degree but which he does not succeed in suppressing entirely in the pages of *Unbelief and Revolution*. By contrast, his knowledge of medieval authors, as we have seen, is second-hand. Then again, Lecture VI (132ff) shows that when it comes to modern authors he appears to know his Grotius intimately—although he does not quote him in the original Latin but in French translation (for which he would be rapped over the knuckles[22]). In other political writers since 1500 he is sufficiently at home to be able to cite them at will (though he may be using Chateaubriand and Haller as a shortcut here). In all his reading of these authors Groen appears guided, as we shall now examine, by a basic theme adopted from Haller. Groen depended on Haller for the view

---

19. Cf. Groen van Prinsterer, *Verspreide Geschriften*, II, 271.

20. Cousin brought Hegelianism to France and subscribed to a three-stage theory of progress and a great-men view of history, without however adopting the strict doctrine of a World Spirit who strides with sovereign unconcern from one philosophical conception to the next for the sole purpose of arriving at his full Self-realization. Zwaan notes that Groen borrowed many systematic and terminological distinctions in philosophy from Cousin (cf. *Bescheiden*, ed. Zwaan, p. 453n53a); on a more fundamental point (whether the Enlightenment represented progress), see Groen's disagreement with Cousin in Lecture VIII (188).

21. This is exhaustively documented, with incredible completeness, in Zwaan's dissertation of 1973; cf. in addition to his 150 pages of endnotes, the 110 pages of indices in his *Groen van Prinsterer en de klassieke Oudheid*, pp. 532–642.

22. By De Bosch Kemper, in his review of *Ongeloof en Revolutie*, p. 215; cf. Zwaan, *Groen van Prinsterer en de klassieke Oudheid*, p. 408, n. 425.

that traditional European kingship was of a private-legal nature. It was a dependence that few found comfortable—then or later.

The correspondence of the years prior to 1845 contains a number of interesting letters relative to Groen's relation to Haller. Koenen, from the earliest years of his acquaintance with Groen, remonstrated with him that Haller's views might be valid for certain feudal monarchies but should not be applied to modern Western European states. Haller, so ran Koenen's objection, essentially wanted to return to a pre-revolutionary order of things; he based authority on landed property; and he was far too Roman Catholic in outlook. Groen tried to defend Haller, but admitted that his sympathies concerned mainly the "egg of Columbus" (brilliant truism) found in the *Restauration der Staats-Wissenschaft*: namely, the obvious truth that states are institutions inseparable from history and human nature rather than creations of convention and contract.[23] In Lecture II (37f) Groen relates how thrilled he had been in the mid-twenties by his discovery of Haller, whose famous work provided the tools with which to expose the artificiality of the social contract theory.[24] Without further analysis Groen had bracketed the positivist Haller with the historical school of Savigny which he had grown to love.[25] But Haller's conversion to Catholicism and his view that the Protestant Reformation represented a fundamental principle of dissolution was enough to ensure that Groen should never turn into a "Hallerian." Groen did pay Haller a visit on one of his trips to Switzerland and he periodically mailed him complimentary copies of new volumes of the *Archives*. "You will find here abundant evidence," he wrote on one such occasion, "that the principles of the Reformation are the strongest refutation of Jacobinism." Haller politely replied that for Switzerland, in any event, the "two revolutions," of the 16th and the 18th centuries, were "identical."[26] When Groen had given his third lecture (on the nature of pre-revolutionary principles of government), it was Koenen who repeated his complaint of many years' standing that Groen was far

---

23. *Briefwisseling*, II, 79f, 106. As of so many other works, Groen preferred to use the French edition prepared by the author, *Restauration de la Science politique* (2 vols.; Lyon and Paris, 1824/25).

24. Cf. also Groen's *Proeve* (1834), p. 158n.

25. Cf. Brants, *Groen's geestelijke groei*, pp. 41–46.

26. *Briefwisseling*, II, 119, 140, 152, 179.

too much influenced by Haller.[27] The complaint is addressed at the end of
Lecture VI (144ff).

SOURCES ON THE REVOLUTION

Under this heading fall the books and authors that functioned as Groen's
sources for piecing together the story of the revolution, both its "natural
history" (the revolution in ideas) and its "biography" (that revolution as
it was put into practice). Thus, while our previous section tried to assess
Groen's sources on the old order, with the present section we say farewell
to him as a political theorist and constitutional historian, to turn to him
as an intellectual and political historian.

As we do so, however, a word of caution is in order. We need to remind
ourselves that Groen lived and worked in an age still dominated by "poli-
tisierende Tendenzhistoriker."[28] This type of historian was not exactly in
danger of sinking into a class of sterile academics producing anemic history,[29] nor did he aspire to the professional status of full-time scientific
historian then emerging under the inspiring example of Ranke and his
school. Groen hailed the latter development, contributed to it through his
archival publications and his *Handbook*, appreciated the need for source
criticism and the demands of the historian's craft in general, and did his
part to advance the careers of budding historians like Bakhuizen van den
Brink and Fruin; but to a large extent he was an admirer and patron, not
a practitioner of the new history. Thus in *Unbelief and Revolution* he has
no pretension of giving an original study of the French Revolution based
on critically evaluated documentary evidence. When he declares toward
the close of Lecture I (17) that "history alone will be our instructor," and
when he states ingenuously at the beginning of Lecture VI (121) that "true
to the historical standpoint, I do not wish to judge but to describe," then he
has something else in mind. His purpose with the lecture series, according to the Preface, is to contribute to the debate then raging in his country
about history and constitutional law, and his contribution comes in the
form of an interpretation of the recent past that shows where the present

---

27. *Briefwisseling*, II, 966; cf. also 335, 644, 787, 894.

28. Cf. Fueter, *Geschichte der neueren Historiographie*, p. 537.

29. Cf. Butterfield, *Christianity and History*, chap. I; idem, *Writings on Christianity and History*, pp. 172–82; Dawson, *Dynamics of World History*, pp. 287–93.

has come from and what it holds in store. In short, Groen is an engaged historian, a historian-publicist. In Groen, the historian is qualified by his political purpose, as the publicist is qualified by his historical orientation. With that reminder, we are ready to examine his historical craftsmanship.

From the previous chapter it is evident that key ingredients in Groen's interpretation of the age of revolution, as he developed these from 1829 to 1834, had solidified into a rather consistent overall view or coherent vision. After 1834, continued study of the subject had resulted, first of all, in the portfolio of notes and drafts labeled "Studies on the revolution," and, secondly, in the lectures on unbelief and revolution. A closer examination of *Unbelief and Revolution* reveals that the intervening decade had produced no real change in Groen's basic interpretation. Groen had his authorities ready, this time in greater number than ever,[30] and the embattled debater marshalled his carefully selected references and citations with powerful rhetorical effect. Groen's "biography" of the revolution takes the form of an ongoing polemic with historical accounts that offer rival interpretations; a continuous narrative, had he been capable of it, would not have suited his purpose. Sometimes it seems that authors are not even introduced and their views reproduced for rebuttal, but merely for the purpose of organizing points to be discussed—such as Ancillon in Lecture XI (287) and De Clercq in Lecture XII (297).[31] The net effect of this entire procedure is a long sustained argument in the form of a composition that could not fail to impress his audience with its erudition as well as conceptual unity.

Both its conceptual unity, born of the guiding vision, and its impressive erudition, fruit of long study, impart to *Unbelief and Revolution* an aura of definitiveness. To be sure, Groen disclaims offering anything more than an "essay" needing further study, revision, polish (Preface, pp. vi, vii), and he politely requests "contradiction and correction where I fail to be convincing" (Lecture I, p. 17). But despite these and other protestations of its tentativeness, the thesis is presented and the argument developed in a

---

30. The chief ones are: Madame de Staël (47 references in total), Lamennais (35), Mignet (31), Thiers (23), Buonarrotti (22), Burke (20), Ancillon (11), Wachsmuth (11), Guizot (10) and Necker (9). This list refers to the 1st ed.; new citations in the 2nd ed. are reviewed in chap. 12 below.

31. Many years later Groen recalled that he had incorporated De Clercq's article "as a theme for refutation" partly because of its "excellent argumentation." *Brieven van Da Costa*, I, 209n.

sure and self-confident tone. Only once does he admit that an interpretation different from his own had given him pause. This happens toward the end of Lecture V (112f), in a manner that is revealing of the way in which Groen went about his work.

The passage in question introduces an anonymous author who derives the revolution "strictly from political causes," namely by tracing it back to the decline of the privileged orders during the eighteenth century: with their decay the supports of the throne vanished and the king stood alone as he faced a rising populace. This line of argument, says Groen, has something to commend it. "Until I had weighed it carefully, it made a considerable impression upon me." Could it be true that the revolution resulted from the decline of clergy and nobility who lost their power to serve as a buffer between king and commoners? This is what is capably argued—Groen tells his audience—in the incisive, and in places prophetic, pamphlet of 1829 entitled *De nos réformes*. He then proceeds to quote from it for more than a page, in a digression, he says, that is only intended to give a sample of how shrewd, intelligent and insightful the unknown author is on another question, namely the causes of the July Revolution of 1830; hence his view of the causes of the Great Revolution deserves careful consideration. (By this time the reader is beginning to wonder when Groen will announce that he has had to give in and give up.) But Groen might not have shown such respect for the excellent pamphlet if he did not also see his way clear to offering a rebuttal. He replies that the author's reasoning about 1789 sounds disturbingly right until it dawns on one that the man is confused about his constitutional categories: his argument would indeed hold for the present *trias politica*, that artificial separation of the three powers of government à la Montesquieu: remove the aristocratic element, and indeed the equilibrium will be gone and the king will be the helpless toy of the democratic element. But under the mixed forms of government of the old regime there were in place, next to the privileged orders, a host of other intermediate bodies to keep king and commoners in their respective places.[32] Thus the brilliant author of *De nos réformes* has been misled by a terminological confusion occasioned by conceptual misapprehension.

---

32. For the distinction in Groen between the mixed constitution and the *trias politica*, see Zwaan, *Groen van Prinsterer en de klassieke Oudheid*, pp. 353, 360.

Groen's tactic of elevating an author he is about to bring low is used to great rhetorical effect in *Unbelief and Revolution* as he prosecutes his case.

By the time Groen lectured on unbelief and revolution it had been thirty years since Waterloo and the historiography of the French Revolution had definitely entered a new phase. Groen uses as his chief sources the second-generation historians of the French Revolution who were able to build their chronicles on the earlier memoirs, reflections and considerations of eyewitnesses and participants. The historians in question had done so, by and large, with some appearance of critical judgment and scientific detachment; nevertheless, they had had very few primary documents at their disposal since archives covering the period were as yet closed or, if open, unorganized. The histories of the revolution that first utilized primary documents to any significant degree, those of Michelet and Blanc, did not appear until 1847. Records of the Assembly's debates remained scattered over a number of semi-official newspapers[33]; the full account of their proceedings, the *Archives parlementaires*, did not start to come out till 1862. Selected portions of the debates had appeared in the enormous collection of Buchez and Roux,[34] but Groen does not appear to have had access to it. (One may discount the possibility that Groen, whose "eclecticism" allowed him to utilize any source whatever, shied away from Buchez merely because his prefaces and editorial passages pushed an interpretation diametrically opposed to his own, namely that the revolution's mission of bringing social justice and equality sprang from the principles of the gospel and therefore represented the culmination of Christianity,[35] though it is certainly the case that this vision guided the selection of the extracts from the Assembly debates and the many other documents reproduced by Buchez.[36]) The largest collection of revolutionary pamphlets, assembled by the Englishman Croker, remained uncataloged. Thus in 1845, even if he had wanted it otherwise, Groen had virtually nothing but secondary literature

---

33. E.g. the *Gazette de France*, the *Journal des débats*, and the *Moniteur*. The latter was reprinted in 32 vols., 1840–45. Groen uses none of the three.

34. *Histoire parlementaire de la Révolution française, ou Journal des assemblées nationales depuis 1789 jusqu'en 1815* (40 vols.; 1834–38).

35. Philippe Joseph Benjamin Buchez (1776–1860) had been a follower of Saint-Simon.

36. Cf. Geyl, "French Historians For and Against the Revolution," pp. 99–102.

readily available to him.[37] Only his strong conceptual scheme kept his work from turning into a mere compilation or a loose-strung narrative.

Turning now to the works cited, we find that in *Unbelief and Revolution* the references to primary sources (in the strict sense of that term) are few in number. We hear of the revolutionaries, their aspirations, their careers, and their speeches in the Assembly, only through the mouth of other historians. And the *philosophes*, whose thought presumably started it all, make their appearance only as shadowy background figures in cursory overviews. With one exception. Clearly stealing the limelight is Jean Jacques! In Lecture IX it is Rousseau who takes center stage, while he makes frequent appearances in Lecture XIII.[38] In the former case, it is by means of statement after statement occurring in *Du Contract social* that Groen draws up his indictment of Enlightenment political thought as a whole. In the latter case, Groen rehearses the dogmas of Rousseau to compare them to the deeds of Robespierre. In both cases we are permitted to listen to Rousseau himself—Groen plays no tricks of ventriloquism on him. But is the reader brought directly in touch with the flesh-and-blood Rousseau of history? The broader backdrop—his intentions, his contradictions, his hopes and fears—are only sparingly mentioned, in remarks scattered over several lectures. Unfair? Unscholarly? Groen is not writing a scientific biography, or a social history of the *philosophes*. In his eyes Rousseau stands for a coherent body of thought that has done its work in history, deceiving thousands, and victimizing millions. To exhibit the unique dynamics of its iron logic is a service to his fellow-man.

After Rousseau, Madame de Staël (1766–1817) belonged to Groen's earliest favorite authors of the revolutionary age.[39] Her renowned *Considérations sur les principaux événemens de la Révolution françoise* came out posthumously in 1818. Though not a formal history of the revolution—her book

---

37. The only primary source Groen appears to have consulted at one time (though it is not cited in *Unbelief and Revolution*) is the selection edited by Guillaume N. Lallement, *Choix de rapports, opinions et discours prononcés à la tribune nationale* (24 vols.; Paris, 1818–23); cf. *Bescheiden*, ed. Zwaan, pp. 522-55, notes 64, 71, 84–87 and 170. This source collection was designed to serve as ammunition in the liberal campaign to "sell the Revolution to the Restoration"; cf. Mellon, *The Political Uses of History*, p. 6.

38. Rousseau figured among Groen's favorite authors in his youth; no other author held greater attraction for him as none could match him in combining such unflinching logic with such passionate eloquence. Cf. Tazelaar, *De Jeugd van Groen*, p. 126.

39. Cf. *Bescheiden*, ed. Gerretson, pp. 3–14, theses 48 and 73.

is a mixture of eyewitness reports and emigrant ruminations, both patently partisan—it did launch an interpretation that was to stir Restoration society for many years.[40] The three-volume work is a bold defense of the revolution as a sublime event whose fruits must not be undone in the nineteenth century. For this gifted writer, the revolution had begun a great work of emancipation, bringing to a people of frustrated enterprise and untapped talent a long-awaited deliverance from the triple burden of an intolerant church, an unproductive nobility and an absolute monarchy. The revolution was prepared by the whole spirit of the eighteenth century and aimed peaceably at erecting institutions for curbing royal despotism. In its early phase it succeeded in enshrining principles of lasting value, such as limited monarchy and individual rights. Regrettably, the revolution went wrong, first, when the Constituent Assembly failed to give the king independent power and sacrificed principles to greed in its struggle to control patronage (a theme to which Groen pays scant attention), and next, when the Legislative Assembly in many hasty decisions imposed party-law and sacrificed principles to administrative expediency.

In Lecture XI Groen makes grateful use of Staël's more felicitous formulations regarding the irrepressible coming of the revolution. As well, he quotes several of her statements about the peaceful intentions and expectations of 1789 to bring out that indeed not the French nation but a sect of believers in a new dogma was responsible for the crises to come. Particularly in Lecture XII Groen skillfully weaves into his interpretation of the moderate phase of the revolution a number of passages where Staël can be shown to contradict herself in blaming certain people and circumstances for the revolution's derailment. If public opinion was so overwhelmingly strong, as she recognizes, how can she blame the king's vacillation or the Assembly's weakness? If the privileged orders started the revolt, how can she speak accusingly of their "thoughtless resistance"?[41] If the constitution of '91 had no real moral authority, how can she deplore the lack of opportunity to work with it? Mockingly Groen dismisses her self-serving opinion that the opening phase was altogether

---

40. Cf. Farmer, *France Reviews Its Revolutionary Origins*, p. 11.

41. In Groen's account, the aristocratic revolt of 1787–88 against royal absolutism is of a piece with the nobles' participation in the abolition of the old regime during 1789–91.

sweetness and light and that the panicky emigration of 1791 was premature.[42] He is more approving of her account as the revolution progresses.
At the top of Lecture XIII he quotes her characterization of the Terror as
a "descent into Inferno" and as a regime not of anarchy but of deliberate
policy defended in the name of "public safety." Her calling Robespierre
a hypocrite must be a slip, for later she refers to his political fanaticism,
describing it as "calm and austere." Finally, Groen agrees with her assessment that the only way Napoleon could have stayed in power was through
foreign adventure. In sum, the frequent and varied invocation of Madame
de Staël's *Considérations* shows Groen at his rhetorical best: she is called
upon alternately as a witness for the defense and as a witness for the prosecution—at Groen's bidding. Whether his overall interpretation has been
significantly influenced by hers is difficult to document, but is probable
for at least one important theme: the impact of the spirit of the age on
the deliberations of men.

Before we turn to a different genre of history-writing, we should briefly
examine Groen's use of a work by Madame de Staël's father, the Genevan
financier and French finance minister of revolutionary fame, Necker.

One of the earliest "histories" of the French Revolution—it really still
belongs to the genre of memoirs—is the two-volume work *De la Révolution
française*, written in retirement by a minister of the constitutional king who
lived to tell the tale, Jacques Necker (1732–1804). Groen invokes Necker's testimony to substantiate an important point in his whole argument, namely
that violent excesses had been part and parcel of the revolutionary experiment not just later but from the very first. Therefore even prior to 1792 any
decision to emigrate was fully justified, and so the self-serving charges of a
"partisan decision" made by Madame de Staël are once for all laid to rest in
Lecture XII (307) by the recollections of her father. In Lecture XIII (332, 334)
a number of Necker's observations about the Girondins—they perished
as victims of their own methods—are reproduced by Groen in support of
his contention that the Jacobin terror did not mark a bizarre shift in policy
but was the natural climax of a trend that had but escalated since the time

---

42. Anne Louise Germaine Necker could afford to delay her departure for a year because
she enjoyed a degree of diplomatic immunity, being married at the time to Sweden's ambas-
sador to France, Baron de Staël Holstein.

the Girondins were in the vanguard. In this connection Necker is quoted as having predicted on one occasion that the bloodstained track would be followed to the finish. At the same time, for that very reason Groen will not allow Necker to do in the end, from puzzlement, what so many other interpreters of the revolution have resorted to for the purpose of whitewashing the revolution, namely to make an exception for Robespierre as a monster beyond human comprehension. For this Jacobin, too, can be made perfectly comprehensible in his monstrous deeds simply by appreciating him for what he was: a religious fanatic, prepared to wade through a sea of blood in order to realize the theory he so sincerely believed in.

After Madame de Staël and Monsieur Necker the next sources to consider are by three pioneers of modern French scientific historiography: Guizot, Mignet and Thiers.

Guizot's famous twin lecture series on civilization in Europe and civilization in France (given at the Sorbonne in the early twenties)[43] are quoted several times in connection with both the Reformation and the Enlightenment—but only for the purpose of taking issue with Guizot's liberalist characterization of these historic movements. Guizot had used his university rostrum to attack the ultra-royalist version of history, which condemned the revolution *en bloc*. In his view, the revolution, while in need of being purged of "lamentable digressions," represented the final stage in the centuries-long struggle for liberty in France.[44] Groen agreed with Guizot that the Restoration "established France on the terrain of the Revolution," but drew the opposite conclusion. More positively, it was Guizot who suggested a peculiar method to Groen. This will be discussed in our closing chapter.

Coming next to Mignet and Thiers, we note that Groen calls them "excellent in form" but willfully partisan, and obviously written from a standpoint that "derives from the revolutionary ideas themselves" (Lecture XI, p. 274). François Mignet (1796–1884) wrote his *Histoire de la Révolution française* (1824) in a few months' time, making no attempt at research other than interviewing survivors. Conceived as an occasional piece for the purpose

---

43. *Histoire générale de la civilisation en Europe depuis la chûte de l'Empire romain jusqu'à la Révolution française* (Paris, 1828); *Histoire de la civilisation en France depuis la chûte de l'Empire romain jusqu'en 1789* (Paris, 1829).

44. Mellon, *The Political Uses of History*, pp. 7, 12–14, 23, 29, 48.

of attacking the Bourbon Restoration by glorifying the revolution, the publication was an overnight success.[45] Since ultra-royalism was on the rise, threatening the restoration of the old regime in its most repressive form, Mignet's analysis seeks to prove that the revolution was the inevitable outcome of a process by which the third estate had risen in wealth and prominence—an irreversible process in fact, whose natural sequel, the overthrow of the Bourbons, could be just around the corner.[46] In an effort to persuade his generation that the ultimate ascendancy of the bourgeoisie was historically inevitable, Mignet's account of the revolution emphasizes how vast movements irresistibly overrode individual interests and wills (almost in a secular version of *Man proposes, God disposes*).

For all his "determinism" or "fatalism," however, Mignet does not deny himself a historical speculation here and there and thus indulges occasionally in "history in the subjunctive"[47]: if Louis XVI had not been so weak, if the Legislative Assembly had not been so inexperienced, etc., etc. A partial explanation for such seeming inconsistency might be that for Mignet history is nothing if not *action*; events take their course from what political leaders do (though they are condemned to historical unproductivity if they resist the inevitable). In any event, Groen is not persuaded by Mignet (who scarcely mentions the *philosophes*) that events rather than ideas and theories functioned as the motors of the revolution. The dramatization of human acts is a feature of Mignet's book that is less useful to Groen and accordingly is passed over in silence.

Groen does appreciate Mignet's "compact sketch" and cites many a pithy statement from it. In Lecture XIII he utilizes Mignet over and over again for his depiction of the leading Jacobins as fanatical believers in the new social theory, of the Jacobin terror as a political necessity, and thus of the radicalization of the revolution as the hard-fought triumph of a "system." But where Mignet follows a different track—in emphasizing the adventitious role played by the personal character of the king, or the spontaneous

---

45. Mignet's reputation as a pioneer of scientific history is based on his more mature works published in his capacity as director of the Foreign Ministry Archives; cf. Gooch, *History and Historians in the Nineteenth Century*, pp. 184–89.

46. Cf. McManners, "The Historiography of the French Revolution," p. 626.

47. A term of Crane Brinton, *A Decade of Revolution*, p. 9, where the author scoffs at it as a "useless genre to indulge in" (only to indulge in it himself on p. 12).

act of self-exclusion by the Constituent—there Groen duly quotes him, but not in order to follow him in downplaying any determinism but only for the purpose of being able to refute him with contrary statements taken from Thiers and Madame de Staël, authors whom he has discredited a paragraph earlier. And so Groen plays one interpreter off against two others, according to the stratagem, "We are victors after being but spectators."[48]

Adolphe Thiers (1797-1877) composed a much longer *Histoire de la Revolution française* (10 vols.; 1823-27). Unlike the work of his friend Mignet, it engages in little analysis; its strength lies in the use of material derived from surviving eyewitnesses, especially soldiers. Like Mignet's, this work too, as it narrates the events of the revolution in great detail, vindicates its cause and by implication indicts the repression under the restored Bourbons. Thiers is not a dogmatic democrat but a pragmatic liberal who believes that power should pass to the bourgeoisie.[49] In his fifth volume Thiers credits the Jacobins for having saved France in a perilous crisis, even though he expresses abhorrence at the violence that was required to do it.[50] The ten volumes, though they sold very well, were produced with careless haste and before long were shown to be less than reliable in many of their factual accounts.[51]

Already in his *Essay on Truth* Groen had given his estimate of this work: written with much talent but of little value if one desires a faithful and accurate account of events. This is stated, moreover, in conjunction with a much more serious charge. Thiers's is a type of history-writing that is "despicable" in Groen's eyes because of its moral indifference: it reduces society to a machine and men to mere tools by presenting crime and virtue alike as "necessary outworkings of relations and circumstances."[52] Because

---

48. See Lecture IV, 176 or ²70.

49. Cf. Fueter, *Geschichte der neueren Historiographie*, pp. 509–11; Gooch, *History and Historians in the Nineteenth Century*, pp. 189–96.

50. Much as he shuddered at the means but believed in the end when he crushed the Commune in 1871.

51. Noted by Groen on p. 274n2 (not included in our abridgment). It was Van Assen who drew Groen's attention to a devastating critique [by Croker] of Thiers's *Histories* in the *Quarterly Review* of Sept. 1845, hence only a few months before Groen started quoting from them in his lectures; cf. *Briefwisseling*, II, 704.

52. *Proeve* (1834), p. 127n.

Groen's own treatment of the revolution lies open to a similar charge we shall return to this question in our last chapter.

Groen draws on Thiers for descriptive details of Louis XVI's dignified behavior at his trial and of Danton's brazen self-defense at his (Lecture XII, XIII, 300, 336). Again, in order to be able to set off to advantage the calm reasoning and self-control of Robespierre and Saint-Just he is happy to quote Thiers's characterization of Marat as a "dogmatic and reckless" maniac (Lecture XIII, 337). On the other hand, Thiers's "lessons" in political psychology, which run counter to the lessons taught in *Unbelief and Revolution*, are stood on their head by Groen for the sake of buttressing his own case. Where Thiers (hopeful of an audience in Restoration France?) holds forth that Louis XVI should have given in early and generously in order to allay the revolutionary fever, there Groen (mindful of the Belgian Revolt?) disagrees, countering that no concessions by any sovereign could have satisfied a movement that aimed, consciously or unconsciously, at establishing the sovereignty of the people (Lecture XI, 291f). And where Thiers explains how the Committee of Public Safety had no choice but to permit atrocities and commit terrible executions in order to appease the revolutionary wrath, there Groen momentarily goes along with this "explanation from expedience" (Lecture XIII, 354): indeed it was only right that this fanatical minority, once in power, fought a war to the death to preserve the revolution—assuming, that is, that the revolutionary ideology provides the only valid standard by which to judge their conduct. Given their premises, Groen is only too glad to pass on Thiers's conclusion that the Terror, however gruesome, was politically justified and that posterity owes the engineers of the Terror a debt of gratitude for having saved France from foreign invasion. To Groen, such an explanation only highlights the diabolical nature of the whole revolutionary experiment.

Again, it fits Groen's scheme of interpretation very well to quote, in Lecture XII (318), from just a few pages of Thiers's first volume where he explains how the stage of constitutional monarchy suffered from internal contradiction. Since Thiers notes correctly that monarchy was indeed understood at that time only in the sense of a republic in which the king simply executed the popular will—and how else could it have been understood, given the wide diffusion of the "revolutionary constitutional law"?

—then of course it is easy to see why genuine monarchy could not possibly have worked for very long.

Typically, Groen does not use any of Thiers's lucid discussions of inflation and price controls. He will not be sidetracked from his main argument by such "secondary" considerations.[53]

In sum, Groen finds Thiers extremely useful for his wealth of narrative detail, for his emphasis on the inevitable succession of the moderates by the radicals, and for his "explanation" of the Terror. But were Thiers's explanations indeed intended as exonerations, as many of his critics claimed and Groen too implied? Thiers himself denied it, boasting that "no one could point to a word which excused crime."[54] Such sophistry would not have impressed Groen, who makes a point of passing on, in Lecture XIII (356), Thiers's stated preference for the moral "superiority" of those Jacobins who chose to institute a regime of terror "purely from policy" over the short-sightedness of the Girondins who failed to see that violent means were required to save the cause of France. The Jacobins in question are of course the very ones who serve as Groen's star witnesses in his indictment of the revolutionary theory, and he cannot but agree with Thiers's characterization of them as acting on the basis of revolutionary expediency. Especially useful to Groen's argument is Thiers's explanation that the men of the Mountain prevailed over their opponents because they had a single mind, a fixed goal and an iron will. But for Thiers actually to prefer these cold-blooded killers who saw what France's safety "required" over the Girondins who opposed further killing from lack of political "realism"—that is tantamount in Groen's eyes to excusing the most heinous of crimes.[55]

---

53. This one-sidedness is severely censured by De Pater, "Groen's beschouwing over het beloop der Franse Revolutie," pp. 100-17, where he draws attention to such "co-determinants" as the opposition of profiteers and enragés and the uprisings by counter-revolutionaries to account for the rise of the Reign of Terror. Groen's view of the progress of the revolution in terms of a logically developing ideology, says De Pater, is "an optical illusion caused by the deficient factual material he worked with" (116). Deficient—or deliberately ignored? At any rate, De Pater faults Groen for ignoring the problem caused by the printing of the *assignats*, whose dizzying drop in purchasing power "for the greater part determined the subsequent course of the Revolution" (111). More about this in our concluding chapter.

54. Quoted in Gooch, *History and Historians in the Nineteenth Century*, p. 190.

55. His indignation at Thiers's standpoint, only tacitly present in Lecture XIII where it is veiled in irony, is very explicit in *Proeve* (1834), p. 128n.

The question of the moral implications of any view that wishes to speak of inevitability in the course of the revolution comes to a head in a debate that Groen engages in with Ancillon. This Restoration conservative wrote a number of essays which Groen finds useful to cite.[56] Ancillon is quoted as recognizing the power of revolutionary movements in general to override the deeds of individuals (Lecture VIII, p. 181), yet also as making an exception for a very specific series of deeds that did make a crucial difference at the outset of the revolution (Lecture XI, p. 287). Groen lists the deeds, and then deflates their significance with the single argument that none of the alternative courses of action suggested by Ancillon were realistic options to the actors involved, committed as the opposition was to radical changes that would be consistent with the universally accepted ideas.

In this exchange with Ancillon Groen again resorts to a rhetorical stratagem that he seems quite fond of. During the phase of preparation, Groen argues in Lecture XI (287-92), all men became infected with the revolutionary ideology—court, notables and commoners. This made the pressure to see it implemented irresistible. At this point in the discussion Ancillon is introduced, who argues that the revolution could have been prevented if only the king had offered greater resistance. This view is then contrasted with that of Staël and Thiers, both of whom are quoted as arguing that the revolution could have been prevented if only the king had offered *less* resistance. Once again the reader is reminded of the stratagem employed earlier: "We are victors after being but spectators."[57] Having thus played one position off against the other, Groen next dismisses both possibilities by maintaining that since the revolution had conquered men's minds it was bound to be reinforced by resistance and indulgence alike.

A curious use is made of Lelarge's *Appel à la France contre la division des opinions*. When first introduced in Lecture XI (285), Groen calls the (then still anonymous) work a "masterful survey of the Revolution, with clear insight into the interconnections between events seemingly the most diverse." Yet as he begins to quote it at length he does so only to show how

---

56. *Nouveaux essais de politique et de philosophie* (2 vols.: Paris and Berlin, 1824).

57. To clinch his victory, as it were, he would add two more quotations from Ancillon in the 2nd ed. (footnotes, pp. 278, 282) to show that Ancillon, too, at a certain point admits to the inevitability of the revolution.

it misinterprets the true nature of, for example, the *cahiers*. The famous *cahiers*, rather than revealing a "genuinely monarchical spirit," as the *Appel* contends, amounted to nothing short of a "declaration of war" on the monarchy. (For this contrary interpretation Groen chooses to quote the pithy formulation found in the *Geschichte der Staatsveränderung* discussed in our next paragraph below.) In the next lecture Groen employs rather lengthy citations from the *Appel* to demonstrate that it also fails to appreciate the essential significance of the events of 1789 and following. After approvingly quoting its sharp observations on the unlawful act by which the National Assembly was constituted and on the tyranny of revolutionary centralism and its elimination of every opposition (316, 322), Groen continues by commenting that these events, here so keenly characterized, are of course not to be interpreted as regrettable excesses but can and must be seen as perfectly consistent applications of the revolutionary theory about establishing the general will. Thus this work, too, is quoted only to show how well its author describes the revolution's events and yet how critically misleading he is in interpreting them.

The anonymous work that is cited to contradict the *Appel* regarding the *cahiers* had a subtitle which suggests that it may have been a favorite with Groen: *The Rise, Progress and Effects of the So-called New Philosophy in This Country*.[58] He had long been acquainted with it and had referred to it in the *Essay on Truth* for an illustration of the type of democratic recommendation made in the same *cahiers* (the king should appoint judges from nominations made by the people).[59] This time Groen makes use of it in Lecture XI (283), quoting from its pages several statements made by Turgot and Necker which clearly show—from their invoking of the *common good* as the criterion for public policy—that Louis XVI's advisers, too, were infected with the revolutionary ideology. In Lecture V (101, 105) Groen uses this work as a source for relativizing (if not belittling) the incidence of abuses under the old regime.[60] Groen appears to have owned only the first

58. *Geschichte der Staatsveränderung in Frankreich unter König Ludwig XVI; oder Entstehung, Fortschritt und Wirkungen der sogenannten neuen Philosophie in diesem Lande* (6 vols.; Leipzig, 1827–33). It was written by Carl Heinrich von Schütz; cf. Holzmann-Bohatta, *Deutsches Anonymen-Lexikon*, II, 193.

59. *Proeve* (1834), p. 202; earlier references in *Nederlandsche Gedachten*, 1831, III, 130, 171.

60. See also his numerous marginal notes citing this work in the manuscript *Study III*; published in *Bescheiden*, ed. Zwaan, pp. 509-21.

five volumes of the work[61]; yet even though these cover the story down to June 1791 he chooses not to refer to it for his own analysis of events from 1789 on. Nevertheless, broadly speaking, his interpretation accords well with the one presented in the German work, which stresses the impact of prevailing ideas on the coming of the revolution.

"I wish you would look through Wachsmuth on the French Revolution some time and compare it with Thiers." Thus wrote Professor Van Assen, who had spotted the histories by Alison and Thiers on Groen's table during his most recent visit, some months before the lectures commenced.[62] This hint proved most helpful. Not that there is any evidence that Groen's reading of the Geschichte Frankreichs im Revolutionszeitalter (4 vols.; Hamburg, 1840-1844) by Ernst Wilhelm Gottlieb Wachsmuth (1784-1866) caused any substantial shift in Groen's view of the revolution. At this late date, that would have been highly unlikely in any case. When he introduced the work to his audience that winter he spoke of its virtues of correctness and vividness yet also of its stamp of "faint liberalism" and of its "one-sided and superficial" treatment of the Restoration (Lecture XI, p. 274). Nevertheless, Wachsmuth's volumes did furnish Groen with certain materials derived from primary sources that could be used with good effect to support and illustrate his own overall conception. There were, for example, the statements by counsellors of Louis XIV, establishing that they already taught that kings were bound by a contract with their peoples (Lecture VI, p. 135). There was also the report to the National Assembly the day before feudalism was abolished, indicating clearly that already very early in the revolution the nobles faced anarchy throughout France (Lecture XII, p. 306). There were texts of speeches by Robespierre that reveal the genius par excellence of the Terror to have been moved by egalitarian idealism and moral earnestness—qualities that Groen is particularly eager to highlight in his portrait of the man who more than any other revolutionary leader was written off as a monstrous freak rather than appreciated as a faithful proponent and practitioner of revolutionary orthodoxy (Lecture XIII, pp. 340, 341, 347). There were to be found as well in the pages

---

61. Cf. Verslag van de aanwinsten der Koninklijke Bibliotheek gedurende het jaar 1881 (met inbegrip van de boekerij Groen van Prinsterer) (The Hague, 1882), p. 321.

62. Briefwisseling, II, 698, 702.

of Wachsmuth characteristic statements by Napoleon, showing how much the Emperor wished to see himself as embodying the nation—statements which Groen insists are not to be interpreted as cynical but as sincere, and above all as consistent: the sovereignty of the people, after all, was the basis of Napoleon's absolute authority and no liberal author may fault him for having used it to the full (Lecture XIV, pp. 378f). Finally, there were some typical quotes in Wachsmuth's pages from early nineteenth-century sympathizers with the revolution, exemplifying ways in which they sought to come to terms with the Reign of Terror: they range from Buchez's eulogy of the Jacobin regime as the glorious culmination of the revolution's humanitarian program, to Desmarais's condemnation of it as a barbaric deviation from the revolution's goal of establishing liberty (Lecture XIII, pp. 347, 355). Groen's reliance on the "faintly liberal" Wachsmuth is illustrative of his general utilization of authorities: they provide additional arguments that can be lifted off their pages regardless of their context, but in no way do they change Groen's mind as he elaborates his own case. Every new fact that comes to his attention is subordinated to his basic interpretation— just as he believed that in reality every fact had been subservient to the overriding cause.

The well-phrased summation, the witty epigram, the insightful quip were favorites of a man of Groen's tastes and erudition, and he noted hundreds of them during his many years of reading. Unless this be remembered one would find it passing strange to see Nodier quoted in a serious work of history. Charles Nodier (1780–1844), that precocious boy orator at Jacobin functions early in the revolution who later developed into a pioneer of romantic literature in France, seemed congenitally unable (or unwilling) to distinguish too sharply between historical fact and historical fiction. Known for his beguiling *Histoire secrète* about army plots against Napoleon, he fabricated a number of spurious memoirs during the 1820s to cover the hoax. His *Souvenirs, épisodes et portraits pour servir à l'histoire de la Révolution et de l'Empire* began to appear in serial form in the *Revue de Paris* from 1829 on and seemed designed to justify the principal actors of Revolutionary times, not excluding Robespierre and Napoleon. Yet when they were published under the collective title in 1831, the prominence of Nodier's own role in the recollected events aroused the suspicion in certain knowledgeable readers that he had abandoned the "original historiographical design in favor of a fictional one ..."[63] Was Groen aware of the dubious character of Nodier's *Souvenirs*? Did he trust him because he used to write in the *Journal des Débats* in its royalist days? But what difference does it make? Nodier's calling the Jacobins cruel but logical suited Groen's purpose exactly and so was reproduced verbatim, as were the almost touching details showing how Robespierre believed himself to have a clear conscience to the very end (Lecture XIII, 349, 361).[64]

Surprisingly, the works of Edmund Burke, which had caused the scales to fall from Groen's eyes in 1829-30,[65] are cited only sparingly. Whenever they are, however, it is done at crucial junctures in the argument, where the words of the great statesman provide solid backing to Groen's case. Burke's *Reflections* are quoted especially in Lecture XII (306, 313n, 315), where Groen analyzes the initial development of the revolution, a phase which neither in his nor in Burke's estimation deserves to be called a "moderate" phase. Support for the monarchy, for instance, though apparently widespread, was largely illusory. Instead, the power of republican principles was triumphing. Burke observed shrewdly and contemptuously that with the ancient orders destroyed the National Assembly inherited an immense authority based on counting heads. Already in the *Reflections*, which dates from November 1790, Burke was able to point to "treasons, robberies, rapes, assassinations, slaughters and burnings," authorized with little opposition. Groen copies a long footnote from the *Reflections*—Lally-Tollendal's horror story of 6 October 1789—to illustrate how powerless the moderates really were at that early date, and how irresistible were the radicals—"the most vehement party"—as they set the course events would take.

Earlier, in Lectures IV (90f) and V (106), it is with an appeal to Burke that Groen confidently maintains that the old regime was perfectly susceptible of reform, that its abuses were greatly exaggerated, and that no revolution—at any rate, no wholesale *social* revolution—was required to rectify

---

63. Cf. A. Richard Oliver, *Charles Nodier: Pilot of Romanticism* (Syracuse University Press, 1964), pp. 78f, 200-202.

64. In the 2nd edition Groen would add nine more footnotes quoting in particular Nodier's relative praise of Robespierre as the courageous opponent of licentious atheism; see footnotes, 2nd ed., pp. 354, 355, 356, and 311, 319, 323, 347.

65. See his glowing account in *Nederlandsche Gedachten*, 1875/74, V, 323-36.

any existing wrongs. He concludes Lecture V on the Burkean note that *the*
revolution must have had a "*theoretic* origin," and the following week he
leads off with the thesis that the revolution was born of "... doctrine, of a
philosophic *theory* ..." This is, of course, the key to the whole interpretation,
and it is so much part of Groen's mind that he does not credit Burke with
the notion until ... Lecture XI, in a footnote added only in the 2nd edition!
There, sandwiched between other quotations, appears Burke's final verdict, in a single sentence: "*It is a Revolution of doctrine and theoretic dogma.*"[66]
The sentence is lifted from the *Thoughts on French Affairs*, the first work
of Burke's which Groen ever read and which, as he recalled later, became
his *vade-mecum* in the fall of 1829 when he witnessed the alarming tide of
liberalism in Brussels.

Burke might have been quoted more frequently if Groen had not run
out of time. Forced to compress his view of international affairs into a short
section at the beginning of the final lecture, he sketches the evil effects of
revolutionary thinking on Europe's international law and international
relations. A criminal faction, says Groen, had withdrawn revolutionary
France from the European family of nations, while the opposing Coalition
partners (England excepted) were more out to enlarge themselves than
to punish the offender. It is, again, not until the 2nd edition twenty years
later that he supplies supporting footnotes with trenchant formulations
taken from the second (he mistakenly says: the third) of Burke's *Letters on
a Regicide Peace*: Revolutionary France was by no means a legitimate state
but a nation held hostage by a "sect of fanatical and ambitious atheists ...
aiming at universal empire ..."[67]

From Groen's reliance on Burke one is tempted to conclude that *Unbelief
and Revolution* is very much an elaboration of the tracts to which the
founder of conservatism owes his greatest fame.[68] The sole (but significant) difference between the two (other than the obvious fact that Groen
carries the story of the revolution down to his own time) is that *Unbelief
and Revolution* in addition provides a theologico-philosophical account

---

66. See footnote, 2nd ed., p. 251 (emphasis in the original).

67. See footnotes, 2nd ed., pp. 404, 405.

68. In his twilight years Groen once did the *Reflections* the honour of referring to it as "a
pamphlet which, as a Christian-historical protest against the revolution, is of world-historical
significance." *Nederlandsche Gedachten*, 1871, III, 192.

of the path by which the impugned "theoretic dogma" had evolved from infidelity to the gospel. That brings us to another one of Groen's sources.

Whereas Burke had identified fanatical atheism as the "principal feature of the French Revolution," a verdict which Groen is glad to quote in Lecture VIII (199), it was not from Burke that Groen had learned to dissect Enlightenment thought and trace the connection—the intellectual links—between rationalism and atheism. This he had learned from Lamennais.[69] Hugues Félicité Robert de Lamennais (1782-1854), before he turned into a passionate democrat, had written equally passionate yet devoutly Catholic treatises such as the *Essai sur l'indifférence en matière de religion* (4 vols.; 1817-1823) and *Des Progrès de la révolution et de la guerre contre l'église* (1829). Especially the youthful *Essay on Indifference* served Groen well in demonstrating how eighteenth-century rationalism had of necessity to evolve from skepticism, through phases of deism and irreligion, to militant atheism. Thus the entire *exposé* of rationalist religion and morality as set out in Lecture VIII—including the telling quotations from Rousseau, Raynal and Bolingbroke—is taken directly from the scintillating pages of Lamennais, as is the deduction in Lecture IX of arbitrary innovationism and political radicalism from the new theory of liberty and equality. These twin chapters constitute the "natural history" of the revolutionary ideology and are therefore of crucial importance to Groen's argument. It is Lamennais who is the chief author he draws on in these lectures, and in the following chapter, the pivotal Lecture X, he gratefully records how the author of the *Essay on Indifference* also unravels the practical consequences of the revolutionary ideology for the contemporary scene; "I should not finish," says Groen there (227), "if I wished to bring together all the striking passages ... in which he so eloquently describes the malady of the age": our age has come to disdain truth and has made numb all sense of religion and morality.

---

69. For the German part of this story, Groen relies in particular on a lengthy essay by August Tholuck, "Abrisz einer Geschichte der Umwälzung, welche seit 1750 auf dem Gebiete der Theologie in Deutschland stattgefunden," first published in the review *Litterarische Anzeiger* 7 (1836): 345ff and reprinted in Tholuck, *Vermischte Schriften* (1839), II, 1-147. Groen's sketch of the rise of German liberal theology since 1750, given in response to a critical observation by one of his auditors, was inserted at the beginning of Lecture IX but not included in the printed version of the lectures; cf. chapter 7 below, note 10.

Perhaps it was precisely because of his heavy dependence on the early Lamennais that Groen felt it necessary to dissociate himself in very clear terms from Lamennais's Roman Catholic sympathies and consequent misrepresentation of the Reformation. This he does in Lecture VII (153) on the Reformation, where on this question Lamennais is lumped with De Maistre and De Bonald and all other Catholics who not only see the Reformation as a revolt against authority but who also draw a direct line from 1517 to 1789. This flaw in his witness for the prosecution, though serious, is not fatal in Groen's eyes. In keeping with his professed "eclecticism" he once wrote about Lamennais's other work that had meant so much to him: replace its ultramontanism with the pure gospel and substitute Scripture wherever it talks of the Pope, and you have a book that every Christian can read with profit![70]

The book referred to is *Des Progrès*. In 1829 it had meant at least as much to Groen as the works of Burke—a handbook for constant reference, always within reach. Though this inflammatory work, he noted later, had intensified the revolutionary aspirations of the day, notably among Belgian liberals and Catholics, nevertheless its intention had been to combat unbelief. The tract was of great help to Groen at the time in his initial struggle to understand the true nature of liberalism, for its analysis persuaded him of three cardinal conclusions: that the revolution must destroy all social bonds inasmuch as it represents the practical denial of God and the negation of everything that rests upon belief; that the supremacy of reason always leads to spiritual anarchy; and that the practical outcome of mankind's emancipation from God oscillates between anarchy and tyranny.[71]

In spite of Lamennais's altered reputation by 1845, Groen does not hesitate to quote from his *Progrès*. Statements from this work turn up particularly in Lecture X (237, 250), where Groen tries to demonstrate at great length how the see-saw between anarchy and tyranny is inevitable once the divine right of government has been denied. Strategic use is made as well of long passages in which Lamennais argues the futility of seeking to safeguard liberty by means of the doctrine of individual rights as propounded by contemporary authors like Benjamin Constant and Guizot.

---

70. Cf. *Nederlandsche Gedachten*, 1873/74, V, 306.
71. Cf. *Nederlandsche Gedachten*, 1873/74, V, 245f, 304, 306-11, 321-23.

Originally these passages must have helped Groen—and he is sure they will now help his audience—not to be tempted to take his stand in the *juste milieu* but rather to strike out for a radically different third way. It is clear from the use he makes of Lamennais that Groen especially appreciates his ability to argue cogently for the absolute necessity of a doctrine of divine right—of respect for the *given* order for society and law—if liberty is to be preserved. Groen has no difficulty invoking this Catholic author's interpretation of that all-important text in Romans 13, which he does in Lecture III (56) with words from, again, the *Essay on Indifference*. On this foundation the Protestant and the Catholic take their common stand against what they see as the forces from the abyss.

Nothing quite illustrated the abyss so graphically as the emergence of modern socialism. A work that is introduced in Lecture IX as "exceedingly helpful in illustrating the character of the Revolution" bears the title *Conspiration pour l'égalité dite de Babeuf* (2 vols.; 1828). Its subject was an object of reverence during working-class uprisings in Paris in 1848 and again in 1871 and holds a special place in Communist literature to this day. Its author, Philippe (Filippo) Buonarrotti (1761-1837), was neither a historian nor a revolutionist but a music teacher, with in fact an eighteenth-century rationalist cast of mind. A participant in the Conspiracy of the Equals, Buonarrotti wrote what was essentially an elaborate apologia, complete with "pièces justificatives," of the abortive communist *coup* of 1796 and its guillotined ring-leader François-Noël ("Gracchus") Babeuf. The reliability of the work (which was translated before long into English by Bronterre O'Brien for the edification of Chartists[72]) does not extend beyond that of memoirs written late in life in the service of a cause and in memory of a long departed comrade. It is certainly helpful to Groen as he argues the "logical irreproachability" of the position of those whom he classes among the *ultras* of the revolution (Lecture II, 219-22). For Babeuf's accomplice and apologist indeed paints a convincing picture of the inevitable radicalization of the revolution: according to Buonarrotti, the principle of equality implies a radical movement toward socialism, a movement which cannot be halted just because the economic interests of the middle classes have

---

72. See our Select Bibliography under Buonarrotti.

been satisfied; *sans-culottism* is the wave of the future, and the Friends of Equality, an enlightened vanguard, succumbed only under the superior force of bourgeois violence. The warning is ominous in its clarity, says Groen in Lecture IX (222): admit the revolutionary view of freedom and equality, and the logical consequence is nothing short of communism. In Lecture XIII he quotes Buonarrotti frequently (339, 356–59) in order to show his celebration of Robespierre as a martyr in the cause of equality and as a loyal pupil of his master Rousseau. Other quotations (350–52) are given to show his unabashed justification of the September massacres, of the proscription of the Girondins, in fact of every extra-legal measure found "deplorable but necessary" during the Terror in the interest of preserving liberty and preparing the day of full equality. The work is also Groen's source for the text of the still-born Declaration of Rights of 1793 and of speeches by Robespierre extolling virtue, popular sovereignty, and the pre-eminence of the general will over private property (357–59). No doubt what Groen appreciated about this work, next to its portrayal of the inner logic of revolutionary thought, was its uninhibited confession of the principles from which such extreme conclusions were rationally derived. These features made it especially valuable for supporting his interpretation of the Reign of Terror in Lecture XIII.[73]

Our examination of Groen as a working historian yields some definite conclusions. The sources he uses and the way he uses them combine to create a patchwork of views and opinions that is fairly representative of major themes in the debate on the French Revolution up to his time. Apart from accounts by certain well-known eyewitnesses, participants and contemporary commentators (Necker and his daughter, Burke, Buonarrotti, Nodier), he relies exclusively on secondary sources. Some of these have scholarly pretensions (Guizot, Mignet, Thiers, Schütz), but anonymous pamphlets by Restoration publicists are not spurned. In a masterfully orchestrated discussion of views and counterviews Groen's sustained polemic summons up a variety of authors at will, eclectically quoting them

---

73. Lecture XIII is a chapter that Groen appears to have spent much time on. The longest in the series, it contains pages with some of the most impassioned prose in the entire book and was literally written down with trembling hand. See his complaint in *Briefwisseling*, II, 731.

out of their immediate contexts so long as they bolster his case. Where liberal writers are mutually contradictory they are allowed to say their piece in order to cancel each other out. Groen guides his audience through the labyrinth by means of the continuous thread identified at the start of the investigation. Thus the details supplied by his sources are marshalled specifically to illustrate the *irresistible* sweep of the revolutionary tide under the driving force of the regnant *ideas*. Other themes (the weakness of key actors, the greed for patronage, the threat of invasion, the impact of inflation, etc.), if mentioned at all, are swiftly and deftly annexed in behalf of Groen's own interpretation. What sympathizers with the revolution describe as accidental excesses Groen insists on portraying as necessary consequences.—Indeed we are watching a practicing historian at work who respects facts and weighs evidence yet for all that is an engaged publicist bent on drawing out what recent history *teaches*.

In summary we can say that *Unbelief and Revolution* is a synthesis of evidence in support of a vision, a bringing to bear upon a single question— *What is the Revolution?*—a mass of diverse material gathered in support of a prior interpretation. This interpretation had first been recorded in 1831 and had been reinforced during a decade of extensive reading when a basic outline for its presentation had taken shape and much material was collected for future use: key formulations—a phrase, a passage—to quote, issues to address, interpretations to refute. Thus the work of 1847 is not just a vision thrown on paper, as it were, but a long-standing personal interpretation carefully buttressed by facts selected from a fund of detailed knowledge of the event in question as well as from a thorough acquaintance with the historiography of that event. It is the mature work of a historian-publicist who put it together not merely to instruct and inform, but above all to understand and to warn. Convinced of the utter relevance of recent history, he had resolved to present the truth as he saw it in accordance with the accepted canons of historical scholarship. The result was a serious work of historical interpretation constructed from a select number of respectable (and a few not so respectable) historical sources. But unlike conventional scientific history the work was at the same time a philosophical treatise and a socio-political manifesto. The combination of all these elements accounts for the book's attractive but also controversial character.

7
—
AUDIENCE

In an age not blessed with electronic media, lecture attendance seems to have been a popular pastime. Da Costa virtually made his living holding series of lectures on advertised subjects to which one subscribed at a fee often at one's own discretion. After the Belgian Revolt, he had opened with a series of public lectures on Dutch history (attended, among others, by Koenen, who sent copious notes to Groen). Da Costa's themes were the pious memories of Old Holland, God's providential rule in the history of the fatherland, and the signs in past and present of Christ's imminent return. He held these lectures in Amsterdam, but at friends' urging began them in Haarlem and Utrecht as well; the latter were continued well into the fifties. In January of 1845, on Groen's invitation, Da Costa started a bi-weekly public lecture series in The Hague, which had an average audience of 250 men and women.[1] Another series was given in 1845/46 (thus during the same season when Groen's private series on unbelief and revolution was running), and still another in 1846/47. The first series in The Hague dealt with *The Apostle Paul and His Epistles* and the second had as topic *Christ According to the Gospels*. They were held every other Thursday and Groen attended them faithfully.[2]

Da Costa's friends followed suit, though on a much more modest scale and in the privacy of their homes. For example, when Koenen became city councillor in 1842 and soon thereafter curator of his alma mater, the Amsterdam Atheneum (precursor of the City University), he took an active

---

1. Cf. Da Costa to Groen, 20 Nov. 1844: "I have no objection to any publicity the friends deem proper. I am quite content with the designated hall; the presence of ladies I think perfectly fine." *Brieven van Da Costa*, I, 190f.

2. Cf. *Briefwisseling*, II, 637, 640, 645, 653, 660, 730, 941; *Brieven van Da Costa*, I, 188–94, 249, 349; III, 183, 194, 202–5, 207, 208, 251.

interest in the students and for years had a group of them come to his home every other week for "tea lectures" on history and literature.[3]

As for Groen van Prinsterer, he was no stranger to this sort of role either. He had led Bible studies at his house, for which he used to prepare himself thoroughly; often he would see to it that prior to the meeting "theses for discussion" were delivered to the members of the group. Lecturing on a learned topic in history and politics, however, was a new thing to him.

From the beginning it was Groen's intention to hold his lectures on unbelief and revolution privately, in his study, to a select number of intimate friends—so privately in fact that certain members of the inner circle of Réveil brothers in The Hague got to know about the plan only indirectly. This we learn from a letter by Capadose to Da Costa. "I haven't written you anything about Groen's plan to give lectures," Capadose rambled to his friend in Amsterdam,

> but you wouldn't take it ill of me, dear friend, if you knew how things went over here. It was all very muted. You know that our good friend is overly afraid of appearing pretentious. In this matter, too, he had suggested the *possibility* to only one of us in a few lines, adding that it would be all right to confidentially inform any other brother he might meet. In this way we all gradually got to hear about it and since I receive a note from our beloved friend almost every day, in which he mentioned nothing of the plan, I spoke to him about it one time and then he assured me that the only reason he had not written me earlier about it was that he had forgotten the whole matter, which he had mentioned only to Elout—and this is the literal truth, as I noticed again just yesterday; he had sat with me as usual and though I was still half ill had talked most entertainingly about all sorts of things; afterwards we were joined by Singendonck and before we parted we talked yet about your lecture series and then, when he was already at the door, he turns back, and

---

3. Kluit, *Het Protestants Réveil in Nederland en daarbuiten*, p. 416. A number of these lectures resulted in respectable historical monographs on such subjects as Jews in the Netherlands (1843), Dutch trade (1853), industry (1856), mercantile policy (1857) and the Dutch agricultural class (1858).

with that childlike simplicity of his and actually blushing, he takes my hand and says: I should be very pleased if you would be able to attend my first lecture this Saturday.

Apparently Capadose was beginning to feel better when he wrote this to Da Costa, for he concluded his account by informing him that he hoped "to be able to go—even though I shall have to take a carriage, which I don't use very often because it runs into such high costs."[4]

Unfortunately we have to do without certain colorful details. For example, who would greet the invited guests at the door and conduct them upstairs[5] to the "book-room"? Was tea or coffee served, and if so, before, during or after the session? Did the men smoke their pipes, or did they confine themselves to snuff? This kind of *couleur locale* can only be guessed at, alas.

The party that sat and listened in the spacious "book-room" or study of Groen's home numbered twelve for the first three lectures but grew to a size of twenty-one. They included Groen's two brothers-in-law; a dozen or so friends, some of whom he had known since university days and who were now prominent civil servants, members of parliament or judges; three barristers; two university professors; and two physicians. It is interesting to take a closer look at each, assisted in part by the research done by Bastiaan de Gaay Fortman (1884–1961).[6] The first group that merits attention consists of men who had been Groen's friends since university days at Leyden. They were Boreel, De Greve, Delprat, and Philipse.

Willem Boreel van Hogelanden (1800–83) was a member of the Second Chamber and would later serve as its speaker in the unsettled days of March 1848.[7] He was speaker again in 1851–55 when the government leader Thorbecke once stated that a member of the opposition (Groen van Prinsterer) was really "out of order" most of the time for insisting on mixing religion with politics; the speaker, however, let Groen have

---

4. De Gaay Fortman, *Figuren uit het Réveil*, p. 379n62.

5. Cf. *Briefwisseling*, IV, 927.

6. *Figuren uit het Réveil*, esp. pp. 436–54, which is a reprint of the article "Groen van Prinsterer's voorlezingen over ongeloof en revolutie," which appeared in *Anti-Revolutionaire Staatkunde* (quarterly edition) 14 (1940): 35–57.

7. Boogman, *Rondom 1848*, p. 30.

his say. A few years later he would become governor of the province of North Holland. At one time a disciple of Bilderdijk, whose lectures he had attended at the same time as Groen, Boreel had developed into a moderate liberal.

Frans de Greve (1803-77) had been professor in the Atheneum of Franeker from 1828 until the year before it closed its doors in 1842. Appointed to the Supreme Court in that year, he would become its vice-president in 1855 and soon thereafter its president.[8] In church matters he tended to side with the irenic party and valued piety above doctrinal precision. It was De Greve who objected orally to Groen's ideal of church-state cooperation as outlined toward the end of Lecture III. After the session Groen tried to answer him more fully in writing, but De Greve wrote back that the meddling of the modern Dutch state with the Reformed Church went "much too far," whereas on the other hand he could not approve either of the "exaggerated North American institution of the isolation of church and state."[9] Responding to Lecture VIII, De Greve also wondered whether Groen was not generalizing for all of Europe what may have been true only of France. Groen's answer[10] was given at the beginning of Lecture IX but not included in the book.[11]

Guillaume Delprat (1801-1900) was a practicing lawyer who later joined the Ministry of Finance as advisor. A deacon in the Walloon Church of The Hague, he found his spiritual nourishment in the Réveil.

Johan Antoni Philipse (1800-84) at this time was vice-chairman of the Supreme Court of South Holland; in 1849 he would become its president. Appointed to the First Chamber in 1850, he served as its speaker till 1870. Conservative in outlook and political allegiance, he was married to Groen's younger sister.[12]

Also present was the man who had married Groen's older sister, Marie Aert Frédéric Henri Hoffman (1795-1874), a Rotterdam merchant

---

8. *Briefwisseling*, II, 402n; *Nederland's Patriciaat anno 1918*, vol. 9, p. 140.

9. *Briefwisseling*, II, 714.

10. Algemeen Rijksarchief, The Hague, Archief Groen van Prinsterer, No. 59; Eng. trans. of this fragment in G. Groen van Prinsterer, *Unbelief in Religion and Politics* (Amsterdam, 1975), pp. 76-79.

11. Cf. *Briefwisseling*, II, 967; Mackay Notebook (see end of this chapter), p. 58.

12. Cf. *Nieuw Nederlandsch Biografisch Woordenboek* (Amsterdam, 1911-37), VIII, 1253; hereafter cited as *NNBW*.

and a member since the previous year of the First Chamber, which he would exchange for the Second Chamber (1850-73), where he often sided with anti-revolutionary members in educational matters.[13]

Then comes a pair of men of decided anti-revolutionary leanings: Gefken and Singendonck.

Jan Willem Gefken (1807-87) was installed as solicitor-general in the Court of The Hague on 10 November 1845. Soon after, he became a regular attendant at the lectures. Gefken had studied law in Amsterdam and Leyden and had befriended H. J. Koenen. Intellectually he had broken with liberalism under the influence of Groen's *Nederlandsche Gedachten* which he read while serving with the volunteer corps during the Belgian Revolt. Of Lutheran origin, his nominal faith had been stirred back to life under the sermons he went to hear in the Walloon Church by pastor Secrétan. He was a charter member of the Abolition Society. Gefken respected Groen as an evangelical and a historian but would grow critical of his contributions to practical politics. He would distinguish himself as attorney-general with the Ministry of Justice in Surinam between 1856-67, and return to The Hague to take a seat in the Second Chamber between 1868-69. Gefken was loath to commit himself to any "party" and never followed the growing radicalism of the aging Groen.[14]

Johan Anne Singendonck (1809-93) was employed as clerk with the Council of State. In 1850 he would become recording secretary of the First Chamber. Fully of one mind with his host at this time, he enjoyed the "sublime poetry" contained in Groen's evening lectures and wrote about it to Da Costa (whose winter lectures in The Hague he organized and administered). In later years Singendonck was to take more distance from Groen and become an adherent of the irenic school which advocated exerting a *moral* influence for good in church and nation and disapproved more and more of the anti-revolutionaries' insistence on *legal* rights and *organizational* safeguards for preserving the Christian character of the national institutions.[15]

---

13. De Gaay Fortman, *Figuren uit het Réveil*, p. 441; see also *NNBW*, V, 238.

14. De Gaay Fortman, *Figuren uit het Réveil*, pp. 93-114, 200-19.

15. *Ibid.*, pp. 45-60.

Close contacts from the Réveil brotherhood were Gevaerts, Gevers, Voûte, and Ernst van Bylandt.

Leonard Robert Gevaerts (1774-1864), a lawyer by training,[16] had been a member of the provincial government of Holland since 1815, where he tried in vain to get a favorable hearing for appeals by Groen and his friends to intervene on their behalf against local authorities who refused permission to establish a private Christian school. A member of the Réveil brothers of The Hague, Gevaerts took part in their communal activities. Gevaerts's signature is the first to appear under the request to the king for a charter for an Abolition Society in 1842.

Marinus Benudinus Helenus Gevers (1789-1873) had been a member of the audit department since 1822 and would become the auditor general in 1851.[17] A Réveil brother, he had cosigned the overture to Synod in 1842 drawn up by Groen. Gevers had also attended the first meeting earlier in the year of the "Christian Friends."

Jean Pierre Estienne Voûte (1793-1851) had been touched by the awakening through reading the periodical *Nederlandsche Stemmen*. He was born in Amsterdam of French stock and had studied in Edinburgh between 1810–14; awarded an M.A., he had transferred to Leyden where he completed a doctorate in mathematics and physics after another four years. Since then he had devoted himself to an academic career.[18] Before resigning his professorship for reasons of health, he had taught philosophy, physics and astronomy in the Atheneum of Amsterdam for a decade, during which time he attended Da Costa's lectures on Dutch history. Since 1834 he had been living in The Hague in semi-retirement, spending his days as philanthropist and evangelist by visiting the poor with material and spiritual aid.[19] A meek man, he wondered about the legitimacy of polemical journalism, also as practiced by Groen: How can the Christian submit himself to the authorities and honor the king, as is his duty, yet freely pass judgment on government action? he asked Groen by letter after the second session.[20]

---

16. *Nederlands Adelsboek*, 1913, vol. 11, p. 407.
17. *NNBW*, III, 466.
18. De Gaay Fortman, *Figuren uit het Réveil*, pp. 406–10.
19. Kluit, *Het Protestantse Réveil in Nederland en daarbuiten*, p. 394.
20. *Briefwisseling*, II, 711f.

Ernst Ferdinand Hubert Marcus van Bylandt (1813–71) had studied medicine in Bonn (until his naturalization his name was written as "von"). Born in the Rhineland of Catholic nobility, he had joined the revival in Germany through the influence of his mother. Late 1840 he had set up a practice in The Hague. As a member of the Walloon Church he had become very involved in the activities of the Réveil circle and also developed personal friendships with some of its members, particularly the Groens. He was Groen's (and Elout's) doctor and in 1851 would be appointed personal physician to Prince Frederick, the late king's brother.[21] In the years 1855–57 Count van Bylandt would be one of the foremost founding members of the German Evangelical Church in The Hague.[22] In 1866 the former Prussian subject would side with Groen (against many Christian conservatives in both The Hague and Berlin) when his friend detected "the Revolution" at work in Bismarck's successful foreign policy of aggression.[23]

Distinctly not of Groen's political school were the following four men with whom Groen would have social or business contact and who may well have been invited for courtesy's sake: Eugène van Bylandt, Gockinga, Noordziek, and Vollenhoven.

Eugène Jean Alexander van Bylandt (1807–76), a brother of Ernst, was referendary of the Royal Cabinet, a position Groen had held a decade and a half earlier. In 1848 he would become governor of the province of South Holland, and later of the province of Overyssel. A follower of Thorbecke, he was a faithful churchgoer and a man of truly liberal principles, who used his office to promote greater freedom and tolerance especially in the area of education.[24]

Campegius Hermanus Gockinga (1804–82) hailed from Groningen and the year before had been appointed justice in the Supreme Court in The

21. De Gaay Fortman, *Figuren uit het Réveil*, pp. 46, 419, 430, 444; *NNBW*, IV, 376; *Briefwisseling*, II, 233, 250-52, 328, 334; III, 367; IV, 374, 924; V, 262, 541, 585, 691.

22. Paul von Tschudi, *Geschichte der deutschen evangelischen Gemeinde im Haag* (Göttingen, 1932), pp. 12-26.

23. *Briefwisseling*, III, 845n; IV, 3; see also IV, 43-90; H. Smitskamp, "Groen van Prinsterer en de politick van Bismarck," *Antirevolutionaire Staatkunde* 10 (1936): 112-93. Cf. *Neue Preussische Kreuzzeitung*, 18 April 1867, and the *Pall Mall Gazette*, 27 April 1867, for reactions to Groen's broadside, *La Prusse et les Pays-Bas; à mes amis de Berlin* (Amsterdam, Paris, Geneva, 1867).

24. *Briefwisseling*, II, 459, 801, 887f, 933-35, 954f; *NNBW*, IV, 376.

Hague. A brilliant jurist, he was a Christian of practical inclination and unassuming deportment.[25]

Jan Jacobus Frederik Noordziek (1811–86) had been second librarian at the *Koninklijke Bibliotheek* in The Hague since 1840. Two years hence he would become editor of the *Nederlandsche Staatscourant* and afterward supervisor of the parliamentary stenographers. A professional relationship may well have been the main reason for Groen to have invited Noordziek and for the latter to have accepted, for there is no evidence of spiritual kinship. In fact, Noordziek later turns up as a member of the Grand Lodge of the Masonic Order in the Netherlands.[26]

Hendrik Vollenhoven (1816–89) did not participate until halfway through the series. Perhaps it was young Hendrik's father, who remembered Groen from government circles in Brussels in the days of the Revolution of 1830, who had requested that his son be invited.[27] Employed since 1840 at the Ministry of Internal Affairs, Vollenhoven Junior would be promoted in 1848 to become head of the new Subdepartment of Education, where he was an influential civil servant for thirty-three years, bearing chief responsibility, among other things, for drafting the school bill of 1857 that would cause so much grief to the supporters of Christian education. Raised in the Remonstrant church, he was also in other respects no co-religionist of Groen's.[28]

Two listeners of the Bilderdijk school were Capadose and De Quertenmont.

Abraham Capadose (1795–1874) had settled in The Hague in 1833. Having given up his doctor's practice, he spent his days organizing Bible evenings at his home and writing pamphlets against small-pox vaccination, desecration of houses of prayer by music festivals, and other matters that roused his ire. A true son of Bilderdijk, he would not make use of his constitutional right to vote since that would make him an "accessory to the Revolution." After the second lecture Capadose wrote Groen to complain that he had emphasized his differences with Bilderdijk more than his agreement; in

---

25. *Briefwisseling*, II, 813; *NNBW*, V, 203.
26. *Briefwisseling*, II, 809; *NNBW*, IV, 1033.
27. De Gaay Fortman, *Figuren uit het Réveil*, p. 422.
28. *Briefwisseling*, II, 809.

fact, was not the theme of the lectures the same as the message Bilderdijk had protested to the world for almost half a century?[29]

C. D. A. de Quertenmont (1806–81), born in Brussels and also trained in Belgium, had studied law in Leyden for a brief spell and become a disciple of Bilderdijk. He had held a position in the Registry Office of The Hague since 1831 and in 1847 would move to a similar position in Dordrecht. He was introduced to Groen by Capadose after two sessions had already been held.[30]

One listener who is difficult to categorize was Anthony Jacob van der Heim (1809–46). Of noble descent, Van der Heim was recording secretary of the Second Chamber at this time.[31] He had studied in Leyden where he completed a doctoral dissertation in 1834 on Anthony Heinsius (whose correspondence with William III had been in the possession of the Van der Heim family). Groen's lectures made a deep impression on Van der Heim and he summarized a number of them in correspondence with a friend at the Dutch embassy in London.[32] Van der Heim died some time during 1846, thus a year before the lectures were published; consequently his name does not appear under the communal letter of thanks sent to Groen by all auditors on 30 October 1847.[33]

By far Groen's closest comrades were Elout and Mackay.

Pieter Jacob Elout van Soeterwoude (1805–93) had just begun his career as justice in the Provincial Court at The Hague, after filling a number of functions connected with the Council of State and with the Crown Prince in the latter's function of commander-in-chief of the armed forces (in which capacity Elout had once refused the use of his unit for being billeted in homes of Seceders). Elout's father had served the state in a number of high positions, including the governorship of the East Indies; the son would later edit and publish four collections of documents relating to colonial history and policy drawn from Elout Senior's estate. Elout Junior, as we have seen, belonged to the inner circle of the Réveil brothers of The Hague and

---

29. *Briefwisseling*, II, 713.

30. *Briefwisseling*, II, 257, 821, 909, 944.

31. *BWN*, IX, 353.

32. *Briefwisseling*, II, 27n5, 430n4, 814.

33. This circumstance may explain why he was not included among the listeners enumerated by De Gaay Fortman, who wrote his article many years before Volume II of the *Briefwisseling* was published.

participated in its activities for church and school reforms. In the Second
Chamber, where he would hold a seat between 1853 and 1862, he spoke on
a wide range of topics and distinguished himself especially in debates
defending freedom of education and urging reform of the exploitative
Cultivation System in the Indies (the obligation of the natives to grow certain crops prescribed by the colonial government). Other causes that were
to find their champion in Pieter Elout were open access to the colonies for
Christian missions, retention of capital punishment for more than treason
and first-degree murder, emancipation of slaves, and abolition of the state
lottery. His appointment to the Council of State was to follow in 1864. He
retired ten years later.[34]

Aeneas Mackay (1806–76) at this time was referendary with the Council
of State. He was the descendant of a colonel who had come over from
Scotland in the second half of the seventeenth century to command a
Mackay Regiment in the service of the Dutch Republic. His father had
been raised to the Dutch peerage in the days of the Restoration, and
shortly thereafter had inherited through the maternal line the seigniory of
Ophemert and Zennewijnen in Gelderland. Aeneas's doctorate was earned
in Utrecht with a "historical-political" dissertation on the Triple Alliance of
1668. He dated his conversion from 1830 and had attended Secrétan's Friday
evenings since 1840. Aeneas would be a member of the Second Chamber in
1848 and again from 1850–62; his parliamentary speeches would do much to
propagate the political philosophy and program of the anti-revolutionaries
in its opposition to such policies and practices as the following: bureaucratic centralism, in part alleviated only by a "rational" policy of uniform
decentralization; public relief that would absorb the church's diaconal
ministry as well as private philanthropy; slavery and opium traffic in the
colonies, and the protection of Islam against Christian evangelism there; a
system of common, public, non-sectarian schools financed from the public
purse and regulated by public authorities who continued to refuse permission to establish private Christian schools in spite of constitutional freedom of education. In church matters Mackay defended the right, if not the
wisdom, of Secession, and like Groen he fought for many years against the
confessional erosion of the Reformed Church, of which he was a lifelong

---

34. De Gaay Fortman, *Figuren uit het Réveil*, pp. 319, 331; *Briefwisseling*, II, 684.

member (though he attended the German church in the latter years of his
life, when modernism was becoming too blatant in the Reformed pulpits
of The Hague). In 1848 he would translate a German work, *On the Rise of
Radicalism and Communism*, which he published with a foreword outlining
the practical implications of the Christian-historical school for Dutch politics as distinct from the progressive liberalism which had just triumphed
in March of that year. (This foreword is a direct echo of Groen's *Unbelief
and Revolution*.) Another practical contribution of Mackay's consisted of
many articles on political subjects written for the periodical *De Vereeniging:
Christelijke Stemmen* between 1850-56. Since 1835 Mackay had been "gentleman in waiting" to the Crown Prince and his wife, sister of the Czar of
Russia, a function from which he would resign in 1846 because of depress-
ing domestic quarrels. After his years in parliament, he was appointed
vice-president of the Council of State in 1862 and would remain on that
body till his death.[35]

Finally, the audience included Van der Kemp, perhaps one of Groen's
closest associates and correspondents at this time of his life.

Carel Maria van der Kemp (1799-1862) was a deputy district judge.
He would spend the last few years of his life as justice in the Provincial
Court of South Holland. Van der Kemp, we recall, distinguished himself
in the struggle for church reform; already ten years earlier he had written a sharp attack against the Groningen School in which he charged that
every Reformed minister who ignored the teachings of Dordt was guilty
of breaking his oath to uphold them. In 1837 he had entered the lists on
Groen's side to defend the latter's condemnation of the government measures against the Seceders.[36] He had cosigned the petition to Synod of 1842.
Like Groen, Van der Kemp had studied law and letters at Leyden, and had

---

35. De Gaay Fortman, *Figuren uit het Réveil*, pp. 147-99. Mackay's private journals, containing much inside information on parliamentary crises and cabinet formations during
1853-70, have been capably abstracted by J. P. Duyverman, *Uit de geheime dagboeken van Aeneas
Mackay, dienaar des Konings 1806-1876* (Houten: De Haan/Unieboeken, 1987). For interest's
sake it may also be recorded here that Aeneas Mackay's nephew, also called Aeneas, headed
the first confessional cabinet, 1888-91, and that Mackay's son Donald returned to the land of
his forefathers when the Dutch branch inherited the title of Lord Reay: Donald Mackay took
his seat in the House of Lords as a Liberal, was appointed Governor of Bombay by Gladstone's
Third Ministry, 1885-90, and served briefly as undersecretary for India, 1894/95. Cf. De Gaay
Fortman, "Een Liberaal van anti-revolutionaire huize," pp. 113-23.

36. *Brieven van Da Costa*, I, 42.

earned his doctorate there in 1822. He came from a long line of staunch supporters of Orange and warm defenders of Calvinism, which he himself had come to love early in his writing career through historical studies. These studies had borne fruit in what were really so many volumes of pleas-for-the-defense, supplemented by reams of authentic documents, vindicating Prince Maurice and other heroes of 1618/19.[37] On occasion Van der Kemp assisted Groen in deciphering letters-in-code for publication in the *Archives*.[38] The Tuesday after the first lecture had been held, Van der Kemp let Groen know that he did not believe the correlation between the revolution and material decline always held: were not the very countries most influenced by the revolutionary principles now witnessing a strong increase in wealth and luxury, while a return to anti-revolutionary principles, though morally imperative, might well prove materially disadvantageous? After the second lecture he wrote that in his view Grotius had not been so historically minded when he introduced the notion of abstract human rights—thus anticipating Groen's estimate of Grotius in Lecture VI (132–34). Having heard Lecture X, Van der Kemp reminded Groen that, next to the drive for self-preservation, surely the presence of devout Christians prevented the revolutionary theory from ever coming to full development.[39]

So much for the twenty-one who were in attendance at the lectures. The mixed nature of the audience explains why Groen, while assuming their general sympathy for his person, did not presume their basic agreement with his position. He tried to persuade, offer arguments for their "consideration," "begged to point out" things they might have overlooked or interpreted differently, appealed to the verdict of "historical investigation," and in particular expressed his willingness to be corrected. What had been intended as a religious-political *soirée* of kindred minds had turned into a forum representing a wider spectrum of religious beliefs and political outlook than the host had first envisioned.

Looking at the company as a whole, we note that it was a rather elite group. Next to the brothers Van Bijlandt, both of whom bore the title of

37. *Briefwisseling*, II, 39; Kluit, *Het Protestantse Réveil in Nederland en daarbuiten*, p. 259.
38. Cf. *Briefwisseling*, II, 779.
39. *Briefwisseling*, II, 708f, 727f.

count, Mackay was a baron and six others bore titles comparable to squire (*jonkheer*). The only commoners among them were, like the host, learned commoners. Next to the speaker, fourteen men held university degrees; two held medical doctorates. Thus it was a company of notables and near-notables, most of whom were approaching middle age and were settled in their careers without having reached the zenith of their responsibilities or achievements. Six of the company were born in the eighteenth century; the oldest of these, Gevaerts, was 71. The remaining fifteen members of the audience, all born since 1800, had an average age of 39.

Present in spirit—a haunting spirit during some of Groen's discussions—was a friend in Amsterdam, Koenen.

Hendrik Jacob Koenen (1809-74) had written pioneering works in economic history as well as works on the history of Jews and French Huguenot refugees in the Low Countries. He and Groen carried on a very active correspondence throughout their lives, recommending (and lending) books to each other and exchanging opinions on them as well as on a host of other subjects, political, organizational, ecclesiastical. A member since 1842 of the city council of Amsterdam, Koenen would be appointed alderman in 1847, followed in 1850 by his election to the Provincial Estates of North Holland.

Unable to make the trip to The Hague, Koenen was informed after the third or fourth session by Van der Kemp of the subject-matter treated thus far. His rather serious objections, communicated to Van der Kemp who passed them on to Groen, are reflected in the passage in Lecture VI (144ff) on the "democratic principle of the Genevan Reformation" and in the allusion to a "Christian liberalism." Van der Kemp faithfully reported back to Amsterdam that the lecturer had offered an explicit rebuttal of the point at issue. In his next letter to Groen, Koenen thanked him for the honor and added: "May I come over some time this winter and be a guest at your lecture?" It appears unlikely that he ever did.[40]

One further detail surrounding the lectures on unbelief and revolution is of more than anecdotal interest. Van der Kemp would on occasion, as

---

40. *Briefwisseling*, II, 716, 718, 966. There is no hint in any of the subsequent (published) correspondence that he was ever present.

we have just noted, offer written comments to Groen. In one of these he complained of the rapid delivery and asked for repetition of main points; apparently he was taking notes as fast as he could. Mackay, too, took notes. When the series was over Mackay lent his notes to Van der Kemp, who had a clerk rewrite the whole in a hardcover notebook. Mackay's notes, along with the notebook, was returned to Mackay in the summer of 1846, and in an accompanying letter Van der Kemp said that he had found the notes useful in supplementing his own notes in places, especially in the French quotations. He further suggested that Mackay reread the text to catch errors by the copyist and to fill in a few spaces left blank. Finally, he pointed to two mistakes in their notes on Lecture III, the text of which had just appeared in print in a separate article in the *Stemmen*, and added: "How I would shudder to let Groen see my notes; he would discover in them blunder upon blunder."[41]

The "Mackay Notebook," as one might name it, ended up as an item in an auction at the family estate some time in the 1950s and has since made its way to the *Mr. H. Bos-Bibliotheek* in the Free University at Amsterdam.[42] As lecture notes go, the Mackay Notebook is often unreliable yet not without its own usefulness; in a number of instances its compact text suggests a term or an idea that captures the marrow of Groen's sometimes convoluted sentences or involved arguments; in several other instances, however, it misconstrues the point or the drift of the spoken word as compared to the published version.

When Groen published the lectures in book form a year later, he wrote Mackay, rather puckishly, that he realized he had really stolen a march on him by publishing the book, because it now invalidated a painstakingly prepared notebook.[43]

The Mackay Notebook records the exact date of each session: November 8, 15, 22, 29; December 13, 20, 1845; and January 3, 17, 24; February 7, 21; March 7, 14, 28; and April 4, 1846.

---

41. *Briefwisseling*, V, 800.

42. The university's former head librarian, Dr. J. Stellingwerff, who first drew my attention to its existence, kindly allowed me to make a photocopy of its 120 pages.

43. *Briefwisseling*, V, 156.

8

—

STYLE

"Apples of gold in pictures of silver." With this biblical metaphor Nicolaas Beets, on receiving the completed *Handbook*, praised not only its author's balanced judgment but also his felicitous style.[1] This verdict by Beets, who was himself a literary figure of some authority, merits separate consideration.

Groen's style, praised by many for a variety of qualities, is so highly original that one might almost say it is eccentric. The Dutch prose of *Unbelief and Revolution* is anything but plain and fluent; in fact, to the modern reader it labors under an unmistakable artificiality. Many eulogists have felt constrained to observe that for all its superb qualities Groen's prose is "difficult." A number of these qualities may here be enumerated for the English reader, who is not in a position to savor the original.

Apart from the subject-matter, a variety of special stylistic elements employed in *Unbelief and Revolution* challenge the reader's powers of comprehension. There is, first of all, a certain stiffness to this prose that results from a predilection for abstract nouns, often strung together to achieve balance and prepare a climax; the effect, quite often, can be overpowering, but it is not always convincing and so forces the critical reader to retrace his steps. Nor is instant readability enhanced by the abundant use of long periods and numerous foreign phrases and classical quotations. To be sure, this is a feature that Groen had in common with the best writers of his time (though it is especially marked in him). Other idiosyncrasies, however, do not conform to any contemporary patterns. For instance,

---

1. Prov 25:11; see *Briefwisseling*, II, 761. A number of representative sections of the *Handbook*—§§ 823–847, i.e. the "General Observations" introducing Part Three: The Age of Revolution (1795–1840)—were later included in an anthology of Dutch literature for use in schools; see J. P. de Keyser, ed., *Neerland's Letterkunde in de Negentiende Eeuw* (The Hague, 1877), I, 484–91.

the convoluted sentence, peppered with adverbial phrases of time, place, manner, degree, agency, etc., alternating (especially in his later writings) with cryptic comments and aphoristic turns of phrase: these are Groen's personal trademarks. His sentences, moreover, are riddled with qualifications and interjections. All these elements make for lively prose but not easy reading. Other stylistic devices which have a similar effect and at which Groen is a master are the sentence fragment, the euphonious alliteration, the sustained metaphor, and the aphoristic contraction.

Easier to identify in English translation are several traits of composition that deserve particular notice. There is, first of all, Groen's frequent use of the rhetorical question. Not merely a device to enliven the prose, it reflects the author's searching and deliberative intellect, his "inquiring mind."[2] Furthermore, a mind like this also has a predilection for devices like the indirect statement, the double negation (i.e., the obverse iteration: denying the negative instead of affirming the positive), the subtle allusion, the guarded assertion. In a private letter, in which he insists on being nominated for election to the Second Chamber rather than the First, Groen can write sentences like this one:

> I venture almost to feel assured that after this confidential com-
> munication you too will be of a mind with me that I shall have to
> await the results of a difference of opinion, which I greatly regret,
> and that by withdrawing my announcement I should not be able to
> escape the reproach of eccentricity.[3]

In *Unbelief and Revolution* he writes sentences like the following:

> So if we should now take the system as a whole, in its full import for
> religion and politics, and recall that its success is expected to usher
> in an endless future of bliss for mankind, and then set it opposite
> the inexorable Word of Revelation (of which the Revolution might
> well say, as Demosthenes was wont to say of Phocion, "This is the
> axe that cuts down all my discourses"),—should we then have any
> doubt that with respect to this terrain, too, the enmity between the

---

2. Cf. Morton, "A Christian Heroism," p. 104.
3. Groen to C. A. Nairac, 25 Nov. 1848; *Briefwisseling*, III, 9.

seed of the woman and the seed of the devil is inevitable? (Lect. IX, p. 215.)

The mind that employs this style rarely finds people "at home"; it finds them "not out." Groen seldom states simply that he is right; he submits, rather, that the case he wishes to defend is "not dubitable."

While the repeated occurrence of the double negation and the constant use of litotes at times become exasperating, another recurring feature, related to the one above, may be rather appealing to many readers. Groen has the habit of the scholastics of introducing possible objections—again, often in the form of rhetorical questions—in order to give himself the opportunity of showing that such objections, though seemingly weakening his argument, actually strengthen his case.

A final distinguishing feature of Groen's writings that may conveniently be treated under style is his abundant use of the direct quotation. Quotable quotes, gathered from like-minded writers but no less from authors who are in disagreement with him on virtually everything else, are Groen's stock-in-trade. In fact, he seems to prefer citing authors of the opposing camp, with the result that the reader is alternately befuddled and irritated: What, liberals and radicals, agnostics and materialists cited in support of what Groen is arguing—how can this be? By what sleight of hand is the orator playing tricks on his audience and misusing his "authorities"? Groen was criticized many times during his lifetime for creating this dubious impression. On one occasion, having been accused in an academic address of "artfully grouping names to metamorphose antagonists into allies," he replies indignantly that when antagonists testify to moments of truth it only heightens the value of the testimony; to invoke them is not deceitful name-dropping but a perfectly proper utilization of supporting evidence wherever it is found.[4] Thus he could write (Lecture II, 36) that he has the right to cite any author "who has paid his respect, even if involuntarily, through inconsistent reasoning, to the principles that I uphold." In other words, some of Groen's quotations actually say: Look here, not even Author A has been able to get around this bit of truth; or better still: Notice how no one less than Authority B has seen the same truth—of which I give you

---

4. *Ter Nagedachtenis van Stahl*, pp. 78–83.

the full story, the only correct interpretative framework. Thus, to cite an isolated truthful insight, no matter who said it or in what context, seems to Groen not only permissible but commendable. This is especially the case when the testimony comes from "established authorities," for their word buttresses his argument with the wisdom of the ages, with that "universal consensus" which according to the *Essay on Truth* is one of the distinguishing marks of truth.[5] Of course, the habit is particularly noticeable on his pages because he prefers the literal quotation to the indirect citation or the summarizing paraphrase. Rhetorical effectiveness is his instinctive guide here. Groen has an ear for the eloquent saying and loves the striking formulation and the felicitous turn of phrase. As well, he knows the value of the well-placed citation from a celebrated author in the course of pleading one's case, be it in a court of law or elsewhere.[6]

A fellow parliamentarian was struck by the humor, irony and witty persiflage of this consummate master of the art of rhetoric. Groen's speeches, this colleague testified in 1853, if they do not convince, at any rate are a welcome relief in the otherwise exhausting debates of the house, as the speaker manages to clothe his thoughts in words that say far more than they express, thanks to his "rare powers of combination and unusual talent for brilliant allusiveness."[7]

Koenen once thought Groen's style distinctive enough to make it the topic of a paper which he read to the *Maatschappij voor Letterkunde* meeting in Leyden. Analyzing Groen, Koenen compared him to Van der Palm the pulpit orator, to Thorbecke the parliamentary debater and academic scholar, and to P. C. Hooft the Renaissance man of letters, the Dutch Tacitus.[8]

Allard Pierson (1831–96), who as a boy had observed Groen van Prinsterer in action as chairman of the meetings of the Christian Friends, recalled many years later that Groen spoke softly yet clearly, at a rapid clip, never raising his voice and making only the simplest of gestures with his hands. His diction was precise, his sentences finely honed; he knew the

---

5. *Proeve* (1834), pp. 172–88.

6. Cf. Zwaan, *Groen van Prinsterer en de klassieke Oudheid*, pp. 9n15, 74n73, 177f, 184n31.

7. Quoted by Groen in *Nederlandsche Gedachten*, 1873/74, V, 329.

8. *Briefwisseling*, III, 352.

power of words, so needed few. Groen could speak, Pierson remembered, "with almost feminine tenderness," but also with an irony that spared no one. Both his motherly concern to shield and to nurture and his vehemence in dogged pursuit and relentless attack stemmed, Pierson believed, from his passionate nature. Groen's was a passion, however, that remained concealed under quiet manners and urbane correctness. Outwardly calm, he

> always held himself in, and he had to, for his inmost being glowed as if it were boiling; he had an intensity of love and hate which with less self-restraint would have caused the flames to shoot out.[9]

The need for self-restraint made itself felt no less during the course of the lectures. Reading between the lines in *Unbelief and Revolution*, one gets the distinct impression that the Groen who presented lectures in the privacy of his home did not differ greatly from the Groen who presided over public meetings. Underneath many a passage in *Unbelief and Revolution* there smoulders the fire of "bridled passion."[10]

In addition to Groen's repressed passion, many commentators have noted his subtle irony and biting sarcasm. They do indeed constitute two of Groen's favorite ingredients and call for a separate comment. A person often has a keen eye for what he has in common with, and most admires in, someone else. In the Introduction which he wrote for the posthumous reprint of Wormser's book on infant baptism[11] Groen makes a revealing comment on his friend's style. The pages where Wormser "alludes to unbelief," he writes, "scintillate with irony, with that smile of indignation which, in a man of his temperament, is one of the most unmistakable hallmarks of unshakable faith and holiness of purpose." Is this an indirect rationalization of his own use of irony, or does it go deeper and put the finger on the quiet conviction that infuses his own style as well as Wormser's? In his old age Groen calls irony the *safety-valve of self-control*: "[Irony] can be caustic, overly caustic. But one forgets that this safety-valve of self-control often represents, in the guise of humor, the anguished cry of indignation

---

9. A. Pierson, *Oudere Tijdgenooten*, p. 119; see also p. 13.

10. Phrase of Conrad Busken Huet, the cultural historian and younger contemporary, as he described Groen in his *Nieuwe litterarische Fantasieën*, vol. I (2nd impr., 1874), p. 126; quoted by Smitskamp, "Het boek 'Ongeloof en Revolutie,'" p. 24n4.

11. J. A. Wormser, *De Kinderdoop*, 2nd printing (Amsterdam, 1864), pp. v–xiv.

and grief, in which polemic, far more than many people suspect, was not seldom coupled with pain."[12]

To what extent does the style betray the man? A modern literary critic, after poring over hundreds of pages in the published correspondence as well as pondering what graphologists have said about Groen's handwriting, concludes that Groen's diction is suffused with the objectivity of the lawyer and reveals a constant repression of human emotions; his circuitous sentence structure betrays the timidity and caution of a man who is painstakingly scrupulous in representing the cause he champions.[13]

How does such a style develop? Groen's earliest letters are precocious notes to his parents, in the French learned from his mother and his governess.[14] At the academy, the Greek and French of Plato and Rousseau belonged to his favorite reading, while Dutch and Latin alternated as the languages he listened to and spoke himself.[15] No doubt this early training, so successfully completed, helped shape his style.

One possible explanation for the indirectness and allusiveness of Groen's mode of expression is the circumstance that very early in his writing career he was a state employee close to the throne. He did not hide from the king the fact that the anonymous political commentator of the *Nederlandsche Gedachten* was none other than his loyal secretary, but at the same time he tried to avoid embarrassing king and government by writing a cautious, circumspect, and conciliatory prose that was sparing of persons even while forceful about issues and principles. Groen himself remembered in his old age that it was especially during the tension-filled years of 1829-32 that he had learned to pick and choose his words carefully; to this recollection he appended this revealing footnote: "The English call this 'a guarded language,' which is a language on which the fault-finder can get no handle."[16] It is a language that serves the purpose not only of the political observer but also of the historian called upon to treat complex

---

12. *Nederlandsche Gedachten*, 1875, V, 4.

13. Rijnsdorp, "Groen in zijn brieven over zichzelf en zijn reputatie," pp. 192f.

14. *Briefwisseling*, I, 2; cf. 725.

15. "To speak Latin like Wim Groen" for a while was a proverb in Holland's small academic world; cf. Schutte, *Mr. G. Groen van Prinsterer*, p. 20.

16. *Nederlandsche Gedachten*, 1873/74, V, 297.

issues; a "great authority" like Mr. Ranke, Groen records somewhere, is noted for his judicious use of guarded language.[17]

Still, he seems also to have been born to the habit of indirectness of expression. Take the following early sample of his style, long before he was a civil servant *cum* publicist. In 1822 the young Groen attended the service in which Da Costa, his wife, and Capadose were baptized. He witnessed it all, standing behind the choir railing in St. Peter's Church of Leyden, and he faithfully reported the event in a letter to his parents. When he came to the point where he had to confess that he was very much moved by the whole ceremony, he wrote: "All this created such an impression that at the solemn moment when they knelt one by one and the benediction was pronounced over them and they were scarcely able to get up, one truly would have had no feelings if one had not felt quite differently at that moment than the way one normally feels ..."[18]

Naturally, all these stylistic features occur in the book-length *Ongeloof en Revolutie*. When it came out, contemporary authorities praised its "powerful, captivating and refined style" and reckoned its author among the "most accomplished stylists in our national literature."[19] One aspect that strikes the modern reader, however, was not noted by the polite reviewers of the mid-nineteenth century. It is undeniable that in places the published lectures, even for that time, are long-winded. Let us allow that this may be due in part to the fact that what we have in print presumably is very close to the text as it was meant to be read aloud to a patient audience in an intimate setting.[20] Yet we know also that Groen could not afford to take a leisurely pace. At least two circumstances imposed definite limits on each lecture.

First, Groen had to be able to read it in a single evening. He had collected (and was still collecting) more material than he could possibly squeeze into a session, so he had to force himself to stick to the essentials. It has been

---

17. *Maurice et Barnevelt*, p. 149.

18. *Briefwisseling*, I, 32.

19. Quoted by Smitskamp, "Het boek 'Ongeloof en Revolutie,'" p. 21.

20. No manuscripts of the lectures have survived, so comparison with the printed version is impossible. Earlier we quoted Groen's explanation in a letter to his publisher: "I am giving the lectures without recasting them, just as they are ..." *Briefwisseling*, II, 790.

plausibly estimated that the actual reading time ranged between forty-five minutes to an hour and a half.[21]

In the second place, Groen was afflicted these very months by a tremor in the right hand which caused him increasing discomfort. Just four days before starting the series Groen wrote to Bodel that "writing is still difficult for me, so I am practising *le style lapidaire*." To Da Costa he wrote on the Friday before Christmas, in the middle of preparing the lecture on the perversion of constitutional law: "Writing is still difficult, and I am not yet ready for Saturday evening. That is costing me considerably more work than I had anticipated." Toward the end of the season, in the week that he was working on Lecture XIII (about the Reign of Terror), he wrote to Koenen that his right hand had become so subject to tremors "as to render it almost unfit for writing."[22]

These two restraints probably prevented the text of *Ongeloof en Revolutie* from becoming longer than it might otherwise have become. So why, nevertheless, its unmistakable long-windedness in places? One authority detects in the book's prose the belabored effort of an undogmatic mind at sustaining a systematic argument.[23] This observation has merit but I would add that the book's prose also reflects the Herculean effort of a Christian historian who is breaking new ground.

The foregoing raises the interesting question: What peculiar challenges does one face when this type of prose is to be rendered into another language? To the present writer, no aspect of Groen's style is more frustrating than the indirect and circuitous formulations in which many of his thoughts are couched. Regardless of whether this trait goes back to an ingrained habit from youth on, as we have suggested above, in later years his circumlocutions alternated with something equally maddening: now his sentences are at times so carved down to the bone, so compressed and pointed, as to become enigmatic. Such is all too frequently the case, for example, in the 2nd edition of 1868. The first edition of *Ongeloof en Revolutie*

---

21. De Gaay Fortman, *Figuren uit het Réveil*, p. 439.

22. *Briefwisseling*, II, 706, 717, 731. Groen wrote a good hand, but at times almost illegibly small. The right hand was never strong. Many copies of letters and memos in the archives are in Betsy's handwriting. For some time during the early fifties, when he was editor-in-chief of a daily, he had to resort to the dictation services of a hired stenographer; cf. *Briefwisseling*, VI, 590.

23. Gerretson, *Verzamelde Werken*, II, 134.

stands roughly halfway through that development between endless cir-
cumlocution and increasingly compact brevity; as a result, it suffers by
turns from both shortcomings. Is it any wonder that the idea of an edited
abridgment has occurred more than once, that the author himself accomplished it in 1860, that Diepenhorst tried his hand at it in 1922, that the
present writer was urged to do so in English by the late Professor Hans
Rookmaaker? In any event, I hope that the abridged translation available
in a separate volume has retained many of the strengths of Groen's style
but eliminated at least some of its weaknesses.

In conclusion, I should like to pass on some of the observations made
by the American translator of portions of Groen's work, Herbert Donald
Morton. While describing Groen's prose as "trenchant, incisive, pithy, terse,
animated, spare" as well as "lean, strong, rich in imagery and allusion, and
surprising in its combinations," he notes at the same time that at least some
of Groen's periodic sentences are "like late summer gardens, heavy with
ripe fruits and wild vines that have overgrown the gardener's classical,
ordered intentions."[24] Characteristic of this style, Morton notes, are the
devastating volleys of sentence fragments and rhetorical questions, and
no less the playful but on occasion exasperating "quest for the better metaphor": that peculiar way in which figures of speech, whether Groen's own
or someone else's, are first recorded and then corrected or improved upon,
often resulting in "a colorful kaleidoscope of carelessly altering images."[25]
In tone and polish, says Morton, this is the style of a fighter whose punches
jab and sting, whose "fencing wordplay/swordplay" penetrates the chinks
in the opponents' armor with unerring accuracy. The style betrays the
Christian heroism of a dauntless knight who confidently invites his opponent to enter the lists and joust. All considered, Morton serves notice to
every aspiring translator of Groen:

> The short, choppy assault, the pithy statement, the ironic nuance
> were his trademarks, even if they often occurred within a matrix
> of compound-complex sentences and interrogative devices. Groen's
> native gifts, his early training in the classics, his scarcely controlled
> passion, his inexorable logic and, above all, his high sense of calling

---

24. Morton, "A Christian Heroism," pp. 101, 105.
25. *Ibid.*, p. 106.

to fight the good fight of faith, impart to his prose a brilliance which no translation can hope to equal.[26]

_____

26. *Ibid.*, p. 108.

9

—

ARGUMENT

Unbelief and Revolution has a well-considered structure or plan. Two opening lectures with introductory material are followed by three more that
expound the *negative* part of the author's case: why the revolution *cannot*
be attributed to the principles (Lecture III), the constitutions (IV) or the
abuses (V) of the old regime. Lectures VI-XIV then present the *positive*
part of the argument: how unbelief gave rise to the new *theory* of liberty,
which in turn led to the revolutionary *practice*.

This positive demonstration comes in two parts: a *physiological* analysis of the revolution, or: what kind of theory of liberty develops from
unbelief (VI-IX); and a *biography* of the revolution, or: how the theory of
liberty operated in historical practice (XI-XIV). Bridging the two parts is
a discussion of the interaction—really: the collision—between the theory
in the abstract and the nature of historical reality (X).

The physiology of the revolution shows that its advent was prepared
by the rise of a new theory of government (VI) and ushered in by a decline
in Christianity and the growth of unbelief (VII). As unbelief unfolded a
double revolution ensued: revelation was replaced by reason (VIII) and
divine right by popular sovereignty (IX).

The biography of the revolution traces the historical events as they
were shaped by the theory through the five *phases* of Preparation (XI),
Development (XII and XIII), and Reaction, Renewed Experimentation, and
Despondent Resignation (XIV).

A final lecture surveys international relations and closes with an
exhortation.

Putting it all together, we can expand the author's Table of Contents
(represented below in small capitals) into the following Outline:

I. INTRODUCTION: how contemporary history is the direct product of
prevailing revolutionary ideas

II. Science against the Political Theory of the Revolution: how the doctrine of the revolution is in stark contrast with the wisdom of the ages

PART ONE: NEGATIVE DEMONSTRATION

III. Anti-Revolutionary Principles: how the constitutional principles underlying the old order cannot account for the rise of the revolution

IV. Historical Forms of Government: how the type of state found under the old order does not explain the coming of the revolution

V. Abuses: how the shortcomings of the old regime constituted an insufficient cause of the revolution

PART TWO: POSITIVE DEMONSTRATION

a: Physiological investigation of the hidden causes governing events: how the theory of revolution conquered the European mind

VI. Perversion of Constitutional Law: how the republicanizing tenor of political theory acted as a long-term preparation of the theory of revolution

VII. Reformation: how the Protestant Reformation of the sixteenth century acted as a temporary suspension of the spread of unbelief

VIII. Unbelief: how the supremacy of reason became the new basis of religion and morality

IX. Unbelief (continued): how popular sovereignty and social contract became the new basis of society

X. The Revolution Doctrine in Conflict with Nature and Law: how the revolutionary theory cannot but operate in constant collision with the divine world order

b: Biography of the revolution: how the theory of revolution operated in historical practice

XI. First Phase: Preparation: how the theory became master of the minds (till 1789)

XII. Second Phase: Development (1789-1794): how the theory unfolded in practice

XIII. Reign of Terror: how the final stage of the second phase carried the development through to the bitter end

XIV. Overview, 1794–1845: how the third, fourth, and fifth phases exhibit the reaction, resurgence, and resignation of the revolutionary mind

XV. Conclusion: how international relations likewise developed in accordance with the revolution and, finally, how the condition of the fatherland imposes certain duties upon Christians

Guided by the structure of *Unbelief and Revolution* as outlined above, one may summarize its subject-matter as follows.

I. INTRODUCTION

The lecturer invites his audience to follow him as he leads them in a thoroughgoing investigation into the driving forces of contemporary history, in order to understand the current *malaise*.

Economically there is declining prosperity, harmful competition, domination by capitalists. Socially there is a growing rift between classes and an alarming increase in pauperism. Politically there is dull routine, lack of direction and initiative. Subjectivism is breaking up the foundations of law and morality. Skepticism is fragmenting the Christian church.

All these symptoms point to a *general* cause. That cause is found in the intellectual and spiritual revolution evident in the *inversion* of the thinking and attitudes of all Christendom. The lecturer proposes to show that the current malaise is due to the revolutionary ideas which have gained ascendancy in Europe since the Enlightenment and which have been elaborated into a coherent system, the theory or doctrine of revolution.

The lectures will try to demonstrate that the revolution *cannot* be explained from the nature of the old order or the abuses that had crept in (III–V), but instead *can only* be explained from the action of revolutionary ideas, both in theory (VI–X) and in practice (XI–XIV).

Armed with this insight, Christians will be able to oppose and counteract the evil of the day in an appropriate manner (XV).

II. KNOWLEDGE AND SCIENCE
VERSUS THE REVOLUTION

Those who oppose the modern revolution in the European consciousness may feel isolated. Yet, although they are in the minority today, they have the wisdom of the ages on their side. The revolutionary ideas conflict with the Bible and history and contradict political thinkers ancient and modern. The belief that earthly authority is *not* grounded in human approval has been maintained throughout history: law was never made to depend upon the will of the majority, and every civilization in every age (with the exception of the Sophists in ancient Greece) acknowledged the divine origin of justice. Even in the age of revolution, the revolutionary doctrine has never been without its challengers (foremost Pitt and Burke, but also Van Alphen, Gentz, Bonald, Maistre, Lamennais, finally Haller and Bilderdijk). Today its dissenters are multiplying in every country of Europe.

III. ANTI-REVOLUTIONARY PRINCIPLES

The old regimes were founded on a number of specific principles which can hardly be said to have necessitated the revolution. On the contrary, they are of enduring significance for any state and society that wishes to be stable and viable.

First, there was respect for *historically acquired rights*, though never in disregard of universal principles of justice.

Second, there was respect for the *autonomy* of provinces, municipalities, estates, corporations, guilds, families—forms of self-rule which, rather than weakening the state, forestalled the stifling effect of artificial centralization and promoted free organic activity.

Third, there was acknowledgment of the *divine right* of civil authority, without leading to tyranny. Government was seen as instituted by God, a "minister to thee for good," not a usurpation by the strong or a contractual agency for looking after common interests. By analogy, all forms of authority in human society exist by divine right and must be so honored; thus civil government, though sacred, is necessarily restricted by the equally sacred rights of the people. This principle alone guarantees a harmonious symbiosis of authority and freedom, for it firmly entrenches both in a higher order, thereby removing them from the arbitrary decisions of an omnipotent state or the good pleasure of a popular majority.

Fourth, there was *union of church and state*, a principle which, though sometimes misapplied in constraint of conscience or in curtailment of religious worship, nevertheless allowed for mutual consultation and cooperation between church and state in providing for the most sacred interests of civil society.

IV. HISTORICAL FORMS OF GOVERNMENT

While the political arrangements of pre-revolutionary times were by no means perfect, they were altogether tolerable. They were rooted in history and suited the respective nationalities. The states were tempered monarchies: sovereignty rested solely with the kings, who had much power but who faced a variety of intermediate bodies in society such as estates, guilds, and towns, each of which had unassailable rights and privileges of its own. Mutual respect for one another's specific competence and calling guaranteed a healthy balance between authority and freedom.

Any shortcomings in these states were certainly not beyond remedy. With the necessary adjustments these governments could have served well for the future. Open to reform, they cannot be said to have warranted revolution.

V. ABUSES

The old regimes suffered from many abuses (though their incidence is often exaggerated in the literature). These abuses could have been alleviated by patient and careful reform efforts, not rash innovation. Modern revolutions are waged by outraged fanatics who condemn everything in sight and seek to erect a brand-new society overnight.

Note, too, that the revolutions of modern times were not started by the people who would have been most affected by any existing abuses; they were started by the notables—in Holland by the regents, in France by the estates; the common people joined only later. In short, former abuses were a secondary, contributing cause of the revolution, not its main cause. When the French Revolution broke out, Edmund Burke saw at once: this revolution originates from a theory.

VI. THE PERVERSION OF
CONSTITUTIONAL LAW

If neither the constitutional principles nor the forms of government nor the abuses of the old regime can account for the revolution of our time, how then is it to be explained? The revolution is a distinctive phenomenon of its own. It was born of doctrines, of a philosophic theory of liberty. The remaining lectures will be devoted to analyzing the rise of this theory (VI–X), and then to narrating its effect in practice (XI–XIV).

The rise of the theory was *promoted* by the corruption of constitutional law. When learning revived in the Middle Ages, the understanding of the nature of the state was perverted by the one-sided orientation to the republics of classical antiquity. As a result, a grave misconception arose in political theory: namely, that all states are at bottom republics, that is, *associations* for the *common good* whose members agree by *contract* to form a state and be ruled over by a government.

This erroneous premise was worked out in two directions. In Hobbes, the association surrendered its rights, and sovereign power came to reside in a single despot. In Sidney, the association retained its sovereignty, and government was virtually destroyed since its powers could be revoked whenever the people wished. In neither version of the contract theory was the limited nature of political authority any longer recognized. The authority of government, irrespective of whether a prince or the people were held to be the sovereign, was believed to encompass everything. Thus, on this view, states were *omnipotent* by definition.

The harmful effect of this republicanizing degeneration of constitutional law was greatly increased when in addition another principle gradually began to assert itself. Unbelief, which was systematized into a doctrine of revolution, transformed the error in *political* theory into a comprehensive misconception about *society* as such.

VII. THE REFORMATION

Whereas the perversion of constitutional law was conducive to the development of the revolutionary theory, another historical force *counteracted* the corruption and for some time worked in the opposite direction. The influence of the Protestant Reformation, far from having paved the way for the revolution, as both liberal and Catholic authors have claimed, actually stemmed the tide of dissolution and fostered a moral rebirth of European society.

The fundamental principle of the Reformation was *submission* to God and the authority of His Word, rather than the repudiation of authority and freedom of inquiry. The leading reformers condemned popular uprisings and the excesses of enthusiasm. Protestants learned from Scripture that civil government is both sacred and restricted. This evangelical salt was a powerful antidote against the spreading poison of revolutionary ideas.

Alas, the awakening was short-lived. Protestants lost their first love; they gave themselves over to internal disputes and spent their energies on refining dogmatic distinctions rather than on reforming scholarship and society in the light of biblical principles. Retreating into confessional orthodoxy, the church of the Reformation was outflanked by the most flagrant misconceptions of philosophy.

Compared to the revolution, the Reformation is its very antithesis. Only when its influence began to recede was Europe overrun by unbelief and thus made ripe for a spiritual and intellectual revolution that has exerted its pernicious influence to this day.

VIII. UNBELIEF

The lecturer is now ready to develop his central thesis. The revolution, in all its schools and shapes, is the logical consequence, the consistent application, the natural unfolding of unbelief. The formative power of the age of revolution lies, literally, in its *godlessness*. A biography of the revolution is therefore best preceded by a physiological investigation of the hidden laws governing the surface events.

It all began with the new faith in *reason*. Once human reason was declared supreme, all the rest followed. The rationalism of the 18th century could not but replace revelation with the human intellect and worship of God with atheism and the religion of humanity, while self-interest and materialism became the new basis of morality. Inevitably, intolerance toward Christianity arose, since the program for human *emancipation* cannot tolerate an authoritarian faith, nor can the claim to human *autonomy* brook submission to revelation. Any halfway position will be swept away by the *unfolding logic* of the new faith. Two rival systems claiming ultimate truth will lock in mortal combat, and where the revolution conquers and prevails, any remaining witnesses to revealed truth will sooner or later be outlawed, prosecuted, and banished or executed.

IX. UNBELIEF (CONTINUED)

Once man is free to follow his autonomous reason wherever it leads him in his thinking, he will also want to be guided by it in his actions. And indeed, the project of the Enlightenment embraced the whole of society. Before long, the fiction of a social contract is utilized to supplant divine right as the only legitimate foundation of authority. God's sovereignty is denied in favor of the *sovereignty of the people*, who are presumed to have instituted governments among themselves to secure their individual, unalienable rights. A government therefore is henceforth regarded as deriving its just powers from the consent of the governed and as answerable to the majority of its subjects, the people, who have the right to alter or abolish it whenever they deem such action in their best interest.

In his *Social Contract*, Rousseau unraveled the full consequences of this revolutionary theory. On the one hand, the new state is *absolute:* the citizens enjoy their freedom and pursuit of happiness as conditional grants from the state; their lives and fortunes are at the free disposal of the state; the education of their children is entrusted to the state; their religious beliefs are free provided they do not conflict with the civil religion approved and prescribed by the state. True freedom is ensured to all members of the community through the dominance of the *general will*. Individual dissenters do not know what is good for them; they will be forced to be free.

On the other hand, the government of such a state has *no independence:* its only mandate is to carry out the will of the people as represented by its deputies, who in turn are subject to recall by the people. Such a government is either the toy of political factions or the slave of public opinion, and can neither guarantee the freedom of all nor safeguard the rights of the minority.

From the standpoint of the theory, the so-called *radicals* alone are consistent and therefore correct, whereas the *moderates* are clearly wrong because they are inconsistent and thus will be continually overruled. The half-hearted system of Montesquieu must yield to the rigorous logic of Rousseau's absolute democracy. In light of the revolutionary premises, the anarchism preached by the "friends of light," who wished to abolish civil society altogether and return to the state of nature, is irrefutable. So also is the communism promoted by the "conspirators for equality" led by Babeuf, which at the time could only be repudiated on selfish grounds, in clear violation of the universally accepted theory.

Now then, is the theory of revolution, as sketched so far in its full consequences, the key to the history of the revolution? Not quite. The theory is not free to run its natural course. The moment it is applied it will clash with man's true needs (the order of nature, the ordinances of God). The history of the revolution, in other words, is the resultant of two factors: the wholesale onslaught of the *theoretical* revolution, and the resistance offered by historical *reality*. The ensuing contest accounts for the many transformations and metamorphoses that the revolution will undergo, even while its unvarying principle guarantees its permanent identity.

X. THE DOCTRINE OF REVOLUTION IN CONFLICT WITH NATURE AND LAW

The revolutionary theory flies in the face of natural and historical realities. When applied, it must constantly be adjusted and readjusted if the experiment is to go on. *Religiously*, atheism will not satisfy for very long. People will turn to spiritualism, mysticism, pantheism, or the Christian communism of a Saint-Simon. *Politically*, the demolition of hated institutions and the abolition of odious rights and privileges threatens the state with anarchy. As more and more people are affected, resistance will mount and a clamor for moderation will magnify. As a result, the revolution will inevitably pass through the following *five phases*.

1. *Preparation*: the theory will gain acceptance. 2. *Development*: the theory will be applied, but as its consequences unfold in ever more radical manifestations, some people will fail to see its logical necessity and begin to deny its legitimacy, others will put their personal interests foremost, while still others will recoil in pity and horror. In the ensuing struggle between moderates and radicals, the latter will at last impose a reign of terror to safeguard the revolution. 3. *Reaction*: when the scales are turned, the revolution will be frozen at the point reached, and a regime of naked force and compulsion will be imposed at the expense of liberty. 4. *Renewed Experimentation*: at last the yoke of tyranny is thrown off and men, taught by experience, will resume the application of the theory, this time via the golden mean, in an unstable compromise between order and liberty. 5. *Despondent Resignation*: repeated outbursts of revolutionary violence will induce men to acquiesce in strong government, to sacrifice the theory, and to concentrate on the pursuit of material wealth instead.

Throughout these successive phases the principle of the revolution remains invariably the same. Thus the *absolute state* persists. The state born of the revolution is omnipotent, indivisible, meddlesome, autocratic,

and atheistic. In idolatrous worship of the "general welfare," this centralized and bureaucratic state will function like an iron network spread over
the entire population, forcing everybody to conform to the regime. This
amounts to an all-encompassing despotism that destroys civil and political liberty and defeats the true interests of nation and people. It cannot be
vanquished except by a return to the sovereignty of God.

XI. FIRST PHASE: PREPARATION

This lecture commences the "life story" of the revolution. Thus far, the logical consequences implied by the revolutionary theory have been *deduced*
from the nature of systematic unbelief; now the actual, historical consequences will be traced in order to *demonstrate* that they were indeed the
manifestations of systematic unbelief. As the fruit could be predicted from
the tree, so the tree shall now be identified by its fruit.

Throughout the five phases sketched above, the revolution has exhibited the following abiding characteristics: (a) it is a unique revolution, not
comparable to any other revolution inasmuch as it is a full-scale social (or
rather anti-social) and anti-Christian revolution; (b) it has affected all of
Christendom, not one European country excepted; (c) it destroys the very
foundations of law and in its place honors mere "legality," an arbitrary
"legal order," irrespective of universal justice; (d) it has never been implemented in full, for the simple reason that it is false, impracticable, and out
of tune with reality; (e) it has passed through many different forms yet has
always retained its identity: Jacobinism, Bonapartism, Constitutionalism—
they all perpetuate the absolute state; (f) it has never been opposed except
from within its own bosom; that is to say, certain of its premises as well
as consequences have been attacked, but no one has ever taken issue with
the revolution as such: symptoms have been combatted, but the cause of
the disease remains unknown; and (g) it loses its power when confronted
with the gospel, which alone is a match for systematic unbelief.

Though erupting first in France, the revolution was a general European
phenomenon. Throughout the 18th century, the doctrine of revolution
made converts everywhere, as witness the enlightened despots. In France,
too, the revolution was long prepared—in the minds of men, in public
deeds and official utterances, in fashionable talk and public opinion.
Louis XVI was a pioneer of revolutionary change; his edicts reflect the

new theories. His ministers led the way; his subjects followed in adopting their views. The three estates sought to reduce the monarchy to mere executive power; the third estate attacked the rights of nobility and clergy as so many intolerable injustices. No matter what the court might have done or avoided doing in the heady days of 1789, the theory of popular sovereignty, master of the minds owing to the spirit of the age, was not to be stopped in its pursuit of a corresponding state.

XII. SECOND PHASE: DEVELOPMENT (1789–1794)

The atrocities of the French Revolution were not due to adventitious circumstances. They cannot be blamed on the king's behavior, on the attitude of the privileged estates, on the intervention of foreign powers. Nor would revolutionary violence have been stayed if Mirabeau had lived longer or if the Constituent Assembly had acted more wisely. No exaggeration provoked by resistance, but consistent application of the theory, is reflected in such characteristic events as the formation of the National Assembly, the constitution of 1791, the founding of the Republic, the death-sentence of the king, the fall of the Girondins. The means employed were likewise consistent with the theory: centralization of bureaucratic state omnipotence, exclusion of dissenters, suppression and violation of laws just made, forcible displacement of timid authorities. At every turn a minority of radicals prevailed over a growing throng of moderates who were inconsistent with their own professed beliefs. The sweep of revolution carried men far beyond what they had intended, for ideas held sway, not the wills of men: men were dragged along willy-nilly by the momentum of triumphant principles.

XIII. THE REIGN OF TERROR

The last stage in the phase of development was the much maligned reign of terror. For all its frightful horror, it was perfectly consistent with the accepted theory. Its principal leaders were sincere believers in the revolution and sought to advance it faithfully. Robespierre's strength lay in his selfless and uncompromising devotion to the doctrines especially of Rousseau. To safeguard the gains of the revolution, the Republic had to be preserved by any means, however harsh. A "revolutionary government" mercilessly crushed all opposition in the name of "general welfare" and "public safety." As the revolution devoured more and more of its children, however, the only escape from the "organized anarchy" was a definitive *coup d'état* by the forces of reaction, ending in the enthronement of a "strong man." Never more than in these years did the revolution exhibit its connection with unbelief.

XIV. OVERVIEW, 1794–1845

Third Phase: Reaction (1794–1815). The terror was replaced by a regime of moderate, that is, inconsistent revolutionaries. Since no party disavowed the original theory, this regime owed its strength only to circumstances, and was vulnerable because it was arbitrary and unprincipled in resorting to intrigue and concessions, force and compulsion. Pressed by extremists on the right and on the left, the Convention, and after it the Directory, sought in vain to maintain peace, order, and stable government. So, to end the uncertainty, Napoleon was elevated to power, and he, in order to consolidate the revolution, suppressed the warring factions, curtailed the press, and on behalf of the sovereign people wielded a complete despotism. This dictatorship was the revolution's only answer to the constant threat of anarchy. It was also in the interest of domestic peace that Napoleon diverted attention to the military conquest of Europe.

Fourth Phase: Renewed Experimentation (1815–1830). The fall of Napoleon ended the Reaction but did not spell a return to anti-revolutionary principles. Rather, men tried again to apply the theory. The constitutionalism of the Restoration was intended to ensure a moderate continuation of the original experiment, but, suffering from internal contradictions, the reign of the Bourbon kings succumbed once more to the liberals' demand for greater freedom.

Fifth Phase: Despondent Resignation (1830–present). No sooner had the revolution of 1830 installed a new dynasty under a revised charter than fear of a revived radicalism restored the forces of reaction. Hopes of greater freedom were dashed by the necessity of suppressing anarchy. Liberals themselves lapsed into despondent resignation, unconsoled by vague promises of a future day for liberty. Political indifference and lethargy set in, as men turned their energies to the pursuit of material prosperity.

XV. CONCLUSION

1. *International law.* Throughout the age of revolution the theory and practice of international law has been as revolutionary as that of constitutional law. Its cornerstone is the sovereignty of humanity and its criterion the well-being of the world. These take precedence over sacred treaties and acquired rights. France overran Europe to spread the blessings of the revolution. The great Powers acted with equal arbitrariness. In the phase of preparation, treaties were sacrificed to the advantages of territorial aggrandizement. In the phase of development, the Coalition spared France by refusing to root out her revolutionary usurpers and resisting only her foreign aggression. During the phase of reaction, each Power in turn (with the exception of Britain) made pacts with Napoleon to mitigate the injustice rather than to oppose it without compromise. During the phase of renewed experimentation, nations were bartered away, liberal constitutions were tolerated, and liberal agitation in Restoration France was encouraged. No sooner was the July Monarchy an accomplished fact than it was granted diplomatic recognition for opportunistic reasons of expediency. International relations are now in a phase where the Powers acquiesce in revolutions that succeed and try to appease those whose violations of the law really call for armed intervention.

2. *The signs of the times.* Conservatism is firmly in the saddle, but radicalism is brewing among the lower classes. Fresh eruptions of revolutionary violence may take place, more terrible than heretofore. The resurgence of Catholicism may prepare the way for ultramontanism as the new civil religion. Everywhere there is a renewal of evangelical Christianity, but will it be able to overcome the apathy of Christians and prove a match for the forces of unbelief in the present world crisis? Perhaps we will see a new reformation. Or perhaps radicalism will triumph. More probably, we are living in a lull before the storm and are heading for a war between light and darkness unprecedented in world history. The Scriptures at any rate foretell increasing apostasy and tribulations until the Lord returns.

3. *The influence of the revolutionary principles in Holland.* This has been enormous. After initial stirrings, a consistent application (not excluding a regime of terror) was forestalled only by the intervention of Prussia in 1787, of France in 1795. The Restoration of 1813 did not bring repudiation of the revolutionary doctrine. On the contrary, we voluntarily adopted

the trappings of constitutionalism. We lost Belgium because we were tainted with the same liberalism and lacked a firm policy rooted in anti-revolutionary principles. At present, we acquiesce in the stagnant routine of conservatism and seem resigned to the status quo.

4. *The calling of the Christian.* We all know that our country is in dire need of liberating reforms. Yet it has become clear that liberalism is incapable of providing them. The Reformed Church must recover her right to rule her own house according to her confessional standards; and the educational system must not be monopolized for the dominant group, but should allow for alternative schools, for conscience's sake. Christians must never tire of testifying to the truth. They are called, in whatever station, to be faithful; not to spurn the humble; and to bring every thought captive to the obedience of Christ—while praying for forgiveness, and for revival by the Word.

10

—

EDITIONS

Ongeloof en Revolutie has been published 12 times to date. The two editions published during the author's lifetime were followed by 10 reissues, of which 5 are simple reprintings of authorial editions and 3 are edited versions, one of which saw two reprints. The ten reissues involved five different publishers, who do not always acknowledge each other's numbering. Five different authors have written forewords to the work. The history of the editions and reprints can be diagrammed as shown in Figure 10.1, where each rectangle represents an "edition" and vertical lines represent the stemma of related "editions." A short description of each follows here. For convenience's sake, we will call each printing an "edition."

THE FIRST EDITION OF 1847

Publisher: S. en J. Luchtmans, Leyden.
Pages: xii, 432.

As the author explained to the publisher, he was releasing the text as it had been delivered orally, personal comments and all, to save himself the trouble of having to rewrite it.[1] Accordingly the Preface (vi) states that the book contains the text of the lectures "except for a few minor changes." Any plans for careful revision had to be laid aside by the author, for this was no time to "sharpen and polish his weapons, but rather to put them to use."

In a brief exchange the following year, when revolutions broke out all over Europe and the Dutch king invited prominent liberals to draft a new constitution, the author suggested to the publisher, "Do you not think it would be appropriate for S. and J. Luchtmans in these circumstances to advertise once more that there are copies available of my *Contribution Toward a Revision of the Constitution* and

---

1. *Briefwisseling*, II, 790.

Unbelief and Revolution?"[2] Since financial return played absolutely no role, Groen's motive for promoting sales must have been purely altruistic. The number of copies printed and the quantity sold are not known.[3]

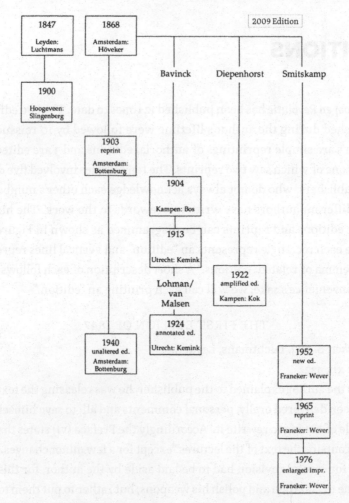

Figure 10.1: Editions of *Ongeloof en Revolutie*

---

2. *Briefwisseling*, II, 871.

3. Groen's published correspondence contains no data. Nor does the (still voluminous) unpublished correspondence and other papers in the Archief-Groen van Prinsterer (Algemeen Rijksarchief, The Hague). The records of the Luchtmans firm (which was dissolved in the course of 1848), on deposit in the archives of the *Vereniging ter bevordering van de belangen des boekhandels* (Library, City University of Amsterdam), contain annual totals only, not figures for separate titles; for 1847, moreover, the record is very incomplete. Letters to the author from J. L. van Essen, 24 Nov. 1987 and 3 Feb. 1988.

THE REVISED EDITION OF 1868

Publisher: H. Höveker, Amsterdam.

Pages: xx, 456.

Title page: "Tweede uitgaaf" (second edition).

We note here that precise terms are hard to come by; not only are the authorial editions of 1847 and 1868 designated *"uitgaaf"* (a term which might as easily be rendered "issue" or "publication"), but so are the reprints of 1903, 1904, 1913 and 1940 described below. Strictly speaking, only the versions edited by Diepenhorst (1922), Van Malsen (1924) and Smitskamp (1952), who correctly refer to their products as *"bewerkingen"* (edited versions), deserve to be called "editions."

A blurb on the back of Groen's *Heiligerlee en Ultramontaansche kritiek*, published by the same firm in early 1868, announced this edition as a "second, revised printing." As much as a decade earlier, in July 1858, the author had tried, without success, to interest the publisher in a reprint; not until June of 1867 was the subject raised again.[4]

Although the new preface called the text "virtually unchanged," the revisions, upon closer inspection, turn out to be substantial. They consisted of numerous deletions, substitutions, and additions. These are examined in the next chapter.

For this revised edition Groen wrote a brief Preface, dated July 1868. He also added an Index of Subjects (pp. 445–53), a List of Authors Cited (pp. 454–55), and a List of Errata (p. 456), each of which is very incomplete. The total run was 550; six years later, more than half were still unsold.[5]

THE EDITION OF 1900

Publisher: R. Slingenberg, Hoogeveen.

This is a reprint of the 1st edition of 1847, in identical page layout but in a different type-face. Planned as a publication in installments, only the first installment is extant; it consists of a printer's sheet of 16 pages and stops in the middle of a sentence. The copy in the library of the Free University bears the following hand-written note: "This is a reprint of the *first* printing and as such a bibliographic curiosity. Publication discontinued."

---

4. *Briefwisseling*, III, 490n5; IV, 78.

5. Figures of sales in Smitskamp, "Het boek 'Ongeloof en Revolutie,' " p. 21.

Why the plan misfired is not known, but see chapter II below, p. 211n1. All reprints after this date reprint the 2nd edition of 1868.

THE EDITION OF 1903

Publisher: H. A. van Bottenburg, Amsterdam.
Pages: xvi, 428.
Title page: "Third edition."

This is a reprint of the 2nd edition of 1868. The text has been entirely reset. The publisher guarantees: "This third edition is unchanged from the second."

THE EDITION OF 1904

Publisher: J. H. Bos, Kampen.
Pages: xxviii, 406, x.
Title page: "Third edition. With a foreword by Dr. H. Bavinck." The numbering ignores the Bottenburg edition of the previous year.

Bavinck, attached until 1902 to the Theological School in Kampen,[6] but since then professor of systematic theology in the Free University at Amsterdam, dates his foreword "April 1904." He begins rather oddly by observing that the ideas which Groen combated are now defended by almost no one; Rousseau has been replaced by Darwin, Kant by Hegel, and revolution by evolution: whereas man used to be regarded as an angel, he is now considered an evolved animal. And yet, Bavinck continues, Groen's work is not antiquated, because the enemy he fought may have changed its face but not its spirit. It is still man who is said to originate language and religion, law and morality, state and society, while God, his Word and law, are still left out of consideration. In fact, Bavinck observes, from this point of view one must say that the situation has not improved but grown worse. "There has been progress, but in the sense of further dissolution; there has been development, but in a downward direction." Science has been completely secularized and today explains the phenomena purely historically, or psycho-genetically, and in the final analysis mechanistically.

---

6. Bookseller/publisher J. H. Bos had many connections with the Theological School and counted Professor Bavinck, whose *magnum opus* he had published—*Gereformeerde Dogmatiek* (4 vols.; 1895–1901)—among his personal friends; cf. Jaap van Gelderen, *Boekenbos 1883-1983* (Kampen: n.p., 1983), pp. 11–13, 35f.

Groen had learned to see this spiritual revolution as the consequences of systematic unbelief. Ever since then, Bavinck goes on, history has demonstrated the correctness of this insight from year to year. In every domain—in family and society, in science and art, in religion and morality, in law and history—the consequences are being drawn which Groen had seen as implicitly present in seminal form in the principle of the revolution. If at present these consequences are not—or not fully—being applied in life, then we certainly do not owe this to the principle, but only to the forces with which God counteracts it in nature and history; we owe it to the return to the gospel which his Spirit has brought forth in a portion of Christendom. That is also the reason, Bavinck believes, why Groen did not lose hope. The gospel is the sole, and also efficacious, cure for the ills of the age. Groen did not long for a return of dead orthodoxy or old-fashioned forms, but for earnest faith, personal conversion, submission to God's Word and law—for sincere believers who heartily embraced and practiced the unchangeable truths of the Reformation.

Here the foreword moves on to underscore what gives the book its special significance. "Groen did not stop at the demand for a personal return to the gospel. However much he emphasized the need for individual, true conversion, he was always on guard against the danger of pietism and world-flight. From the gospel he deduced principles which would bring blessing to family and society, science and art, law and politics. After all, the power of the gospel to effect order, freedom and prosperity had been substantiated by world history. Whatever is useful and beneficial to man is promoted by the fear of God and thwarted by the denial of God."

All these things, Bavinck concludes, "reveal the significance of Groen's work not only for the past and the present but also for the future. Like the staff of Moses before those of the Egyptians, it is a book that devours many other books."

Bavinck's foreword, which here covers nine pages, is reprinted in the editions of 1913 and 1924.

THE EDITION OF 1913

Publisher: Kemink, Utrecht.

Pages: xxviii, 406, x.

Title page: "Fourth edition."

This edition by Kemink is a reprint of the "third edition" of 1904 by Bos. In fact, it uses identical plates and thus includes the foreword by Bavinck, which the "third edition" of 1903 by Bottenburg lacked.

THE DIEPENHORST EDITION OF 1922

Publisher: J. H. Kok, Kampen.

Pages: [viii], 344.

Title page: "Edited and amplified for our time by P. A. Diepenhorst, LL.D., professor in the Free University at Amsterdam."

This edition is in the nature of an abridgment. The text is that of the 2nd edition, but shortened so as to achieve easier reading while retaining the flow of the argument. Lengthy passages judged less relevant to the present are summarized in short paragraphs enclosed in parentheses. In all, the text is reduced by at least one third. Foreign quotations are translated into Dutch if essential to the argument, deleted if merely illustrative of a point first made in Groen's own words. Each chapter is headed by an extensive Argument; its phrases recur in marginal notes at the appropriate places. An Index of Names and an Analytical Table of Contents are placed at the end of the book. In Lectures I, II, III, and VII, subheadings are introduced.

Modest annotation at the foot of the page is provided as well. Of the thirty notes added by the editor, eighteen provide information on authors cited (e.g. Lamennais, Guizot, Burke, Dumont), five identify historical figures (e.g. Turgot, Babeuf), four clarify events or issues (e.g. the background of Article 14 of the charter in Restoration France, the distinction made by Groen between constitutional monarchy and constitutionalism), while three do other things (a running translation of a French poem, a reference to a recent doctoral dissertation on the Monarchomachs, and a recommendation of Doumergue's 1902 study of Calvin).

Of far greater interest is the editor's 55-page Epilogue, in which he traces the drift to the left of Western politics as predicted by Groen. Diepenhorst outlines the growth of the "theory of revolution" from economic liberalism, over socialism and anarchism as their inevitable reactions, to the Commune of Paris and the Bolshevist ideology and revolution in Russia.

The aim of this edition, the foreword explains, is "to give all our actively involved men and women, not least our Christian labor organization, a book that provides principial nourishment on life's journey."

THE VAN MALSEN EDITION OF 1924

Publisher: Kemink & Zoon, Utrecht.

Pages: xxxiv, 583, xxvi.

On the cover: "Fifth Impression." This numbering is consistent with the publisher's edition of 1913.

Title page: "Fifth Edition, prepared from the second edition by H. Van Malsen, with an introduction by A. F. de Savornin Lohman, minister of state, former member of parliament."

Turning the pages of this hefty volume bound in gilt-stamped, dark blue cloth, one meets successively: a foreword by Van Malsen; the introduction by Lohman; Bavinck's foreword "to the third and fourth edition," and finally, the two original prefaces by Groen van Prinsterer.

Following the text of *Unbelief and Revolution*, Van Malsen adds an Epilogue of 33 pages and an Appendix of 138 pages containing literally hundreds of citations from other works of Groen bearing on points in the text (the citations are grouped and numbered 1–305, which numbers also appear boldface, in parentheses, in the text at appropriate places, the same number often being used more than once). The book closes with a List of Works Cited and Consulted [by the editor]; an Index [of both names and subjects]; a List of Authors Cited [by Groen]; and, finally, an Index to the Appendix. Of the 641 pages of this volume, 417 are given over to the text of *Unbelief and Revolution*, 224 to other things; in other words, the editorial additions account for more than one-third of the total.

Van Malsen explains in his foreword that *Unbelief and Revolution* is a scholarly work requiring serious study, especially of the entire "universe of Groen's thought" as manifested in his later writings. To popularize the work in the sense of transplanting it to the soil of an "unscholarly *socio-economic* milieu" must therefore be considered a mistake. Having studied Groen's entire oeuvre for more than ten years, Van Malsen feels he has yet to come near the center of it. Groen has turned out to be, in the good sense of the word, an exceedingly "lively model" whose true portrait is not easy to capture. The annotation, the editor advises, can only be a limited sampling of the "awesome amount" of material he has collected on Groen and hopes to publish before long. Van Malsen ends by inviting criticism of "*serious* students of Groen" (italics in original).

Lohman's introduction covers six pages and recommends both the work and this particular edition. He commends *Unbelief and Revolution* warmly because it provides a firm guide and compass for determining both what men have done in the past and what they ought to have done. That compass was for Groen "simply the gospel, which is, for whoever will read and obey, be he a lowly citizen or a lofty statesman, not just a revelation of divine wisdom but also a practical guide for living." Therefore, since the gospel never grows old, every new edition of *Unbelief and Revolution* will continue to be of immense value to the Christian. However, cautions Lohman, Groen did not just write for a party; his sympathies went out to all the people, to "*the entire nation*," and for this reason he wrote innumerable pamphlets and articles to communicate his profound thought and prodigious knowledge to whoever would listen. "But," Lohman goes on, "this is where a difficulty arises for the common man. Not that Groen is difficult to understand. He may not have been a popular writer in the ordinary sense of the word— although few match Groen in having given currency virtually throughout the nation to so many slogans. His style is concise; never a word too much, but never a word too little either. Reading the same thing over two or three times is often more profitable and less time-consuming than the reading of countless popular writings. Only, one must read with care! But the great difficulty is: *what* to read?"

At this point Lohman draws attention to the peculiar merits of the anno-tated edition here presented to the public. The annotations of his friend Van Malsen greatly illumine the original work with the very words of the author himself. I have no doubt, Lohman concludes, "that *this* edition of Groen's basic work will be considered a welcome addition by many."

Transparent in the words of both Van Malsen and Lohman are the allusions to an edition of *Unbelief and Revolution* which they consider infe-rior and partisan. The butt of their critique is no doubt the Diepenhorst edition of two years earlier, which immediately upon publication had been severely castigated in the pages of Lohman's paper *De Nederlander*,[7] especially for having dared to violate the original by abridging portions of it. An ulterior motive behind this critique may have been the fact that Diepenhorst was a disciple of Abrahm Kuyper, but Van Malsen of Lohman, who always underscored Groen's Réveil antecedents and scorned Kuyper's annexation of Groen for his neo-Calvinism.[8]

THE EDITION OF 1940

Publisher: H. A. van Bottenburg N.V., Amsterdam.

Pages: xiv, 373.

Title page: "Fourth Edition, unaltered from the last edition published by the author."

This edition by Bottenburg is a reprint, from new plates, of its own "third edition" of 1903. The numbering ignores the successive Bos and Kemink editions issued in 1904, 1913 and 1924. This edition may have been occasioned by a renewed interest in Groen especially in circles of the Anti-Revolutionary Party. Hendrik Smitskamp had published his dissertation on *Groen van Prinsterer as Historian* in February, 1940; that fall he wrote a study outline of *Unbelief and Revolution* for the first issue of the party's new monthly (called *Nederlandsche Gedachten*, thus reviving the name of Groen's periodical). No doubt Nazi Germany's juggernaut over Holland, ending in military defeat and occupation, added to the interest in *Unbelief and Revolution*.[9] The Bottenburg reprint is warmly recommended to the readers as late as March 1941, in the seventh issue of *Nederlandsche Gedachten*, shortly before it ceased publication when the party went underground.

On balance, then, the publication history of *Ongeloof en Revolutie* up to the Second World War is as follows. If we allow "editions" to include simple reissues with a new foreword, we can say that between 1847–1940 eight complete editions have appeared, to wit: two during the author's lifetime (1847, 1868), four in the twentieth century (1903, 1904, 1913, 1940), and two editions of a special kind: the abridged and amplified edition of 1922, and

---

7. *Veertiendaags Bijblad*, 20 Dec. 1922, 17 and 31 Jan. 1923.

8. See H. van Malsen, *Lohman, ontwikkelingsgang van zijn denken en handelen* (Haarlem: Bohn, 1931), pp. 198, 201.

9. See note 10 below.

the annotated edition of 1924. As well, there is the abortive edition of 1900. That makes for a total of nine editions. Three more will follow after the war.

THE SMITSKAMP EDITION OF 1952

Publisher: T. Wever, Franeker.

Pages: 344.

Title page: "New Edition, prepared by Dr. H. Smitskamp, professor in the Free University."

Professor Smitskamp explains in a foreword dated January 1951 that the aim of the new edition, which is based on that of 1868, is to make the work accessible to as broad a circle as possible. In a possible allusion to the Diepenhorst edition Smitskamp assures the reader that although "neither the difficulty of the subject-matter nor the pithy, compressed style can be remedied without violating the work as such," yet there is help in the case of other obstacles. He then lists the five changes he has made: all quotations in foreign languages have been translated into Dutch; spelling and punctuation have been brought into line with modern usage, and longer paragraphs have been split up; the Index of Subjects and the List of Authors Cited have been replaced by an Analytical Table of Contents; a Chronology has been appended of dates and facts that one needs to know to be able to follow the historical chapters; and finally, extra annotation has been inserted at the foot of the page in order to facilitate comprehension of the text by elucidating a number of allusions to events and persons now largely unfamiliar to the modern reader. Thus what is offered here is a *revised* edition, but the revisions, the editor hastens to assure us, touch only the form: the content has been left unchanged. No mention is made of the Diepenhorst edition.

Was a more radical procedure not advisable? Smitskamp raises this question because, after all, various passages and citations could very well, he concedes, have been abridged or even deleted; in places the work is dated and contains inaccuracies; nor does it always reflect Groen's *definitive* views, as witness the discrepancy here and there between the main text of 1847 and the notes added in 1868. But no, answers Smitskamp in reply to his own question, the less drastic method followed here is preferable: *Ongeloof en Revolutie* has become a classic with the content Groen himself gave to it. One should accept it as it stands, or write a new book on the same subject.

As for the annotation, the editor informs the reader that his additional footnotes are not intended to enlarge upon the correctness or incorrectness of Groen's expositions. And indeed, Smitskamp's scores of brief explanatory notes are written with sober detachment. Two exceptions are the notes on pages 41 and 117, where he takes issue, respectively, with Groen's patrimonial view of the state and with his questionable reading of the Act of Abjuration of 1581.

About the contemporary relevance of the work Smitskamp comments: "This masterful depiction of the spirit of revolution, the compelling logic with which it is analyzed and the clarity with which its manifestations are pointed out in the political domain, have retained their value for the present time. ... It was no coincidence that during the German occupation many people, for the first time or once again, drew strength from this book for principled resistance against national socialism.[10] It can still render the same service in the face of all systems and currents that expect the salvation of society from human power and effort alone."

A total run of 2000 copies was sold out by 1960.[11]

THE REPRINT OF 1965

Publisher: T. Wever, Franeker.

Pages: 336.

This is an unaltered but completely reset printing of the Smitskamp edition of 1952.

A total run of 2,000 copies was sold out by 1976.[12]

---

10. Passages from the work, stencilled by the underground, went from hand to hand. Groen's analysis suddenly seemed acutely relevant for assessing the "revolution of the twentieth century"; cf. H. Algra, *De Revolutie permanent?*, p. 44. One passage in particular, from Lecture III (51)—"I will not subscribe to any interpretation that would oblige us ... to hail today as a power ordained of God the crowned robber who yesterday banished our legitimate prince"—played a curious role: it helped persuade Calvinists that active resistance against the German occupation authorities was permissible; cf. C. Smeenk and J. A. de Wilde, *Het Volk ten baat* (Groningen: Jan Haan, 1949), p. 699; see also V. H. Rutgers, "Toetsingsrecht," *Nederlandsch Juristenblad*, 29 Nov. 1941, pp. 749–60. E. van Ruller, "De Anti-Revolutionaire Partij en het verzet," *Anti-Revolutionaire Staatkunde* 24 (1954): 143, relates a telling anecdote: During the first few months of the occupation, when leaders of the Anti-Revolutionary electoral associations inquired at their party's national secretariat what should be on the agenda for their meetings "in these unusual times," Chairman Colijn had but one short answer: "Read and discuss Groen's *Unbelief and Revolution!*"

11. Information kindly provided by the firm's Mr. J. Beintema.

12. See previous note.

THE COMMEMORATIVE EDITION OF 1976

Publisher: T. Wever B.V., Franeker.
Pages: 342.
Title page: "Third enlarged impression."
On the cover: "Newly edited by Prof. Dr. H. Smitskamp."

This is a photographic reproduction of the 1965 reprint. The enlargement consists of three additional passages: two from the 1st edition of 1847, and one whose omission was noted by Van der Kemp when the book first came out. On page 7 the publisher notes that this new edition has undoubtedly gained in significance as a result of the incorporation of the three passages.

The first passage is reproduced on page 189. Deleted in the second edition, it contains Groen's confession, at the end of Lecture X, that the pressure of the weekly preparations had become so burdensome that he had seriously considered quitting for the year, "now that we have finished about half the journey." However, the author continues, "in the light of the brevity of life and my desire once for all to submit my political ideas as a whole to competent and sympathetic judges, and in reliance on friends whose indulgence will be extended according to need, and above all in reliance on Him who gives strength to the weary," he had decided to go forward and make a beginning of the *history* of the revolution.

The second passage is appended on page 329 and consists of what might be called the book's *envoi*. At the end of Lecture XV, immediately after the Bible verse "quicken me according to thy word," Groen had continued for almost another whole page, in which he expressed, first of all, his thanks to the hearers for their sympathetic ear and their constant encouragement; secondly, his doubt that he would be able very soon to realize his wish to give another series of this kind devoted to a new topic; next, his hopes that the frank communication of his views had strengthened the bond of friendship; and, finally, his testimony that "if there has been anything good or useful in my presentation, I return the praise with thankful prayer to Him who gave me strength, while I ask Him forgiveness for the sins and shortcomings mingled with it through my own doing."

The third passage, appended on pages 330-32, consists of the hitherto unpublished text of Groen's provisional answer, at the beginning of Lecture IX, to the question whether he was applying what may have been true of

France too broadly to the rest of Europe. The publisher had been alerted to the existence of this text by the English edition of Lecture IX, which had meanwhile appeared.[13]

The occasion of this reprint, which was lavishly bound in gilt-stamped maroon cloth, was the commemoration on 19 May 1976 of the centennial of Groen's death. The event saw a score of radio and television programs, special "Groen Issues" of dozens of periodicals and magazines, a commemorative stamp issued by the Post Office, a graveside ceremony led by the Minister of Interior Affairs, a commemorative gathering featuring three prominent speakers and attended by hundreds of educators, journalists and politicians, and the publication of a new popular biography[14] and of a memorial volume of some forty papers on Groen, entitled *Een Staatsman ter navolging*. Pre-publication orders for Wever's anniversary edition of *Ongeloof en Revolutie* ran so high that the publisher increased his run from two to four thousand.[15] It quickly sold out.

Carefully monitored advertising seemed to indicate[16] a slightly higher interest in the book, geographically, from the province of Zealand, and denominationally, from the Liberated Reformed Churches[17] (a rough datum which may tell something only to those who are intimately acquainted with Dutch relationships, and which will be variously interpreted even by them).

In all, then, the publishing firm Wever sold 8,000 copies of the Smitskamp edition in a quarter century. That figure must be judged substantial for a nineteenth-century work, yet is but modest for a population whose per capita rate of personal book purchases is reputed to be among the highest in the world.

After this examination of the editions, another look at our diagram of their history can be very enlightening for solving a little puzzle connected with them: namely, their confused numbering. Our stemma makes visible at a glance a plausible reason for the confusion: it may well reflect a minor publishers' war. If our conjecture is correct, Zwaan is too

---

13. It was the editor of that publication who also drew the publisher's attention to the two other passages described above.

14. G. J. Schutte, *Mr. G. Groen van Prinsterer*; 2nd ed. 1977.

15. Private communication to the author by Mr. L. Wever.

16. See previous note.

17. Gereformeerde Kerken (vrijgemaakt).

charitable when he writes that the publishers "lost count."[18] Only in the case of the two "third" editions of 1903 and 1904 may this at all be the case. But once this error was made, company mergers or sellouts were bound to perpetuate it. Bottenburg, so our conjecture goes, somehow must have taken over Höveker's interest in *Ongeloof en Revolutie* around the turn of the century, and from then on must have assumed first rights to Groen's (non-copyrighted) work.[19] Kemink, meanwhile, appears to have taken over part of the publisher's list of J. H. Bos[20] and must have felt justified thereafter in numbering its 1913 reprint (using Bos's plates) the "fourth" and Van Malsen's subsequent edition of 1924 the "fifth." Mr. Van Bottenburg, for his part, can hardly have felt bound to yield to this arrogation, and so, understandably, his reprint of the work in 1940 (as in 1903, without any foreword by Bavinck or anyone else) was likewise designated the "fourth". Wever wisely side-stepped the question of numbering by calling the Smitskamp edition simply a "new" edition.

THE MODERNIZED EDITION OF 2008

Publisher: Nederlands Dagblad, Barneveld
Pages: 390
Title page: Edited and introduced by Arie Kuiper and Roel Kuiper

Another edition of *Ongeloof en Revolutie* saw the light in 2008. It was published in the series "Klassiek klicht" by the Christian daily *Nederlands Dagblad*. This edition was offered to the public as a *hertaling* (rewording). It simplifies syntax, diction, and sentence structure, and translates all foreign terms and quotations into modern Dutch—a process similar to the one applied in the English translation of 1989. A modest number of clarifying footnotes add to the usefulness of this edition for the modern reader. Print run and volume of sales could not be traced.

From the Introduction: "*Ongeloof en Revolutie* appeared in 1847 and slowly grew to the monumental significance it acquired later. Groen van

---

18. Zwaan, *Groen van Prinsterer en de klassieke Oudheid*, p. 473.

19. The proprietor of the Bottenburg firm, Mr. Ton Bolland, reported that its archives were damaged, incomplete and no longer contained any data on the firm's editions of *Unbelief and Revolution*. Letter to the author, 25 June 1988.

20. This would have been shortly after 1911, when Bos (who as a young man had apprenticed at the venerable firm of Kemink's) began to run into financial difficulties; cf. Van Gelderen, *Boekenbos 1883-1983*, pp. 11-14.

Prinsterer published his work on the eve of the revolution year 1848, thus at a pivotal moment in European history. ... *Unbelief and Revolution* probes the spirit of modernity that broke to the surface in the Enlightenment. In this book a Christian is speaking who has discovered modernity's intention to tear Western Civilization from its Christian roots. In [our] ideologically charged times, Groen's thought compels one to choose, and in those moments the radical message of *Unbelief and Revolution* is most forcefully recognized by his spiritual kin."

THE MODERNIZED EDITION OF 2009

Publisher: Nederlands Dagblad, Barneveld. Series *Klassiek Licht*.
Pages: 389.
Title Page: Edited and introduced by Arie and Roel Kuiper.

Since the publication in 1989 of the present study, another, most remarkable edition of *Unbelief and Revolution* has come out, edited by father and son Roel and Arie Kuiper. Their treatment of Groen's text has the explicit intention of making the work more accessible to the modern reader. To that end they have transposed some old-fashioned diction into present-day Dutch idiom, briefly expanded passages to bring out their intended ironic character, recast and at times reformulated obscure passages, simplified complex sentence and paragraph structure, and added a modest amount of annotation, all the while endeavoring to retain Groen's style and guarding against merely abridging or popularizing the work. Most of Smitskamp's translations of foreign quotations have been adopted. The introduction recounts the significant role that this classic has played in the history of Dutch society and politics, and argues that it has kept its relevance in the twenty-first century.

11
—

THE FIRST AND SECOND EDITIONS COMPARED

As promised, we shall now examine the deletions, substitutions and additions which the author saw fit to make as he prepared the 2nd edition. A comparison shows that the text of the 1st edition often provides a solution to a problem occasioned by the text of the 2nd edition. Thus both editions have significance in their own right for establishing the full meaning of the work.

This conclusion runs counter to the general rule that when a work has gone through more than one edition during an author's lifetime it is the last authorial edition that counts as "authoritative for study and critique" since it must be presumed to contain the final "authorized" version of the author's "authentic" views on the subject-matter of the book. This rule appears to have been followed without question in almost every posthumous republication of Groen's famous book.[1] Yet in the case of *Unbelief and Revolution* there are good reasons not to adhere too strictly to the rule. For one thing, what we have designated "the revised edition of 1868" is not referred to by Groen as a revision but as a "reissue" (*tweede uitgaaf*) consisting of a "virtually unchanged" text; this alone would justify regarding the 1st edition as equally authoritative. More importantly, as we shall see in a moment, the type of changes incorporated in the 2nd edition of 1868 are such that one cannot dispense with the earlier version of 1847. That the changes are not negligible is already intimated by the fact that Smitskamp, although he faithfully repeats the author's statement that the text is "virtually unchanged,"[2] saw himself compelled, when giving

---

1. Infraction of this rule may have spoiled the market for the edition of 1900.
2. Preface, Smitskamp edition, 1952, p. 7.

a bibliographic introduction of *Unbelief and Revolution* to the Society of Christian Historians, to revert at several points to the text of the 1st edition.[3] Again, Zwaan remarks somewhere, with a hint of irritation, that certain deletions in the 2nd edition are anything but improvements, and that Groen's intended meaning comes out much more clearly in the 1st edition.[4] The following comparison of the two editions, consequently, illustrates interesting changes not only in style but also in substance. Especially the fact that some of the changes in substance appear to be unintended warrants the conclusion that next to the 2nd edition the 1st edition has retained its own intrinsic value, so that both editions should be read together in order to be able to do justice to the book's intentions.

DELETIONS

The first most obvious feature of the revision of 1868, when compared with the original edition of 1847, is the prodigal manner in which the author-editor has seen fit to expunge words, phrases, whole sentences, even paragraphs. The deletions are of various kinds.

The personal addresses that were woven into the original text are removed, as are other vestiges of the original lecture setting. One no longer reads words like "My friends!" "Follow me now as," "I crave your indulgence," "I should like to recall to your mind," etc. Apart from such dispensable features, a number of other deletions of this kind must be considered a real loss. For example, toward the close of Lecture V a whole page reciting objections raised by the hearers is eliminated; they expressed nuances but also disagreement with respect to Groen's depiction of pre-revolutionary monarchies. Again, toward the end of Lecture X Groen has removed nearly a page in which he confides to his audience that he has seriously considered ending the series at this point. Also, a final word of farewell and thanks on the very last page of the book has been struck. At the opening of each lecture, the summaries of what has been discussed so far are greatly reduced if not deleted altogether. Similarly, at the close of each lecture

---

3. See *Lustrumbundel*, pp. 11, 12, 13, 14, 16; the same need was felt in the contributions by Drs. Smit and Sneller, *ibid.*, pp. 53, 192.

4. Zwaan, *Groen van Prinsterer en de klassieke Oudheid*, p. 378n179.

the recapitulation of the evening and the introduction of questions to be treated next time are dropped.

Moreover, about half the internal cross-references and nearly as much of the source documentation are deleted from the foot of the page. Footnotes that once identified Bible passages quoted in the text have more than once gotten lost in the scramble for space at the foot of the page.

Furthermore, like any careful writer, Groen has attempted to weed out all needless verbiage. Many articles, definite or indefinite, have been deleted, and prepositions in a series are sometimes not repeated, as they invariably were before; compare the following sentence[5] in Lecture V:

Let us look at the principle, at the form, and at the abuses. ([1]114)	Let us, also here, look at principle, form, abuse. ([2]104)

While some of this rewriting is done to good effect, other changes seem less than helpful. Much of Groen's weeding is certainly not demanded by good Dutch style. On occasion the result is downright cryptic. The result is likewise mystifying when connectives like *and, but, yet, however, accordingly, nevertheless*—helpful hinges in any argumentative prose and certainly useful logical links which an intricate case such as that presented in *Unbelief and Revolution* can scarcely do without—are greatly reduced in number. On the other hand, clarity and brevity are served when old-fashioned subjunctives are replaced by indicatives, the present perfect is shortened to the simple present, compound sentences are broken up into a series of independent clauses, and convoluted figures of speech are streamlined. Excessive use of capital letters is toned down by a reversion to lower case (though not consistently), while in some lectures sections are given numbers or letters of the alphabet (though in other lectures they are dropped).

Many intensifiers, like *even, very, own, itself*, have been removed, resulting in leaner prose, but here and there with loss of impact. To be sure, no

---

5. Throughout this chapter, the column on the left represents the 1st edition, that on the right the 2nd edition.

meaning is lost when Groen erases an occasional *thereof* and *herein*, but
the reader wonders whether it was really necessary for him to discard so
many of those particles like *toch, al, wel, nog, mede, dan*—which are best
left "untranslated" in English but which are the fairies, not the gremlins,
of Dutch prose. Terseness must have been the aim but denseness is the
result when subordinate clauses are stripped of their verbs and turned
into participial phrases or absolute constructions reminiscent of Latin.

What may possibly account for these changes? The older Groen of 1868
is more hardened, more radical than the middle-aged Groen, who was
above all intent on persuading his contemporaries (and perhaps somewhat
himself) of the correctness of his unconventional views and interpretations; moreover, in 1868 he claims in the Preface that in the intervening
two decades his worldview has not just remained the same but has been
reinforced. These biographical factors help explain why there is a certain
directness, starkness, bluntness to the revised edition; they help explain,
for example, why nearly all restrictive modifiers and extenuating qualifications have been removed. Gone are such guarded phrases as *to some
extent, in large measure, in many respects*. All but vanished are parentheses like *as it were, so to speak, it would seem*. Excised, almost defiantly, are
safety valves like *almost, perhaps, as yet*—only to reappear, it is true, in
other places, albeit far less frequently (there the qualifiers seem to reflect
Groen's sensitivity to the advancement in historical studies and also wider
reading on his part).

An obvious conclusion to draw from all this, already at this juncture, is
that the modern reader is well served by consulting both authorial editions
of this work. Equally, the modern translator is well advised when adopting one edition as his or her copy-text, continually to check the other for
possible hints as to nuances and hidden connotations.

Below are some examples (here italicized) of modifiers and qualifiers
deleted from the 2nd edition (but retained in our abridged translation).

"The eighteenth century must have contained much that was, *in
part*, good." (Lecture VIII, 184)

"The Revolution doctrine is the Religion, *as it were*, of unbelief."
(Lecture VIII, 192)

"The apologia, published by one of them, Buonarrotti, in 1828, is exceedingly helpful, *it seems to me*, in illustrating the character of the Revolution." (Lecture IX, 219)

"If we want to know the natural history of the doctrine of unbelief we have to view it in the context of the atmosphere of reality, *which cannot but modify it*." (Lecture X, 225)

"... then the gravest responsibility lies, not with those who *in their ignorance* devoted themselves to illusions of liberty and morality ..." (Lecture XIII, 364)

"... the House [of Orange], which the Lord himself in former days had appointed, *as it were*, to be watchmen over Religion and Liberty ..." (Lecture XV, 409)

Deletions such as these, though not always felicitous, are not grave. Others are more serious. For instance, in the important discussion about fatalism at the beginning of Lecture VIII (180f), the deletion of a single sentence has created a puzzling gap between text and footnote. The text used to read: "Just as there are forces and laws in the physical world, so there are forces and laws in the moral realm. There are times when the power of men is powerless against the action of these principles." Following these two sentences the text had continued with a quotation from Ancillon about people's inability to stop an ideological revolution once it has been set in motion. Now, in the 2nd edition, the second sentence is deleted altogether, while the quotation is relegated to a footnote. This (invisible) change has occasioned the observation by one serious student of Groen, who is relying on the 2nd edition only, that the quotation in the footnote, in terms of content, distinguishes itself essentially from the main text.[6] In itself this observation is correct; things become almost comical, however, when the discrepancy is invoked to illustrate the otherwise valid point that Groen had the habit of quoting authorities "without giving up his intellectual independence or the integrity of his own distinctive position."

A final hidden change of some consequence is the following. Deletions have made it especially difficult to ascertain Groen's view of historical causality. Once again it pays to consult not just the 2nd edition (as so many

---

6. Algra, "Beginsel en causaliteit," p. 213.

interpreters have done thus far) but also the first. To illustrate which version is more helpful for appreciating the view of causality carefully advanced here, consider:

I do not deny that abuses were among the secondary causes of the Revolution. ... I fully admit the influence of every wrong that had become commingled with the political arrangements. Yet I am convinced that, compared to the influence of the Revolution ideas, the harmful operation, even if acknowledged in its full force, was nothing but very subordinate cooperation. (Lecture V, [1]96)	Abuses were subordinate causes of the Revolution. I fully admit the influence of the wrong commingled with the political arrangements. But in the harmful operation these abuses were not comparable to the Revolution ideas. ([2]88)

Similarly, which version gives the reader a fuller understanding of Groen's awareness of the hierarchy of causes he was choosing:

Whatever may have been the subordinate action of secondary causes, as to the principal cause the history of Europe for more than half a century has been the inevitable result of the errors that have made themselves master of the predominant mode of thinking. (Lecture I, [1]5)	The history of Europe for more than half a century has been the inevitable result of the errors that have made themselves master of the predominant mode of thinking. ([2]4)

Let me end this discussion of *deletions* by deploring the fact that Groen chose to strike one trenchant clause on page 2 of the second edition from his enumeration of the "lack of order" throughout society: "Workingmen are helpless over against the factory owners ..."

SUBSTITUTIONS

Of course a revision of a text involves replacing words with better ones. This is an author's unquestioned prerogative, and Groen made ample use of it (a right he was known to practice liberally even when proofreading his speeches in the Dutch Hansard). Still, in the case of the revision of *Ongeloof en Revolutie* the reader sometimes questions whether his substitutions are really improvements. For example, Groen may achieve brevity but not always clarity when he reduces prepositional phrases as shown in Table 11.1.

1st edition	2nd edition
op grond van	uit
ter wille van	om
een soort van	een
te midden van	in
ten gevolge van	door
ten behoeve van	voor

Table 11.1: Reduction of prepositional phrases

A good example of the unclarity produced by substitutions is found in Lecture VIII. After Groen has cleared himself of the charge of partiality by praising the relative justice of the cause of the Enlightenment, he resumes his main theme by saying: "I now proceed ...

I now proceed ... to the elaboration of my opinion that the Revolution, in its entire compass, is nothing other than systematic unbelief, the forsaking of the Gospel in its consequences. (Lecture VIII, ¹191)	... I come to the argument that the Revolution is systematic unbelief, forsaking the gospel with the appurtenances thereof. (²176)

In his critical appraisal of 1949, Professor A. M. Donner, who consulted only the text of the 2nd edition, complains that in the sentence reproduced above, as well as in other, similar passages, Groen clearly posits the *identity* of unbelief and revolution whereas he had begun by promising to demonstrate the *causal connection* between the two: the lecturer had promised rashly at the outset that he would show how unbelief had led irresistibly to revolution, but he ended by simply telescoping the two, thus forgetting to prove his main thesis. Donner spends five pages pleading his interpretation.[7] A look at the 1st-edition variant of the sentence in question might have given him pause. "Appurtenances" is much less a temporal-historical term than is "consequences." It is only after one has compared the two versions, here *et passim*, that one realizes the eminently historical sense in which Groen uses terms like "systematic" (systematized; developed or elaborated into a full-blown system) and "forsaking the Gospel" (a renouncing, one after the other, of the tenets of Christianity in their full import for man and society). Our translation has tried to avoid any possible ambiguity in either version: "... nothing other than the logical outcome of systematic unbelief, the outworking of apostasy from the Gospel."

Another type of substitution betrays an unmistakably purist attitude. The version of 1868 shows a tendency, though not consistently followed, to Dutchify words of foreign derivation. The translator into English—and I dare say in some cases even the modern Dutch reader—is delighted, after staring at a number of "pure" Dutch-sounding words in the 2nd edition, to discover their "foreign" equivalents originally used in the 1st edition.[8] See Table 11.2.[9]

---

7. *Lustrumbundel*, pp. 138–42, citing the 4th ed. of 1940.

8. In the Smitskamp edition, the annotation to a number of these terms are presented as if they provide "more contemporary Dutch equivalents"; in actual fact they turn out to be the same as originally used in the 1st edition.

9. Our tables record only the place of first occurrence of the substitution.

page	1st edition	2nd edition	page
363	genealogie	geslachtslijst	357
113	genivelleerd	effen gemaakt	103
155	hypothese	onderstelling	141
82	identiteit	eenzelvigheid	76
214	sociabiliteit	gezelligheid	201
375	transitie	overgang	368

Table 11.2: Dutchification of foreign words

Almost equally as helpful to the English translator is the discovery of the foreign "impurities" shown in Table 11.3.

The proclivity to Dutchify appears almost to have become a fetish, for how else can one explain the substitutions shown in Table 11.4? Or is Groen trying to become more readable to the common man? In that case he is inconsistent when, inversely, native Dutch words are replaced as shown in Table 11.5. From this point of view it would also seem self-defeating that Groen added, in 1868, new words like *fantasmagorisch, intermezzo, ochlocratisme, omnipotent, philippica* and *theocratisme*,[10] while resurrecting, in his new notes, words purged from earlier passages in the text of the 1st edition like *anarchie, interventie* and *representant*.[11] No scoffer at purism, however, will fault Groen for making the substitutions in diction as shown in Table 11.6.

One of Groen's former teachers, Professor Siegenbeek of Leyden's literary faculty,[12] fought valiantly for the purity of Dutch. In 1847, thus in the same year that *Ongeloof en Revolutie* first came out, Siegenbeek published a *List* of 177 words and expressions which he considered incompatible with Dutch idiom.[13] The vast majority of them were Germanisms. Interestingly, *Ongeloof en Revolutie* has no more than two of the words Siegenbeek disapproves of: *onbevangen* (297) and *vrijzinnigheid* (411).[14] Two decades later,

---

10. See 2nd ed., pp. 127, 314, 364, 411n, 439n, 136.

11. See 2nd ed., pp. 396n, 407, 246n.

12. He held his chair from 1797 to 1847; cf. *Briefwisseling*, II, 118, 598. Groen probably attended his lectures in literature and history; cf. Tazelaar, *De Jeugd van Groen*, pp. 68, 80.

13. Matthijs Siegenbeek, *Lijst van woorden en uitdrukkingen, met het Nederlandsch taaleigen strijdende* (Leyden: S. & J. Luchtmans, 1847), 56 pp. My attention was drawn to this list by Dr. J. Noordegraaf.

14. The latter was coming into vogue as a "more Netherlandic" synonym for *liberalisme* and *liberalismus*.

page	1st edition	2nd edition	page
360	analogie	overeenkomst	353
95	artificieel	kunstmatig	87
351	elastisch	rekbaar	344
78	energie	veerkracht	72
73	geconcentererd	zaamgetrokken	67
99	geprivilegeerd	bevoorregt	90
191	gradatiën	trappen	176
388	impulsie	stoot	388
75	incompetent	onbevoegd	69
84	interventie	tusschenkomst	78
391	intimidatie	afschrik	393
43	patriarchaal	aartsvaderlijk	39
325	proscriptie	vogelvrijverklaring	316
9	ramificatie	vertakking	8
98	representatie	vertegenwoordiging	90
122	systematisch	stelselmatig	109
76	verifieren	nagaan	70

Table 11.3: Substitution of "impurities"

page	1st edition	2nd edition	page
238	anarchie	regeringloosheid	228
98	despotisme	dwinglandij	90
343	fanatisme	geestdrijverij	336
137	materieel	stoffelijk	124
400	rebel	oproerling	405
80	resultaten	uitkomsten	74
166	suprematie	oppertoezicht	153

Table 11.4: Puristic Dutchifications

page	1st edition	2nd edition	page
77	gebied	territoir	71
80	navorsching	studiën	74
174	strijd voeren	polemizeren	160
163	vreemd	heterogeen	150

Table 11.5: Substitution of native Dutch words

page	1st edition	2nd edition	page
353	apologist	lofredenaar	345
379	derisie	spotternij	374
192	eclectiek	keursteen	177
xii	fyzionomie	gelaat	xix
383	geëscamoteerd	weggegoocheld	381
324	irregulariteit	onregelmatigheid	315
203	nomenclatuur	woordenboek	189
150	objectie	tegenwerping	136
415	repartieert	verdeelt	427

Table 11.6: Understandable substitutions

in his 2nd edition, Groen, referring to the French word *incarné*, replaces *geconcentererd* (¹361) with *belichaamd* (²355), a word which had appeared on Siegenbeek's black list of 1847 but was probably naturalized by 1868. From the purists' point of view it was indeed a losing battle. Of the Gallicisms condemned by Siegenbeek, none occurs in *Ongeloof en Revolutie*. Groen was equally at home in French and Dutch and thus could keep them apart.[15] He deplored it when a nation's language was "larded" and "disfigured" by loan words and foreign phrases.[16] Although Groen made a special effort to guard against contamination, he confessed to his editor Bodel that he did not always know equivalents for loan words or their adaptations.[17]

---

15. This may have been true of his audience as well. In any case, greater familiarity with French than with German was universal for Dutch society at mid-century. German quotations in *Ongeloof en Revolutie* are invariably translated, French quotations are given only in the original.

16. *Bescheiden*, ed. Gerretson, p. 144.

17. *Briefwisseling*, II, 905.

Apart from Dutchifications there were, of course, other changes in diction. In several (though not all) places Groen deemed it advisable to replace his designation of "the despotism of the revolutionary State"[18] with "the absolutism of the revolutionary State."[19]

One final point of interest under the heading of diction: the word *wereldbeschouwing* makes its debut in the 1868 edition. It is used in the new Preface, and in Lecture XIII ([2]334) it replaces the word *leer* (doctrine), to denote the coherent set of views to which Robespierre and company had dedicated their lives.

A more sensitive substitution involves the adjective *anti-revolutionary*. As Groen never tired of explaining: we are Christian-historical and *for that reason also* anti-revolutionary. For many years, if not all his life, Groen's critics, in parliament and press, insisted on equating "anti-revolutionary" with counter-revolutionary reaction and legitimist disapproval of any and all revolutions, while bracketing "Christian-historical" with nostalgic conservatism and theocratic aspirations. Nevertheless Groen persisted in using both terms equally—and interchangeably; for, as he explained over and over again, the two are inseparable: "Christian-historical" denotes our positive program, but "anti-revolutionary" reminds us of the polemical stance we must take in our time, out of self-defense.[20] His ethical-irenic friends felt less than comfortable with the former epithet but were decidedly offended by the latter, "repellent" one. No stickler for terms, Groen seems to have been willing to downplay the negative designation of his "party" and push the positive one to the foreground, especially when its positive program became more articulated as time went on. We see this shift also reflected in the 2nd edition of *Unbelief and Revolution*. Not that Groen now suppresses the term *anti-revolutionary* altogether. Page ix of the original Preface (faithfully reprinted in the 2nd edition) still talks of the case he defends as his "anti-revolutionary argument." And in one of the closing pages of the book ([1]423f, [2]437) he still exhorts his friends always to remember that the "recommendation of the anti-revolutionary truths is practical, even when the revolution principle retains the upper

---

18. See 1st ed., pp. 241, 253, 254, 255.

19. See 2nd ed., pp. 231, 244, 245, 247.

20. Cf. Diepenhorst, *Groen van Prinsterer*, pp. 309–15.

hand." Moreover, in the new Preface he refers to his basic conviction as a "Christian-historical or anti-revolutionary worldview." In other critical places, however, *anti-revolutionary* is replaced by *Christian-historical*.[21] Two straightforward instances in the 2nd edition illustrate the effect of the substitution.

The first goes like this (we italicize): What was lamentable about the Restoration was that "to acknowledge the *Christian-historical* principles as rule and guide continued to be regarded by the rulers, scribes and wise men of this world as absurd and harmful" ([2]380; cf. [1]382).

And the second: Until 1830, Belgium could have been saved for Holland "if the king could have been induced to follow a *Christian-historical* policy" ([2]422; cf. [1]410).

A third instance is more complex. Speaking of the calling of Christians to protest and to warn against the spirit of the age, Groen makes this change in Lecture XV:

Our principles lead us also more directly to political improvement, [even though] I shall not detain you by sketching the particulars of a utopia according to anti-revolutionary maxims ... ([1]422)	The Christian-historical principle leads also more directly to political gain, [even though] I shall not sketch for you the particulars of a utopia. ([2]436)

---

21. That one must not infer a permanent change in position from this change in wording is borne out the following year, when Groen launches his second series of *Nederlandsche Gedachten* and writes: "Anti-revolutionary: it is not permissible to give up a title with which our party, in tenor and essence, stands or falls. Some people say, I am indeed Christian-historical, but not anti-revolutionary. I reject this distinction. After all, the hallmark of the Christian-historical school is that it combats the principle of the revolution. Inversely, the strength of the anti-revolutionary party lies in its Christian and historical foundation." *Ned. Ged.*, 1868, I, 11f.

In Lecture XI the revision uses neither term but opts for "the Gospel":

... the power of anti-revolutionary ideas, comparatively at least, to effect order, liberty and prosperity has been in evidence in all earlier times. (^{1}271)	the power of the Gospel to effect order, liberty and prosperity has been substantiated by world history. (^{2}260)

Smitskamp too has put his finger on a number of other, perhaps more substantial and in any case rather interesting substitutions in the 2nd edition.[22] For example, he concludes that in 1868 Groen appears to have felt less of an urgency than in 1847 to dissociate himself sharply from Bilderdijk, the teacher whom he had "followed" and whom some men in his original audience still followed:

... I do not wish to hide the fact that I am very far from subscribing to all his contentions in history and political philosophy. (^{1}39)	... I do not subscribe to everything he taught in history and political philosophy. (^{2}35)

Again, the revisions of 1868 indicate that Groen had mitigated his view of Catholicism since 1847. Whereas the 1st edition (165) attributed skepticism and agnosticism to the late medieval "corrupt clergy" in general, the 2nd edition (152) restricts these lamentable corruptions to "a part of the clergy" (Lecture VII). Similarly, popery's "most blasphemous superstitions" of 1847 have been softened in 1868 to "half-forgotten, pitiful superstitions" (^{1}406, ^{2}415).[23] Incidentally, on the same page of Lecture XV in the 2nd edition (415), in a similar exercise of moderation, an apparent contradiction has resulted from the addition of a new footnote: the original text, which is maintained, speculates that ultramontanism has a good

---

22. Cf. Smitskamp, "Het boek 'Ongeloof en Revolutie,'" pp. 19f.
23. Cf. Smitskamp, ibid., p. 20.

chance of becoming the oppressive civil religion of the future—to which the reassuring footnote is now added that "our Christian bond with Roman Catholicism in the face of unbelief" has never been in doubt, that philosophical skepticism, not Rome, is the identifiable Antichrist, and that "humiliation of the Papacy is not always a gain for the Gospel," assertions supported by quotations from Stahl and Tocqueville. This addition (in a new footnote) does not amount to self-contradiction, however, but reflects a re-evaluation of nineteenth-century Roman Catholicism by a contemporary Protestant and does not necessarily require a reassessment (in the main text) of Roman Catholicism in the sixteenth century. Groen at any rate has no problem retaining his statements, on the last page of Lecture VII in the 2nd edition, that in the Reformation the fundamental truths of the Christian religion overcame the world, the "Antichrist of Rome" and the devil. By not observing the difference in century one commentator has been deceived into making the cavalier remark that *Unbelief and Revolution* "is such a passionate work that Groen first tells his readers that the Pope is the Antichrist and in the end argues explicitly that the Pope is not the Antichrist."[24]

Still another instance of substitution to which Smitskamp draws attention reveals that by 1868 Groen had also modified his view of Calvinism. The change occurs in the concluding section of Lecture VI. Whereas the 1st edition (147) had explained that sixteenth-century Calvinists, because they were driven to self-defense by bloody persecutions, were more than others disposed "to look upon questionable resistance as a legitimate means of defending popular rights," in the 2nd edition (133) they are said to have looked upon "vigorous resistance as a dutiful means" of achieving this end.[25] In the same context, incidentally, the 1868 revision gives rise to another odd discrepancy. The 1st edition (148) had denied that Calvinism contributed to the republicanizing corruption of constitutional law; this statement is retained in the 2nd edition (135), yet at the close of the discussion of Calvinism a lengthy footnote is added (^{2}137n) which concedes that Calvinist church polity did encourage revolutions such as those inspired by Puritanism in England, Scotland, and North America; the concession is

---

24. Kasteel, "Groen en de Roomsgezinden," in *Een Staatsman ter navolging*, p. 158.
25. Cf. Smitskamp, "Het boek 'Ongeloof en Revolutie,' " p. 20.

made in the form of an exchange with Stahl, who is quoted at great length and with obvious deference to his authority, although Groen does not refrain from pointing out explicitly that Stahl at the same time appears very much aware of the ideological contrast between Puritanism and the revolution, for example when he (Stahl) writes: "The Revolution establishes everything on the will of man and in the service of man. Puritanism establishes everything on the commandments of God and to the glory of God."

Discrepancies like those pointed out by Smitskamp reveal that in 1868 Groen did not take the time to subject his original book to the thorough-going revision which his altered views warranted. To judge from the new Preface, the chief aim of his new edition seems to have been to make clear to the reading public that the book's analysis was fully up-to-date, having been validated by events in the intervening years.

ADDITIONS

Our last two examples of substitutions have already pointed to changes resulting from additional footnotes. As announced in the new Preface, the text of the 2nd edition, though "virtually unchanged," has been enlarged with new footnotes in which the author attempts to "turn to good account the experience of twenty years in an exceptionally revolutionary era." In part, this refers to Groen's own production of political commentary since 1847. As well, it refers to one of Groen's favorite polemical weapons: with great relish he appears to have collected quotable quotes as supporting evidence from new publications over the years, as is evident both from numerous pencil ticks in the margin and from page listings in the back of his personal copies of these new books now lodged in the *Koninklijke Bibliotheek* in The Hague. The 1st edition had been rushed into print and lacked broader documentation based on further research. So it must have been very gratifying to the author, not that the unruly events of 1848 had thundered a loud Amen, as it were, to his 1847 prophecy of doom, but that so many books and articles were coming out that supported his basic interpretation of contemporary history.

Scores of new authors are cited in the footnotes that were added to the 2nd edition.[26] Even a cursory glance at the new notes bears out that, understandably, almost all of them were added each time to confirm aspects of his interpretation, thus strengthening the text of 1847 and answering some of its critics.[27] A few, however, seem clearly intended to document—or at least to intimate—modifications in Groen's thinking. Since the main text is rarely revised, discrepancies have arisen between the old text and new footnotes.

Perhaps the most notorious case of such a discrepancy involves Stahl, whose appreciation of common interest, public justice and the rule of law as criteria for the state hardly comport well with Groen's "Hallerian" text.[28] Whereas the (unrevised) text continues to hold up "genuine monarchy" as a private affair administered with absolute power though tempered by intermediate bodies in society, the notes that quote Stahl admit of a different definition of monarchy. In a footnote toward the end of Lecture VI ([2]137), as we have seen, Groen admits to a "nuance" of difference with Stahl on the historical relation between Calvinism and "republicanism" and expresses a willingness to entertain as "plausible" that Calvinism not only encouraged "constitutionalism properly so called" but may in fact have contributed historically to the development of the revolution doctrine! If this concession leaves the reader wondering about the validity of Groen's entire account of the "perversion of constitutional law" in modern times, he is assisted in recovering his bearings as to Groen's basic intention in later lectures. There, newly introduced formulations, borrowed from the writings of Stahl, explain the difference between bad constitutionalism as opposed to constitutional monarchy properly understood.[29] Groen also uses the occasion of

---

26. The chief ones are Stahl (quoted 66 times, using thirteen of his works but particularly his *Philosophie des Rechts* and *Die gegenwärtige Parteien*), Sybel (16 times), Renan (13), Croker (9), Mallet du Pan (8), and Lamartine (6). Publications since 1845 yield 60 further quotes by Guizot (28 from the *Mémoires* alone), and 45 more by Tocqueville (many from *L'Ancien Régime*, of course, but also from the volumes of *Correspondance*). Many of these citations first appear in short form scribbled in the margin of Groen's personal copy of the 1st ed.

27. In the following we shall refer especially to the critical review by Jacob de Witte van Citters in *Themis; regtskundig tijdschrift* IX/1 (1848): 109-32, to the one by Jeronimo de Bosch Kemper in *Nederlandsche Jaarboeken voor Regtsgeleerdheid en Wetgeving* XI (1849): 187-220, and to the attack by Robert Fruin in his two pamphlets of 1853 and 1854 (see our Select Bibliography), reprinted in his *Verspreide Geschriften*, X, 76-167, 168-238.

28. Cf. *Lustrumbundel*, pp. 50-58, 126-35. We shall return to this problem in our concluding chapter.

29. See footnotes, 2nd ed., pp. 308, 384, 427.

his revision to pass on Stahl's more favorable opinion of middle-of-the-road parties in general and of the Doctrinaire party in particular.[30]

As for Guizot, the additional quotes from seven of his works published since 1845 serve in the first place to bring out how Guizot, not Groen, has changed—has in fact come much closer to Groen's religious interpretation of the revolution and has consequently come to revise much of his earlier appreciation of liberalism. The new notes document the statesman-historian's altered opinions, if not outright retractions, with respect to the Reformation, the Enlightenment, democracy, the ideas of 1789, the liberal state, and even Charles X.[31] The most resounding testimony is taken from Guizot's retrospective *De nos mécomptes* of 1855 and is reproduced on page 336, where he is quoted as exclaiming: "Our fathers of 1789 were condemned to pass from prospects of Paradise to scenes of Hell. God forbid we should forget!"

Again, some readers will find it fascinating to watch Groen reproduce a variety of statements made by Guizot as he looks back on the July Monarchy—about its claim to legitimacy, its comparative mildness, its even-handed justice, its policy of non-intervention abroad and its measures for self-preservation at home. These statements are critically examined, discussed, and often found wanting.[32] Only once, in the final lecture, does Groen appear to have been persuaded by Guizot to adjust his views: he now appears willing—at the foot of the page, where he quotes Guizot, but not in the body of the text—to think more positively about contemporary developments in Roman Catholicism.[33]

In Tocqueville we have an author to whom Groen is inclined to defer. He respected him highly and read his posthumous *Oeuvres complètes* from cover to cover.[34] Here was a talented writer who in his own way had seen the persistence of the revolution since 1815 and whose premonition of the eruption of 1848 must have given Groen a shock of recognition. Faithfully Groen reports in Lecture III that Tocqueville has shown on good evidence

---

30. See footnotes, 2nd ed., pp. 211, 384, 394.

31. See footnotes, 2nd ed., pp. 141, 170, 173, 188, 193, 245, 258, 386–88, 400.

32. See footnotes, 2nd ed., pp. 389–91, 395f, 396–99, 408.

33. See footnote, 2nd ed., p. 417.

34. Cf. Groen's praise of Tocqueville, footnotes, 2nd ed., pp. 263, 439. Groen's personal copies of the two volumes of *Correspondance* in particular are heavily marked.

that administrative centralization in France was not a product of the revolution, as Groen had argued, but a development of the old regime.[35] Groen
adds at once, however, that while this may be a *fact*, his quarrel with the revolution is precisely that it raises centralization to a *principle*. One wonders
whether Groen can evade the force of Tocqueville's argument that easily.
The latter's analysis, after all, based as it was on fresh archival research,
represented nothing less than a historiographical revolution in that it established continuity rather than discontinuity—at least on the level of political administration—between the French Revolution and the Old Regime.[36]

If any author could have induced Groen to reconsider or adjust his
account of the revolution it was Tocqueville! But several other places where
he is cited make clear that the 2nd edition is not a true revision in that sense.
In Lecture XII, where Groen had conceded (in a subordinate sentence) that
the hard-pressed clergy of 1789 had themselves contributed to the spread
of the false ideas through unbelief and immorality, he now adds a footnote in which to report, "also for the sake of impartiality," the opinion of
Tocqueville on the clergy *of 1789*: never, on the whole, was a clergy more
enlightened, more public-minded, and of greater faith.[37] Yet Groen seems
loath to let the reader forget in what tradition the clergy stood, for he adds
immediately: "But see above, p. 159." The cross-reference, if followed up,
brings the reader face to face again with Groen's charge that the French
prelacy *of the seventeenth century* had removed a potentially very important
barrier to unbelief in their land: by excommunicating the gospel of free

---

35. See footnote, 2nd ed., p. 44; cf. also p. 104, where it is conceded that this development
made *a* revolution almost inevitable.

36. Cf. Fueter, *Geschichte der neueren Historiographie*, pp. 557–60. That an emphasis on
continuity does not necessarily settle issues of this kind, however, was demonstrated already
in the late nineteenth century by the German-American historian Von Holst, whose comment
on Tocqueville's discovery is curiously similar to Groen's: "To Tocqueville belongs the merit of
having proved that the immoderate centralization ... existed already under the *ancien régime*.
The essential difference ... consists in this, that the revolution made legal what under the
ancien régime was to a great extent only a fact." H. von Holst, *The French Revolution: Illustrated
by the Career of Mirabeau* (2 vols.; Chicago, 1894), I, 10. According to John F. Bosher (in a paper
read to the annual meeting of the Canadian Historical Association, University of Windsor,
9 June 1988), it was Tocqueville's formidable reputation that long discouraged further study of
the political administration under the *ancien régime*, even though his emphasis on continuity
was actually quite misleading: the revolution completely transformed the earlier system
of centralization by rationalizing it and by nationalizing all independent powers in society.

37. See footnote, 2nd ed., p. 293.

grace in the persons of the Jansenists, the Gallican church had crucified the Lord afresh!

In Lecture V, again without revising his main text, Groen significantly softens his criticism of "revolutionary authors" like Madame de Staël where they make bold to assert that Louis XIV actually held that "the properties of his subjects belonged to him." Groen is honest enough to insert a footnote at this place[38] in which he concedes, quoting Tocqueville, that royal edicts of the Sun-King did actually make the claim that all lands in private *possession* were the *property* of the Crown. A nice distinction—nice enough, one would think, to excuse the boldness held up for scorn in the text. Again the discrepancy between text and footnote raises more questions than it settles.

A final instance of fresh annotation that uses Tocqueville and sends the reader's mind in different directions occurs in the discussion of the Illuminists in Lecture IX. There Groen speaks of the sect's "ramifications and conspiracies and ultimate demise." In 1868 he inserts the sentence, "I do not wish to attach too much weight to them," and drops a footnote quoting Tocqueville's verdict that they were the "symptoms of the disease and not the disease itself, its effects and not its causes."[39] The main text continues to characterize them as a "typical crop of the revolutionary soil," thus maintaining the age's intellectual ferment as the primary cause of the social upheaval to follow yet leaving open the possibility that Illuminists hatched a plot to trigger the revolution. The question is not clarified until Lecture XI, in a passage where the diffusion of the revolutionary ideology is said to have prepared Europe for the upheaval: it had captured the minds of the ablest and noblest people, the reader is assured, and was not just festering among obscurantists; a new footnote[40] quotes Tocqueville as making the point that "hidden intrigues are always found, forming as it were the substratum of revolutions; but the change in ideas which ended in changing the facts was enacted in broad daylight by the joint efforts of all—authors, nobles and princes."[41] Groen's overarching interpretation is

---

38. See 2nd ed., p. 91.

39. See 2nd ed., p. 206.

40. See 2nd ed., p. 265.

41. The quote is from a letter to the Count of Gircourt who had asked Tocqueville's opinion about the many plot theories that were still current (in 1852).

broad and flexible enough to shield plot theories, if one insists, though he himself is inclined to dismiss them. He has little need to investigate the possible contribution of sinister conspiracies since his entire vision is focused on the revolution as a gigantic "plot" of a whole generation carried aloft by the inner dynamic force of unbelief.[42] In the meantime, the fact that Groen leaves the reader with the option of incorporating or not incorporating a variety of (contributing) causes is confusing, to say the least. The seams between text and notes are noticeable, imparting to the 2nd edition that impression of patchwork so wearying to the reader of his footnotes.[43]

Groen shows considerable respect as well for the work of Ranke's pupil Heinrich von Sybel (1817-95). Sybel's *Geschichte der Revolutionszeit* (1853; 2nd ed., 3 vols., 1859-60) was a pioneering history based on archival material dug up in Berlin, Paris and The Hague and therefore especially good on international relations during the revolutionary period.[44] Groen, however, does not use Sybel for that aspect (the brief overview at the beginning of Lecture XV was not expanded). Nor does Groen find any use for Sybel's sensitive treatment of social and economic conditions. What he finds appealing about this work is its corroboration of Burkean themes: philosophic equality leads to the destruction of liberty, and popular sovereignty leads to mob-rule or military dictatorship. In a long overdue correction of the liberal focus on the revolution as a constitutional struggle, Sybel brings out how from the very first it overturned normal social life and generated lawlessness: "He boldly challenged the popular distinction between 1789 and 1793, and directed attention to the tyranny and anarchy of the opening months."[45] Groen finds especially Volume I to his purpose and quotes it repeatedly in Lecture XII. He eagerly copies the gist of four passages

---

42. In that sense, *Unbelief and Revolution* foreshadows the interpretation of Hippolyte Taine (1828-93) whose "thèse du complot" reduced the revolution to a triumph of the rationalistic *esprit classique*, or the interpretation of Augustin Cochin (1876-1916) who pictured the revolution as a breakthrough of the doctrine of popular sovereignty hatched by the *sociétés de pensée* and nursed along by a revolutionary minority; cf. Farmer, *France Reviews Its Revolutionary Origins*, pp. 28-37, 78-84; Furet, *Interpreting the French Revolution*, pp. 164-204.

43. This circumstance may justify the omission in my abridged translation of much of the 2nd edition footnote apparatus; unquestionably a critical English edition would have to incorporate all of it—with further editorial commentary.

44. Cf. Fueter, *Geschichte der neueren Historiographie*, pp. 537-39; Gooch, *History and Historians in the Nineteenth Century*, pp. 131-37.

45. Gooch, *History and Historians in the Nineteenth Century*, p. 132.

in which Sybel demonstrates that it was always a resolute minority that gained the upper hand.[46]

In another place, however, Sybel is given the dubious distinction of being classed among the "if only" historians: after listing five contingencies which according to Sybel successively made escalation of the revolution inevitable, Groen comments that Sybel fails to explain *why* no one, not even the ablest and strongest, was able or strong enough to bridle the revolution.[47] Thus Sybel's authority is utilized both positively and negatively to strengthen Groen's case.

A final instance of invoking this historical scholar as a new ally involves Sybel's lectures of 1861 entitled *Die Erhebung Europas gegen Napoleon*. In Groen's rebuttal, in Lecture XII, of the argument that the revolution had derailed because of the ill-advised and unsolicited intervention of the Allies, he had tried to show how this argument entailed the falsification of historical facts. Now he is glad to be able to counter this falsification of history a second time by quoting Sybel's *Erhebung Europas*. In its opening pages Sybel states as one of his main conclusions that while countless books have perpetuated the myth that the revolution was mild and humane until haunted by threats of war, the science of history, after studying the best sources—contemporary documents, letters, diplomatic dispatches—has today reversed the entire picture.[48]

About the remaining authors we can be brief. They yield no fresh insights or clinching arguments for the historiographic debate and appear to be quoted only to enliven a portrait or enhance a verdict appearing in the text. The collected *Essays on the Early Period of the French Revolution* (1857) by John Wilson Croker (1780-1857) are invoked to support Groen's judgment of Robespierre and his personal accountability for the Terror.[49] The *Mémoires et Correspondance* (2 vols.; 1851) of the émigré journalist Jacques Mallet du Pan (1749-1800) yield a number of powerful formulations,[50] but do not alter the picture. From the use of two other sources of "remarkable" observations it is disturbingly evident that the "eclectic"

---

46. See footnote, 2nd ed., p. 318.
47. See footnote, 2nd ed., p. 287.
48. See footnote, 2nd ed., p. 298.
49. See footnotes, 2nd ed., pp. 310, 320, 330, 331, 332, 356.
50. Cf. e.g. footnotes, 2nd ed., pp. 252, 298, 382.

Groen is not very fastidious in his choice of authors to quote. Ernest Renan (1823–92) is cited not only as a critical commentator on Guizot's picture of the July Monarchy, but also as an authority on the constitutional history of France.[51] Our second and final example is Groen's use of that highly unreliable romantic bestseller *Histoire des Girondins* (4 vols.; 1847) by the poet-politician Alphonse de Lamartine (1790–1869).[52] In Lecture XIII[53] Groen cheerfully inserts quotations from this work which portray Robespierre as a pupil of Rousseau whose "very isolation proved his strength" and who prevailed over his adversaries because of his unfaltering devotion to the "philosophic utopia." The point was already well made in the text of the 1st edition, but the reader of the 2nd edition admires the brilliant strokes with which Lamartine has painted his portrait and gladly forgives Groen for adding them to his own.

To what extent, finally, did Groen use the revision to try and satisfy his critics? As was to be expected, not to any great extent. After all, the intervening twenty years (the new Preface declares) had only confirmed him in the essential correctness of his vision. All the same, he cannot resist setting straight certain persistent misunderstandings about his position.

To begin with, there was the charge that what he really wanted was to restore the old regime, that he championed antiquated institutions, that he would like to see guilds and corporations resurrected, etc.[54] In extra notes Groen makes a point of stating in so many words that the old order is irrevocably past and ought to stay that way.[55]

Does this book and its author condemn every revolution that has ever transpired? Of course not, it is patiently explained in new notes; there have been revolutions that were quite legitimate: political overturnings that avenged injustice and restored old rights.[56]

---

51. See footnotes, 2nd ed., pp. 389, 394, 396, 397, 398, and 75, 131, 233, quoting from Renan's review article of the first two volumes of Guizot's *Mémoires* in the *Revue des Deux Mondes* of July 1859.

52. Cf. Gooch, *History and Historians in the Nineteenth Century*, pp. 215f. Groen was aware of its shortcomings and quotes Croker to that effect; see footnotes, 2nd ed., pp. 263, 310, 358. See also *Brieven van Da Costa*, I, 273.

53. See footnotes, 2nd ed., pp. 331, 333, 334, 350.

54. Cf. De Bosch Kemper, review, p. 211; Fruin, X, 143–49, 215–24.

55. See footnotes, 2nd ed., pp. 233, 381.

56. See footnotes, 2nd ed., pp. 137, 227, 250, 251, 252.

One charge that Groen had a hard time living down was that at bottom he still belonged to the school of Bilderdijk and favored absolute monarchy.[57] He now inserts that he has never been opposed to *constitutional* government but only to a kind of *constitutionalism* that turns a king into a mere figurehead.[58] While these assurances may have put certain critics at ease, a new note on page 67 must have made things worse in the eyes of others.[59] To the position argued there, that if taken in the right (limited) sense the adage *L'état, c'est moi* is perfectly correct, Groen now adds the documentation that two authorities are of the same opinion about the adage attributed to Louis XIV: namely, Tocqueville and Stahl!

Had Groen overrated the importance of Rousseau?[60] How wrong, Groen retorts in 1868, and he quotes Tocqueville in reply, reproduces Stahl's verdicts that Rousseau was the foremost writer of liberalism and that the constitution of '91 was the realization of his doctrine, and cites Renan who says of Rousseau that he gave the French Revolution "its definitive stamp."[61]

No fewer than seven new notes appear in Lecture VII to drive home the point that the Reformation cannot be seen as an emancipatory movement, as the liberals insist on doing,[62] but must be appreciated as a religious movement that brought Christendom back to its old basis of authority.[63] Similarly, toward the end of Lecture I Groen now copies a particularly striking paragraph (from one of his own earlier works) which allows for no analogy but only an antithesis between the Reformation and the revolution.[64]

---

57. The complaint antedates the book. It was made in the heat of debates in the chamber of 1840 but became serious in Groen's eyes in 1845 when the historian Bakhuizen van den Brink put it in print. He even used personal channels to have his critic corrected. Cf. Smitskamp, *Groen van Prinsterer als historicus*, p. 155.

58. See footnotes, 2nd ed., pp. 36, 83, 256, 427.

59. Cf. De Witte Van Citters, pp. 126f: How can Groen defend the maxim *L'état, c'est moi*? It stands for nothing short of autocratic despotism.

60. Cf. Fruin, *Verspreide Geschriften*, X, 90: "Of the ideas of Rousseau no traces can be found in the *cahiers*: they do not begin to function until the revolution is well under way." The thesis that Rousseau's *Social Contract* had a pervasive influence both before and during the revolution has in recent years received renewed endorsement; cf. Bronislaw Baczko, "The Social Contract of the French: Sieyès and Rousseau," *Journal of Modern History* 60, supplement (Sept. 1988): 98–125, esp. 100.

61. See footnotes, 2nd ed., pp. 192, 204, 275, 308.

62. Cf. Fruin, *Verspreide Geschriften*, X, 81, 102, 160f.

63. See footnotes, 2nd ed., pp. 141, 143, 148, 149, 155, 157.

64. See footnote, 2nd ed., p. 13.

Does this not necessarily make Groen an anti-papist? In 1868 Groen seems ready to remove unnecessarily harsh criticisms of the Roman church[65] and to bring out what his real quarrel with Rome is: the ultramontane claim, on her behalf, to temporal power.[66] But how then can the state be Christian: does Groen want to replace a dominant Church of Rome with a dominant Reformed Church?[67] Groen cuts through the issue by declaring plainly in new notes that what anti-revolutionaries defend is not a medieval theocracy of one sort or another but the "laic state," the acknowledgment of the divine right of civil government and the state's independence of the clergy in consequence of its own direct submission to God's norms, unmediated by the church.[68]

Possibly against some of his own friends who had let him down over the years Groen takes extra care this time to show that individualism is a product of the revolution and that so-called "Christian individualism" abandons public life to the forces of unbelief.[69]

In 1868 Groen is even less a man of compromise than in 1847. He inserts new notes which repeat his lesson to "resist beginnings": no shade of liberalism is acceptable; moderates, while they may be preferable to radicals, nevertheless prepare the way for them, and where men share a principle the most consistent adherents to it will always win out.[70]

One last charge that Groen tries to counter with renewed effort is the belief that his vision implies some form of determinism.[71] Groen tries— but how successful is he? Does he really think it helps to clear his name of fatalism when at the foot of the page he takes to task some more of those typical "if-only" arguments used by historians to deny the inevitability of the course of the revolution, or when he adds a note saying that circumstances can doom a person to impotence?[72] But perhaps a proper balance is achieved between freedom and necessity with his new note on page 175:

---

65. See the instances discussed above under "Substitutions."

66. See footnotes, 2nd ed., pp. 60, 144, 153, 156, 416.

67. This had been the critical question of some of his own friends; cf. *Briefwisseling*, II, 810, 967.

68. See footnotes, 2nd ed., pp. 52, 60, 156.

69. See footnotes, 2nd ed., pp. 61, 189, 439.

70. See footnotes, 2nd ed., pp. 176, 183, 211, 292.

71. Fruin, X, 87, had bracketed him with Mignet and Thiers on this score.

72. See footnotes, 2nd ed., pp. 168, 281, 286.

"One could also underestimate the influence of persons," followed by a quotation from Guizot, who writes that history is by no means a "drama that is fixed from the moment it begins"? The balance does not last for the remainder of the book, for we are told in a new note on page 378 not to *overestimate* the influence of the person in the case of Napoleon, whose career instead exhibits the triumph each time of the ideology. The stigma of determinism is anything but removed and the book would continue to attract it far into the twentieth century.[73]

---

73. Cf. Smitskamp, *Groen van Prinsterer als historicus*, pp. 70–82; De Pater, in *Lustrumbundel*, pp. 100–103.

12

TRANSLATIONS

" 'Tis a pity our language is so confined," the marine historian De Jonge wrote to the author when the book first came out; "else I should predict a European name for it."[1] Although short citations and summaries of Groen's "system" have since appeared in English, French and German, until quite recently no attempt was ever made in any of these languages to translate integral portions (let alone the whole) of *Unbelief and Revolution*.

FRAGMENTS

In the year that the author himself gave a synopsis of *Ongeloof en Revolutie* in French,[2] the first attempt to convey at least something of *Ongeloof en Revolutie* into German occurred in the third volume of Polenz's *History of French Calvinism*, where a "free translation" is given of the closing section of Lecture VI, dealing with the so-called democratic principle of the Genevan Reformation.[3] In his highly readable *In Memoriam Groen van Prinsterer* of 1877, Theodor Wenzelburger, a teacher of German in a secondary school in Delft, included a German translation of a few passages from Lecture II (2nd ed., pp. 35-37) about Groen's relation to Bilderdijk.[4] Another rendition in German, this time giving the tenor of the whole work, is found in Kolfhaus's biography of Kuyper.[5] The next attempt at summarizing the

---

1. J. C. de Jonge to Groen, 22 Aug. 1847; *Briefwisseling*, II, 809.

2. *Le Parti anti-révolutionnaire* (1860), pp. 33-41.

3. Gottlob von Polenz, *Geschichte des französischen Calvinismus bis zur Nationalversammlung im Jahre 1789* (5 vols.; Gotha, 1857-69), III, 410-16. (Polenz unfortunately reads a contrast between French and Dutch Calvinists where Groen intended to draw a contrast between "political" and ultra-Calvinists within both countries.) In this work, incidentally, Polenz also cites lengthy extracts from letters published in the *Archives*; cf. e.g. *ibid.*, I, 581-84; II, 333-36, 552-56, 709-16; IV, 868-72, 875f.

4. *Preussische Jahrbücher* 40 (1877): 203-24, esp. 204.

5. Wilhelm Kolfhaus, *Dr. Abraham Kuyper, 1837-1920; ein Lebensbericht* (Elberfeld: Buchhandlung des Erziehungs-Vereins, 1924), pp. 45-50, 106-8.

work was made by the American pastor-theologian Gerrit H. Hospers, Sr., whose very informative article, "Groen van Prinsterer and His Book," to my knowledge the first of its kind in the English language, came out in 1935.[6]

A more ambitious attempt in the English language led indirectly to the present translation. In 1955, a number of Dutch-speaking Canadian and American students on the campus of Calvin College and Seminary in Grand Rapids, Michigan, while studying the work in meetings of the Groen van Prinsterer Society, resolved to undertake a complete translation of *Ongeloof en Revolutie* (in the Smitskamp edition) with a view to eventual publication. The result of their labors was never published[7] but was consulted at every point in the preparation of the present translation. In 1974 and 1975, finally, Herbert Donald Morton and the present writer published annotated translations of, respectively, Lecture XI and Lectures VIII and IX.[8]

In the meantime, paralleling Hosper's article, other English publications have rendered fragments in translation as they discussed the contents of *Ongeloof en Revolutie*. H. Evan Runner did so in his third Unionville Lectures of 1962, where large sections are devoted to the work,[9] as did McKendree

---

6. *Evangelical Quarterly* 7 (1935): 267-86.

7. Dividing the work among them, they completed draft translations of Lectures III through XIII (respectively by Jack Quartel, Fred Hofman, Peter van Nuis, Harry Mennega, Bernard Zylstra, John Kunst, Peter van Egmond, Aaldert Mennega, Albert Huls, and Louis Tamminga). From its inception the communal project was carried out under the general supervision of Professor H. Evan Runner, who committed the translation after some years to Professor Henry Van Zyl. The latter spent a number of his retirement years patiently revising and completing it. In 1963 the entire manuscript translation was passed on to the present writer for extensive revision. In the course of that revision he reverted from the Smitskamp edition to the 2nd edition of 1868, initially to retrieve the original text of quotations in foreign languages. The project was again shelved until 1972, when in Amsterdam H. Donald Morton became involved in it. Collaborative efforts on a portion of the translation by way of experiment led to the decision jointly to begin publishing an English translation in serial form. As we prepared the first installment, Morton bought himself a copy of *Ongeloof en Revolutie* at an antiquarian bookseller. It was a first edition, presumably superseded by the second, but much to our amazement we discovered that its text—contrary to the author's assurances, repeated by Smitskamp—differed so significantly from that of the 2nd edition that many obscure points and cryptic formulations were instantaneously cleared up. The next decision was only natural: to prepare an English edition translated virtually from scratch. Three installments of this critical edition have appeared, containing Lectures VII, VIII, IX, and XI.

8. See the Select Bibliography.

9. Cf. *Scriptural Religion and Political Task* (Toronto: Wedge, 1974), pp. 98f; see also 1, 64, 75, 89–91, 107. His high estimate of the work is documented in the interview that concludes the first of his two *festschriften*, eds. J. Kraay and A. Tol, *Hearing and Doing: Philosophical Essays Dedicated to H. Evan Runner* (Toronto: Wedge, 1979), pp. 348, 352.

R. Langley, who introduced the work in its immediate historical context
and summarized its central thesis in several popular articles written since
1971.[10] E. L. Hebden Taylor provided a number of very readable abstracts
in his book on political philosophy,[11] while Dr. D. Martyn Lloyd-Jones
included long quotations from Lecture XI in his closing address at one
of the Westminster Conferences.[12] Finally, on the hundredth anniversary
of Groen's death Bernard Zylstra included key statements from the book
in an article in which he compared it to Eric Voegelin's book of 1975, *From
Enlightenment to Revolution.*[13]

Recently, access to Groen's work was created in another international language. A Spanish version of Lecture XI, translated by Humberto
Casanova from the English publication of 1974, came out in 1982. In 2010,
a complete translation, prepared by Adolfo García de la Sienra, was published in Mexico under the title *Incredulidad y Revolución.*

THE PRESENT TRANSLATION

Our translation is at the same time an abridgment. As an abridgment it
strives after clarity and economy without sacrificing the complexity essential to Groen's argument. As a translation it seeks to provide a text that
reads smoothly and idiomatically without losing the forcefulness peculiar
to Groen's diction. An abridged translation (or translated abridgment) must
therefore come to terms with both content and style.

As to *content*, a translated abridgment, while it cannot pretend to be
a historical source for the serious scholar, can highlight essentials and
facilitate comprehension, especially for those who are making their first
acquaintance with the book. In making the abridgment, my policy has
been, wherever feasible,

---

10. E.g. "Pioneers of Christian Politics I," *Vanguard* (Toronto) (April 1971): 7–9, 22; "What
Does It Mean to Be a Christian in the World?" *The Presbyterian Guardian* (Jan. 1976): 8–13;
"The Witness of a World View," *Pro Rege* (faculty quarterly of Dordt College, Sioux Center,
Iowa) VIII/2 (Dec. 1979): 2–11; "The Legacy of Groen van Prinsterer," *Reformed Perspective*
(Jan. 1985): 25–28.

11. *The Christian Philosophy of Law, Politics and the State*, (n.pl., n.d.), pp. 18–42, 238–47.

12. "The French Revolution and After," chap. 6 in *The Christian and the State in Revolutionary
Times* (London: Westminster Conference, 1975), pp. 94–99.

13. "Voegelin on Unbelief and Revolution," in *Anti-Revolutionaire Staatkunde* 46 (1976):
155–65; reprinted in *Een Staatsman ter navolging*, pp. 191–200.

- to drop all summaries and recapitulations if they merely repeat, but retain of them any fresh wordings that add meaning;

- to reduce florid passages to their bare essentials;

- to omit inessential digressions and dated allusions;

- where three or more examples are given to illustrate a point, to incorporate the best and to drop the others.

It did not seem advisable at this time—or feasible, for that matter—to provide a complete text along with a critical apparatus recording all the variants, and so on. Thus the translation offers a straightforward and smooth, uninterrupted text, based on countless admittedly subjective—but I hope not high-handed—choices. My method of editing was quite simple. In all cases I took the text of the 1st edition as my point of departure. Variants from the 2nd edition are interwoven wherever they seem to clarify the meaning intended. In addition I have included (with proper identification) some of the longer footnotes that were new in the 2nd edition; my selection here was governed by the consideration that the English reader should have access to any additional material that draws significantly on post-1847 publications or that indicates a possible shift in Groen's emphasis or interpretation. To keep down interruptions of the flow of thought, the shorter footnotes added in the 2nd edition have been left out, unless they document significant revision. For those who wish to have the author's *ipsissima verba*, there will of course always be the Dutch original (in both editions) to consult.

As to *style*, an abridged translation, while it cannot hope to duplicate the impact of the original, can approximate it sufficiently to convey some of the power of the original. In making the translation, my policy has been, wherever feasible,

- to reduce the asides, allocutions, apostrophes and apologies occasioned solely by the lecture setting;

- to simplify tortuous figures of speech, or else to restate the point in non-figurative language;

- to eliminate those rhetorical flourishes, effusions and interjections that seem to make the prose, especially for today's
  reader, top-heavy;

- to avoid linguistic anachronisms, however tempting; for
  example, in 1847 bills could not be "steamrolled" through parliament, omnipotent governments were not called "totalitarian," and atheistic law systems and worldviews were not yet
  described as instances of "secularism."

No attempt has been made to construct the kind of translation that an
English-speaking contemporary of Groen's might have made. Although the
idea was alluring, the endeavor would have been foolhardy and the result
no doubt ludicrous. Nevertheless I have incorporated an occasional archaic
term or obsolete expression if for no other purpose than to remind the sensitive reader that he is, after all, perusing a mid-nineteenth-century work.
My task has been to tune in to Groen at the right frequency and transmit
him at the correct wavelength—at the appropriate level of diction: neither too formal nor too colloquial, neither too Dutch nor too British, etc.

GROEN ON TRANSLATIONS

What would the author himself have thought of the whole venture? Groen
was wary of translation. For example, when preparing for the first publication of letters from the family archives of the House of Orange he ran
into the official requirement that every item not written in French be
accompanied by a French translation; he advised the king against it for
a well-considered reason: "Mediocre translations are of little use [while]
good translations are an exceedingly difficult task for which capable persons are not easily found and which demand time and care that would be
better spent on editing the original documents."[14] He got his wish and when
the work came out he explained in the Preface:

Mediocre translations serve no purpose other than to mislead; good
translations are difficult to make and always inadequate, since the

---

14. *Briefwisseling*, V, 37.

slightest nuance in the wording causes an appreciable change in meaning.[15]

More than once the translator of *Ongeloof en Revolutie* needed to remind himself of this sobering thought.

Happily, Groen knew how to appreciate good translations when he saw them (which, admittedly, was rare). Some translators from German into Dutch did succeed, he granted, in doing justice to the idiom of a Luther or the diction of a Stahl, though even then "those who are familiar with such writings would rather read them in the original."[16] A careful stylist like Groen, master of the "guarded word," could not but be sensitive to the semantic aspects of translation:

> The difficulties of translation are not inconsiderable. It is not an easy task, when conveying [into another language] the writings of those who are masters in their own tongue, to retain the force of words and correctness of expression. Often these writings may as well be called *untranslatable*.[17]

As for the aesthetic aspect, ancient and modern authors alike posed similar difficulties. In his D.Litt. thesis Groen recorded that none of the Plato translations he had consulted left him satisfied; but then again, he expressed his doubt whether any translator could even come close to the beauties of the original.[18] We would certainly not begrudge Groen the pleasure of seeing applied to himself what he at one time remarked about a contemporary publicist whom he much admired:

> In effect Monsieur Tocqueville is one of those classic authors in whom substance is so inseparable from form that they defy the talent even of the most skillful translator.[19]

Who would not feel hesitant about introducing Groen's substance in a different form, about clothing his thoughts in words other than his own?

---

15. *Archives*, I, xi.

16. *Briefwisseling*, II, 645; III, 817n6; *Parlementaire Studiën en Schetsen*, II, 348.

17. *Nederlandsche Gedachten*, 1873/74, V, 262.

18. *Prosopographia Platonica* (Leyden: Hazenberg, 1823), p. 4.

19. *Maurice et Barnevelt*, p. 166.

Tone and style, therefore, posed special problems of their own. Fidelity to *Ongeloof en Revolutie* requires reproducing a prose that is alternately guarded and blunt, plain and ornate, prosaic and allusive, profuse and concise, fiercely polemical and gently urbane. I can only hope that we truly hear the voice of Groen, transmitted across the distances of time, culture and tongue, inescapably distorted, yet not beyond recognition.

In conclusion, a few examples of key choices made by the translator are accounted for below. They deal with some of Groen's technical terms and neologisms, for which either concordant or dynamic equivalents had to be selected.

A BRIEF ANNOTATED GLOSSARY OF TERMS

"Unbelief" for Ongeloof

Central to the book as a whole, this term is charged with a meaning and scope that is not set forth until Lectures VIII and IX. There we see that *ongeloof* for Groen carries all the biblical connotations of (a) disbelief in revelation, (b) apostasy from God, and (c) defiant rebellion against God. The English term *unbelief* can serve to evoke the same connotations, but English usage around 1850 would also have allowed *infidelity, irreligion*, and even *incredulity*, while it would appear that semantic usage did not differentiate between them.[20] If one suspects, however, that their ranges of meaning and their connotations surely did not always overlap neatly, one needs to consider whether there may actually have been a shade of difference between, say, *unbelief* and *incredulity*. It is doubtful. Or was it really anything other than considerations of style which made Dickens open his *Tale of Two Cities* (1859) with the following pairs of opposites: "It was the best of times, it was the worst of times, it was the age of wisdom, it was the age of foolishness, it was the epoch of belief, it was the epoch of incredulity ..."

One can easily see why "epoch of unbelief" would not have been half as felicitous—but would it have been an inexact antithesis of "epoch of

---

20. In instances such as these, Murray's *Oxford English Dictionary Based on Historical Principles* proved an indispensable tool.

belief"? I have found no evidence to support this supposition; for all intents and purposes *incredulity* was synonymous with *unbelief*.

The same can be said about the term *infidelity*. Consider the widely popular work by the Rev. David Nelson, *The Cause and Cure of Infidelity; with an account of the author's conversion* (New York, 1837). The British reprint of this American work had its subtitle changed to: *including notice of the author's unbelief, and the means of his rescue* (London and Calcutta, 1853). Interestingly, the 1870 Spanish translation of Nelson's book talks of *incredulidad* in both title and subtitle, while a Dutch translation came out in 1874[21] under the title *Het Ongeloof, de grootste krankheid van onzen tijd, in haar oorsprong en genezing.*[22]

The term *apostasy* seems less satisfactory since it covers only part of the range of meaning desired; it does, however, highlight one connotation also present in Groen's term *ongeloof*: this was not just any unbelief, but the anti-Christian, post-Christian unbelief of the Enlightenment, which consciously rejected the gospel.

The term *secularism* I had to disqualify, not only because it has a different root entirely, but also because it was not introduced into the English language until G. J. Holyoake coined it in 1851.

The word *unbelief* was finally selected because, once the ear gets used to it, it seems to take on the functions required by the various contexts in which Groen uses *ongeloof*.

"The Revolution" for de Revolutie

Groen writes the term variously with a capital letter or in lower case, with the article sometimes italicized: *"de* revolutie," "de revolutie," *"de* Revolutie," and most often "de Revolutie."

As we expect, Groen has invested this term with new meaning. In 1847, the word *revolutie* does not yet seem to have been completely naturalized in the Dutch language. At least, one reviewer of the book remarked that he did not understand why the author continually uses the "foreign term" *revolutie*, since the good Dutch word *omwenteling* (which he notes Groen

---

21. With a foreword by the Christian Reformed (Secession) minister W. H. Gispen.
22. Fifth impression: Enkhuizen, 1895.

does use as well here and there) "seems to us to express the same idea."[23] The answer is, of course, as the reviewer also acknowledges, that Groen required a special term to carry his special meaning. To be sure, the meaning of *revolutie* as a "general, mostly unexpected inversion in the political and/or social conditions of a country" was at least as old as 1732, but the first recorded usage of *revolutie* to denote "changes in the religious and philosophical realm" occurs in ... Groen's *Ongeloof en Revolutie!*[24]

At a very early stage I decided to capitalize the word *revolutie* wherever it stands for that complex of meanings intended by Groen: the revolution is an error of the mind proceeding from an unbelieving heart, a profound and far-reaching error, one from which men cannot be dissuaded by mere logical arguments since it is firmly rooted in a heart commitment. The revolution is a mental habitus, a spiritual posture fed by the soul's craving for self-emancipation, man's defiant revolt against any and all authority, first of all divine authority (*ni Dieu*) but also every earthly kind (*ni maître*). It is, above all, a collective mentality, a reorientation in the consciousness of Western man: the revolution is an antipathy to Christianity converted into mutiny against Christendom. Thus, for Groen the French Revolution is a visible manifestation or symptom of "the revolution" in a way in which the American and certain other revolutions are not. To leave this term uncapitalized would make it look too unspecific in contexts where Groen's specific sense had to be conveyed. This did necessitate going against current English rules for capitalization, so that our translation refers to concrete historical instances of revolution by the names "the American revolution" and "the French Revolution." The context here usually prevents confusion, as is shown, for example, in the discussion in the opening paragraphs (262f) and again in the closing section (293) of Lecture XI: the French Revolution of 1789 is not an instance of political reformation that brought wholesome change; also, it is far more than a political revolution that led to radicalism; it is nothing less than "the Revolution: with its systematic application of the philosophy of unbelief ... with its self-deification and its adoration of Reason on the ruins of the ancient state."

---

23. De Witte van Citters, in *Themis* 9 (1848): 115.
24. *Woordenboek der Nederlandsche Taal*, XII/4, 696–99.

"The Revolution Doctrine" for de Revolutieleer

By analogy, we also get the revolution theory, the revolution principle: for *de revolutietheorie, het revolutiebeginsel.*

These terms should not present any problem to the readers once their ears have grown accustomed to them.

To translate *leer* with "ideology" was tempting, but rejected as somewhat anachronistic: Groen used *ideologie* only twice, in Lecture XIV (378, 392), and then in the sense known to Napoleon: impractical dreaming, visionary theorizing. To be sure, a modern writer on the same subject would capture Groen's *revolutieleer* very well if he talked of "the ideology of secular humanism." At the same time one must today be on guard against Marxian overtones: "ideology" can be understood simply as a set of self-serving rationalizations protective of class interests. In Groen, by contrast, the *revolutieleer* is a product of religious unbelief, which people embrace or reject irrespective of class.

"The Revolution Ideas" for de Revolutie-begrippen

This term is used interchangeably by Groen with *de revolutie-beginsels, -grondstellingen, -denkbeelden, -leerstellingen,* which we render by "the revolution principles, premises, notions, maxims."

The opening sentence of the book calls the *revolutie-begrippen* disastrous *denkbeelden* (notions). Too many commentators, misled by Groen's "logicism," take the term *begrip* in a narrow, logically restricted sense of *concept.* As Algra has pointed out, *begrippen* can stand for more than just "concepts": the Dutch Education Act of 1922, for example, prescribes respect for everyone's religious *begrippen;* throughout the 18th and 19th centuries Dutch prose speaks of religious, moral, social, political, liberal *begrippen.*[25] Hence the term denotes, not just logically defined and sharply delineated concepts, but as often as not something closer to ideas, beliefs, convictions, notions that involve human *choices* and *judgments.*[26]

In Lecture I (5f) these ideas—sometimes Groen will adopt the common phrase "the ideas of 1789," though of course he never limits them to that

---

25. Algra, "Beginsel en causaliteit," p. 215.

26. Cf. *Woordenboek der Nederlandsche Taal,* II/1, 1435–38. See also Zwaan, *Groen van Prinsterer en de klassieke Oudheid,* p. 69n44, where he warns against seeing affinity here with Plato's idealism or Von Humboldt's historical idealism.

year or even to the French Revolution—are said to include the following *grondstellingen* (basic premises or maxims): liberty and equality, popular sovereignty, social contract, conventional re-creation (i.e. artifical reconstruction of state and society by common consent).

"Phases of the Revolution" for Revolutie-tijdperken

A rendering of Groen's *tijdperken* by "periods" or "time-periods" was rejected as too bland. "Stages" might have done, but "phases" emphasizes the inevitability Groen sees in their regular succession, as in astronomy (phases of the moon) or biology (cycles in the life history of insects, or seasonal changes in the color of fur-bearing animals). According to Groen, the historical metamorphoses of the revolution reflect its "natural history," i.e., the logical unfolding of all the consequences implicit in the revolution's principle or controlling starting-point.

Admittedly, using a term like "phases" runs the risk of leading one to associate Groen's analysis too closely with a school of sociology which, positivistically, seeks to formulate law-like regularities in human phenomena, in such a way as to disallow or disparage, in keeping with its methodological determinism, the possibility of free, responsible choice. Since we believe, however, that Groen transcends the freedom-determinism polarity into which critics have tried to press him, we have not hesitated to use "phases" as our translation of *tijdperken*. The risk involved in doing so may have an added benefit. Any critique of Groen must consider all angles of his periodization of history: the term *tijdperken* reflects his philosophy of history and the term "phases" serves well in pinpointing a key problem in that philosophy: if that problem can be tackled head-on and be resolved, Groen's case will come out all the stronger.

The five successive *tijdperken* that divide the history of the one revolution (which is still with us, says Groen) must be distinguished from the *Revolutietijd,* i.e. the entire era in which the revolution holds sway, the whole "age of revolution." This distinction must be clearly reflected in the terminology for each. It must have been while reading the proofs of the first edition that Groen noticed a lapse in terminological precision on his part, for on the list of errata (appended in the back of the 1st edition) he notes that on page 256 (*read:* 257), line 22, one should read *den Revolutietijd* (the Age of Revolution, the revolution era) instead of *het Revolutie-Tijdperk* (the revolution phase or period); regrettably, he fails to note a similar lack of precision a few pages further on (page 261, line 2, and page 270, line 19).[27]

As for the characteristic names given to the phases, they permit of a straightforward translation: 1. *Voorbereiding* (Preparation); 2. *Ontwikkeling* (Development); 3. *Reactie* (Reaction); 4. *Hernieuwde Proefneming* (Renewed Experimentation); and 5. *Moedelooze Berusting* (Despondent Resignation).

Phase Two might also be called the phase of Unfolding, since in this period the revolution ideas, having conquered the minds, unfold themselves, like the petals of a rosebud, to reveal their contents (or implications) as men seek to apply them.

Phase Five comes close to being a period of Disillusionment or Demoralization.

One might be tempted to push the naturalistic analogy to the point of labeling the five phases Gestation, Evolution, Remission, Resuscitation, and Deterioration. Such labels, however, would obviously overshoot the mark, or at least go beyond Groen's intention as reflected in his word choice. Nevertheless, it would be fair to summarize his periodization of the Age of Revolution in the following metaphor: the revolution, nourished by unbelief, is like a vine whose flowers bud, bloom, close, revive, and wilt.

"Constitutional Law" / "Political Theory" / "Political Philosophy" for the single term Staatsregt

"State law" obviously will not do, referring as it does to a piece of legislation on the books, a statute.

"Public law," a much more likely candidate, is less than satisfactory because it is too broad in meaning: it comprises administrative law, international law, constitutional law, and according to some authorities, even criminal law; in common parlance, moreover, "public law" usually refers only to international law.

For *Staatsregt* we needed a term whose meaning is strictly limited to the basic rules that are to govern the functioning of a state (relations between governmental organs, relations between government and citizens, etc.). The term is "constitutional law."

---

27. The passages in which the errors occurred were altered or deleted in the 2nd edition.

The choice once made, our problems are far from over. For what is constitutional law? Is it positive law, or also theory? When Groen uses *Staatsregt* he is referring first of all to the law governing a state, i.e. to that body of laws or rules and principles which underlie a state's political arrangements—as actually in effect or presumed to be in effect. Of course Groen is aware of another meaning of *Staatsregt*, but only in one instance does he feel compelled to add the adjective "positive": at the beginning of Lecture XI (260) he characterizes Lectures III, IV and V as an examination of the old regime's *positieve Staatsregt*. Yet from this area of positive law the meaning easily slides into the area of legal theory and legal philosophy. By *Staatsregt* Groen seems to mean almost as frequently "constitutional theory" or "political philosophy."

The sliding scale of meanings is not strange. Positive constitutional law is notoriously open to divergent interpretation and controversial debate since its written rules (or, in the British system, its tacit conventions) are linked to principles of a different order which constantly play in the background. This background order is denied only by legal positivists; most other legal thinkers hesitate to distinguish too sharply between constitutional law and political theory and philosophy.

In consequence of all these considerations, we have on occasion, where the context warranted, chosen for unambiguous clarity and rendered *Staatsregt* variously by "constitutional theory," "political philosophy," or simply "view of the state."

These variants comport well with Groen's whole approach to law. No legal positivist but a jurist sympathetic to the Historical Law School, and moreover a believer in the Supreme Lawgiver, he neither spurned positive law nor accepted it as the final word. This approach is illustrated very well in his 1837 treatise on the government measures against the Seceders. The title of the treatise, it will be remembered, announces that it will "test the government measures against the *Staatsregt*" of the Netherlands. And what grounds does the treatise then proceed to adduce in order to reach its (negative) verdict? Curiously, the term *Staatsregt* occurs only in the title, not once in the body of the piece. A close reading shows that Groen draws his arguments:— first of all, naturally, from *positive law* and *the fundamental law*: namely, from a careful juridical interpretation of specific articles in the Penal Code and in the constitution of 1814/15; but also from the nation's *history* and the national *spirit:* to wit, from Holland's legacy of religious toleration, its people's traditional aversion to anything resembling constraint of conscience, and the generous intentions of the Restoration of 1814/15; and no less from the *memory* of its ruling dynasty: that is to say, from the historic record of members of the House of Orange for coming to the protection of religious minorities; and even—perhaps surprising for a declared opponent of abstract, ahistorical human rights—from *universal principles of justice and equity!* Truly, this is an appeal to *Staatsregt* in the broadest possible sense of the term.[28] Groen's understanding of the term appears equally broad in *Unbelief and Revolution.* In the face of such a wide range of meanings,[29] a concordant translation of this term, however faithful "literally," would semantically have been unfaithful to the original.

"Science" / "Scholarship" / "Learning" / "Knowledge" for the single term Wetenschap

A not unusual range of meaning for this term. The context must decide.

In the opening sentence of the Preface, Groen announces that the lectures will deal with the revolutionary school of thought which dominates constitutional law and *wetenschap* (learning).

In Lecture I (11) Groen observes that the fear of the Lord is the beginning of *wetenschap* (knowledge), but the beginning is not the whole of it: Christians must do their homework, all the while allowing the gospel to do its work as a leaven, both in the pursuit and in the products of *wetenschap* (learning).

In Lecture II (20) Groen asserts that throughout the ages thoughtful *wetenschap* (science) speaks out against the political doctrine of the revolution.

At the beginning of Lecture XI, in a recapitulation (not included in our abridgment) of what has been demonstrated so far, Lecture VI is said by Groen to have shown that the revolution did not arise from the perversion of *wetenschap* (science—i.e. the science of constitutional law) as such.

---

28. See also Gerretson, *Verzamelde Werken,* V, 79.

29. The definition of "staatsrecht" in *Woordenboek der Nederlandsche Taal,* XV, 337, is too restrictive.

At the very end of the concluding Lecture XV (427), Groen exhorts his friends to do whatsoever their hand finds to do in the world of *wetenschap* (scholarship) and politics.

Examples like these remind one that "perfect" one-to-one equivalents, even in cognate languages like Dutch and English, are not always at hand.

"Omnipotence (Omnicompetence) of the State" for Almagt (Alvermogen) van den Staat

These terms capture Groen's basic quarrel with the revolutionary state: its despotism; its centralized machinery, spread out over the populace like an iron network; its meddlesome interference in every domain of life (Lecture X, 241–55); its destruction of every mediating structure or "intermediary body" (Lectures V and XIV, 113, 375); its unlimited power to dispose of people's children, property and lives and to impose upon them a creed of civil religion that takes precedence over every other, "private" religion (Lecture IX, 207f, 212ff).

There is only one word in modern English that captures the nature of such rule: *totalitarianism*. Unfortunately, the word is too recent a creation to function legitimately in a work of 1847.

13
—

CONTROVERSIAL ISSUES

Our study is designed to open up a source document, not to recount its critical reception. At the same time it might be useful to outline the main points of controversy engendered by the work since its first appearance more than a century ago. Such an outline, necessarily brief though it must be, may not only spark interest among new readers of *Unbelief and Revolution* in the perennial debate around the book, but it may also help them to avoid certain persistent misinterpretations that have plagued its reception for too long.

Most of the controversial issues raised by the book stem from Groen's methodology and philosophy of history. Before we examine these, one contentious issue of a different kind may conveniently be discussed first, and that is Groen's monarchical bias.

MONARCHICAL BIAS

As many commentators have noted, there is a certain stubbornness with which Groen clung to the Hallerian interpretation of old-order monarchy as a kind of property right. On this view, royal authority was but the natural power exercised by the proprietor of lands, whether acquired through conquest or inheritance. Thus monarchy rested on a purely personal type of power, as opposed to the public nature of governmental authority in republics. This "private-legal" definition of kingship informs Groen's analysis of pre-revolutionary monarchy in Lecture IV as well as his line of reasoning in Lecture VI as he outlines the "perversion" of constitutional law since the Middle Ages. Groen could not be budged from utilizing Haller's interpretative reconstruction, not even after critics pointed out how untenable this reconstruction really was.

Whence this stubbornness? One reason is easily adduced. Groen wanted to demolish the historical credentials of ancient "royal democracy" which liberal writers believed existed in the early Middle Ages and which they equated, anachronistically, with participatory government under a representative electoral system. These Restoration authors revived Mably and Montesquieu's picture of the empire of Charlemagne as a kind of constitutional republic. In opposition, Groen defended, from very early on,[1] the view of early medieval kings as "possessors" of absolute authority. He sums up his all too brief discussion of it in *Unbelief and Revolution* with a quotation from Guizot[2] to the effect that the "distinguishing and fundamental character of barbarian kingship was that it was a personal, not a public power; a force in the presence of other forces, not a magistracy in the midst of society."[3] Unfortunately, Groen leaves out the word "barbarian" in the quotation! Negligently—or deliberately, so as not to weaken his case?[4] Though it refers only to the nature of kingship as it first emerged among the Franks, Guizot's interpretative description is presented by Groen, along with a number of other "authoritative" statements, as holding for pre-revolutionary monarchy in general, in whatever phase or historical period.

An early critic complained, not unjustly, that Groen's so-called "historical forms of government" were really composite pictures containing details collected from different centuries.[5] More recent critics have noted a lamentable dependence on Haller here. The mildest among them comes to the verdict that Groen's patrimonial conception of pre-revolutionary monarchies is "not quite historical": those situations which in any way resemble his picture were created under political and economic duress, were deviations from the norm, and were gradually overcome as feudalism made way (again) for public-legal administration; Groen simply ignored the tendencies leading to modern constitutions that were in fact operative

---

1. See e.g. his eight articles in the *Journal de la Haye* of Nov./Dec. 1832, written in reply to the *Gazette de France*; cf. *Bescheiden*, ed. Zwaan, no. 28; *Briefwisseling*, I, 631, 636.

2. *Essais sur l'histoire de France* (Paris, 1823), p. 305.

3. Lecture IV, p. 81 (not included in our abridgment).

4. In general, Groen's quotations are rarely letter-perfect, but comparison with the originals has satisfied me that this lack of precision does not (except perhaps in the above instance) result in an unreliable or tendentious text.

5. Cf. De Bosch Kemper, review of *Unbelief and Revolution*, p. 194.

from the very beginning of the Middle Ages.[6] A more severe critic deplores Groen's debt to Restoration conservatives, who knew of no defense against the innovationism of the revolution save in the respect owed to whatever grows over time and crystallizes in the historical process—a "historicist" mode of thought which fails to recognize constant creation structures behind the variable forms of history and is capable of acknowledging at most a relative, not a fundamental, distinction between the "undifferentiated" structures of medieval, feudal society and the "differentiated" structures that have been part of the modern scene since the French Revolution; as a result, Groen thought he could wed his later (revised) public-legal view of the state (learned from Stahl) to his earlier private-legal conception (adopted from Haller) by simply adding to the function of the intermediate bodies in society the task of exercising their autonomous powers with a view also to the public interest or common good.[7] Zwaan speaks of a "conceptual confusion" in Groen's "doctrine of the state"[8] between "monarchy" as described by authors of classical antiquity and as defined by Haller; yet often a "light breaks through" that leaves his monarchism in the shade and brings out the "republican" sympathies and love of liberty that he always displayed in practical politics.[9]

Many students of Groen have criticized him severely for his tendency to assume continuity, if not identity, between public-legal ("republican") government and bureaucratic centralism, state absolutism and political radicalism.[10] A more balanced view would have resulted if they had emphasized that Groen's aim throughout was to safeguard liberty against the governments of modern nation-states, which were spreading their imperial wings in the name of the "common good." In Groen's estimation this criterion lacked firm delimitation, indeed seemed to warrant government claims to omnicompetence. If the revolution did establish the

---

6. Cf. Smit, "Groen en de prae-revolutionaire staatsvormen," pp. 61–72; the conclusion is based in part on studies by such twentieth-century historians as G. von Below, C. H. McIlwain, F. Meinecke and H. Mitteis.

7. Dooyeweerd, "Het historisch element in Groen's staatsleer," pp. 124–35; see also Dengerink, *De sociologische ontwikkeling van het beginsel der "Souvereiniteit in eigen kring,"* chap. II.

8. Zwaan, *Groen van Prinsterer en de klassieke Oudheid,* chap. III (pp. 214–424 [sic]).

9. Zwaan, *Groen van Prinsterer en de klassieke Oudheid,* pp. 283f, 293.

10. See the discussion in Zwaan, *Groen van Prinsterer en de klassieke Oudheid,* pp. 294–98.

public-legal nature of government it had seemed to imply at the same time that the community formed the collective sovereign, against whom no intermediate body could stand. In Lecture X (253) Groen stated his whole-hearted agreement with Tocqueville that this inordinate concentration of power posed a grave threat to liberty. In reaction, Groen held a brief for a private-legal form of monarchy (which he assumed to have obtained under the old regime) because it was by definition tempered: the absolute kings, sovereignly independent in their sphere, which in fact embraced the entire national community, were nevertheless surrounded by a host of dependent authorities who each wielded power in their respective subordinate spheres; such vibrant intermediate bodies throughout society, secure in their private-legal rights, automatically functioned as checks and balances on absolute kings. We agree with Dooyeweerd that what is needed here is an *intrinsic* criterion for delimiting the task of government, one based on a structure of creation rather than on what seems like a time-bound historical configuration. At the same time we would like to note that, historically speaking, such a correction of Groen is itself indebted to his early struggle to find a solution: his intellectual heirs, like Kuyper and Dooyeweerd, were able to bring the complex and thorny problem to a more satisfying solution precisely as a fruit of the seminal ideas of Groen van Prinsterer.

Groen's own "solution," *genuine* and therefore *tempered* monarchy, was an earnest attempt to guarantee liberty while respecting the sanctity and integrity of government. Admittedly, his ideal of monarchy—the king rules in strict independence of the people yet in constant consultation with them—was mainly an ideal-type, hardly suited for historical realization. No contemporary reader of *Unbelief and Revolution* seems to have taken his ideal solution seriously.[11] Sane and practical as always, Koenen brought Groen back to reality by reminding him, upon receipt of the published book, that his ideal of a monarchy independent of the people was quite unfeasible for modern states like Holland, since the King, lacking sufficient income from private domains, would always be in need of approved taxes to run the state.[12]

---

11. Not even the reactionary conservative Bakker Korff, who deplored this aspect of the book since it could not but weaken the impact of the "voice of [true] conservatism and the correct observations" which it also contained; see his review, p. 402.

12. *Briefwisseling*, II, 811.

Meanwhile, the reader senses from the close of Lecture IV (89–91) that Groen's optimism about the possibility of a tempered monarchy was based on his anti-oligarchic, pro-Orange reading of the history of the Dutch Republic[13] and his admiration of the British system as a mixed constitution organically rooted in that nation's history. By the same token his monarchist bias was inspired by his contempt, not only for "unbelief's formula for politics," viz. "power to the people" (^{2}193n), but also for the artificial imitations of Restoration constitutionalism (383), which meant in practice that monarchs ruled like autocrats and the constitutional organs languished (6, 414f).[14] In the place of both "revolutionary autocracy" and "radical democracy" he advocated constitutions under which kings had the power and the people had influence (^{2}427n). That the rightful influence of the people (including the "people behind the voters") was not nugatory in his mind is apparent from his own parliamentary career, and never more so than in 1866, when he proved willing to risk the displeasure of the entire conservative establishment for the sake of defending the rights of parliament against a cabinet that hid behind the royal prerogative in order to withdraw areas of administration from parliamentary control.

It should also be remembered that Groen did not write his book out of blindness to the improvements brought by the revolution (190f). He grants that old-regime abuses constituted a *sufficient cause* (though not *ground*) for revolution (118). He admits that excessive centralization had long made a revolution almost unavoidable (^{2}104n). The root of the revolutionary evil, however, "lies at a deeper level than the political surface" (117f). The destabilizing struggle between court, nobility and commoners before 1789 goes a long way toward explaining the ensuing political upheaval, but not the social cataclysm, which is the real revolution. *The revolution is not the political inversion that was accomplished but rather the new basis of authority that was installed* (293). In the course of history, *forms* of government come and go, but the new political philosophy undermines them all! Groen could protest with some justification that he was

---

13. Cf. Zwaan, *Groen van Prinsterer en de klassieke Oudheid*, p. 314.

14. Geyl's fulminations in *Reacties*, pp. 27–42, against the "reactionary tenor" of *Unbelief and Revolution* are to some extent justified by the book's monarchist passages but disregard its author's intentions.

no legitimist (144, 264f).[15] His indictment of the revolution did not in the first place concern the acute symptoms that attended it, such as its reduction of monarchy and aristocracy, its nationalization of property, or even its bloodshed; what alarmed him far more was the chronic disease with which it had infected Europe's body politic: its systematic undermining of peace, order, and good government; its whirl of paper constitutions; its elevation of expedience as the basic rule of international law; and its installation of the omnicompetent state, which curtailed civil rights and imposed a civil religion.

This last point is important to keep in mind as one tries to assess the extent of Groen's "monarchical bias." His reading of the French Revolution stood in the traditions of Burkean conservatism, French Traditionalism, and Prussian throne and altar thinking, yet was distinct from each.[16] He preferred to characterize his position as anti-revolutionary and Christian-historical. As a Dutch Calvinist he was a passionate lover of liberty, a defender of "lawful" revolutions, and the heir to a mature political tradition steeped in religious thought and democratic sentiment alike. As an evangelical historian he was eager to prove the healing power of the gospel from the history of the nations and the historical force of guiding beliefs in the great events of the past. Such a man is a confessor of the Christian faith more than Burke ever was, a champion of religious toleration more than the Traditionalists ever were, and a critic of authoritarian monarchy more than the Germans Stahl and Gerlach could ever have been.

None of the above considerations, however, diminishes the fact that the picture of the old regime in *Unbelief and Revolution* is rosier than history warrants. If Groen is to be believed, the incidence of oppressive dues was almost negligible (100–7) and the need for reform was not so great that it could not have been met by constitutional means (90). At the close of his review of pre-revolutionary monarchies Groen briefly recites the critical comments and questions that have been raised by some of his auditors: Are kings correctly defined as "sole possessors of authority"? Should constitutional law be treated as a species of private law? Is liberty to depend

---

15. See *Brieven van Da Costa*, I, 264.

16. The various themes in their interrelation with the Historical Law School are explored in René van Woudenberg, *De geschiedbeschouwing van Groen van Prinsterer en haar achtergronden* (unpub. qualifying thesis, Free University, Amsterdam, 1980), esp. pp. 12–29, 46–66.

on the character of the person on the throne? Has the separation of church and state, though since carried too far, not been a good thing?[17] Groen's only reply is that it is enough that they are all of one mind as to the main issues: *viz.* that the old regimes were *legitimate*; that sovereignty is a sacred trust from *God*, not a mandate delegated by man; and that the revolution essentially destroys *all* government.

In his rosy picture of the old regime (esp. 98–107) Groen to some degree anticipated Tocqueville, who was to write a decade later that his research in the provincial archives indicated that by 1750 the greater part of French feudalism had become extinct.[18] Of course the part that was left, particularly some manorial dues, remained, Groen admitted, irksome. But that they too were at last abolished (on 4 August 1789) is portrayed by Groen neither as a long-overdue reform, nor even as an act of spiteful vengeance, but as a simple demand of ideology (292). He also, as we have seen, shared Tocqueville's appreciation for the advantage of having intermediary bodies in society. Under the old regime, rights and privileges of all kinds prevented absolute rulers from turning into despots: "a strange kind of liberty allowed every group to hold up its head before the royal officials."[19] Groen may not, in 1845, simply have wished to resurrect the former power of the estates, but he certainly painted a bright picture of their erstwhile contribution to liberty in the state (83–85). In a letter written to Groen shortly before the lectures commenced, De Bosch Kemper conceded that under the old regime the estates had been mediators of the different interests in society, but he added that in his opinion they had not been very effective and in any event could be such no longer: the times had changed and demanded different forms.[20]

As a result of his view of monarchy Groen even came to espouse a questionable interpretation of the Dutch Revolt. For, regrettably,[21] his vindication of old-regime royal absolutism left him no choice but to dismiss

---

17. Lect. V, pp. 117f (removed from the 2nd ed. and not included in our abridgment).

18. It is out of character for Groen not to add this authoritative opinion to his earlier documentation when he revised his book in 1868.

19. Richard Herr, *Tocqueville and the Old Regime* (Princeton University Press, 1962), p. 128.

20. *Briefwisseling*, II, 706.

21. Cf. Donner, in *Lustrumbundel*, p. 144.

libertatis causa, the defense of political and civil liberties, as a legitimate ground for the revolt against Philip II of Spain.[22]

Indeed, Groen's monarchical bias was stronger than he cared to admit or his friend Koenen could abide. It is to his credit that he silently passed over the fanciful reconstruction of Merovingian rule in Michelet's *Histoire de France* (1833–43). But his reliance on Moreau was a decided weakness in that it led him to depict old-style kings as having sole legislative authority, limited only by natural law or their conscience. Thus, in line with his scornful dismissal of the presence of "royal democracy" in the early Middle Ages, he accepted Moreau's reading of the *Edictum Pistense* as an instruction for judges presiding over town court proceedings (78).[23] He would have been wise to take Koenen's remark more seriously that Moreau should not be relied on since he had worked without the benefit of the modern, critical studies in feudalism, a circumstance which might explain why he mistook the power wielded by the Merovingians and the early Carolingians for entirely "monarchical" rather than in part also "military." Moreau may have proved that the Frankish kingdom was no "republic à la Rousseau," yet did he understand the workings of the feudal system and its effect on the Frankish monarchy? Besides, Moreau had been an official court historian, easily tempted to project the absolutism of his royal master back into the early Middle Ages.[24]

Groen felt misunderstood in his reliance on Haller. Haller's epochmaking book on the *Restoration of Political Science* had been a revelation to him in the twenties, and although it left him unsatisfied in some respects, at least it demolished a prevailing falsehood and prepared the ground for something better (37f). In later years Groen explained that what had struck him about Haller was "the negative side, the refutation of liberalism."[25]

---

22. Smitskamp, "Groen's denkbeelden over het recht van opstand," pp. 182ff; idem, *Groen van Prinsterer als historicus,* pp. 155–59.

23. A modern authority like A. J. Carlyle, *Political Liberty* (1941; repr. London, 1963), p. 205, does not hesitate to take the edict as evidence that the king was not the sole legislator but needed the counsel and consent, if not of "the people," at least of the great men of the realm; see also his *History of Mediaeval Political Theory in the West* (Edinburgh and London: Blackwood, 1903), I, 238.

24. *Briefwisseling,* II, 411, 644. Koenen's letters show that unlike Groen he was acquainted with more recent research into the nature of feudalism and medieval relations in general.

25. *Le parti anti-révolutionnaire* (1860), p. 42.

Still later he modified his qualified endorsement even further: "My praise does not extend beyond Volume I—the *polemics*; the mighty political *deed*; the penetrating vehemence with which [Haller] struck down and pulverized the dangerous doctrine of social contract and popular sovereignty."[26]

To sum up, Groen's assessment of the old regime and of modern constitutional law, rooted as it was in his conception of the nature of kingship, is perhaps the weakest part of *Unbelief and Revolution*. His dependence on Haller clearly prevented him from properly appreciating the "general welfare" as a criterion of public administration. In consequence, he could but see the "republicanizing" assault on the tempered monarchies of old— especially when *philosophes* mounted the assault in terms of a secularized conception of what constitutes the "general welfare" and of how the "general will" is to be constituted—as leading straight to a totalitarian form of government. Groen's later conversion to Stahl's political philosophy necessitated a complete reappraisal and recasting of at least that part of his book. The mere incorporation of Stahlian footnotes in the 2nd edition was hardly likely to strengthen *Unbelief and Revolution's* internal consistency; from that point of view, in fact, the revision decidedly weakened its impact.[27]

METHODOLOGY

The method used in *Unbelief and Revolution* has come in for a great deal of criticism. The opening lecture states that the case will be argued solely in terms of historical *facts*, with the proviso, following Guizot, that facts are not restricted to phenomena on the empirical surface but include as well the "general laws that control them"—remote and obscure though they be, and difficult to observe and describe, yet facts all the same, facts which have their legitimate place in historical analysis alongside empirical facts and "which man is no less obliged to study and to know" (17). The implied organic relationship between facts-as-surface-phenomena and facts-as-general-laws is clarified later, at the beginning of Lecture VIII (182).

---

26. *Nederlandsche Gedachten*, 1873/74, V, 250.

27. For a parallel (though far too general) critique of the revision of the *Handboek*, see Geyl, *Reacties*, p. 20: "It succeeded only in making the work unpalatably ambivalent. Untenable statements were deleted, bold formulations softened, but in other places passages just as offensive remained unchanged. And in particular: the system was essentially maintained, only it now seemed to have become even more arbitrary, while certain concessions had left component parts utterly without foundation."

At this point in the series, the lecturer first reminds us that his purpose is to present an "essay at biography" (which is now further described as a "survey of the revolution's history in connection with its doctrine"); but then he informs us that he will preface that survey with something else. Borrowing another terminological distinction from Guizot, Groen explains that before engaging in the *anatomy* of the period he will first present its *physiology*. The anatomy will establish the facts, while the physiology will establish the interrelations between the facts. Since these interrelations are said to be the "hidden laws that preside over the course of events," it makes good sense to try to establish them first. Hence, wherever possible, a physiological examination should come *prior to* an anatomical examination. And thus was introduced into *Unbelief and Revolution* that questionable feature which has since been referred to as Groen's "apriorism." In a literal sense the term is quite appropriate, for as Groen himself says on the same page, he will first analyze the "natural history of the revolution ideas" and "only after this analysis" turn to the "actual events of the revolution," a procedure that will enable him, as he claims on the next page, to "predict" the drift of events "even without the light of history" (183; see also 15). More about this apriorism in a moment.

It should be noted that both the anatomy and physiology of history are here further distinguished from a third dimension, history's *physiognomy*.[28] In addition to the first two operations, the historian is also assigned the task of recreating the past by reproducing the external shapes and features of events. This task comes third not only in order but also in rank. For the externals of history may be very colorful and entertaining but of course by themselves can hardly be considered very instructive: staying on the surface, after all, does not enlighten one about the "hidden laws that preside over the course of events."[29]

This methodology with its threefold distinction suited Guizot, for whom the main task of the historian was "to teach and to warn."[30] It also

---

28. See the use of this term, 1st ed., pp. xii, 165.

29. There is an uncanny resemblance, at least formally, between this early nineteenth-century theory of history in France and the doctrine of "structures" adhered to in our century by the school of the *Annales*. But see note 31 below.

30. Cf. Gooch, *History and Historians in the Nineteenth Century*, p. 183.

suited Groen, who wanted history above all to be instructive in a moral and a religious sense.

PHILOSOPHY

Obviously, distinguishing three dimensions in which the historian works presupposes a particular philosophy of history. As with many of his generation, there was no doubt in Guizot's mind—nor in Groen's—that the "hidden laws" of historical physiology were *spiritual* in nature.[31] To be exact, Guizot identified them as "man's ideas, sentiments, moral and intellectual dispositions," or, in another place, as man's "beliefs, sentiments, ideas, manners." These are the elements that are habitually employed by Guizot to establish "man's interior state," a state which "precedes the exterior condition, the social relations, the political institutions," in short, the state or condition on which "depends the visible state of society."[32] Thus from man's interior state issues the whole external world that he builds up for himself.

The implications of this view of history for the writing of history are not difficult to imagine. If all of external society can be shown to flow from man's beliefs and ideas, history must appear quite predictable and rational. Understandably, this is an approach to history that has never lacked critics, from the time when it first came into vogue. Sainte-Beuve, for example, once commented: "History seen from a distance ... produces the illusion that it is rational. ... Guizot's history is far too logical to be true."[33]

The same has been said of Groen's history. Groen far too readily assigns a subordinate role to other than ideal factors. The opening lecture of *Unbelief and Revolution* states very bluntly: "Whatever may have been the subordinate action of secondary causes, as to the principal cause the history of Europe for more than half a century has been the inevitable result of the errors that have made themselves master of the predominant mode of

---

31. This is what distinguishes them from the structuralists of our own day, who turn instead, as if by instinct it would seem, to *material* factors.

32. Cf. *Civilisation en Europe*, Leçon 3, and *Civilisation en France*, I, 38, as quoted in Smitskamp, *Groen van Prinsterer als historicus*, p. 57.

33. Quoted in *History and Historians in the Nineteenth Century*, p. 182, by Gooch, whose own verdict of Guizot reminds one of critics of Groen: "No one has surpassed him in his capacity to seize the ideas which underlie events, to discern the inner changes which govern outward transformations, to recover the intellectual tendencies of an epoch. ... The influence of individuals, however, and the chapter of accidents are underestimated, and the epochs dovetail too neatly into one another." *Ibid.*, pp. 180f.

thinking" (5). Groen's choice for this "hierarchy of causes"[34] and his consistent application of it in *Unbelief and Revolution* as well as other works have prompted the criticism that his history-writing labors under *apriorism*, *idealism*, and *determinism*, and that his approach to history suffers from *logicism* and sociological *schematism*.[35] We shall devote a short discussion to each of these critical designations.

APRIORISM

The first issue that could bear some further clarification is the charge of "apriorism." Groen does indeed present his ultimate explanation abruptly, up front, on the first page. And halfway through his book he first devotes three lectures (VIII–X) to the "natural history" of the revolution before tackling the revolution's "biography." This is done, he says, to predict the fruit from the known tree. The apriori method could not have been stated with more painful candor.

But something worse than an apriorist mode of presentation is at stake here. The very integrity of Groen's hermeneutic is at issue. Did he allow himself to be instructed at all by his material as he combed the past for proof of his theory? It is rather disturbing to learn (as we have from our study of prototypes in chapter 5) that Groen's main thesis and train of argument were fixed quite some time before he gave the lectures. Worse still, his mind appears to have settled on the "root cause" as early as 1831, thus many years in advance of his ability to provide the full proof.

Unbelief and Revolution makes clear that the historical investigation has been guided from the start by an explanatory theory. The book's logic of explanation is deliberately deductive, openly reflecting the logic of Groen's discovery. Groen makes no secret of the fact that he approaches his subject-matter with a preconceived interpretation and thus knows the outcome of his investigation before it has begun.

Now it cannot be denied that a mode of presentation in which the conclusions do not follow the evidence but precede it creates the uncomfortable impression that the interpretation is filtering the facts rather than

---

34. A useful concept, elaborated in E. H. Carr, *What Is History?*, chap. iv.

35. See the informative discussion in Smitskamp, *Groen van Prinsterer als historicus*, pp. 50–82.

flowing out of them. In its strict form, however, this impression is mis-leading. Granted, Groen first hit upon his interpretative key. But this key then became, not his magic wand, but his heuristic tool. In the years that followed—more than a decade of intensive study—he took great pains to find support for his interpretation in the facts. Moreover, we have evidence that familiarity with the details of the revolutionary age preceded his abil-ity to interpret them. *Unbelief and Revolution*, as will be remembered, also functioned as a detour in preparation for writing the final installment of the *Handbook*, which had to deal with Holland in the revolution era, and we know from Groen's correspondence that what daunted him about that project was not so much the mass of intricate and turbulent facts and events to be related as the lack of clarity he felt about the "principles to be outlined"[36]; in other words, he seems to have felt quite in command of the raw material for the "anatomy" and would be ready to start writing as soon as he saw his way clear in terms of the "physiology" with which to give structure to his account. From all this one can only conclude that the lectures rightfully claim to be reporting on a genuine historical inquiry, and although one cannot suppress a smile when reading that "history alone" is the author's guide (17) and that his story of the revolution is intended to be the "pure result of unbiased historical investigation" (297), nevertheless one must acknowledge that the expressed intention is sincere, not feigned. It will not do, therefore, to try to exempt *Unbelief and Revolution* from his-torical critique by classifying it as a political treatise or as a tract for the times; this tendency is noticeable among some friends of the book[37] but one of its most relentless critics is correct: its claim is to be a historical study.[38]

From the above we may conclude that Groen's approach is as much *apos-teriori* as it is *apriori*. His early discovery of "unbelief the root, revolution the fruit" became his tentative theory—his working hypothesis or, as we have referred to it in chapter 6, his guiding vision—which he then sought honestly to prove on the basis of empirical evidence. Whether his proof stands up to scrutiny—whether his conclusions follow cogently *from* the evidence—is a different issue, quite distinct from his alleged "apriorism."

36. Cf. *Brieven van Da Costa*, I, 239f; III, 267.

37. Cf. Smitskamp and De Pater in *Lustrumbundel*, pp. 24-26, 101, and Donner, "Groen van Prinsterer als staatsman en evangeliebelijder," in *ibid.*, p. 62.

38. Geyl, *Reacties*, p. 10.

And I believe we are today in a better position to judge the merits of this type of history-writing than fifty or even twenty-five years ago. Forever gone, let us hope, are the days when scientific objectivity was chained to a naive inductivism, and theory-directed historical research was considered an ill-advised and unscholarly undertaking.[39]

In a formal sense, therefore, the extent of Groen's apriorism is much less objectionable than would appear at first sight. Nevertheless, that does not lessen the suspicion and distrust with which the modern historian regards the whole procedure, especially when it is so openly advertised. Just how strongly, he can't help but wonder, has the preconceived explanation determined the selection of supporting facts while suppressing many others? Geyl, no "objectivist" of the old school, nevertheless states that in his judgment the "aprioristic, monolithic principle" wielded by Groen eventually became an "obsession" to him, rendering him more a visionary than a reliable historian—a judgment Geyl arrived at in 1931 and which he was inclined to soften in 1937 but felt constrained to reiterate in 1951, after renewed study of the book and its critics.[40]

However one finally judges Groen's apriorism, it must be admitted that the peculiar method of first deducing governing principles in the abstract and then demonstrating their active presence in concrete reality—of

39. Cf. e.g. Fueter's critical remark, in the 3rd enlarged ed. (1936; repr. as recently as 1968) of his standard reference work, directed at Hippolyte Taine's pseudo-inductive procedure: "er trat mit vorgefassten Meinungen an sie [scil. die geschichtlichen Phänomene] heran und sah nur das, was zu seiner Theorie passte." *Geschichte der neueren Historiographie*, p. 584. In Anglo-Saxon countries historians have long resisted "theories" in order to safeguard their discipline as one of the "humanities." In 1950, G. J. Renier sounded decidedly progressive when he granted, in his handbook *History, Its Purpose and Method* (2nd impr.; London: George Allen & Unwin, 1961), p. 117, that a prior reading of the "views of sociologists" might be useful to the historian to guide his research and save time in its preliminary stage. In America it was lingering positivism, parading as respectably conservative "Rankeanism" (sic), that accounts for much of the resistance to the notorious *Bulletin 54* (1946) and *Bulletin 64* (1954) of the Social Science Research Council, which urged historians, respectively, to acknowledge the relativity of their subjective "frames of reference" and to avail themselves of the theories produced by social scientists; cf. Cushing Strout, *The Pragmatic Revolt in American History* (Yale University Press, 1958), pp. 18–29, 157–62, and H. R. Guggisberg, *Alte und neue Welt in historischer Perspektive; sieben Studien zum amerikanischen Geschichts- und Selbstverständnis* (Bern and Frankfort: Herbert Lang, 1973), chap. VII. I have discussed these and related issues in *The Debate Among American Historians About Generalizations* (unpubl. qualifying thesis, Free Univiversity, Amsterdam, 1970).

40. Geyl, *Kernproblemen*, pp. 15, 242, 261, 265f; *Reacties*, pp. 20, 447; *Encounters*, p. 325. In many of Geyl's debates with historians past and present, there is an element of aggressive self-assertion; cf. Puchinger, *Herinneringen aan Geyl*, p. 28.

examining inner logic before external life—has something forced about it. It is ironic that there are passages in *Unbelief and Revolution* where it is to some extent noticeable that the facts have *aposteriori* dictated the shape of at least certain subthemes of the overall interpretative theory. This happens to a greater extent, apparently, than the author would like. Groen appears bothered by the fact that despite his claim that he can predict the nature and course of the revolution purely from its starting principle, without consulting history, he is not always successful in keeping his later "anatomy" of the events from contaminating his prior "physiology" of the general laws governing those events. For example, halfway through Lecture X, thus prior to dealing with the history, he forecasts what the revolution's phases will look like but cuts the discussion short by confessing that he wants to avoid appearing to be making allusions to *actual* conditions (241). And a little earlier (236), where he predicts an inescapable phase of reaction under a strong man, he concedes that he is drawing the descriptive details of his *hypothetical* dictator from the *historical* career of Napoleon. Concessions such as these indicate that not even Groen can conceal from himself that his methodological separation of logic and life has something artificial about it.

In the 2nd edition of 1868 another small crack shows up in the imposing *apriori* structure. While still maintaining that Lecture XI(^{2}261) marks the *transition* from logic to life, Groen cheerfully inserts a new sentence at the outset of Lecture X(^{2}214) to the effect that the transition starts already there: "We do not now inquire into the *logical* but into the *historical* biography." Though confusing, this insertion is more like a cosmetic blot, detracting in no way, as will become clear below, from the overall integrity of the approach.[41] That approach is: Tell me what was taught, and I shall tell you what was done. His book is "the story of what was taught and consequently came to pass" (16).

---

41. The sentence would properly introduce Lecture X if made to read: We do not now inquire into the logical biography in the abstract but in its relation to history, in its logically inevitable clash with historical reality.

IDEALISM

Can such a complex event as the French Revolution indeed be deduced from prevailing teachings? Do doctrines shape history? Do ideas have legs? Does history bring to light what has been "concluded in the sphere of thought" (292)? To brand Groen's positive answers to these questions as "idealism" is to invite closer examination and definition of the term.

To begin with, Groen was not an idealist in the sense of Platonic realism. The Platonizing interpretation of Groen is at least as old as 1883, when Allard Pierson published his essay on Réveil personalities.[42] It bore fruit at the turn of the century in a doctoral dissertation that portrayed Groen as a Platonic idealist who fought for the ideal church and the ideal state and whose whole method of thinking and arguing proceeded from intellectual abstractions like revelation as such, the Reformation in itself, the revolution in its essence.[43] In a sense, this sort of interpretation was to be expected sooner or later. When Western thinkers educated in the classical tradition seek to acknowledge transcendental norms for earthly life, immutable "objective" standards for human conduct and cultural formation, then they often resort naturally to a mode of discourse reminiscent of Platonism.[44] Groen does that in places, and Pierson, eager to come close to Groen through sympathetic understanding, seized upon it. But it has not proved to be the hermeneutic key to his thought. This has been fortunate for Groen's reputation as a Christian thinker. His anti-revolutionary world-view, it is now generally recognized, was not a baptized Platonism, even though some of its formulations have that appearance. The new consensus on this point in Groen studies, which liberates us from an unfruitful tradition of interpretation, was bound to come about once his works were systematically analyzed with something like philosophical rigor.[45] Moreover, Groen's critical reservation with respect to the "peerless" yet pagan author (26) is entirely

---

42. *De Gids* 47 (1883): III, 92–130. Reprinted in *Oudere Tijdgenooten* (Amsterdam: Van Kampen, 1888), pp. 102–43; see esp. pp. 120ff.

43. Cf. Fokke J. Fokkema, *De Godsdienstig-wijsgeerige beginselen van Mr. G. Groen van Prinsterer* (Groningen, 1907), pp. 15–20, 228f.

44. A prime example is Eric Voegelin and his study, *From Enlightenment to Revolution*, ed. John H. Hallowell (Durham, North Carolina: Duke University Press, 1975), pp. viii, 51n, 180; and, with impressive consistency, his 5-vol. work *Order and History* (Baton Rouge: Louisiana S. U., 1956).

45. See above, chap. 3, notes 36–38.

in character. For that matter, even those whose thinking selectively borrows and assimilates thought-forms of Plato need not always adopt the fundamental thrust of his philosophy; the tensions inherent in a synthesis like Christian Platonism do not necessarily resolve themselves in an (involuntary) endorsement of a pagan ground-motive. That this is true in the case of Groen van Prinsterer has been established—definitively, it would seem—by Zwaan, whose ample documentation makes clear that the influence of Plato on Groen has in any event been grossly overrated.[46]

Neither was Groen an "intellectualist" in the Platonic tradition. For he states plainly that the channel by which the transcendental norms are known is not the mental effort of the philosopher but the childlike faith of the believer (177, 426f). No doubt this gave him reason to feel understood by the common people of the Reformed persuasion. Groen was not surprised when Wormser once reported to him that a medical doctor, asked about his opinion of *Unbelief and Revolution*, had replied that he "could not make head or tail of it," whereas a "simple office-clerk" had said that the book pleased him very much.[47]

Other meanings of "idealism" have also to be declared ill-fitting. Smitskamp has argued persuasively that the approach taken by Groen is not the philosophically tinted historical idealism of German contemporaries; if anything, it resembles the intellectual-spiritual treatment of history that he saw modeled in Guizot and defended in Burke and especially Lamennais.[48]

What kind of idealism, then, is present in *Unbelief and Revolution*? It is the view that ideas play a leading (though not exclusive) role in constituting human affairs, and that ideas were the main cause of the revolution. Up to a point such a view is expressed in its simplest form when a historian writes: "The Revolution was due to the union of concrete grievances ... with an intellectual ferment ... "[49] Essentially the same, but in a more complicated formulation, is another historian's summarizing conclusion: "Certainly if the old regime had been threatened only by ideas it

---

46. Cf. "Groen van Prinsterer over de wijsbegeerte," pp. 29–45; *Groen van Prinsterer en de klassieke Oudheid*, pp. 132–61.

47. *Brieven van Wormser*, I, 188; see also II, 81.

48. Smitskamp, *Groen van Prinsterer als historicus*, pp. 50–62.

49. G. P. Gooch, *Maria Theresa and Other Studies* (London: Longmans, 1951), p. 262.

would not have been in danger. To be effective, ideas needed a fulcrum: popular misery and political malaise. Yet no doubt this political factor would not have sufficed to bring about the revolution, at least not as rapidly. It was ideas that demonstrated and systematized its implications and led to a demand for the Estates-General ... which led to the Revolution."[50] Here the outbreak of the revolution is judiciously attributed to a conjunction of ideas and political circumstances, with a certain preponderance assigned to the ideas.[51]

As indicated, Groen's explanatory model is essentially the same: preponderance of ideas as they operate in a given context. The model, though debatable, is hardly novel or particularly shocking. Yet many commentators of Groen have criticized the "mechanical" manner in which he emphasizes ideas as the decisive factor. This criticism is not without ground and is relatively easy to substantiate from the text. For we read: the history of the last fifty years is the inevitable result of errors that have prevailed (5), events reveal that the revolution ideas work themselves out according to the dictates of logic (15), it was the necessary consequences of these ideas that determined the way things went (182), the horrors during the revolution stem from a consistent application of the ideas (296), whatever men might have wanted, it was always the power of principles that triumphed (328), the terror was implicit in the ideas of 1789 (328), there is a direct link connecting Robespierre's deeds to Rousseau's dogmas (357) and to Montesquieu's principles (364), and so on. As we hope to make clear in a moment from other passages in the text, in these sentences with their stark formulations Groen overstates his own case. But there have been critics who likewise overstate their objections, as when Geyl insists that Groen comes to the past with "the false conception that ideas are everything in history,"[52] thus peremptorily dismissing what Groen says about the subordinate, contributory status of all the other factors.

Ideas are not everything for Groen. His concept of causality incorporates a wide variety of factors operative in history, such as political unrest

---

50. Daniel Mornet, *Les origines intellectuelles de la Révolution française* (2nd ed.; Paris: Armand Colin, 1934), p. 477.

51. A related point made by Mornet, that the causes of its outbreak did not necessarily determine its subsequent course, is discussed below.

52. Geyl, *Reacties*, p. 11; but see his concession tucked away in the footnote on p. 5.

arising from constitutional abuses (96, 118), or shrewd political calculation (141, 151), or even the cooperation of favorable circumstances.[53] When he writes in the Preface that history is shaped "not just by the succession of deeds, but especially by the unfolding of ideas" (xi), then his "idealism" is transparent, but so are its limits. The sentence means, as the book will show, that the historical analysis, if it is to be instructive, must concentrate on human action, but in particular insofar as this action reveals the influence of the ideas humans gave their heart to and believed in. An early critic of the book surmised astutely that Groen did not mean to present unbelief as the *only* cause, knowing full well "that no event in world history arises from a single cause but from the confluence and cooperation of many causes and circumstances," but that he (Groen) had chosen to highlight unbelief as the principal cause, in a manner as though in his eyes it were the only cause, "under the influence of certain theological notions" (which the reviewer respected but did not share.)[54]

That brings us to still another, equally weighty, reason for dismissing the view that ideas are everything for Groen. Most fundamental to Groen's causal analysis is the role in history of the moral world-order. For this is what restrains the revolutionary doctrines from running their logical course to the very end, a subject to which all of Lecture X is devoted. That restraining order, in Groen's fluctuating terminology, includes all of the following:

> the ordinances of God (222)
> man's constitution and man's needs (222)
> man's conscience and man's true needs (224)
> the human disposition (225)
> the nature of things (222)
> historical reality (223)
> truth and law (223)
> nature (223)
> law and history (205)

---

53. Cf. 1st ed., p. 169. At the end of the Middle Ages the invention of printing, the discovery of America and the revival of letters all contributed to the rejuvenation of Europe.

54. T. Roorda to Groen, 22 Oct. 1847; *Briefwisseling*, II, 824.

nature and history (224)

the action of nature and time (204)

the historical rise of states (224)

the organic growth of societies[55] (224)

divine right (50–56)

the sacred origin of law and authority (224)

the universal principles of justice and right (45–47)

the simple pronouncements of nature and revelation (44)

the necessary relation between church and state (57f, 224) —

all of them "eternal and unshakable principles" (67), "immutable laws which the Maker and Sustainer of all things prescribes for his creatures and subjects" (116), "unchangeable ordinances of God" ([2]218).

Faced with this panoply of forces and factors, ideas nevertheless hold a place of paramount importance in the shaping of history. And that for a reason that is in line with a long-standing tradition among Christian historians. Groen sees ideas operating at the nerve center of history, where man responds to the fundamental issues of life and reacts to the metahistorical dimension of his existence. Consequently, *Unbelief and Revolution* is "idealist history" of a special kind. Groen claims he can explain the history of the revolution from prevailing ideas, yet at crucial points it becomes apparent that he wants to lay hold of something behind or beneath the ideas. Thus, his conceptual framework repeatedly refers only to the force of powerful ideas, yet when his argument has advanced to the stage where the historical impact of these ideas is to be analyzed and described they are at once spoken of as deriving their force from a more profound, spiritual source beyond them (143, 181). Again, the revolution is emphatically said to have a "theoretic origin" (119), yet when the fateful theoretical ideas have at last been sketched, in Lecture VI, Groen directs the reader beyond mere ideas to the dynamic force that gave them strength: warfare against

---

55. That Groen in practice bases these more on the concrete particulars of historical evolution than on the *created order* for the world is attributed by Dengerink, *De sociologische ontwikkeling van het beginsel der S.i.e.k.*, pp. 71, 87, 93, 267, to Groen's failure to acknowledge Scripture not merely as an external control on social philosophy but as a dynamic force for its inner reformation, a failure which prevented him from fully overcoming the influence of historicism. See also Dooyeweerd, *Roots of Western Culture*, pp. 53–55.

the gospel (144). Therefore, the real meaning of Groen's "idealism" does not become apparent until he begins to explain that the ideas in question owe their overwhelming historical influence to a particular spiritual impulse, a pernicious principle animating them (143). That impulse is called *unbelief* for short; the notion is expanded to comprise the *spirit of the age* (5, 189), marking a *crisis in Christendom* (144); it is further identified as an *invasion of evil spirits* (178), a *corruption of the human heart* (197), an *error* (197), a *lie* (198), a *force from hell* (200), or, simply, as *systematic godlessness* (215). Thus Groen's interpretation comes in two stages. The ideas, which presumably explain all, themselves require explanation before their historical action can be understood. Without the latter explanation they appear greatly overrated; the explanation given, they assume a status far above mere ideas. The ideas that make history are anything but strictly logical concepts.[56] Groen sums up the two-stage explanation at the end of his book: "The Revolution, to the full extent of its pernicious fruits, is the consequence of the Revolution doctrine—just as that doctrine itself is the consequence of the systematic rejection of the Gospel" (426). If a label is desired, one might call this a "deepened idealism."

That unbelief is here conceived as operating at the religious depth-level of life—at the level of the human heart—is borne out by the whole tenor of the book. Groen calls unbelief the underlying cause, the *first principle*, of the revolution. The revolution arose from an *inversion* of Christendom through a rejection of the gospel (5f), a setting aside of the God of revelation (183). This revolutionary *principle*, he says, proceeded to generate the revolution doctrine as its "natural organism" (121), by which he means to say that the revolution doctrine is the "manifestation of *unbelief in systematic form*" (122). The diagnosis therefore does not stop until it has penetrated to the human heart, for the heart is the wellspring of human life.[57]

Our interpretation is further borne out by Groen's word-choice at one point. It occurs in a passage that repays careful examination. Given that systematic exposition (many have remarked upon it) is not Groen's forte, and that he does not always take care to ensure terminological consistency and precision, it is therefore all the more interesting to observe

---

56. Cf. glossary, chapter 12 above, s.v. *the Revolution ideas.*
57. Cf. Prov. 4:23.

how carefully he reserves the term *Religie* (translated by us as "Religion") for a particular semantic usage, in contradistinction to *godsdienst* (translated "religion"). The term *godsdienst* (sometimes written with a capital: *Godsdienst*) is used throughout the book to designate "religion" in the sense of religious faith and worship, religious beliefs and practices, conscious service of God (or of that which takes His place, an idol). The term *Religie*, by contrast, is used in four places only, two of which may be left out of consideration here.[58] A third place occurs early in Lecture VIII (192), where we read: "The Revolution doctrine is the Religie, as it were, of unbelief."

This word-choice is deliberate and significant. In the context of Lecture VIII where this sentence occurs, the reader has just been informed that the revolution doctrine (now identified as "the *Religie*, as it were, of unbelief") concerns both *godsdienst* and *politiek* (subjects sucessively dealt with in Lectures VIII and IX). From this we must conclude that *Religie* is the more comprehensive term, embracing as it does doctrines and beliefs in both religion and politics, in a single system which is said to derive, in the eighteenth century, from unbelief. Hence unbelief denotes a more encompassing reality or a deeper layer: it is the wellspring of both the religious (or moral) philosophy[59] and the political philosophy of the eighteenth century.

Our reading is further corroborated by the fourth place where Groen uses the word *Religie*. On page 406 he speaks of "the universal need for a 'Religie,' of whatever kind," thus pointing to an ineradicable human trait to hold to something that transcends our finite existence, to embrace an absolute, non-negotiable value, whether accompanied by a form of formal worship or not, some ultimate commitment, with or without a set of articulated beliefs. This wholistic meaning of the word "religion" is a staple in the neo-Calvinist worldview since Abraham Kuyper, who observed in his *Lectures on Calvinism* (1898) that religion is a universal phenomenon, a comprehensive "life-system," one that covers not a part but the whole of

---

58. Page 45 refers to the *"religie-oorlogen"* (religious wars) of the sixteenth century, and page 346 talks of executions *"om der religie wille"* (for the sake of religion), which is a standard rendering in Dutch of *religionis causa*.

59. Groen refers to this as "philosophy in the broad sense—the 'science of things divine and human,' as it has been called" (192).

human life which all human creatures inescapably live *coram Deo*, before the face of God their Creator.[60]

A close reading of the text yields the following result. As the unbelief of the age generates a mode of thinking inimical to Christianity, it comes to systematic expression in a dual set of doctrines or beliefs that have the force of a new religion. Lectures VIII and IX identify these two sets, respectively, as rationalism and popular sovereignty. The logical outcome is atheism and materialism in the one case, and radicalism, despotism and liberalism in the other. Or, tracing the argument of Lectures VIII and IX in reverse order, from fruits to system to root, we ask: Where do the practical atheism and materialism of our age and its cycle of radicalism–despotism–liberalism come from? *Answer*: From the moral and political philosophy of the Enlightenment, which teaches the supremacy of man's reason and will; this dual philosophy comprises the complete revolution doctrine, which is the Religion of unbelief—apostasy from God elevated into a system. The lines of force can be sketched as in Fig. 13.1. Unbelief can be pictured as generating a Religion embodied in the revolution doctrine. This doctrine bifurcates into two fields of application: (i) in moral philosophy, it negates divine revelation and posits the supremacy of human reason, producing rationalism and its offshoots: atheism in religion and materialism in morality; (ii) in political philosophy, it denies divine right and declares the supremacy of the human will, leading to the endorsement of popular sovereignty and its alternating manifestations in a recurring cycle[61] of radicalism, despotism, liberalism.

One tacit assumption behind all this should not be allowed to pass unnoticed. How can Groen be so sure that a *spiritual* force like unbelief will serve as the animating impulse of an *intellectual* system and be elaborated into a full-fledged *philosophic* doctrine? He has answered this question in Lecture VI. Unbelief is able to have its concrete impact on history because it lodges in the hearts and minds of men and causes a crisis in Christendom that prepares popular opinion—the "universal mode of thinking"—to wage a "war against the Gospel in every field of learning and practice" (144).

---

60. Abraham Kuyper, *Lectures on Calvinism*, pp. 11–20, 43–54. See also note 63 below.
61. A "circle" (6), "vicious circle" (271), or escalating "spiral" (267f, 405–7).

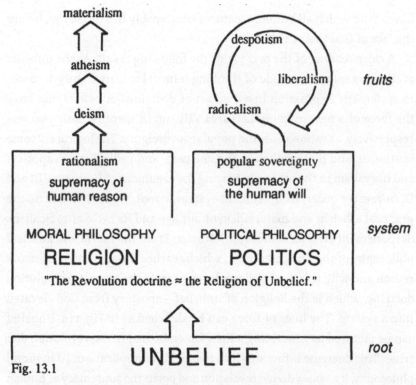

Fig. 13.1

One may be willing to entertain the notion that unbelief can, in certain times and under certain circumstances, have this historical effect, and yet be skeptical that unbelieving *ideas* have this effect *always*. A measure of ambivalence is undeniably present in Groen's explanatory model, straining its credibility. His "two-stage, deepened idealism" requires that one stage be interpreted in light of the other. "There are places," Algra remarks with insight, "where Groen seems to reason as though ideas govern men with the reins of logic; but time and again it becomes apparent that he knows it is not just a question here of abstract theories or doctrines, of systems or mental constructs, but of *that which rises with great force from the depths of human existence.* And it depends on many factors whether that force will prove sufficient to become of decisive historical significance."[62] Kamphuis explains rather convincingly that Groen's idealism makes the claim, not that just any theory, system or idea has the power to shape the course of history, but that this particular revolutionary theory rooted in unbelief

---

62. Algra, "Beginsel en causaliteit," p. 218 (emphasis added).

always has that power: it is in the very nature of a *religiously apostate* ideology that it operates irresistibly and relentlessly. Generated and energized by an existential choice against divine revelation, its inner dynamics propel its devotees ever onward as they develop its practical consequences. And although this development is often arrested or diverted by external obstacles, *internally* the choice has set the course; "in Groen's eyes, however, that choice, even when it works itself out in a theory, an idea, a system, is not a theoretical choice but a religious decision."[63]

Even more important, of course, than the terms Groen uses is his causal framework, in which religion constitutes the base line. As a Calvinist he takes "religion" in the comprehensive sense of *relation to God*. This relation is fundamental everywhere, also in the history of the revolution. It defines man, and he can never divest himself of it. Nor is it a merely formal concept. The relation to God, as it functions in Groen's view of history, is always one of two things: it is either obedience or disobedience with respect to revelation. Created human life is lived out before the eyes of the Creator, one way or the other, in a *covenantal* relationship, in which humans respond to their Maker either in a faithful imaging of Him or in a rebellious distorting of His image. The "human condition" is religious; life is religion.[64] Consequently, Groen sees religion where others see nothing of the kind because a theology or a cult is absent. He must have been pleased to note Tocqueville's observation in his famous book[65] that the general discredit of all "forms of religious belief" exerted a "preponderant influence on the course of the French Revolution." At the place where Tocqueville averred, however, that the revolutionary generation "attacked the Christian religion with almost frenzied violence, without replacing it with another," Groen scribbled in the margin: "that other Religion was that of Rousseau!"[66] He must have given his whole-hearted consent again when Tocqueville draws his

---

63. Kamphuis, *Causaliteit bij Groen*, p. 40.

64. Cf. Calvin, *Institutes*, I, ii, 1-2; xv, 3; II, i, 3. See also H. Evan Runner, in *Christian Perspectives 1960*, pp. 102-13; *Christian Perspectives 1961*, pp. 11-16, 48-51 (esp. p. 50); *Christian Perspectives 1962*, pp. 136-50 (esp. p. 148); and S. G. de Graaf, *Promise and Deliverance*, 4 vols. (St. Catharines: Paideia, 1977-81), I, 29-55, and the Translator's Introductions, I, 10-14, and III, 11-21.

65. *L'Ancien Régime et la Révolution*, Part III, chap. 2.

66. *"Die andere rel. was die van Rousseau!"* Penciled gloss in Groen's handwriting on p. 229 of his copy of Tocqueville's book.

discussion in the chapter to an unexpected close: when Frenchmen had "religion expelled from their souls" the vacuum thus created was promptly filled with "a host of new loyalties and secular ideals": they now believed in the perfectibility of man, and in their own sacred calling to regenerate society and the whole human race. "Of this passionate idealism was born what was in fact a new *religion* ..."[67] How much more sure-handed is Groen's own characterization: "At its deepest level, the revolution is the world-historical *war of Religion*"![68] His greater clarity on the issue stems from his profounder insight into the comprehensive nature of religion.[69]

Meanwhile, the recognition of a religious substratum beneath all cultural expressions and historical actions does not, for Groen, obviate the task of historical explanation. Religious unbelief was bound to change the face of Christendom—yes, but *how* did that come about? This is the focus of Groen's inquiry, provisionally answered by the thesis that the age revealed (empirically) the rule of ideas that had their (deep-seated) origin in unbelief (5f). Accordingly, most of his explanations are cast in terms of ideas rather than their underlying impulse or origin. About the origin he says comparatively little. With it, after all, he has reached the limit of his historical diagnosis; for to call unbelief the "origin" is also to mark the end of one's regressive search for causes in empirical history. An origin cannot be further "explained." All Groen says by way of explanation is that unbelief filled the vacuum left by a retreating Christianity. It was this fundamental substitution that prepared men to embrace the tenets of *natural* religion and to endorse a *philosophic* legitimation of authority. The ensuing woes can be explained by unraveling the logical consequences of the new surrogates. But the wellspring of these surrogates, the apostasy of human hearts, Groen

---

67. *L' Ancien Régime et la Révolution*, pt. III, ch. 2 (emphasis added). Tocqueville wrestled with the concept of religion as it applies to his subject: the Revolutionary movement *resembled* a religion, "assumed many of the aspects" of a religious revival, yet also "it would perhaps be truer to say that it developed into a species of religion, though a very incomplete one, since it lacked a god, a ritual, and the promise of an afterlife" *Ibid.*, pt. I, ch. 3.

68. *Handboek*, 3rd ed., § 827 (orig.: "De Revolutie is, in haar diepsten grond, de wereldhistorische *religie-krijg* (Gen. 3 v. 15) ..."

69. It is ironic, in light of Groen's analysis, that Carl Becker observed in 1932 that Tocqueville's contemporaries, unlike modern historians, could not "grasp the significance of his pregnant observations" because they were not yet "sufficiently *detached* from religions." Carl L. Becker, *The Heavenly City of the Eighteenth-Century Philosophers* (Yale Paperbound ed., 1959), p. 155 (emph. added).

does not try to explain. He merely notes (186, 196, 200, 203, 205, 226–29, 257, 267) that men were left to their own devices—to their mundane, temporal, frail and fallible resources—once they stopped listening to revelation. Here his principal cause touches on his remote or final cause.

With a similar degree of reticence Groen is sparing of *direct* explanations from unbelief. His purpose, after all, is to exhibit the truth of Christianity in a "narrative sequence of indisputable facts" (11). The pursuit of this purpose can be illustrated from his treatment of the Reign of Terror. Groen deduces it rigorously from the prevailing *ideas*: this infernal regime rested on *popular sovereignty* exercised by committee; a contract theory sanctioned the *general will* as the highest law; the state's ultimate end, the *general welfare*, legitimated the use of the *ultima ratio*: terror, violence, death (332f, 350, 358). The reader wonders, is this deduction from ideas not tantamount to an "idealist" reduction? Not finally, for at the end of the lecture the whole episode is summarized in the lesson: "The removal of submission to divine revelation removes the barrier against every error and every crime" (363). So even though the final emphasis falls on the original inspiration behind the revolution doctrine, the preceding analysis first takes the reader through the step-by-step unfolding, the practical outworking, the intermediate agency, of the doctrine. Not until the lecture's summarizing conclusion (and perhaps also in between the lines) does the reader hear Groen giving his witness as a confessor of the gospel: godless men will do godless things; when the Christian moral law is abolished this outcome is predictable: it has been foretold, and it has come to pass. In the main text, by comparison, we see Groen developing his argument as a historian-publicist: when Christian principles of constitutional law were abandoned, a purely secular, utilitarian conception of public justice supplied grounds for the harshest measures, including mass judicial murder.

The alarming thing is that the fatal doctrine which caused all this to happen has not been repudiated and replaced. The deadly disease of his time, according to Groen, is its anti-Christian religion, in whatever form this manifests itself: as recognizable cults and rituals, complete with hymns and catechisms,[70] or, much more pervasively, as the dominant spirit

---

70. For aspects of propaganda during the revolution, see the publications by James A. Leith, e.g. *Media and Revolution,* 2nd impr. (Toronto: CBC Publications, 1974).

in society, deceiving men into surrendering to the religion of humanity and the deification of reason in science and in politics. To do battle with that spirit requires penetrating beyond the prevailing theories to the hearts of men. The reason why neither the Reaction nor the Restoration broke with liberalism is due not to any ideological inertia but to human failure, namely to repent (238, 271). That is why the mere propagation of alternative theories will not accomplish very much. Philosophy and theology cannot effectively counteract the revolution; only Christian proclamation and personal conversions can do that (177, 422ff). To refute the ideas is necessary and useful; but to contend for the highest truth is the *sine qua non* for the healing of society (191).

Smitskamp has tried to account for Groen's idealism by pointing to his evident *predisposition* for it. It was Groen's personal wish "to have his life ruled by fixed principles." This must have sharpened his eyes for the power of ideas and induced him to portray the progress of the revolution as a march of ideas, and the conduct of its leaders—those who rode the crest of its onrolling tide—as the pure result of their unconditional dedication to those ideas, ruling out all personal considerations and passions. Thus Groen's interpretation is, in part at least, a case of projection.[71]

This explanation from psychology, interesting though it be, lends itself less easily to verification than the explanation from historiographical pragmatism. De Pater suggests that Groen's one-sided emphasis on the decisive role of ideas serves the *purpose* of his book: to warn his contemporaries against liberalism's *logical consequences*, namely the chain of errors and train of woes that *must*—as history presumably *teaches*—follow upon its treacherous starting point.[72] This suggestion is much easier to test against the text. There is much to be said for classifying *Unbelief and Revolution* under the pragmatic genre of history-writing. Here, history is a school for politics. Groen's major historical works are variants of this genre.[73] To stretch the point: *Unbelief and Revolution* is written for the next vote in

---

71. Smitskamp, *Groen van Prinsterer als historicus*, pp. 58, 81.

72. *Lustrumbundel*, p. 104.

73. Despite the fact that at the outset of his career he had termed the habit of (Enlightenment) historians to pass judgment on the past both "unnecessary" and "hazardous"; cf. Tazelaar, *De Jeugd van Groen*, pp. 68f, citing *Proeve* (1826), pp. 28ff.

parliament, for the next election. Like Thucydides and Polybius[74] of old, Groen is looking for the universal in the particular, for "the lesson" of the past fifty years (11, 144, 212, 271, 414). That is why he trains the floodlights on that part of the story that falls under man's responsibility: namely, the choice of ruling principle for shaping society and determining conduct.

But is that not hopelessly one-sided? What then does he do with all the other strands that make up the story? To state, as some critics have done,[75] that Groen is so one-sided that he simply neglects or ignores them, does not advance our insight into his method. Of course he takes factors other than principles into account. Only, as Lectures XI–XIII show, he treats them as co-determinants in the sense of cooperating and conditioning forces and circumstances, as causes which account for much of the "physiognomy" of the history but which do not touch the crucial role played by man.

These other causes are recognized as *modifying* the course of events, never as decisively *altering* it. In the march of history highlighted by Groen they represent historical accidents. To treat them as anything more would be to obscure the significant, to muddle the meaningful interpretation guiding this historical inquiry.[76] Therefore, to complain that causal factors other than ideas—call them contributory and conditioning causes if you will—are given short shrift is not wrong, but it is superficial. Those factors are recognized, in Smitskamp's phrase, as functioning "on the second plane" only, not really "making history" but at most promoting or thwarting the realization of ideas.[77] One need not go so far as De Pater and say that, after the printing of the *assignats*, spiraling inflation "for the greater part deter-mined the subsequent course of the Revolution"[78] to concede the point that economic factors, for example, do not, in Groen's account, receive their due in terms of their own intrinsic dynamics. But in this idealist interpretation, the factors are not equal or even comparable in effect. The revolution is not the simultaneous converging of a number of distinct factors into one

---

74. Zwaan, *Groen van Prinsterer en de klassieke Oudheid*, p. 463n113, notes at least four "closely interrelated" points of resemblance between Groen's historical method and that of Polybius: an interest in (1) chains of cause and effect, (2) cyclical repetition, and (3) lessons of history; as well as (4) an aversion to philosophical speculations.

75. Smitskamp and De Pater, in *Lustrumbundel*, pp. 26, 109; Geyl, *Reacties*, p. 11.

76. Cf. Carr, *What Is History?*, pp. 103–7.

77. Smitskamp, *Groen van Prinsterter als historicus*, pp. 59f.

78. *Lustrumbundel*, p. 111.

prevailing direction, but it is the triumphant march of a single ideology that gathers every other movement into its sweep, engulfs every contributory cause in its tidal wave (Lecture VI, 120).[79] Inflation, but also the war scare, the selfish ambitions of men, historical accidents like the untimely death of Mirabeau and the assassination of Marat, they may all belong to causal chains of their own, but Groen has them enter the picture only to illustrate how they came to be swept up by the overriding cause.

DETERMINISM

Why did Groen not make more of the political merit and patriotic intention of the eighteenth-century aristocracy? asked Da Costa in a letter to the author after leafing through the fourth installment of the *Handboek*. Many years later, when editing the correspondence for publication, Groen noted that it had been his particular concern "to bring out the *tragic* as well as the *logical*" unfolding of unbelief and revolution: men of no mean talents and devotion had been involved in the experiment with the promising theories, only to reap anarchy and tyranny.[80]

Notes like this seem to confirm an impression many have received from *Unbelief and Revolution*. Its account is deterministic. It presents the age of revolution as a tragedy, the course of history as beyond man's control, bringing inevitable doom. Just what is the nature of Groen's "determinism," and its corollary, "fatalism"?

Following our examination of the precise nature of Groen's idealism, we are now in a better position to sketch his view of causality in history. By taking stock of Groen's entire oeuvre but especially of illuminating passages in Lectures I (4f), VI (143f), X (224f, 230f), and XIII (342–47), we can draw up the following hierarchy of factors and causes.

1. First, there is the role of the moral world-order or the "ordinances of God." It sets the stage, inviting Christian-historical action and restraining willful revolutionary action.

---

79. For an analogous form of this argument, cf. Butterfield, *The Origins of Modern Science*, p. 197.

80. *Brieven van Da Costa*, I, 215f, 220n.

2. Against this backdrop, the main or "principal" cause in history is always *ideas*, which comprise notions, principles, doctrines and theories. These ideas are rooted in a religious standpoint or a personal existential choice, as every human's inescapable response to revelation in Scripture and history, a response that is necessarily characterized by either obedience or disobedience. Thus ideas represent what men believe, profess, and wish to live by. Because ideas reflect the communal spirit or direction of an age, they constitute the "general" cause of events in that age.

3. A class of "secondary" causes, subordinate to the main cause, is made up of the ordinary *human* causes that arise from personal consciousness—such as faith, hope, love, trust, patience, passion, fear, hate, egoism, ambition—as well as from interpersonal relationships—like coercion, intimidation, indoctrination, persuasion, believing, obeying, following, defending, teaching and learning. In this last category are also found thinking, reasoning, conceptualizing, organizing knowledge and developing theories—in short, human theorizing as it is guided by the main causal factor: religious presuppositions or regulative *ideas*.

4. Another class of secondary, hence subordinate, causes consists of such *impersonal* factors as natural events, circumstances favorable and unfavorable, historical accidents, psychological mechanisms, military events and economic exigencies.

Now, the complex whole called history is conceived as moving through time *conditioned* by category 4, *shaped* by category 3, and *determined* by category 2 in *interaction* with category 1. To further complicate the picture it must be noted that Groen acknowledges two other dynamic forces as actively present in history. They are clearly of a metahistorical nature: the Spirit of God and the spirit of the evil one, who compete for the hearts of men (178, 187).

To sum up, in this conception history moves under the *guidance* and *direction* of ideas which are either in harmony or in disharmony with divine revelation and the divine world-order. The resultant is a drama in which God's promise to bless obedience and His threat to visit judgment on disobedience are fulfilled (Preface, p. xii). Consistent with this whole conception, finally, is Groen's statement that the history of the revolution is essentially *determined* by two factors: (i) the unbelieving theory, (ii) in its encounter with historical reality. The course of revolutionary events can therefore be anticipated by looking at both together: the revolution's assault, and nature's resistance (223).

Groen's causal hierarchy, without making man and his ideas the sole cause of history, is obviously designed to give human freedom and responsibility their full due. Man reaps what he sows (p. v). He lives under a universal covenant: it is predetermined that to walk in God's ways is to live, and that the alternative is the way of death (255). Such is the nature of Groen's "determinism," if the term is to be maintained. Man does not embrace unbelief with impunity. The revolution doctrine, whose reception was prepared by a corruption of constitutional law, became a historical force when "animated by a much more pernicious principle" (143). The threefold thesis—that the revolution's coming was irrepressible, its progress irresistible, and its outcome inescapable—is predicated on the fact that the eighteenth century had embraced unbelief (181f). One must recognize the figure of speech in statements like this one: "The theory of the supremacy of the people, master of the minds owing to the spirit of the age, was not to be stopped in its pursuit of a corresponding state" (^{2}283).[81] The entire discussion makes clear that the statement does not mean to imply that a mere theory was pushing ahead, but rather that human beings, persuaded of an ideology, were striving hard to realize a society that would be in harmony with it. Groen's subject is not a natural phenomenon or a mechanical process, but a historical development governed by moral laws that presuppose the inescapable responsibility of free human

---

81. In terms of the "linguistic protocols" analyzed by Hayden White, *Metahistory: The Historical Imagination in Nineteenth-Century Europe* (Baltimore: Johns Hopkins University Press, 1973), Groen's explanatory strategy uses the trope of Metonymy, his theory of truth and mode of argument is Organicism, his mode of emplotment is Tragedy, and the ideological implication of his work follows the tactic of Liberalism.

agents.[82] Other passages employ similar figures of speech and in no way imply a "determinism" of a mechanistic or naturalistic sort.

A final insidious implication of determinism is fatalism. What student of the French Revolution has not been struck by the *seemingly* impersonal momentum of its progress and the *apparent* impotence of its actors? Or was its momentum *truly* impersonal, and men's impotence *all too real*? One of Tocqueville's jottings for his unfinished history reads: "Impotence of individuals and even of entire groups at the beginning of the revolution and as long as its peculiar impulse lasted."[83] The observation is Groen's precisely. The question I want to raise here is: Do observations of this sort point to the influence on Groen of "fatalists" like Thiers and Mignet, as has been suggested?[84]

The question is not hard to answer for the discerning reader. The above-mentioned "smear by association" is anticipated by Groen, who takes pains to clear himself of the moral indifference which might seem inherent in his account and which he himself sees exemplified in the account of Thiers. While he argues repeatedly that the ideas of '89 were *bound* to lead to a terror à la '93, nevertheless he maintains that this "inevitability" does not annul human responsibility or absolve crime. It is in accordance with laws in the moral world that the ideas were pushed to their limit (180): the corruption of the human heart ensured a rich harvest of errors and crimes (258), and a universal intoxication overpowered all, rendering individual resistance largely illusory, and in any event impotent (289). In a simile that is open to misinterpretation (180), Groen contends that the moral laws which obtain here are every bit as compelling as physical laws.[85]

---

82. Cf. a saying of Martin Kähler: "Man is like King Midas, for whom everything he touched turned into gold: he encounters moral decisions everywhere he turns." Quoted in Reinhard Wittram, *Das Interesse an der Geschichte*, 2nd ed. (Göttingen: Vandenhoeck & Ruprecht, 1963), p. 169 (my trans.).

83. Tocqueville, *Fragments*, in *Oeuvres complètes*, ed. J. P. Mayer, t. II/2 (Paris: Gallimard, 1953), p. 176.

84. Cf. Fruin, *Verspreide Geschriften*, X, 87: De Pater, in *Lustrumbundel*, p. 103; Geyl, *Reacties*, p. 7.

85. Cf. Smitskamp, *Groen van Prinsterer als historicus*, p. 73: "This identification [sic] of mechanical and historical causality is telling. It reveals the weak spot in Groen's interpretation. ... [H]e sees the operation of historical causality much too mechanically." Cf. however Kamphuis, *Causaliteit bij Groen*, p. 11: The two types of causality are not declared equal or

Nevertheless, individual participation in what is historically irresistible remains a personal responsibility.

One of the overriding themes in Groen's book is that the force of ideas gave the revolution its irresistible momentum. Yet the story of what "came to pass" (16) is especially the story of *what was done* (363). The deeds of responsible human agents are central—*conditioned*, to be sure, by their context (physical challenges, moral resistance, economic and legal obstacles, etc.), but *determined* by human choices. Hence the question, What *moved* men to choose this course? The moving forces turn out to be partly conscious, partly unconscious. Nevertheless men are to be held accountable for both types: as much for the revolutionary hysteria that drove them on and the ideological delirium that led to the next step, as for their greed, fear, ambitions and the perverted logic that exonerated blasphemy and condoned crimes against humanity. Thus in Groen's eyes the seemingly "impersonal" force of the revolutionary tide never absolved human persons from their share of accountability for the sweep of events. "Woe to that man by whom the offence cometh!" he quotes in Lecture XI. Those who resist will not be blamed for being continually overruled, but those who assist and applaud will go down in history as culpable accessories (288). When ideas triumph rather than men (328), its bearers are not robots. For the ideas in question, as we have seen, are not a set of merely abstract theories—a type of disembodied concepts that lead a life of their own, metaphysical principles that actualize themselves in the historical process thanks to or in spite of men, or even mere logical premises from which to deduce human actions. In Groen's profoundly religious vision of the revolution, the triumph of ideas is due to the dynamic unfolding of unbelief, which is never a mechanical process but a walk of people on paths of rebellion against God and His ordinances.

Algra, at one time a journalist for the Anti-Revolutionary underground press during the Nazi occupation of the Netherlands, observes in this

---

identical but *comparable in respect of their compelling character.* On the point of perceived determinism it would be worthwhile to investigate the similarity and difference between Groen's reference to "moral laws" and Ranke's concept of the "moralische Weltordnung"; cf. Gerhard Frick, *Der handelnde Mensch in Rankes Geschichtsbild* (Zurich, 1953), pp. 116ff, 159f, 167-70, 180-92, and Heinrich Hauser, *Leopold von Rankes protestantisches Geschichtsbild* (Zurich, 1950), pp. 23, 57-67, 94, two insightful studies from the seminar of Professor L. von Muralt.

connection that it is proper to man to embrace ideas, think through their implications, proclaim these as his goals, and then work for their realization; this is the typically human factor in history, and this factor was as decisive in the French Revolution as it was in the Third Reich. Algra is fully in line with Groen when he continues: "But this always happens in a combination of head and heart, of logic and fanaticism." And he adds that what his generation had learned from Groen was hideously borne out by their historical experience: when the unbeliever gives his heart to an anti-Christian theory, it will seek and find the ways and means toward a godless practice. The relation between unbelief and revolution is not that of a coercive process but that of "people walking on roads of disobedience."[86]

Algra's formulation is valid in both a personal and a corporate sense. As Beets noted: "Your book makes it clear to me: the nations are walking in ways where no return is likely, no halt avails, and progress is the increasing manifestation of the man of sin."[87] At the same time, this corporate thinking affords the individual no alibi. The path of revolution is inevitable, but every step of the way involves human decisions: first, and most momentously, when the choice is made for the ideology; but no less as the ideology is being implemented and choices have to be made about objectives, about the means to achieve them, and so on, right down to the last unspeakable consequence. Along the way, the participants remain personally accountable for every step taken, because every step presupposes a human choice. And by the same token, every next step may be logically necessary, and will appear so after the fact, but it need not actually be taken. Men may have a change of mind—or better, a change of heart—and retrace their steps or break ranks. Surrounded by overwhelming pressures and overpowering facts, men are called to transcend the flux of history and seek to determine it rather than be determined by it.[88] However much Groen is impressed by the permanent character of the revolution of his time, he publishes his book to help break its spell and to call his generation back to the "sole road which leads to the happiness of nations" (191).

---

86. Algra, "Beginsel en causaliteit," pp. 218–21.

87. Beets to Groen, 8 Sept. 1847; *Briefwisseling*, II, 812.

88. Cf. Meyer C. Smit, *Writings on God and History*, I, 89, about the "liberating transcendental relation." See also his *Toward a Christian Conception of History*, p. 241.

The above discussion should make clear why the charge of "mechanical idealism"[89] is beside the mark. True, Groen's thesis is couched in language that makes it sound exceedingly mechanical: the theory overcomes every obstacle and overrules every protest, its logic propels men from one consequence to the next, and its progress is irresistible and predictable. For all that, Groen's actual explanation is placed fully in the flux of *human* history. Lecture X fills out the simplified, mechanical scheme by setting forth how the theory is not free to run its natural course but will be subjected to many transmutations as humans find themselves confronted with the demands of reality. Lecture XIII in turn tries to show how the revolution owes its progress to men whose logic functions in the service of passionate belief. And Lecture XIV, finally, argues that the fact that the theory survives the vicissitudes of revolution is not due to any mechanical *force majeure* but to the faith men continue to place in it.

LOGICISM

Did the desire "to have his life ruled by fixed principles"[90] turn Groen into a logicist? Biographically it is certainly true that logical consistency—internal coherence of position—enabled Groen to accept, in fact *insist on*, his gradual isolation in and out of parliament. He took his increasing isolation, which he discovered in the thick of the fray so to speak, to be the result of his refusal to compromise, of his fidelity to principle. Since he believed that politically speaking this was a virtue and an asset, he coined the watchword, *In our isolation lies our strength!*[91] Isolation that results from adherence to principle gives double strength in the political arena, Groen once explained: it wards off all those who would tear us away from our fundamental moorings; and it attracts all those who are one with us in principle and who are looking for leadership.[92] Groen would rather lose

---

89. De Pater, in *Lustrumbundel*, p. 103; see also Smitskamp, *Groen van Prinsterer als historicus*, p. 73.

90. Smitskamp, *Groen van Prinsterer als historicus*, p. 58.

91. Cf. *Le parti anti-révolutionnaire*, p. 76. The meaning of "isolation" as a political tactic makes its first appearance in 1850; cf. *Brieven van Da Costa*, II, 26, 223, 251, 266; III, 26, 59; *Nederlandsche Gedachten*, 1873/74, V, 71.

92. *Parlementaire Studiën en Schetsen*, XXXIII (1866), pp. 336f; cf. Kamphuis, *Evangelisch isolement*, p. 44.

support, if need be stand alone, than abandon the principle to which the anti-revolutionary movement owed its existence.

Conversely, he believed the opposing camp must be attacked first and foremost on *its* principle, not its persons or even its program. This tactic is captured in that other watchword of Groen's, *Principle against principle!*[93] It is a tactic that he applies on every front. Thus, few contemporaries are criticized more sharply by Groen than the intellectuals who spearhead theological modernism. Because their starting-point is wrong, their initial deviation from orthodoxy, however limited, will inevitably lead to the wholesale destruction of Christian truth, as the accommodation theory already illustrated so clearly (193). Still another watchword applies here: *Resist beginnings!* (190). For once a thinker has chosen his point of departure he will follow it through along a trail blazed by syllogisms. If the path one has chosen can be shown *to lead logically* to a yawning abyss, no further proof is required that this is a dangerous track to follow. Principles once set in motion acquire a momentum of their own, to which persons contribute but which they do not control. Keen thinkers like the philosopher Opzoomer will follow through fearlessly[94]; cautious souls like Allard Pierson may hold back yet will be overtaken by others of the same school. "I do not in any way deny the *conservative* nature of your intentions," Groen writes to the latter; "I only point to the *destructive* character of your *principle.*" To Groen, this is not *Prinzipienreiterei,* or *Konsequenzmacherei* (as Geyl, on his standpoint, is bound to call it[95]), but a lesson from history. To persuade Pierson by means of an analogy Groen adds: "the conservative monarchists of '89 paved the way for the terrorists of '93."[96]

Groen can speak of theologial modernism and political liberalism in one and the same breath because of their common starting-point in human autonomy. The principle of unbelief affected every field of human culture (188, 200). And the adherents to this starting-point who proved to be especially potent were those who followed its logical implications most consistently (215–22). Despite his difference of principle, Groen understands

---

93. Cf. 2nd ed., p. 211n.
94. Cf. *Brieven van Da Costa,* I, 352n2.
95. *Reacties,* p. 15n1.
96. *Briefwisseling,* III, 575.

Robespierre's refusal to shrink back from the ultimate consequence, even if he were to stand alone; for did not his very strength derive from his uncompromising consistency (341)? Though the suggestion that Groen "borrowed" his watchword from Lamartine[97] goes too far, he does quote Lamartine's assessment of Robespierre with approval: "By his very isolation he proved his strength" ([2]333n). Robespierre was the personification of the revolution because he was the most faithful representative of the inner logic that directed its course.

Groen van Prinsterer's life and works indicate that his habit of arguing from first principles may have been *reinforced* by a personal idiosyncrasy, but that this habit had *taken root* in him precisely as a result of his analysis of the revolution. But to what extent was that analysis itself flawed by "logicism"? It is indeed Groen's position that logic gave direction to the revolution because ideas held sway. Not only does he identify ideas as the primary cause leading to the outbreak of the revolution, but he presents them, thanks to the "power of syllogisms," as still controlling events while the revolution unfolds.[98] Thus the revolution's final causes or ends are the same as its initial causes, as the ideas that brought it about: the envisioned goals of the revolutionaries pull the revolution along; their initial vision also directed its course. That the vision-in-action exhibited a different dynamic from the vision-on-paper is explained by Groen from its utopian character. Where the revolution ended up in actuality was due for an important part to the natural resistance it encountered. Yet its *direction* was always in keeping with its original impulse.

From this point of view Groen's book is a veritable *tour de force*. A major purpose of his lectures is to demonstate that the revolution's so-called unfortunate excesses and exaggerations were in reality its consistent development (312–25). The demonstration is first laid out in the abstract,

---

97. Thus I. Lipschits, *De protestants-christelijke stroming tot 1940* (Deventer: Kluwer, 1977), p. 72n4.

98. Furet discredits many histories of the French Revolution because they fail to differentiate the field of forces *before* and *after* the revolution from the forces operative *in* or *during* the revolution—the causes and effects of the revolution, as distinct from the revolution as a "mode of change, a specific dynamic of collective action." Writers of such histories mentally collapse "two different levels of analysis," on the assumption that the course taken by the revolution was an implicate of its causes. Cf. *Interpreting the French Revolution*, p. 18. On Furet's standpoint, *Unbelief and Revolution* is a textbook example of such collapsing.

in the form of a logical deduction from its starting principle, which is then "confirmed" by the demonstration from history. As he announces his switch from the one to the other, the lecturer explains that, having shown what was *bound* to come to pass given the premises, he will find it that much easier to show that in fact it *did* come to pass (256). Lectures XII and XIII, consequently, purport to be the demonstration that between 1789–94 it was the ideology that gained the upper hand, again and again, right up to the Thermidorean reaction. And why? Because the spirit of the age had conquered the minds (292f), producing a public opinion that none could refute (288, 344) and a fanaticism that deliberated with cool reason about how to correlate the means—any means—with the desired ends (230, 324, 346, 351ff).

The Revolutionary Tribunals were the lineal heirs of the Tennis Court Oath. Such is Groen's sustained argument. But his aim is more ambitious yet. He tries to portray every turning point in the revolution and every one of its five phases, from 1789 right down to the year 1845, as ultimately governed by the identical ideology—metamorphosed each time to suit the circumstances, to be sure, yet identifiably ever the same. What remains the same is the revolutionary state, with its inherent despotism, regardless of whether "the will of the people" is expressed by a representative assembly, an appointed committee, an elected directorate, a usurper-emperor, or a restored monarch. Since 1789, neither war nor peace, neither want nor prosperity, neither restricted nor universal suffrage, neither the sway of popular opinion nor the rule of a dictator, neither the ascendancy of the *bourgeoisie* nor the dominance of the *sans-culottes*, neither panic reaction nor rational decision, neither royalist scheming nor clerical protest have effected any fundamental change in the revolutionary state. The European states are caught in a pendulum swing between liberalism and reaction, anarchy and tyranny, because the true principles of government, which combine freedom and authority under God, have been forsaken.

Of those who agree with Groen that ideas launched the revolution, not many will agree that it navigated its course by the same compass and ran into heavy weather because of its inherent conflict with the "nature of things" rather than its hapless encounter with unfortunate contingencies

and unlucky circumstances. Brants does not hesitate to call such an explanation "logicistic."[99]

To stop here would decide the point under investigation: Groen is a
logicist, irredeemably so. But such a conclusion would not do justice to
the full text. Much more than critics have taken into account, the pivotal
Lecture X modifies the straightforward, syllogistic manner in which theory
is said to control practice.

Though the revolution is driven by the logic of its principle, it suffers
from much internal dissension. Why? Because, Groen writes explicitly,
"logic alone is not the guide of the human race" (231). There is first of all
the obvious fact that the road that is marked by syllogisms shows many
"twists and turns" as the revolutionary coachmen seek tenaciously to steer
around the obstacles thrown up by a recalcitrant reality (225). Second, some
revolutionaries recoil before the logical "next step" out of stupidity, fear,
pity, or self-interest (231). And, most important of all, the revolutionary
vanguard obeys logic even against common sense and ordinary human
instinct. Why? Again, because their logic is subservient to their doctrine,
their beliefs (234; see also 342–46). In this way Groen embeds his simple
"logicism" in the complexity of historical causation. Lecture X depicts the
historical action of ideology in conflict with reality, and especially of logic
in league with faith, of syllogisms *fueled by passionately held convictions*. The
champions of the revolutionary terror were caught in a vicious circle of
"logic" *and* "passion." Groen's psychology is decidedly richer than that of
Fruin, who asserted stoutly:

> It shows little knowledge of human nature to derive the acts of
> men and nations, as Groen does, from their ideas. How small is
> their influence upon them! Passion is universally and invariably
> the mainspring of history, and that explains why the deeds of men
> from the most widely separated periods are always similar.[100]

---

99. Brants, *Groen's geestelijke groei*, p. 134. Groen is first called a "*logicist*" in an article of
1914 by Gerretson, "Groens aanleg," reprinted in *Verzamelde Werken*, II, 10–42; see p. 22n1. The
Dutch word *logicist* can denote "one who is given to explaining things logically," or may mean
simply "logician"; the context in Gerretson does not necessarily imply a pejorative sense.

100. Fruin, *Verspreide Geschriften*, X, 84. On this point, Geyl ruefully takes distance from
Fruin, though the suggested alternative—ideas function only "in the context of events"—is
rather trivial; cf. *Reacties*, p. 5n.

In Groen's account, ideas and a certain form of passion both find their place. Ideas prevail, logic develops, but ultimately heartfelt convictions provide the motive force:

> The mind will acquiesce in any pretext when a cause is pleaded before the tribunal of the wicked heart. Cold reason is defenseless in the face of excited passion and vehement self-interest. The temptation becomes irresistible above all when it not only camouflages the evil proclivities in their hideousness but transforms them into principles.[101]

In truth, those who read "logicism" in Groen have stopped reading halfway through. Groen's argument is that "ideas" do not derive their irresistible force from some abstract logic or timeless reason but from the hearts of men who assent to them and who draw up their "syllogisms" in line with them. Man is a religious creature, whose logical reasoning is a function of his heart-commitment. Proceeding from that commitment, he follows his logic as he seeks to lead a consistent and meaningful life. If man had his way, consistent logic based on compelling arguments would always rule the day, in private and in public life. The validity of Groen's line of argument has been frightfully confirmed in the twentieth century, when fanatic adherents even of *irrational* ideologies like fascism proved consistent in following their worldview to its logical conclusions.

SCHEMATISM

Later confirmation of the book's message has not silenced the critics. It may be good prophecy, but is it good history? Many deny it, if for no other reason than that it reduces all to one cause. And monolithic causal explanations seldom satisfy the mind of the historian. He finds multicausal explanations far more convincing. This is the very reason why philosophers of history often say that the historian is uniquely equipped to contribute to interdisciplinary research and discussion, accustomed as he is, as no other "social scientist," to be on the lookout for a plurality of causes to account for social phenomena.

---

101. Groen, *Vrijheid, Gelijkheid, Broederschap*, p. 50.

But the historian's advantage also has its disadvantages. How can he preserve unity in his picture of an event if the lines that compose it keep multiplying in the workshops of historical research? A classic case in point is the historical explanation of the triumph of Christianity in the Roman Empire. (We pick this example here because it involves Edward Gibbon, who will return later when we discuss Groen's criticism of his method.) In the account of the Enlightenment historian Gibbon, Christianity's triumph can be explained from at least five "secondary" causes (his "first" cause is providence, to which he makes a perfunctory bow at the start, to get on with the serious work).[102] By the time the twentieth-century historian Kenneth Scott Latourette writes up his explanation, he identifies as many as eight "contributory" causes.[103] The proliferation of factors that seems to come with renewed or sustained investigation once prompted Jan Romein to talk of the "demolishing" effect of traditional historical research; the more factors are discovered to have been involved in an event or episode, the more fragmented our picture of it becomes, until at last it crumbles to pieces.[104]

Romein's complaint was sparked by the growing fragmentation of the picture of the Dutch Revolt. The same complaint has been raised about our image of the French Revolution. Two centuries of poring over the nature and causes of the French Revolution have certainly tended to fragment its image. The bicentennial commemorations may momentarily have united the minds on some "central significance" or other,[105] but ongoing research will continue to dig deeper into its diverse layers of meaning, its numerous eddies and sundry cross-currents, and thus will only heighten our awareness of its bewildering complexity. Was Lefebvre correct when he emphasized, on the occasion of the celebration of the 150th anniversary,

---

102. Gibbon, *The Decline and Fall of the Roman Empire*, chap. XV.

103. Latourette, *The Expansion of Christianity* (New York: Harper, 1937), I, 162–69.

104. Romein, "Het vergruisde beeld" (1939); in *Historische lijnen en patronen*, pp. 147–62. Romein came with a solution: *integral history*, a holistic approach which does not analyze periods to pieces but continually synthesizes new discoveries into the whole; cf. "Integrale geschiedschrijving" (1956), *ibid.*, pp. 536–51. Romein's own specimen is his *Watershed of Two Eras: Europe in 1900* (Middletown, CT: Wesleyan University Press, 1978), trans. by the indefatigable Arnold J. Pomerans.

105. The dissension that broke out among the French in 1988 as they prepared a national commemoration points in a different direction.

that the French Revolution was not a single or uniform phenomenon but a cascading series of revolts—aristocratic, bourgeois, proletarian, peasant?[106] Or is a much more complex formulation called for? Was the French Revolution in fact a mere temporal conjunction of quite heterogenous movements?[107] Other issues, meanwhile, have stayed on the historians' agenda and many questions remain unanswered: Was the pre-revolution liberal or aristocratic? Is the broader concept of "the Atlantic revolution" helpful in understanding the French one?[108] Did the revolution break out in a context of poverty or prosperity? The questions can easily be multiplied since the vast field of Revolutionary historiography is still expanding. While the Marxian consensus has lost the ground it held previously,[109] it still begs an adequate replacement: If class interpretations never quite "fit," what other paradigm satisfies? The bicentennial commemoration did not surprise us with a new integrated synthesis. In any event, the abiding merit of the synthesis offered by Groen van Prinsterer is that it focuses attention on a factor—call it "secondary" if you will—that falls fully within our human responsibility and control: to what beliefs and principles shall we pledge our allegiance, and what corresponding ideas and programs shall we proclaim and promote? Groen's is a reading of the revolutionary age that makes us all conscious of a most fundamental choice we make in life: by what compass do we, personally but no less communally, chart our course: reason or revelation, self-chosen values or transcendent norms?

The advantage of Groen's book is obvious: its alleged weakness (one overriding cause) is also its admitted strength (the history is all of a piece). In general, Groen's concentration on the power of well-defined principles, Smitskamp observes, imparts a "monumental quality" to his treatment of history: it enables him to penetrate to the unity of complicated epochs and to throw into full relief the towering contours and "grand and imposing antitheses" of historical development.[110] For all his critical reservations with respect to Groen's historical writings, Smitskamp cannot keep from

---

106. Georges Lefebvre, *Quatre-vingt-neuf* (1939); the unity he nevertheless found lay in its cumulative effect: the "liberation of the human person"; cf. Eng. trans., pp. 3-5, 177-87.

107. Furet and Richet, *French Revolution*, p. 406.

108. See R. R. Palmer, *The Age of the Democratic Revolution*.

109. Cf. J. F. Bosher, *The French Revolution* (New York: Norton, 1988), pp. xi, 119, 191f, 283.

110. Smitskamp, *Groen van Prinsterer als historicus*, p. 58, quoting Allard Pierson.

speaking of their "monumental" and "grandiose" qualities. Noting the striking coincidence that *Unbelief and Revolution* was published less than a year before the *Communist Manifesto*, he remarks that "Groen reduces all of history to the single denominator of a battle of principles with the same grandiose one-sidedness with which Marx and Engels reduce the entire course of history to a struggle of classes."[111]

Grandiose or not, *Unbelief and Revolution* certainly has something monumental about it. This is due in large measure, we believe, to its unparalleled degree of unity. Now it is important to note that this unity seems guaranteed by the concept of the "spirit of the age." For consider: once unbelief was the spirit of the age, the "mentality" it inspired accounts fully for the fact that the philosophical theories could come to be held universally (143f): the *philosophes* often said little more than what everybody was already thinking; their chief distinction lay in being mouthpieces of the spirit of the age, marching in the vanguard only because they were more far-sighted (189f).[112] The same universality of outlook is depicted everywhere. From this it follows that Groen's account of the French Revolution resists any serious fragmentation, particularly one virulent form of it: his basic theme is proof against fragmentation into a number of subthemes corresponding to a range of distinct economic "classes"—a dubious concept for the eighteenth century in any event—who each pursue their own interests in the revolution, turning it into a period full of sound and fury but *signifying* nothing. On Groen's view, the revolutionary mode of thought was found everywhere: from king, noble, clergyman, to provincial lawyer, townsman, merchant, peasant and *sans-culotte*. Groen's unified explanatory model, consequently, easily has a place for reactions arising from conflicting *economic* interests (231, 233, 348), just as it can incorporate, for example, different *psychological* reactions to the radicalization of the revolution (231f, 313, 320, 334f). Thus we see that his concentration on an intellectual-spiritual factor transposed into an overarching spirit of the age, whatever its merits or demerits, has at least this advantage that it makes his account of the French Revolution immune to the artifical

---

111. Smitskamp, in *Lustrumbundel*, p. 26.

112. Cf. Gay, "Why Was the Enlightenment?," p. 68: the *philosophes* were "radical mainly in the sense that they pushed emerging values and rising hopes and novel ideas to unexpected and unconventional conclusions."

differentiation along class lines dictated by the Marxian presuppositions of much Revolutionary history from Jaurès to Soboul, which has been seriously challenged only since 1945.[113]

The notion of a "spirit of the age," however, even if it is not of the Hegelian variety, is not without its problems. Groen is praised by Dooyeweerd for having put his finger on the "religious motive power" behind the revolutionary principles.[114] On Dooyeweerd's own understanding of the term, a religious motive power is a spiritual ground-motive or driving force at work in any given society, a spirit that controls persons as members of their community and governs all of life's temporal expressions such as art, philosophy, science, and social structure.[115]

The questionable implications of such a concept for historical study, notably the making of unwarranted generalizations, have not escaped the attention of a number of critics.[116] Its problematic nature is exemplified, *mutatis mutandis*, also in *Unbelief and Revolution*. As with the notion of a dominant *Zeitgeist*, to accept a communal religious ground-motive tends to crowd out any recognition of cross-currents and counter-movements in that time-period. Thus the entire counter-revolution is written off by Groen as not being truly *anti*-revolutionary, that is, as fighting symptoms while ignoring the cause (270f). De Pater, on a similar point, complains that Groen's "schematism" keeps him from doing justice to the "fundamental opposition to the revolutionary ideas" that was offered by pope and clergy after the nationalization of the church's landed property and the Civil Constitution of the Clergy.[117] The point is well taken, though it is also clear that Groen dismisses counter-currents of this sort as ineffectual resistance, of no account in influencing the *direction* of the revolution.

---

113. Cf. Cobban, *The Myth of the French Revolution* (1955), and Furet and Richet, *La Révolution française* (1965). Since then, editor Soboul has been fighting a rear-guard battle in the *Annales historiques de la Révolution française*.

114. Dooyeweerd, in *Lustrumbundel*, p. 118.

115. Dooyeweerd, *Roots of Western Culture*, p. 9.

116. Cf. Dale Van Kley, "Dooyeweerd as Historian," in *A Christian View of History?*, eds. George Marsden and Frank Roberts (Grand Rapids, MI: Eerdmans, 1975), pp. 139–80; C. T. McIntire, "Dooyeweerd's Philosophy of History," in *The Legacy of Herman Dooyeweerd* (Lanham, NY: University Press of America, 1985), pp. 81–117, esp. 108ff; and, more particularly for the history of philosophy, Albert M. Wolters, "Facing the Perplexing History of Philosophy," *Tydskrif vir Christelike Wetenskap* 17 (1981): 1–17, esp. 5.

117. *Lustrumbundel*, pp. 110f.

Nevertheless it cannot be denied that a form of schematism plays a role in *Unbelief and Revolution*, preventing Groen from always being fair. To highlight an overriding cause can easily result in suppressing or distorting whatever has its own distinctive causation. It should challenge students of the French Revolution to test the validity of Groen's interpretation, to see whether the many phenomena that do not fit his scheme are indeed the exceptions that prove the rule, or that instead they bulk so large as to invalidate the main thesis of his book.

A different type of schematism is the one associated with the nomothetic nature of positivistic science. Smitskamp talked in 1940 of Groen's "sociological schematism" and defended the thesis that from a methodological point of view *Unbelief and Revolution* was "more a sociological than a historical study."[118] Groen's procedure is said to "resemble" the positivistic method which is oriented to the natural sciences and which aims at establishing rigorous schemes of historical evolution.[119] This charge bears looking into, preferably by theorists of history and philosophers of science, though historiographers will want to consider as well whether Groen's penchant for launching law-like statements is not much rather inspired by two other factors: (1) his keen eye for the logical development of an ideological revolution, which prompts him to indulge in schematic formulations that can nevertheless be read without assuming determinism (see above); (2) his obvious love of strict periodization,[120] which he has in common with a very old tradition of history-writing.

Be that as it may, Smitskamp believes he can illustrate the untenability of Groen's "schematism" by means of instances in Groen's account where pointed facts force their way through the constrictions of his model.[121] Groen twice betrays inconsistency, says Smitskamp, in applying his five-phase schema for the logical progress of the revolution. In one passage he has to admit, rather lamely, that the English "skipped over, as it were," part or all of a phase, "owing perhaps to events witnessed elsewhere" (264). In another place he hastens to interject that the Dutch saw their democratic

---

118. Thus Thesis I appended to his doctoral dissertation, *Groen van Prinsterer als historicus*.

119. Smitskamp, *Groen van Prinsterer als historicus*, p. 73.

120. Cf. *Handboek*, Table of Contents: Dutch history has three Parts; each Part consists of a number of Periods; each Period subdivides into two or more Sections; all are precisely dated.

121. Smitskamp, *Groen van Prinsterer als historicus*, pp. 74–76.

revolution halted prematurely on two separate occasions—in 1787 by Prussian intervention, in 1795 by the French invasion (409). Thus Groen's model breaks down in his own application of it. He is hoist with his own petard!

In point of fact, however, Smitskamp ignores a critical qualifier. The instances he adduces by no means compromise the validity of Groen's schematization. On the contrary, they corroborate Groen's general thesis, which is that the revolutionary ideas by their very nature are bound to be pushed with systematic regularity to their full consequences ... *unless* "forcibly arrested" (pp. v, 409).

But there is another ground on which Smitskamp's charge of sociological schematism appears justified. Is Lecture VIII not concerned with showing the "general laws" governing the ideology's "natural history," its "necessary consequences under any and all circumstances" (182)? Is it not Groen's stated aim to demonstrate that the phases of the revolution can be predicted "with almost mathematical certainty" (223)? And, to say no more, does Lecture X in particular not offer a general analysis with its depiction of the five predictable phases of the revolution? In short, is Groen not a student of the anatomy or morphology of revolution in the tradition of political theorists ancient and modern, or in a class perhaps with Lyford Edwards, Crane Brinton, Carl Brinkman, and others?[122]

Not really. Although it is true that Groen offers his analysis in the general terms reminiscent of morphological history, inviting the drawing of analogies and suggesting law-like regularities and uniformities of behavior, nevertheless his only claim is to be making valid assertions about one specific instance of revolution: *the* revolution. His is essentially an analysis of the peculiar ideological dynamics of the modern secular revolution as it is bound to affect state and indeed all of society. On no account does it pretend to be an analysis of the world-historical phenomenon of political revolt, nor does it claim to offer a universally valid theory of the

---

122. Cf. Lyford P. Edwards, *A Natural History of Revolution* (University of Chicago Press, 1927; repr. 1970), passim; Crane Brinton, *Anatomy of Revolution* (New York: Prentice-Hall, 1938; rev. ed. 1952), esp. 1–27, 264–93; Carl Brinkman, *Soziologische Theorie der Revolution* (Göttingen, 1948). A quantitative analysis is attempted in Peter Calvert, *A Study of Revolution* (Oxford: Clarendon Press, 1970). A fine recent instance of the genre is Jaroslav Krejci, *Great Revolutions Compared: The Search for a Theory* (New York: St. Martin's, 1983); cf. esp. the sensible opening chapter, "Theoretical Considerations."

"structure of revolutions." Lecture X, for example, wants to open our eyes to the chaos in the abyss, the seething violence inside the volcano, the stampedes of madmen caught in a vicious circle; but its explanation in terms of a God-negating theory on a collision course with the God-ordained world-order is clearly event-specific. The only rule of more general applicability that Groen espouses here is the oft-observed pattern that political upheavals tend to grow more radical, until overthrown in turn by a counter-revolution that resorts to physical force.

One must recognize *Unbelief and Revolution* for what it is. It is not a sociological study at all, but a reading of history that seeks to make sense of specific facts and trends and that is supported (as much serious history is) by an explanatory model rooted in a personal preconception. We are reminded that the work is an occasional piece, written by a concerned observer of and participant in Western Civilization's wrestling with the legacy of the French Revolution.

RELIGIOUS INTERPRETATION

A number of the controversial issues reviewed thus far converge on the book's obvious religious stance. And it is not doubtful that the religious deepening of the explanation from ideas constitutes the most controversial as well as the most intriguing aspect of *Unbelief and Revolution*. Nowhere else does Groen's strong personal "bias" come out more clearly. And is biased history, if sometimes intriguing, not always distorted and therefore highly disputable? One fruitful approach to this problem is to acknowledge that bias does not necessarily mean unwarranted partiality or uncritical prejudice. The critical test, rather, is to raise this question: Does the investigator's bias *help him to open up* his field of inquiry? The test seems particularly pertinent in connection with the historiography of the French Revolution. It has prompted one of its students to observe: "The strong personal opinions of a historian are not just his 'bias,' to be discounted; very often they also constitute the essential groundwork of his originality and insight."[123]

---

123. John McManners, "The Historiography of the French Revolution," in the *New Cambridge Modern History*, vol. VIII (1971), p. 618.

Groen's religious interpretation is unquestionably the key to his appraisal of the revolution. *Being without God* was the real formative power of the revolution (181), hatred of the gospel its defining feature (199), recognition of the sovereignty of God its only antidote (256), and a Christian revival its only remedy (271). The revolution is an incision in modern history that parallels the Reformation (14); as the latter was a mighty work of the Holy Spirit (164), so the former was made possible by an invasion of evil spirits (178). This religious interpretation functions everywhere as the hermeneutic key, in a studied defiance of secularized historical science.

Since 1834, when he wrote his *Essay on Truth*, Groen had had definite ideas about countering secular historical science. History was to be viewed in the light of the gospel and interpreted with Christ as its center and the fortunes of Christianity as its theme.[124] Under the influence of the eighteenth-century philosophy, however, all recognition of God's hand had been eliminated from history.[125] This was intolerably presumptuous. While Groen cautioned, in his turn, that mortal man must not presume "to lift the veil that God has put over the mysteries of the governance of this world," yet he also expressed the conviction that the believing historian may not close his eyes either to the "wonders of history [whereby] God's love and justice did not remain without witness to the nations in the ways of His providence ..."[126] Not that historical outcomes by themselves revealed God's will, or that success or failure as such established divine approval or disapproval. Groen did not regard events as "revelatory" in that sense.[127] For example, to condone *Realpolitik* that succeeds as "manifestly blessed of God," especially when it succeeds at the expense of Catholic powers, was both wrong and reprehensible in Groen's eyes; witness his reproof of his "Christian friends in Berlin" in 1867 and his condemnation of the aggression against Pius IX earlier in the decade.[128] But history, when it is viewed through the

---

124. *Proeve* (1834), pp. 99–144; see chapter 3 above.

125. Cf. *Nederlandsche Gedachten*, 1831, III, 112.

126. *Handboek*, Foreword, p. xi [allusion to Acts 14:17].

127. For examples of Groen's refusal to take facts as normative, cf. Van Essen, "Groen van Prinsterer and His Conception of History," pp. 239f; Kamphuis, *Causaliteit bij Groen*, pp. 31, 38; Smitskamp, *Groen van Prinsterer als historicus*, pp. 46f; Zwaan, *Groen van Prinsterer en de klassieke Oudheid*, pp. 76–78.

128. *Briefwisseling*, III, 504f, 845; IV, 37, 44f, 46f, 54–90; V, 652f, 656f, 667–69, 687–92.

spectacles of Scripture, reflects the reality of God's covenant faithfulness to his Word of blessing and curse.

According to the biblical view of history in the Calvinian tradition,[129] God, in calling history into being, covenanted with man to bless him if he walked in His ways but to curse the ground and commit him to death if he disobeyed. This promise and this threat are not just fulfilled at the end of time but have proved real from the beginning. Groen stands in this tradition, with a personal variation. He sees the realization of God's promise and threat not by preference (as traditionally) in unexpected turns of events, miraculous deliverance, natural disasters, and so on,[130] but in particular (perhaps owing in part to the emphasis in his age on historical growth and continuity) in long-term phenomena like cultural progress and political freedom, economic decline and social disintegration, each of which are to be explained in relation to a people's spiritual resources. Thus modern Holland, in Groen's view, experienced a rise and decline in prosperity in proportion as Reformed orthodoxy formed the backbone of the people, that is to say, in proportion as biblical religion was brought to bear on the life of the nation. On the opening page of his *Handboek* he writes: "The history of the Republic is the confirmation of the promise, 'But seek ye first the kingdom of God, and his righteousness; and all these things shall be added unto you.' Blessed is the nation whose God is the Lord."[131] Thus Groen associates God's providential dealings with the relationship of peoples and nations to Himself.[132]

This association is especially clear in the revolutionary age of modern times. With obvious approval Groen quotes the words of sorrowful resignation uttered by Stadtholder William V early in 1795, as he was about to go into voluntary exile at the approach of the French Revolutionary army: "The true source of our misfortunes lies ... in the national sins and

---

129. Still the best treatment is K. J. Popma, *Calvinistische geschiedenisbeschouwing* (Franeker: Wever, n.d. [1945]), or his more rambling *Evangelie en geschiedenis* (Amsterdam: Buijten & Schipperheijn, 1972). See also J. D. Dengerink, "De geschiedenis als antwoordstructuur," *Groniek*, no. 70 (Oct. 1980), pp. 47–57; A. M. Wolters, *Creation Regained: Biblical Basics for a Reformational Worldview* (Grand Rapids, MI: Eerdmans, 1985), pp. 21–41.

130. For examples in Groen, cf. Van Essen, "Groen van Prinsterer and His Conception of History," p. 234; Smitskamp, *Groen van Prinsterer als historicus*, pp. 42–45.

131. *Handboek*, § 3.

132. Cf. Van Essen, "Groen van Prinsterer and His Conception of History," pp. 234f.

iniquities. God has a controversy with the Netherlands and reveals it in the failure of every [defense] measure and even now in the severe frost which paves the [enemy's] way across the waters. Who shall raise up when God casts down?"[133] In this view, the conditionality of God's covenant with man has not been suspended by the Incarnation and the dispensation of grace which it ushered in, but if anything has been heightened. This is brought out expressly in the *Handbook*, where Groen writes: "Whenever a people blessed with the Gospel chooses unbelief, the prophecy applies, 'I will bring evil upon this people, *even the fruit of their thoughts*, because they have not hearkened unto my words, nor to my law.' "[134] And again: "The bitter fruits of the unremitting practice brought out the nature and tenor of the revolution and at the same time the judgment of God: 'My people would not hearken to my voice, so I gave them up to their own hearts' lust: and they walked in their own counsels.' "[135] As can be seen, Groen bases interpretations of this kind on a corporate conception of God's relation to man, valid not only for the people of the old covenant but also for the nations of Europe who once embraced the Christian gospel.

Unbelief and Revolution's central thesis ultimately rests on this covenantal conception of human history. Groen links the revolution's disastrous outcome to unbelief, not because he holds to some sort of mechanical idealism, but because he believes that the Lord of history is the "God of the Covenant with man, Who carries out the promises and threats of that Covenant in the course of history."[136] This belief is his warrant for extending, as it were, the examples from antiquity of moral decadence and personal wretchedness as they appear in the opening chapters of the Epistle to the Romans, to the political malaise and social disintegration as they are becoming manifest in modern times. Paul's teaching about God's curse on classical paganism is here applied to the neo-paganism of the permanent revolution. God, in his righteous revulsion at man's rebellious disobedience, gives men over to a reprobate mind, to vain imaginations, and abandons the wicked to their sins; for He judges men according to

---

133. Quoted in *Handboek*, § 820 [cf. Ps. 147:6; Ezek. 13:10–14; Hos. 4:1; 12:2; Mic. 6:12]; the inclusion of the quotation had been suggested by Koenen, cf. *Briefwisseling*, II, 558.

134. *Handboek*, 3rd ed., § 822, quoting Jer. 6:19 (emphasis added by Groen).

135. *Handboek*, 3rd ed., § 823, quoting Ps. 81:11, 12.

136. Schutte, *Mr. G. Groen van Prinsterer*, p. 54.

their deeds, in this world and the next. Telescoping the wrath to come (1 Thess. 1:10, Rev. 19:15) and the wrath revealed from heaven in the present age (Rom. 1:18), Groen employs a version of the biblical lesson that those who persevere in well-doing reap the reward of glory, honor, peace, eternal life, while those who disobey the truth reap the punishment of tribulation and anguish, of wrath and perdition (cf. Lecture X, p. 229).

As was to be expected, this whole interpretation has led to many long debates among those who share Groen's orientation to Scripture. We shall not summarize them just yet, other than to say that some think that it does injustice to the wonder of God's grace, others that it glosses over the difference between the Old and the New Testament, and still others that it presumes too much knowledge on the part of fallible human beings. The points of critique will return in a moment.

Our earlier example of the plurality of reasons for the triumph of Christianity in the Roman Empire can also lead us directly to the heart of a final controversial issue that has raged around Groen's work. It is the problem of acknowledging the *hand of God* in history, or perhaps better put: the question of reckoning with history's relation to and interaction with the God of history.[137]

Gibbon, the eighteenth-century skeptic, as we indicated above, sarcastically pays lip-service to it by speaking of the "first cause" in a single sentence, to devote his actual, serious examination, covering many pages, to what he calls the "secondary causes."

Latourette, the twentieth-century Christian, is even more reticent on this score. Though he submits that a possible "cosmic significance" of Jesus cannot but obtrude itself to every "thoughtful mind," yet he notes that questions of this sort "lie outside the realms in which historians are supposed to move."[138] And so, from a wish to make an original but not esoteric contribution to the history of the expansion of Christianity—and perhaps also from a desire to be read by a general public in a secular age— Latourette deliberately confines himself to what he calls a "narrative of facts," in an attempt to "conform to that kind of objectivity extolled by the school of history in which he has been trained." That school, he explains,

---

137. Cf. M. C. Smit, *Writings on God and History*, I, 69–80, 89–91, 136–39, 202, 255–62.
138. Latourette, *The Expansion of Christianity*, I, 168.

"looks askance at the supernatural" and chooses to restrict its explanations to "mechanical and human factors ..."[139] Accordingly, Latourette, as he seeks to deepen his readers' understanding of the astonishing "geographic spread of the Christian faith," focuses their attention on this intriguing question: What was it, "simply as a plain matter of history," that gave all the operative causes their real effectiveness? His answer is that they can all be traced back to some primary impulse; they all arose and received their effectiveness from an initial "burst of energy," a "vast release of creative energy," that was somehow connected with the "uniqueness of Jesus." In short, the one major, underlying, determinative (though "not alone sufficient") cause of the expansion of Christianity is a mighty "impulse which came from Jesus."[140]

What do these two historians illustrate? Both Gibbon and Latourette, albeit for different reasons, restrict their explanation to a *naturalistic* account in terms of purely *innerworldly* factors. In sharp contrast to this all too common approach, Groen refuses to be so restricted. As we have seen, Groen yields to none in recognizing causal chains in the historical process; it is part of the orderliness of the created world that antecedents lead to consequences, and it is part of the normal task of the historian to trace effects back to their probable causes. Yet at the same time he does not for a moment—not even in a suspension of judgment conventionally demanded of the Christian historian *qua* historian—divorce this historical causality from the creational ground and providential governance of history.

It is to be deplored that few analysts have given Groen credit for the integral unity of his approach. Smitskamp and Brants, for example, distinguish in Groen between, on the one hand, a preference for explanations in terms of a natural causality and, on the other, a resorting to supernatural causes as theological shortcuts or stopgaps whenever natural explanations fall short. This interpretation creates the misleading impression that Groen's causal reasoning, alternately and rather arbitrarily, runs along two separate tracks.[141] In actual fact, Groen sees the latter category of causation

---

139. Latourette, *The Expansion of Christianity*, I, x, xvii, xxiii.

140. Latourette, *The Expansion of Christianity*, pp. 165–70.

141. Smitskamp, *Groen van Prinsterer als hisioricus*, pp. 41–45, and, more nuanced, Brants, *Groen's geestelijke groei*, pp. 129–34. I owe this point to Kamphuis, *Causaliteit bij Groen*, pp. 36–39.

as operative *in* and *through* the former, in a kind of interplay between what he in one passage calls *final* and *secondary* causality (where "secondary" this time includes all the causes enumerated under 2, 3 and 4 in his hierarchy described above). Let us examine this passage for a moment. It occurs in the *Essay on Truth* of 1834, in a critical note on Edward Gibbon.

> In the 15th chapter of his great work Gibbon takes pains to prove that the progress and expansion of Christianity can very well be explained without assuming any supernatural influence. Even so, to read this chapter is to see everywhere that, however much the world may in many respects have been prepared for receiving the seed of the gospel, this germ would very soon have been choked if the teaching of Christ had not been far superior to human doctrine and the protection it enjoyed not far stronger than the favor of circumstances. Among the natural causes mentioned by Gibbon surely not the least is: "Virtues of the first Christians"; but how did those virtues, which no philosophy could produce, suddenly arise in the midst of the deepest moral corruption? It is lamentable, above all for the author himself, that he does not seem to have investigated this question, which might have brought him to better insight.[142]

These incisive comments do leave one wondering how Groen would conceive of an investigation that is to take the historian beyond mere "natural" causes. A clue to this problem occurs a few pages further on, in a discussion of the foundations of jurisprudence. What, Groen asks there, is the ultimate ground of law, the source and foundation of justice? He answers: God and His will. Not social utility or moral conscience. Nor human reason, which is but a *means* to get to know law, right and justice. Having posited this, he goes on to make the following profound observation:

> It is very true that science is not advanced by pointing *only* to God [as the source and ground of law]; but it is equally true that by *not* pointing to God the bottom must fall out of science and every system must collapse. To know only the remote cause is not enough; yet

---

142. *Proeve* (1834), p. 139n; Groen adds sarcastically: "Probably he did not very much incline toward such an investigation."

in the proximate ground, too, one ought to acknowledge the final cause. The wish to accord independence to secondary causes has been the source of manifold idolatries, including scientific ones.[143]

To acknowledge the final cause in the proximate ground—this is an essential ingredient in what Groen calls "believing philosophy" and "believing science."[144] The two forms of knowledge, faith and science, are for him inseparable. Accordingly, he writes history in full and open acknowledgment of the inseparable connection between mundane history and the transcendent Lord of history. Here we have the real reason why, for Groen, to write history *sub specie aeternitatis*, with an open eye to its transhistorical relation, is not to dispense with mundane explanations. The modern Christian historian does not use his faith (even if some medieval chroniclers did) to shortcircuit historical explanation and circumvent painstaking research into the facts and their interconnections. But neither does he deny himself (even if modern secular historians insist he should) the use of revelation to illumine history. On the contrary, the "truth of the Gospel" is there to leaven a lump of "dough": the "solid stuff of learning" (11); and, conversely, scholarly learning desperately needs the leaven of the "wisdom that is from above" (186). Thus Groen's historical accounts are fundamentally open to enrichment from revelation, to permeation by Scriptural insights. His explanations of facts and events are designed to take into account the *created* order in which they are grounded and the *metahistorical* framework in which they have their existence. And Scripture and Christian faith have crucial things to say about that order and that framework. This "believing" approach to history at once throws light also on the function of Bible texts in *Unbelief and Revolution*: when Groen there gives what purport to be "historical" explanations of the rise of unbelief, of the development of the revolutionary theory and the deterioration of the revolutionary praxis, then his use of Scripture citations, notably at the close of Lectures VI, X and XIII, reveals how conscious he wants his audience to be of the higher (or deeper) causation that is *simultaneously* at work in these historical processes.

---

143. *Proeve* (1834), p. 150n.

144. Cf. his characterization of "unbelieving philosophy" on pp. 192ff, 198 and its contrast with "Christian learning" on pp. 9–14, 18, 21, 258, 425, 427f.

In pointing to the hand of God in human affairs Groen is actually quite sober. He is not quite like a Joseph de Maistre (1753-1821), who took the "panoramic view of history" in an effort to divine the pattern behind the sweep of history;[145] with an omniscience worthy of a Bossuet, he unhesitatingly placed the revolution in the grand scheme of things: it was, he declared prophetically, a scourge for the sins of the old regime and a purge of France in preparation for the providential restoration of the Bourbons.[146] Groen is much more cautious by comparison. Only in passing and with circumspection does he venture to suggest in what way God's counsel may have been fulfilled in and through specific events: growing decadence "seemed" to have made the generation of 1789 "ripe for the judgments of God" (94), and the great suffering inflicted on the nobles by the revolution was "perhaps" an indication of "the gravity of their guilt and the justice of divine retribution" (304); the Reformation, whose cultural impact can be traced empirically, is at the same time an evident "revival of Christian truth through an outpouring of the Holy Spirit" (164); it is equally evident that only when the Reformation's influence waned did Europe enter a spiritual vacuum soon filled by unbelief—thus fulfilling the prophetic parable of the empty house invaded by evil spirits (178); the revolution's baleful influence was "tempered by the benefactions of a higher providence" (293); the Napoleonic wars manifested the "judgments of the Lord" (382), and Napoleon's final defeat was a "blessing of God" (401).

As implied above, providential pointers of this kind occur only sparingly. They reflect Groen's deepest personal vision of the "remote," ultimate, or final Cause, and he is not ashamed to share this vision, with conviction but also with caution, lest he appear too presumptuous in entering into God's secret counsel and justifying His inscrutable ways to finite man.[147] As a working historian he feels instead called to trace the empirical evidence of the action of providence *in* and *through* the mundane causes. Da Costa, who calls *Unbelief and Revolution* a "powerful witness," still would have

---

145. Cf. Jack Lively, ed. and trans., *The Works of Joseph de Maistre* (New York: Macmillan, 1965), p. 30.

146. Cf. Joseph Marie, comte de Maistre, *Considérations sur la France* (London [Basel], 1796 [1797]), chaps. 2 and 9; Eng. trans. by Richard A. Lebrun, *Considerations on France* (Montreal and London: McGill-Queen's University Press, 1974), pp. 31-50, 131-37.

147. For further examples of this conviction as well as caution, cf. Smitskamp, *Groen van Prinsterer als historicus*, pp. 42-49, 82, 95f, 147-50.

preferred greater directness in explaining the revolution as a "divine nem-
esis" for the sins of the old regime.[148] His friend prefers, however, to focus
on the proximate, mediated causes at work in history.

Groen's historical method deserves to be more carefully analyzed and
defined than has been done so far. In his hands the "proximate" causes do
not in any sense operate independently of, or parallel to, and least of all
in competition with, the remote or final Cause, but rather they operate
continuously by virtue of and in subordination to that Cause. Thus Groen
does not, so to speak, analyze history in terms of two "levels" or "storeys,"
or in something like two modes of discourse or mental operations, requiring the historian by turns to put on his believer's cap and his thinker's cap.
Searching for a more appropriate image, rather, one might say that he reads
history simultaneously on two planes: the foreground and the background.
Groen the historian at one and the same time sees what we might call the
events in the visible foreground, and a metahistorical Presence constantly
shimmering just behind these events in the background.

That this "view of two planes" has implications for the old problem
of a distinctively Christian approach to history is readily apparent. The
Christian historian is here not restricted to reading history as providence's
beautiful work of embroidery of which earthlings can see only the bewildering back side.[149] History *viewed on two planes at once* is translucent, at
times quite transparent. And in principle this transparency holds for the
details as well as for the whole history of the revolution as Groen sees it. As
in viewing a painting, background and foreground come to view in one and
the same glance. One must read the revolution against the metahistorical
background—unmistakable to whomever will "see"[150]—of the great truth:
To forsake God and defy His ordinances for human life is to court disaster. This
penetrating insight into the divine judgment in history, meanwhile, though
it is in one sense known *apriori* by faith, is not perceived as being somehow

---

148. *Brieven van Da Costa*, I, 217, 272, 296.

149. A favorite image of the late Professor Jan Roelink; cf. his commemorative volumes
Vijfenzeventig jaar Vrije Universiteit, 1880/1955 (Kampen: Kok, 1956), pp. 28, 191, and *Een
blinkend spoor; beeld van een eeuw geschiedenis der Vereniging voor Wetenschappelijk Onderwijs
op Gereformeerde Grondslag, 1879-1979* (Kampen: Kok, 1979), p. 23.

150. Cf. Aeneas Mackay to Groen, 26 Aug. 1847: "The *Word* applied to *politics* was new
to me, and now that I have placed that candle in the darkness I see sorry things, but *I see* ..."
Briefwisseling, II, 810.

in tension with ordinary, careful, craftsmanlike historical spadework in the "foreground." As we have noted several times before, in no way does Groen absolve the Christian historian from working on the plane of analysis that demands a close study of the historical process in which the divine judgment is executed. In fact, just such a study must be engaged in if one's contemporaries are to receive convincing proof of the historical judgment revealed in the recent past (11). And so Groen is determined laboriously to trace the empirical connections between unbelief and revolution, while recognizing all the while that divine judgment is also at work in them, to "bring evil upon this people, *even the fruit of their thoughts* ..."[151]

Our conclusion can be no other than that Groen tries to prove from the facts what he knows to be true from revelation and can see with the eyes of faith. He is determined to try, in the words of Donner, to offer an empirical demonstration of a connection which he has "prophetically grasped" or "religiously perceived."[152] Dornner faults him for it—for "short-circuiting" science and faith. But we now understand why Groen cannot find satisfaction in a causal analysis of mere foreground phenomenon—why he cannot even content himself with explaining the revolution strictly from a deep-seated and widespread skepticism concerning the received foundations of Christendom, necessitating the adoption of a new basis for truth, law, authority, justice, civil society. That causal chain is there, but by itself is too superficial, too exclusively proximate (we might say, too much of a surface or foreground explanation) to suit Groen. He feels compelled to give the whole story by penetrating to the cause behind that skepticism. When he identifies that background cause as unbelief—culpable, rebellious apostasy from God—then he clearly transgresses the canons and conventions of secular historical science. He has then crossed the boundary of the inner-worldly dynamics of history and gives full measure to the metahistorical connection or conditionedness of reality—of history's

---

151. Jer. 6:19 (see note 134 above). The same verse from Jeremiah plays a key role in Herbert Butterfield's view of divine judgment in history; cf. his *Writings on Christianity and History*, ed. C. T. McIntire, p. 190, where he quotes another verse that is similarly used by Groen in *Handboek*, § 1103: "In the voice of history was heard the voice of God: 'Thine own wickedness shall correct thee' " (Jer. 2:19).

152. Cf. Donner, "Het oorzakelijk verband tussen ongeloof en revolutie bij Groen van Prinsterer," p. 143.

all-important *"metaphysische Rückbeziehung."*[153] The heart of Groen's critical diagnosis, the core of his historial interpretation, is metahistorical, not intellectual or philosophical. Far more than to unmask mistaken theories, untenable propositions and false ideas, he wishes to unveil, directly behind (or beneath) these ideas, as their hidden motive force, the constant, dynamic impulse of unbelief, infidelity, disobedience.[154] Whoever abandons Christianity, is Groen's conviction, must go from bad to worse. Here too, *It is written!* is his watchword. Apart from God, life lies under judgment. This is a law of history, which man ignores only at his peril.

AN ARGUMENT WITHOUT END?

Not all readers of Scripture will agree that Groen has established a law of history. Several contributions to the *Lustrumbundel* of 1949, published by the Society of Christian Historians in The Netherlands, leave no doubt on that score. Yet, partly in protest to that book, the church historian Kamphuis judges Groen's diagnosis a legitimate application of "covenantal causality." It is in keeping with the clearly revealed terms of the covenant with mankind, he argues, that life lived in obedience may await divine blessing, whereas disobedient living—personally, socially, nationally—will incur divine judgment.[155] Kamphuis does not wish to imply that either outcome is predictable or always visible, but only that when it does manifest itself it must be so interpreted and named.

Pleading for a more nuanced view is Kamphuis's co-religionist, the history teacher J. Schaeffer. Schaeffer expresses his doubt whether a strictly covenantal causality holds for New Testament times, when the faithful are told to expect persecution instead of prosperity and when the corporate entity is the church culled from all nations, not a chosen people set apart.[156] Moreover, says Schaeffer, the way Groen operates with this causality in his book detracts from God's sovereign control over the actual historical impact that evil principles will be permitted to exercise: Groen has the

---

153. Term of Peter Meinhold's, hailed by M. C. Smit, *Toward a Christian Conception of History*, p. 338, as the most "hopeful word" uttered in contemporary discussions about a Christian approach to history. The term may be translated as "metaphysical retro-connection."

154. Cf. H. Algra, *Onder de schijnwerper der historie* (The Hague, n.d.), p. 8.

155. Kamphuis, *Causaliteit bij Groen*, passim.

156. Schaeffer, "Spreken de feiten?," p. 238.

temerity to predict that the revolutionary principles will in fact be followed by their disastrous consequences to the fullest extent.[157]—This last objection overlooks the many things Groen says about the restraining action of the divine world-order, and it insufficiently takes into account his stated belief that the revolution's influence was "tempered by the benefactions of a higher providence" (293).

Algra has more to say on the matter. In his opinion, Kamphuis's attempt "to rescue 'causality in Groen' by throwing it a life preserver from the theological deck" is not a success. Algra roundly dismisses the notion of "covenantal causality" that has thus been introduced into the debate, calling it a "theological construct" that overestimates the scope of human knowledge. Strictly speaking, it also underestimates the evidence of divine grace in human life. God's righteous rule remains shrouded in mystery, Algra insists; it must never be presented as the first link in a causal chain, enabling man to calculate and verify its inscrutable ways. God's rule is, rather, "wonderful in counsel and excellent in working" (Is. 28:29), especially in the manifestation in history of the triumph of His grace. On a more general point, furthermore, Algra agrees with those who consider the very concept of "causality" singularly inappropriate for history. It stems from the study of the physical world, with its predictable regularities. How different the historical world! Here Algra sounds a theme that pervades all his histories:[158] the course of history lacks necessity, and often surprises us with unsuspected possibilities. And one only makes matters worse when one tries to transpose the concept of "historical causality" onto the level of the covenant. For that matter, Algra concludes, "there is not a trace to be found in Groen of an attempt to make world history over into covenantal history."[159] Algra betrays irritation at the attempt to apply the concept of

---

157. Schaeffer, "De leiding Gods in de geschiedenis," pp. 109f, 117.

158. Documented in my *Hendrik Algra als verteller van de vaderlandse geschiedenis* (unpub. qualifying thesis, Free University, Amsterdam, 1970); cf. H. Algra, *Erfdeel der vaderen; handboek der vaderlandsche geschiedenis,* 3 vols. (Amersfoort: Geref. Jongelingsbond, 1932–46); *Dispereert niet; twintig eeuwen historie van de Nederlanden,* 13 vols. (Franeker: Wever, 1941–56; 3rd impr., in 5 vols., 1961–65; 8th impr. 1980); *De eigen weg van het Nederlandse volk* (Franeker: Wever, 1952); and *Het wonder van de 19e eeuw; van vrije kerken en kleine luyden* (Franeker: Wever, 1965; 6th impr. 1979). Hendrik Algra (1896–1982) was made Doctor *honoris causa* at the Free University, Amsterdam, in 1980.

159. Algra, "Beginsel en causaliteit," pp. 219–21.

the covenant to world history. His conclusion, however, is not borne out by Groen's view of history as set forth in the *Essay on Truth*.[160]

A book-length contribution to the more general debate about the hand of God in history was written by Leih, another history teacher. Although Groen is not explicitly mentioned by him, the Groenian tradition in the teaching of history looms large in the background. Leih, then, warns his fellow teachers against moving from their valid confession of God's presence in history to the traditional but unwarranted practice of pointing to concrete historical events and phenomena as visible evidence of that Presence. To be sure, God works in history as the "first cause" of all that happens, guiding history to its appointed end. Only, He works in secret, and therefore no particular event may be identified with His involvement in history in bringing about His plan for the world.[161] Leih cannot, on the other hand, keep himself from reserving certain features of history for believing interpretation, be it ever so cautiously. Fruits of the Spirit, for example, are visible throughout the ages in good people whose lives were loving service of neighbor. Rightly viewed, history is full of "signs" of deliverance and "signs" of the coming of the kingdom.[162]—These are statements that cannot be fully harmonized. Leih is clearly in reaction against the tendency to annex God for finite human causes by means of arbitrary interpretations of history. The strong reaction, both pro and con, which his book provoked, especially in educational circles, indicates that the Calvinian approach to history is still very much alive in the country where it has been practiced for so long.

Bremmer, a pastor-theologian as well as a historian, tries to conciliate the debating partners by calling attention to the element of confession in history-writing. Although Bremmer agrees with Schaeffer and Leih that the old way of telling history should not be imitated today, he asks for greater appreciation of Groen's unique position in time. Groen van Prinsterer was a historian of the Réveil, whose historical research found its natural application in a *testimony*. His book contains moments

---

160. Cf. above, chapter 3.

161. Leih, *Gods hand in de geschiedenis?*, pp. 29, 36.

162. Leih, *Gods hand in de geschiedenis?*, pp. 69, 84.

of *proclamation* about a reality in history for which "causality" is an infe-licitous term. Groen was a *witnessing* historian.[163]

Finally, Van Essen, the editor of Groen's published correspondence, has endorsed Kamphuis's vindication of Groen's view that God's promises and threats are manifestly fulfilled in history. However, by means of illustra-tions from Groen's works she emphasizes that Groen is careful to avoid the simple equation of divine blessing with earthly prosperity and divine judgment with temporal adversity.[164]

It is useful to remind ourselves, as we follow the various arguments, of the distinction between faith that is opposed to sight 2 Cor. 5:7) and faith that is allowed to see (2 Kings 6:17). As the debate continues one early voice has tended to get lost. Early on, Hendrikus Berkhof had emphasized that it is not only permissible but even obligatory for believers every now and then to identify God's hand in specific historical events—not lightly or superficially, but earnestly and thoughtfully, with tentativeness and humble modesty. History does not, of course, function as the ground of Christian belief, Berkhof cautions, but it does invite believing interpreta-tion, in fact demands to be believingly interpreted. Conversely, while faith does not rest on any religious interpretation of history, it does press the believer, who confesses God's providential rule over all things, to advance from faith to sight. Berkhof agrees with Groen that to point to God's hand is "difficult and hazardous." And yet it must be done, as an act of faith and a work of gratitude. Admittedly, the believer will make mistakes, because he is a finite and sinful creature, and also because Christ and antichrist are still hidden in the historical process. But to refuse categorically to iden-tify the handiwork of God in history is to exhibit unbelief and ingratitude. Referring to the calamity of World War II and the renewal of the church that resulted from it, Berkhof states that we may *believe* and therefore also *see* that "what appears to be a purely horizontal event also has a vertical dimension which encompasses the horizontal."[165]

The debate among fellow Calvinists has had the merit of pointing up that Groen's religious vision of history is itself not a finished piece of work

---

163. Bremmer, *Er staat geschreven! er is geschied!*, pp. 42–46, 58–70.

164. Van Essen, "Groen van Prinsterer and His Conception of History," pp. 239–42.

165. H. Berkhof, "Gods hand in de geschiedenis," *Ad Fontes* 6 (1958/59): 2–8; see also his *Christ the Meaning of History* (Richmond, VA: John Knox Press, 1966), esp. chap. 9.

but exhibits tensions and unresolved problems. Here too Groen was a pioneer as he modernized the Calvinian tradition of historical interpretation. That leaves us with one last, critical question to be addressed: Was this attempt at substantiating a religious vision of history by means of evidence from indisputable facts—was this very attempt not "unhistorical" and "unscientific"?[166]

Not so much unscientific, I am inclined to answer, as uncommonly candid and unreservedly radical. For *can* Groen's subject receive adequate treatment at the hands of "historical science" as that branch of learning has come to be defined? Granted, if one agrees with Groen—and most historians today certainly would—that at the root of the age of reason and revolution lies the aspiration to order life *apart from God*, then one will also agree with him that *not* to bring out the overpowering and decisive presence of this *a-theism* in men's beliefs and actions would be inexcusably superficial and therefore gravely inadequate. But—and this is the radical element in Groen's treatment of history—for a historian *not* to see and *not* to say that this movement foundered because it called down judgment upon its head (rather than because it ran afoul of unhappy circumstances) would mean for Groen to miss the root-cause and to withhold the vital explanation, would be for him to "cleave to the dust." Groen's explanation is "religiously biased" in that it entails a confrontation with questions that concern one's ultimate view of life. Much of the irritation and impatience with *Unbelief and Revolution* stems from this confrontation. Its personal tone, subjective standpoint and confessional cast will shock many readers and offend many more scholars. Scientific detachment and dispassionate neutrality seem so much more "reasonable." And so much safer. In the face of history's imponderables—man's restless quest for wholeness, his pursuit of happiness and thirst for truth and justice, his selfless love and buoyant hope; but also man's inhumanity to man, his pride, greed and insatiable ambition, his sin and guilt; the presence of evil, and of the evil one; and the presence of God—in the face of all these profound realities, too deep to fathom, ordinary "technical" historians can feel so overwhelmed that they decide to play it safe and stick to the empirical foreground phenomena, declaring the deeper dimensions to lie beyond their professional competence (and

166. Geyl, *Reacties*, p. 10; Donner, in *Lustrumbundel*, p. 144.

proceeding, more often than not, to write their histories from an implicit scheme of values nonetheless, since their subject-matter defies neutral treatment). But there is also a way of doing history, a self-consciously confessional way, that leaves little room for a non-committal posture, that allows of no escape into a "value-free" zone of "rational" discussion. As in politics, so in history Groen posits *principle against principle*. To dismiss his writing of history on that account is to show lack of critical insight into one's own religious bias, an unscholarly lack of critical reflection on one's own pre-theoretical point of departure.

To conclude, Groen's attempt, whatever its shortcomings, was a valid attempt both historically and scientifically. He worked as a Christian and a historian, inseparably. "With this book," wrote the succeeding anti-revolutionary leader Kuyper to Groen upon receiving a complimentary copy, "you have given me a photograph of your *geest*."[167] Groen's book is a typical specimen of prophetic history-writing—prophetic not in the sense of its predictive power but of its passionate interest in the truth. But what historian is not interested in the truth? Do I mean to imply, then, that historians may speak prophetically? Should they even try? That is, should they aspire to speak the *deepest truth* about their subject as they see it? Actually, they have no choice. This was the conviction of Groen van Prinsterer, and he was not alone in this. Two of his countrymen, living a century later, the one a Christian and the other a humanist, have argued similar positions. Meyer Smit maintained that no practicing historian can escape some philosophy or other about the meaning of the phenomena he studies, and this involves him, whether he likes it or not, in a fundamental choice with respect to the meaning and origin of history.[168] And Pieter Geyl contended that the historian comes to his material "not *only* as a technician, but as a human being," one who in his own way will be a "servant of truth, like the preacher or the prophet"; for: "History must reveal to us a meaning in life, or we are not worth our salt."[169] Since the 1960s "engaged history,"

---

167. *Briefwisseling*, V, 671. *Geest*: mind or spirit.

168. M. C. Smit, *Toward a Christian Conception of History*, pp. 223–46, 327–40.

169. Geyl, *Encounters in History*, pp. 330, 335 (*contra* Butterfield). Perhaps this is why his colleague (and bitter rival) had to admit, in a review of the volume *Reacties*, that Geyl "is often irritating, seldom satisfying, but always fascinating"; thus Gerretson, *Verzamelde Werken*, V, 350. Cf. also Von der Dunk, "Pieter Geyl: History as a Form of Self-Expression," passim.

from a variety of causes, has been taken more seriously again. Historians must not lose this emancipation from the scientific straitjacket.[170] It is a healthy sign when history is occasionally found at the storm-center of public debate. Scientific historians should relish being dragged from their studies to participate in society's periodic refurbishing of its collective memory. They can serve there as no one else can, provided their products are properly researched, reliably documented and open to correction. So conceived, even history as a *machine de guerre* can be a positive index of a society's mental health. To chide historians like Groen van Prinsterer for "mixing science and faith" is to disqualify the very thing that gives history its value. *Unbelief and Revolution* is a polemical series of historical lectures that contends for the highest truth. That is what makes it a classic.

And here I wish to end my discussion of Groen van Prinsterer and his book. This introduction is meant to introduce his work, not to praise it. In my estimation, the value of *Unbelief and Revolution* has been vindicated by at least two outstanding virtues. *First*, after more than a century of inconclusive debate it continues to offer a coherent, comprehensive, commanding and (to some people at least) convincing picture of the French Revolution in every one of its tempestuous phases and contradictory tendencies: its program of humanitarian reform and policy of cruel terror; its love of liberty and embrace of dictatorship; its promise of brotherhood and liberation and its practice of subjugation and oppression; its heights of optimism and depths of despair.[171] *Second*, since the day it was first published the book has enabled readers to understand our secular age in two of its most perplexing enigmas: totalitarian regimes and diabolical ideologies—dark riddles of our time which it explains from the fact, not that men have forsaken reason, but that they have departed from revelation. A work of such enduring value deserves continued study, especially on the score of its "religiously perceived" explanation. I for one would be able to silence or suspend this type of explanation in my work as a teacher

---

170. Cf. G. Puchinger, *Over de hartstocht van de ware geschiedschrijver*, pp. 3–6; but see also p. 13: "Polemical history sometimes betrays ... an author's preoccupation with current issues with which he has not come to terms."

171. Thus a single event that possesses unity in the very diversity that makes Cobban call "the" French Revolution a *myth*; cf. *Aspects of the French Revolution*, p. 108; see also the publications of Richard Cobb.

of history only at the price of intellectual schizophrenia. A scripturally directed, biblically sensitive study of history is an integral, not a partial assignment. To restrict oneself to the surface while glimpsing a dimension underneath—to stay with the factors of the foreground while perceiving a much more vital background—is to relinquish one of the historian's high offices, is to forgo the obligation and the privilege of laying bare the truth about history. Too much does the everyday historian cleave to the dust; his prayer is to be made alive by the Word.

SELECT BIBLIOGRAPHY

Aalders, W. *Theocratie of ideologie; het dilemma van de huidige christenheid.*
  The Hague: Voorhoeve, 1977.

De Afscheiding van 1834 en haar geschiedenis. W. Bakker et al., eds.
  Kampen: Kok, 1984.

Algemene Geschiedenis der Nederlanden. Vol. X: *Liberaal getij,* 1840–1855.
  Utrecht: De Haan, 1955.

[Nieuwe] Algemene Geschiedenis der Nederlanden. Vol. 10: *Nieuwste Tijd.*
  Bussum: Unieboek, 1981.

Algra, H. "Beginsel en causaliteit." *Anti-Revolutionaire Staatkunde* 35
  (1965): 210–22.

———. *De revolutie permanent?* The Hague: Willem de Zwijgerstichting,
  1974.

Aspecten van de Afscheiding. A. de Groot and P. L. Schram, eds. Franeker:
  Wever, 1984.

*Aspecten van het Réveil; opstellen ter gelegenheid van het vijftigjarig bestaan
  van de Stichting Het Réveil-Archief.* J. van den Berg, P. L. Schram
  and S. L. Verheus, eds. Kampen: Kok, 1980.

Bakker, Korff. J. A. Review of *Ongeloof en Revolutie* in *Vaderlandsche
  Letteroefeningen I* (1848): 401–12.

Bavinck, H. "Recent Dogmatic Thought in the Netherlands." *The
  Presbyterian and Reformed Review* 10 (April 1892): 209–28.

Beik, Paul H. *The French Revolution Seen from the Right: Social Theories
  in Motion, 1789–1799.* New York: Howard Fertig, 1970. Reprinted
  from the Transactions of the American Philosophical Society, Vol.
  46, Part I (1956).

Berg, J. van den. "P. Hofstede de Groot en het Réveil." In *Aspecten van het
  Réveil,* pp. 11–34.

Boogman, J. C. "The Dutch Crisis in the Eighteen-Forties." In *Britain and the Netherlands*, Volume I, pp. 192–203.

———. *Romdom 1848; de politieke ontwikkeling van Nederland, 1840–1858.* Bussum: Unieboek, 1978.

Bosch Kemper, J. de. Review of *Ongeloof en Revolutie* in *Nederlandsche Jaarboeken voor Regtsgeleerdheid en Wetgeving* XI (1849): 187–220.

———. "De verhouding tusschen Christendom en Staatswetenschap." *Nederlandsche Jaarboeken voor Regtsgeleerdheid en Wetgeving* X (1848): 545–69.

Brants, J. L. P. *Groen's geestelijke groei; onderzoek naar Groen van Prinsterer's theorieën tot 1834.* Diss. Free University. Amsterdam: Wed. G. van Soest, 1951.

Bremmer, R. H. *Er staat geschreven! Er is geschied! Introductie tot het leven en werk van Groen van Prinsterer als getuigend historicus.* Apeldoorn: Willem de Zwijgerstichting, 1981.

Brinton, Crane. *Decade of Revolution, 1789–1799.* The Rise of Modern Europe, ed. by William L. Langer. New York: Harper, 1934.

Britain and the Netherlands. Volume I. Papers Delivered to the First Anglo-Dutch Historical Conference. Ed. by J. S. Bromley and E. H. Kossmann. London: Chatto & Windus, 1960.

———. Volume VIII: Clio's Mirror: Historiography in Britain and the Netherlands. Papers Delivered to the Eighth Anglo-Dutch Historical Conference. Ed. by A. C. Duke and C. A. Tamse. Zutphen: De Walburg Pers, 1985.

Brugmans, I. J. *De arbeidende klasse in Nederland in de 19e eeuw (1813–1870).* 1925. 7th rev. ed. Utrecht and Antwerp: Het Spectrum, 1967.

———. "Economische en maatschappelijke verhoudingen in het Noorden, 1840–1870." *In Algemene Geschiedenis der Nederlanden*, Volume X, pp. 153–75.

———. *Paardenkracht en mensenmacht; sociaal-economische geschiedenis van Nederland, 1795–1940.* The Hague: Nijhoff, 1961.

———. *Stapvoets voorwaarts; sociale geschiedenis van Nederland in de negentiende eeuw.* 2nd rev. ed. Haarlem: Fibula-Van Dishoeck, 1978.

Bruins Slot, J. A. H. J. S. *Groen van Prinsterer bij het herstel der hierarchie in de Roomsch-Katholieke kerk in Nederland.* Diss. Free University. Amsterdam: S. J. P. Bakker, 1931.

Buitendijk, W. J. C. "De jonge Da Costa, romanticus in de biedermeiertijd." In *Aspecten van het Réveil*, pp. 53-73.

Buonarrotti, Philippe. *History of Babeuf's Conspiracy for Equality*. Trans. by James Bronterre O'Brien. London, 1836.

Butterfield, Herbert. *Christianity and History*. London: Bell, 1949.

———. *The Origins of Modern Science*. Revised ed. New York: Free Press, 1957.

———. *Writings on Christianity and History*. Edited with an introduction by C. T. McIntire. New York: Oxford University Press, 1979.

Carr, E. H. *What Is History?* New York: Penguin, 1964.

Cobban, A. *Aspects of the French Revolution*. London: Jonathan Cape, 1968.

———. *The Myth of the French Revolution*. 1955. In *Aspects of the French Revolution*, pp. 90-112.

Dawson, Christopher. *Dynamics of World History*. New York: Sheed & Ward, 1956.

Dengerink, J. D. *Critisch-historisch onderzoek naar de sociologische ontwikkeling van het beginsel der "Souvereiniteit in eigen kring" in de 19e en 20e eeuw*. Diss. Free University, Amsterdam. Kampen: Kok, 1948.

Deursen, A. Th. van. "De Vrije Universiteit en de geschiedwetenschappen." In M. van Os and W. J. Wieringa, eds., *Wetenschap en rekenschap, 1880-1980; een eeuw wetenschapsbeoefening en wetenschapsbeschouwing aan de Vrije Universiteit* (Kampen: Kok, 1980), pp. 360-400.

Diepenhorst, P. A. *Groen van Prinsterer*. Kampen: Kok, 1932.

———. *Onze strijd in de Staten-Generaal*. Volume I: De schoolstrijd. Amsterdam: Drukkerij De Standaard, 1927.

Donner, A. M. "Het oorzakelijk verband tussen ongeloof en revolutie bij Groen van Prinsterer." In *Lustrumbundel*, pp. 138-54.

Dooyeweerd, H. "Groens 'Ongeloof en Revolutie.'" *Nederlandsche Gedachten*, 28 Feb. 1948, pp. 53-57.

———. "Het historisch element in Groen's staatsleer." In *Lustrumbundel*, pp. 118-37.

———. *Roots of Western Culture: Pagan, Secular, and Christian Options*. Trans. John Kraay. Toronto: Wedge, 1979.

Essen, J. L. van. "Bilderdijk en Groen van Prinsterer." *Het Bilderdijk-Museum* 1 (1984): 6–12.

———. "Guillaume Groen van Prinsterer and His Conception of History." *Westminster Theological Journal* 44 (1982): 205–49. Reprinted in J. L. van Essen and H. Donald Morton, G. *Groen van Prinsterer: Selected Studies* (Jordan Station, ON: Wedge, 1990), 15–54.

Evenhuis, R. B. *Ook dat was Amsterdam*. Volume V: *De kerk der hervorming in de negentiende eeuw: de strijd voor kerkherstel*. Baarn: Ten Have, 1978.

Fafié, G. *Friedrich Julius Stahl; invloeden van zijn leven en werken in Nederland, 1847–1880*. Diss. City University of Amsterdam. Rotterdam: Bronder-Offset, 1975.

Farmer, Paul. *France Reviews Its Revolutionary Origins: Social Politics and Historical Opinion in the Third Republic*. New York: Columbia University Press, 1944.

Fogarty, Michael P. *Christian Democracy in Western Europe: 1820–1953*. Notre Dame University Press, 1957.

Fruin, R. J. *Verspreide Geschriften*. Volume X: *Redevoeringen en opstellen van verschillende aard, II*. The Hague: Nijhoff, 1905.

Fueter, Eduard. *Geschichte der neueren Historiographie*. Munich and Berlin: R. Oldenbourg, 1911. Third, enlarged edition, 1936. Reprinted 1968.

Furet, François. *Penser la Révolution française*. Paris: Gallimard, 1978. English trans. by Elborg Forster, *Interpreting the French Revolution* (Cambridge University Press, 1981).

Furet, François, and D. Richet. *La Révolution française*. 2 vols. Paris, 1965. Eng. trans. *French Revolution* (London, 1970).

Gaay Fortman, B. de. *Figuren uit het Réveil; opstellen uitgegeven door de Stichting Het Réveil-Archief ter gelegenheid van haar vijftigjarig bestaan*. Kampen: Kok, 1980.

———. "Groen van Prinsterers voorlezingen over ongeloof en revolutie." *Anti-Revolutionaire Staatkunde* (quarterly edition) 14 (1940): 35–57. Cited according to the reprinted version in idem, *Figuren uit het Réveil*, pp. 436–54.

———. "Een Liberaal van antirevolutionairen huize; Mr. D. J. Baron
      Mackay van Ophemert (1839-1921)." *Anti-Revolutionnaire
      Staatkunde* (quarterly edition) 14 (1940): 113-23.

Gäbler, U. "De weg naar het Réveil in Genève." *Nederlandsch Theologisch
      Tijdschrift* 38 (1984): 37-44.

Gay, P. "Why Was the Enlightenment?" In *Eighteenth-Century Studies,
      Presented to Arthur Wilson* (University Press of New England,
      1972), pp. 61-71.

Gelderen, J. van. " 'Scheuring' en Vereniging—1837-1869." In *De
      Afscheiding van 1834 en haar geschiedenis*, pp. 100-46.

Gerretson, [F.] C. *Verzamelde Werken*. 6 vols. Baarn: Bosch & Keuning,
      1973-1976.

Geyl, P. [C. A.] *Encounters in History*. Gloucester, MA: Peter Smith, 1977.

———. "French Historians For and Against the Revolution." In idem,
      Encounters in History, pp. 87-142.

———. *Kernproblemen van onze geschiedenis; opstellen en voordrachten
      1925-1936*. Utrecht: Oosthoek, 1937.

———. *Readies*. Utrecht: Oosthoek, 1952.

Gooch, G. P. *History and Historians in the Nineteenth Century*. Boston:
      Beacon Press, 1959.

Griffiths, R. T. *Achterlijk, achter of anders? Aspecten van de economische
      ontwikkeling van Nederland in de 19de eeuw*. Inaugural lecture,
      Free University, Amsterdam, 4 December 1980. Amsterdam:
      VU Boekhandel/Uitgeverij, 1980.

———. "Ambacht en nijverheid in de Noordelijke Nederlanden, 1770-
      1844." In *[Nieuwe] Algemene Geschiedenis der Nederlanden*, vol. 10
      (1981), pp. 219-52.

———. *Industrial Retardation in the Netherlands, 1830-1850*. The Hague:
      1979.

Groen van Prinsterer, Guillaume. *Aan de Hervormde Gemeente in
      Nederland*. Leyden: Luchtmans, 1843.

———. *Adviezen in de Tweede Kamer der Staten-Generaal, in dubbelen getale*.
      Leyden: Luchtmans, 1840.

———. *Archives ou Correspondance inédite de la Maison de l'Orange-Nassau*.
      First series: 9 vols.; Leyden: Luchtmans, 1835-47. Second series:
      6 vols.; Utrecht: Kemink, 1857-61.

————. *Bescheiden*. Ed. by C. Gerretson. Rijks Geschiedkundige
Publicatiën 93. The Hague: Nijhoff, 1951.

————. *Bescheiden*. Ed. by J. Zwaan. 2 vols. The Hague: Institute voor
Nederlandse Geschiedenis, 1990, 1991.

————. *Bijdrage tot herziening der Grondwet in Nederlandschen zin*. Leyden:
Luchtmans, 1840.

————. *Briefwisseling*. Edited by J. L. van Essen, C. Gerretson, A. Goslinga
and H. J. Smit. Volumes I; II; III; IV; V; VI. Rijks Geschiedkundige
Publicatiën 58; 114; 90; 123; 175. The Hague: Nijhoff, 1925; 1964;
1949; 1967; 1980; 1992.

————. *Brieven van J. A. Wormser*. 2 vols. Amsterdam: Höveker, 1874–76.

————. *Brieven van Mr. Isaac da Costa*. 3 vols. Amsterdam: Höveker,
1872–76.

————. *L'Empire Prussien et l'Apocalypse; à mes amis de Berlin*. Essais
historiques sur les événements d'Allemagne en 1866 II.
Amsterdam: Höveker, 1867.

————. *Grondwetherziening en eensgezindheid*. Amsterdam: Müller, 1849.

————. *Handboek der Geschiedenis van het Vaderland*. First edition, Leyden:
Luchtmans, 1841–46. Third, revised edition, Amsterdam: Höveker,
1872.

————. *Historia de la Revolución en su primera fase: la preparación (hasta
1789)*. Conferencia XI sobre *Incredulidad y Revolución; una serie
de conferencias de historia*. Traducido de inglés en castellano por
Humberto Casanova. Madrid: Impresión y Ediciones S.L., 1982.

————. *The History of the Revolution in Its First Phase: (Till 1789)*. Lecture XI
from *Unbelief and Revolution: A Series of Lectures in History*. Ed.
and trans. by Harry Van Dyke and Donald Morton. Amsterdam:
The Groen van Prinsterer Fund, 1973.

————. *De maatregelen tegen de Afgescheidenen aan het staatsregt getoetst*.
Leyden: Luchtmans, 1837.

————. *Maurice et Barnevelt; étude historique*. Utrecht: Kemink, 1875.

————. *Ter nagedachtenis van Stahl*. Amsterdam: Höveker, 1862.

————. *Nederlandsche Gedachten*. First series: 4 vols.; The Hague: Vervloet,
1829–32. Second series: 6 vols.; Amsterdam: Höveker, 1867–76.

————. *Open Brief aan de Kiezersvereeniging: Nederland en Oranje te Leiden*.
The Hague: Van Cleef, 1857.

————. *Parlementaire Studiën en Schetsen*. 3 vols., containing 49 pamphlets, 25 Oct. 1865–15 Nov. 1866. Pp. 498. The Hague: Van Cleef, 1866.

————. *Le Parti Antirévolutionnaire et Confessionnel dans l'Eglise Réformée des Pays-Bas; étude d'histoire contemporaine*. Amsterdam: Höveker, 1860. Eng. trans.: *Christian Political Action in an Age of Revolution*. Aalten, Neth.: Woodbridge, 2015.

————. *Proeve over de middelen waardoor de waarheid wordt gekend en gestaafd*. Leyden: Luchtmans, 1834.

————. *La Prusse et les Pays-Bas; à mes amis de Berlin*. Amsterdam: Höveker, 1867.

————. *Stukken betreffende de afwijzing eener bijzondere school der eerste klasse te 's Gravenhage*. The Hague: Roering, 1844.

————. *Unbelief in Religion and Politics*. Lectures VIII and IX from *Unbelief and Revolution: A Series of Lectures in History*. Ed. and trans. by Harry Van Dyke and Donald Morton. Amsterdam: The Groen van Prinsterer Fund, 1975.

————. *Verspreide Geschriften*. 2 vols. Amsterdam: Höveker, 1859–60.

————. *Vrijheid, Gelijkheid, Broederschap; toelichting van de spreuk der Revolutie*. The Hague: Roering, 1848.

Groot, A. de. "Het vroegnegentiende-eeuwse Nederland." In *De Afscheiding van 1834 en haar geschiedenis*, pp. 9–29.

Hagoort, R. De Christelijk-sociale beweging. Franeker: Wever, 1956.

————. *Patrimonium (vaderlijk erfdeel); gedenkboek bij het gouden jubileum*. Kampen: Kok, 1927.

Hartoch, G. M. den. *Groen van Prinsterer en de verkiezingen van 1871; een keerpunt in de wordingsgeschiedenis der Anti-Revolutionaire Partij*. Diss. Free University, Amsterdam. Kampen: Kok, 1933.

Huizinga, J. *Verzamelde Werken*. Vol. VIII: *Universiteit, wetenschap en kunst*. Haarlem: Tjeenk Willink, 1951.

Kamphuis, J. *De hedendaagse kritiek op de causaliteit bij Groen van Prinsterer als historicus*. 1963. Second impression, Groningen: De Vuurbaak, 1971.

————. *Evangelisch isolement; over de zinspreuk "In ons isolement ligt onze kracht."* Groningen: De Vuurbaak, 1976.

Keijzer, W. P. *Alexandre Rodolphe Vinet, 1797–1847*. Amsterdam: Uitgeversmaatschappij Holland, 1947.

————. *Vinet en Hollande.* Wageningen: Veenman, 1941.

Klapwijk, J. "Calvin and Neo-Calvinism on Non-Christian Philosophy."
    Philosophia Reformata 38 (1973): 43–61.

Kluit, M. Elisabeth. *Het Protestantse Réveil in Nederland en daarbuiten,*
    1815-1865. Amsterdam: H. J. Paris, 1970.

Knetsch, F. R. J. "Louis Gabriel James (1795-1867)." In *Aspecten van het*
    Réveil, pp. 126–49.

————. "Het Réveil en de Afscheiding." In *Aspecten van de Afscheiding,*
    pp. 65–83.

Kuyper, Abraham. *Lectures on Calvinism.* Grand Rapids: Eerdmans, 1931.

Lakke, A. J. *Philip Willem van Heusde.* Diss. Free University, Amsterdam.
    Leyden, 1908.

Langedijk, D. "Groen van Prinsterer's 'Ongeloof en Revolutie' 100 jaar."
    Nieuw Nederland 2, no. 40 (Oct. 1947): 6f.

Lefebvre, G. *Quatre-vingt-neuf.* Paris, 1939. Eng. trans. by R. R. Palmer,
    The Coming of the French Revolution (Princeton University Press,
    1947).

Leih, H. G. *Gods hand in de geschiedenis?* Kampen: Kok, 1976. 2nd impr.
    1977.

Lohman. See Savornin Lohman.

Loo, L. F. van. "De armenzorg in de Noordelijke Nederlanden, 1770-1854."
    In *[Nieuwe] Algemene Geschiedenis der Nederlanden,* vol. 10 (1981),
    pp. 417–34.

Lustrumbundel. See Suttorp.

McManners, J. "The Historiography of the French Revolution." In
    New Cambridge Modern History, VIII (1971), pp. 618–52.

Meere, J. M. M. de. "Sociale verhoudingen en structuren in de
    Noordelijke Nederlanden, 1814-1844." In *[Nieuwe] Algemene*
    Geschiedenis der Nederlanden, vol. 10 (1981), pp. 384–416.

Meijer, R. P. *Literature of the Low Countries.* The Hague: Nijhoff, 1978.

Mellon, S. *The Political Uses of History: A Study of Historians in the French*
    Restoration. Stanford University Press, 1958.

Morton, Herbert Donald. " 'A Christian Heroism': Elements of the Style
    of Guillaume Groen van Prinsterer." In J. L. van Essen and H.
    Donald Morton, *Guillaume Groen van Prinsterer: Selected Studies*
    (Jordan Station, ON: Wedge, 1990).

Mulder, H. W. J. *Groen van Prinsterer, staatsman en profeet*. Franeker: Wever, 1973.

Oostendorp, L. H. P. *Scholte: Leader of the Secession of 1834 and Founder of Pella*. Diss. Free University, Amsterdam. Franeker: Wever, 1964.

Palmer, R. R. *The Age of the Democratic Revolution*. 2 vols. Princeton, NJ: Princeton University Press, 1959.

Pater, J. C. H. de. "Groen's beschouwing over het beloop der Franse Revolutie." In *Lustrumbundel*, pp. 100-17.

Puchinger, G. *Groen van Prinsterer als correspondent, 1848-1866: Strijder-Triomfator; een studie*. Delft: Uitg. J. Stellingwerff, 1952.

———. *Herinneringen aan Geyl*. Delft: Meinema, 1972.

———. *Over de hartstocht van de ware geschiedschrijver*. Delft: Meinema, 1978.

Rasker, A. J. *De Nederlandse Hervormde Kerk vanaf 1795; haar geschiedenis en theologie in de negentiende en twintigste eeuw*. Kampen: Kok, 1974.

Reinsma, R. *Een merkwaardige episode uit de geschiedenis van de slavenemancipatie*. The Hague: Van Goor, 1963.

Rijnsdorp, C. "Groen in zijn brieven over zichzelf en zijn reputatie." *Anti-Revolutionaire Staatkunde* 46 (1976): 188-96. Cited according to the reprint in *Een staatsman ter navolging*, pp. 213-19.

Rullmann, J. C. *De Afscheiding in de Nederlandsch Hervormde Kerk der XIXe eeuw*. Fourth, revised edition. Kampen: Kok, 1930.

———. "De politieke leiding onzer christelijke periodieken in de 19e eeuw." *Anti-Revolutionaire Staatkunde* (quarterly edition) 6 (1932): 496-540.

———. *De Strijd voor kerkherstel in de Nederlandsch Hervormde Kerk der XIXe eeuw*. Third impression. Kampen: Kok, 1928.

Sassen, F. *Geschiedenis van de wijsbegeerte in Nederland tot het einde der negentiende eeuw*. Amsterdam and Brussels: Elsevier, 1959.

Savornin Lohman, W. H. de. "Groen's reis naar Parijs en Besançon in 1836 ten behoeve der 'Archives.'" *Bijdragen en Mededeelingen van het Historisch Genootschap* 42 (1921): 1-106.

Schaeffer, J. "Groens zelfportret." *Radix* 7 (1981): 219-28.

———. "De leiding Gods in de geschiedenis." *Radix* 8 (1980): 100-23.

———. "Spreken de feiten?" *Radix* 8 (1982): 233-39.

Scheel, W. *Das 'Berliner Politische Wochenblatt' und die politische und soziale Revolution in Frankreich und England.* Göttingen: Musterschmidt Verlag, 1964.

Schelven, A. A. van. "Groen's denkbeelden over de Reformatie." In *Lustrumbundel*, pp. 73–99.

Schram, P. L. *Documentatieblad voor de Nederlandse Kerkgeschiedenis van de Negentiende Eeuw*, no. 3 (March 1978): 7–18.

———. "Réveil-relaties met Genève en Neuchatel." *Documentatieblad voor de Nederlandse Kerkgeschiedenis van de Negentiende Eeuw*, no. 4 (Sept. 1978): 27–50.

Schutte, G. J. *Mr. G. Groen van Prinsterer.* Goes: Oosterbaan & Le Cointre, 1976. Eng. trans.: *Groen van Prinsterer: His life and Work.* Neerlandia, AB and Pella, IA: Inheritance Publications, 2016.

Smit, H. J. "Groen en de prae-revolutionaire staatsvormen." In *Lustrumbundel*, pp. 27–72.

Smit, M. C. *Toward a Christian Conception of History.* Lanham, MD: University Press of America, 2002.

Smits, C. De *Afscheiding van 1834.* Volume VI: *Het Réveil en ds. H. P. Scholte; correspondentie.* Dordrecht: Van den Tol, 1984.

———. "Secession, Quarrels, Emigration and Personalities." In Herman Ganzevoort and Mark Bockelman, eds., *Dutch Immigration to North America* (Toronto: Multicultural History Society of Ontario, 1983), pp. 97–110.

Smitskamp, H. "Het boek 'Ongeloof en Revolutie.' " In *Lustrumbundel*, pp. 9–26.

———. *Groen van Prinsterer als historicus.* Diss. Free University. Amsterdam: H. J. Paris, 1940.

———. "Groen's denkbeelden over het recht van opstand." *Anti-revoltionaire Staatkunde* 8 (1934): 182–94.

Sneller, Z. W. "De aanval van Fruin in 1853 op den auteur van 'Ongeloof en Revolutie.' " In *Lustrumbundel*, pp. 155–94.

Een staatsman ter navolging; Groen van Prinsterer herdacht (1876–1976). Ed. by C. Bremmer and M. N. G. Kool. The Hague: Stichtingen Kader-en Vormingswerk ARP, CHU en KVP, 1976.

Steur, J. "De geldelijke nalatenschap van Groen van Prinsterer." *Tot Vrijheid Geroepen* 22 (1976): 78–87.

Suttorp, L. C. et al., eds. *Groen's "Ongeloof and Revolutie"; een bundel studieën*. Wageningen: Zomer & Keuning, 1949. Vijfde Lustrumbundel van het Gezelschap van Christelijke Historici in Nederland.

Tazelaar, C. *De Jeugd van Groen (1801-1827)*. Diss. Free University. Amsterdam: Uitgeversmaatschappij Holland, 1925.

TenZythoff, G. J. *Sources of Secession: The Netherlands Hervormde Kerk on the Eve of the Dutch Immigration to the Midwest*. The Historical Series of the Reformed Church in America 17. Grand Rapids: Eerdmans, 1987.

Velde, M. te. "J. A. Wormser en zijn Vrije Gemeente in Amsterdam (1840-1851)." In M. J. Arntzen et al., *Bezield Verband; opstellen aangeboden aan prof. J. Kamphuis bij gelegenheid van zijn 25-jarig ambtsjubileum* (Kampen: Van den Berg, 1984), pp. 261-76.

Verberne, L. G. J. *Geschiedenis van Nederland in de jaren 1813-1850*. 2 vols. Introduced by L. J. Rogier. Utrecht and Antwerp: Het Spectrum, 1958. Reprint from *Geschiedenis van Nederland*, ed. H. Brugmans, vol. VII, 1937.

Von der Dunk, H. W. "Pieter Geyl: History as a Form of Self-Expression." In *Britain and the Netherlands*, vol. VIII, pp. 185-214.

Vree, J. *De Groninger godgeleerden; de oorsprongen en de eerste periode van hun optreden (1820-1843)*. Diss. Free University, Amsterdam. Kampen: Kok, 1984.

———. "De Nederlandse Hervormde Kerk in de jaren voor de Afscheiding." In *De Afscheiding van 1834 en haar geschiedenis*, pp. 30-61.

Wieringa, W. J. *Economische heroriëntering in Nederland in de negentiende eeuw*. Groningen and Djakarta: Noordhoff, 1955.

Witte Van Citters, J. de. Review of *Ongeloof en Revolutie* in *Themis; regtskundig tijdschrift* IX/1 (1848): 109-32.

Zappey, W. M. "De negentiende eeuw—Deel 1: De periode 1813-1848." In J. H. van Stuijvenberg, ed., *De economische geschiedenis van Nederland* (Groningen: Wolters-Noordhoff, 1977), pp. 201-18.

Zwaan, J. *Groen van Prinsterer en de klassieke Oudheid*. Diss. Free University. Amsterdam: Hakkert, 1973.

———. "Groen van Prinsterer over Grieken en Turken." [D.i. 'Kort ontwerp' van de Bedenkingen tegen een oproeping tot ondersteuning der Grieken (1825).] *Documentatieblad voor de Nederlandse Kerkgeschiedenis van de Negentiende Eeuw*, no. 3 (March 1978): 21–31.

———. "Groen van Prinsterer over de wijsbegeerte." *Correspondentie-bladen van de Vereniging voor Calvinistische Wijsbegeerte* XXXVI/2 (Sept. 1972): 29–45.

INDEX OF NAMES

INDEX OF SUBJECTS

SCRIPTURE REFERENCES